INDIAN MYTH AND LEGEND

INDIAN MYTH AND LEGEND

DONALD A. MACKENZIE

GYAN

Published by

Gyan Publishing House
5, Ansari Road
Daryaganj, New Delhi-110002
Phone: 011-47034999, 9811692060
E-mail: books@gyanbooks.com

Distribution Network
gyanbooks.com
India, USA, Canada, UK, Australia, France

ISBN: 978-81-212-8772-2 (PB)
First Published, 1913

2nd Impression 2023

Printed at: Gyan Press, Delhi.

INDIAN MYTH AND LEGEND
Author: Donald A. Mackenzie

INDIAN MYTH AND LEGEND

INDIAN MYTH AND LEGEND

DONALD A. MACKENZIE

With Illustrations by Warwick Goble and Plates

THE GRESHAM PUBLISHING COMPANY LIMITED
66 CHANDOS STREET COVENT GARDEN LONDON

To My Indian Friends

PREFACE

This volume deals with the myths and legends of India, which survive to us in the rich and abundant storehouse of Sanskrit literature, and with the rise and growth of Brahmanism, Buddhism, Jainism, &c. The reader is introduced to the various sacred works of the Hindus, including the ancient invocatory hymns of the four Vedas, the later speculative and expository "Forest Books" in which "the Absolute is grasped and proclaimed", and those great epic poems the *Râmâyana*, which is three times longer than the *Iliad*, and the *Mâhâbharata*, which is four times longer than the *Râmâyana*. In no other country have the national poets given fuller and finer expression to the beliefs and ideals and traditions of a people, or achieved as a result wider and more enduring fame. At the present day over two hundred million Hindus are familiar in varying degrees with the legendary themes and traditional beliefs which the ancient forest sages and poets of India invested with much beautiful symbolism, and used as mediums for speculative thought and profound spiritual teachings. The sacred books of India are to the Hindus what the Bible is to Christians. Those who read them, or hear them read, are believed to be assured of prosperity in this world and of salvation in the next. To students of history, of ethnology, and of comparative religion they present features of peculiar interest, for they contain an elaborate sociology of the ancient Aryo-Indians, their political organizations, their codes of laws, their high ethical code, and above all their conceptions of God, the soul, and the Universe. Some knowledge of them is necessary for those who desire to approach with sympathy the investigation of the religious beliefs of our Hindu fellow men and to understand their outlook upon life and the world.

The Introduction deals with various aspects of the study of these ancient myths and legends which have been the inspiration of a national literature infused with much grandeur and sublimity. The historic Aryan controversy, of which the science of comparative mythology is a by-product, is passed under review, and it is shown to what extent philological theories regarding race problems have been modified during recent years as a result of the adoption of broader and more exact methods of ethnic and archæological research and the ever-extending study of comparative mythology. There has also been condensed much important data dealing with the early phases of Aryo-Indian civilization accumulated for historical purposes by industrious and painstaking Sanskrit scholars who have been engaged in investigating and systematizing the internal evidence of the various religious poems and treatises. It will be found that no general agreement has yet been reached regarding Aryo-Indian chronology, but it now appears to be well established that although there were early cultural as well as racial "drifts", fresh invasions, which had far-reaching results in the social and religious life of northern India, occurred at a late period in what is known as the Vedic Age. In consequence, the problem presented by this ancient civilization tends rather to grow more complex than to become simplified. Its origin is still wrapped in obscurity. At the very dawn of history Aryo-Indian culture had attained a comparatively high state of development, and a considerable period must be allowed for its growth. Even some of the ancient Vedic hymns, addressed by priests to the deities, are styled "new songs", which suggests the existence of an older collection. Many of them also afford indications that immemorial beliefs were in process of change and fusion. The sublime deities, Varuna and Mitra (Mithra), for instance, were already declining in splendour. Yet they must have been closely associated with Indra, king of the gods, in the unknown Aryan homeland, as is made evident by an inscription recently deciphered at Boghaz Köi, in Asia Minor, which refers to them as deities of the mysterious Mitanni people who were of Aryan speech like the settlers in the Punjab. There is no evidence, however, that the Mitanni rulers gave recognition to the fire god Agni, who in India was exalted as the twin brother of Indra. The problem involved may not be devoid of ethnic significance, although the identity of the Agni-worshipping section of the early raiders remains obscure.

During the early Vedic Age in India prominence was given to the gods: the social organization was of patriarchal character; the goddesses remained shadowy and vague, some being, indeed, little more than figures of speech. A great change took place, however, after the invasions of the Bharata and other tribes who are now referred to as "late comers". Profound and speculative thinkers attained to the pantheistic conception of the world soul; new doctrines, which are not referred to in the Vedic hymns, regarding the ages of the universe and transmigration of souls, received wide acceptance as the result of missionary efforts: the Vedic gods were reduced to the position of minor deities and new goddesses rose into prominence, one indeed being Bharati, the tribal deity of the Bharatas, who became associated with the Saraswati river and under her new name was ultimately made the wife of the supreme god Brahma. It is significant to note that the new culture radiated from the "Middle Country", the area controlled by the "late comers". That it contained elements which were not of Indian origin is made clearly evident when we find that the doctrines of the ages of the universe and transmigration of souls were shared by other peoples, including the Greeks and Celts and a section of the ancient Egyptians. Sumero-Babylonian and Egyptian resemblances may also be traced in post-Vedic religious literature, the former, for instance, in the Deluge legend, and the latter in the myth regarding the avenging goddess Kali, who slaughters the enemies of the gods like Hathor-Sekhet, and has similarly to be restrained by one of the deities. The worship of goddesses was also prominent among the Sumerians, Egyptians, Greeks, and Celts, as contrasted with the worship of gods among broad-headed mountain and wandering peoples. In this connection special interest attaches to the conclusions of prominent ethnologists, who include in the Mediterranean or "Brown" race of brunet "long heads" the early Egyptians and Neolithic Europeans, the Sumerians and present-day "Aryan" types in India, and especially in the old "Middle Country" and Bengal. On the other hand, a broad-headed type is still prominent in the Punjab, the area occupied by the earliest invaders who worshipped the Vedic gods. Dr. Haddon suggests that these pioneers of civilization were mixed with peoples of Mongolian and other affinities. Some such ethnic explanation must be urged to account for the differences between Vedic and post-Vedic mythologies. The invasions of the "late comers", who entered India by a new route, no doubt stimulated thought and promoted culture after settled conditions were secured, as was undoubtedly the result of the mingling of races elsewhere.

"It may be put down as an axiom", says Professor Jastrow, "that nowhere does a high form of culture arise without the commingling of diverse ethnic elements. Civilization, like the spark emitted by the striking of steel on flint, is everywhere the result of stimulus evoked by the friction of one ethnic group upon another": and he supports his theory with the evidence afforded by Egypt, Babylonia, Greece, Rome, France, Germany, and Great Britain, as well as the present-day United States of America, "the melting pot" of many peoples.

Throughout this volume comparative evidence is provided to assist the reader towards the study of this most interesting aspect of the Aryan problem. We trace the cremation custom, which has prevailed in India since Vedic times, to countries as wide apart as Great Britain, into which it was introduced during the Bronze Age, and Southern Siberia, where it is still practised by the Mongolian Buriats. Over the areas occupied by representatives of the Mediterranean race it was unknown prior to the invasions of unidentified fire-worshippers. Special interest also attaches to the horse sacrifice, which was also an Aryo-Indian ceremony even in Vedic times. It is not yet unknown among the Buriats. At one time the horse sacrifice was widely prevalent. White horses were sacrificed to the sun in Ancient Greece; the sun horses are referred to with horror by Ezekiel; the ceremony was also connected with the mysteries of Aricia grove. Indeed, as is pointed out in Chapter V, various ancient peoples offered up this domesticated and historic animal. In the Indian epics and religious treatises there are illuminating references to the horse sacrifice which throw much light on the significance of the immemorial practice. White and black horses were alternately favoured, and it is evident that the practice was not only associated with solar worship, but was also intended to secure fertility—crops, and therefore rain in the first place, increase of flocks, herds, human offspring, &c.—as is undoubtedly the case among the modern-day Buriats. In India the horse was also offered up as a sin offering, a late conception, evidently. A prominent feature of this sacrifice in most countries was the decapitation of the sacrificial victim. Recent evidence from Egypt suggests that the sacrifice of the ass may have preceded the sacrifice of the horse. Professor Flinders Petrie has found in a triple tomb in the early dynastic Tarkhan cemetery the skeletons of three asses with the heads cut off and placed beside them. He suggests that the animals were killed to accompany their owner to the other world. The Buriats still sacrifice horses at graves, professedly for the same reason. As this custom was not prevalent throughout Ancient Egypt, it may have been an importation, connected, perhaps, with the myth about the sun-ass which gallops round a hill-surrounded world followed by the pursuing night serpent. An isolated reference is also made to the sacrifice of the ass in a Twelfth Dynasty story about a Naga-like demigod, a fact which emphasizes the historical importance of the material embedded in folk tales and mythologies. In this connection it may be noted that certain developed myths suggest there may have been either a cultural contact of Ancient Egypt with India, through an unidentified medium, or an infusion of religious ideas into both countries from a common source. In an Indian creation myth Prajápati weeps creative tears like the Egyptian sun-god Ra, whose rays are tears from which all things spring, as Maspero shows.

In India the juice of the soma plant was identified with the vital principle, and the demons were the poisoners of crops and plants; in Egypt honey-flowers and sacred trees sprang from the fertilizing tears of deities, while the tears of demons produced poisonous plants, diseases, &c. Like the Egyptian Horus, the Indian Prajápati, or Brahma, sprang from a lotus bloom floating on the primordial waters. The chaos-egg myth is also common to both mythological systems. Brahma issues from a golden egg like Ra, and a similar myth is connected with the Egyptian Ptah and Khnumu, and with the Chinese P'an Ku, while the egg figures in Eur-Asian folk tales which contain the germs of the various mythologies. All mythologies have animistic bases; they were, to begin with, systematized folk beliefs which were carried hither and thither in various stages of development by migrating and trading peoples. Each separate system bears undoubted traces of racial or local influences; each reflects the civilization in which it flourished, the habits of thought and habits of life of the people, and the religious, ethical, and political ideals of their rulers and teachers. When well-developed myths of similar character are found in widely separated districts, an ethnic or cultural contact is suggested. Such myths may be regarded as evidence of remote racial movements, which, although unsupported by record or tradition, are also indicated by ethnological data. It is hoped that the reader will find much suggestive material in this connection in their study of the myths and legends of India. They will also find that many of the tales retold in this volume have qualities which make universal appeal, and that some are among the most beautiful which survive from the civilizations of the ancient world.

Not a few, we are assured, will follow with interest

the development from primitive myths of great and ennobling ideas which have exercised a culturing influence in India through many long centuries, and are still potent factors in the domestic, social, and religious life of many millions of Hindus.

DONALD A. MACKENZIE.

CONTENTS

CONTENTS

PLATES

PLATES IN MONOCHROME

PLATES IN MONOCHROME

PLATES IN MONOCHROME

INTRODUCTION

The triangular sub-continent of India is cut off from the rest of Asia by the vast barriers of the Himalayas, the Hindu Kush, the Suleiman mountains, and the Indian Ocean. Its population comprises about two hundred and ninety-five millions, and is of greatest density on the fertile northern plain, which is watered by three river systems, the Indus and its tributaries on the west, and the Ganges and Brahmaputra with their tributaries which pour into the Bay of Bengal. South of the Vindhya mountain ranges is the plateau of the Deccan. The climate varies from temperate on the Himalayan slopes to tropical in southern India, and over the entire country there are two pronounced annual seasons, the dry and the rainy.

Our interest abides in this volume chiefly with the northern plain and the people who are familiar in varying degrees with the sacred and heroic literature passed under review; that is, with the scenes of the early Indian civilization known as Aryan and those numerous inheritors of Aryan traditions, the Hindus, who exceed two hundred and seven millions of the population of India. Modern Hinduism embraces a number of cults which are connected with the early religious doctrines of the Aryanized or Brahmanized India of the past; it recognizes, among other things, the ancient caste system which includes distinct racial types varying from what is known as the

Aryan to the pre-Dravidian stocks. Other religious organizations may be referred to in passing. Buddhists are chiefly confined to Burma, Sikhs number two millions, the Mohammedans nearly sixty-three millions, while the Parsees number roughly ninety-five thousand; less than three million natives and half-castes are Christians.

Like Egypt, India is a land of ancient memories, but its history, or rather pre-history, does not begin until about a thousand years after the erection was completed of the great pyramids at Gizeh. Between 2000 B.C. and 1200 B.C. tribes of pastoral and patriarchal peoples of Aryan speech were pouring over the north-western frontier and settling in the Punjab. There are no written or inscribed records, or even native traditions, of this historic migration, but we are able to follow vaguely, from the references found in religious compositions, the gradual conquest of northern India, which covered a period of several centuries. To what extent this invasion was racial, rather than cultural, it is extremely difficult to discover. But no doubt can be entertained regarding the influence exercised by the ancient military aristocracy and their religious teachers. Certain of the Aryan gods still receive recognition in India after a lapse of over three thousand years. This fact makes Indian mythology of special interest to the ever-increasing number of students of comparative religion.

Indian mythology also possesses particular attractions for us on account of its intimate association with what is known as the "Aryan problem". Scholars of a past generation held pronounced views on Aryan matters, and produced a considerable literature of highly controversial character. In fact, theories regarding the Aryan languages and the Aryan "race" are as varied as they are numerous; the wordy warfare which occupied the greater part of the nineteenth century, was waged ever strenuously and not infrequently with much brilliance; occasionally, however, it was not awanting in the undesirable elements of personal feeling and national antipathy. But, happily, we appear to have reached a time when this fascinating and important problem can be considered dispassionately in the proper scientific spirit, and without experiencing that unnecessary dread of having to abandon decided opinions which may have been formed when the accumulated data had less variety and bulk than that which is now available. This change has been brought about by the extended study of comparative religion and the wonderful and engaging results which have attended modern-day methods of ethnic and archæological research.

The Aryan controversy had its origin at the close of the eighteenth century, when that distinguished Oriental scholar Sir William Jones, who acted for a period as a judge of the Supreme Court in Bengal, drew attention to the remarkable resemblances between the Sanskrit, Greek, Latin, German, and Celtic languages. In 1808, Schlegel published his *Language and Wisdom of the Hindus*, and urged the theory that India was the home of an ancestral race and a group of languages that were progenitors of various European ones. Other scholars subsequently favoured Zend, the language of Persia, and transferred the "racial beehive" to that country; rival claims were afterwards set up for Asia Minor and the Iranian plateau.

The science of Comparative Philology was a direct product of these early controversies; it was established in the "thirties" when Bopp published his Comparative Grammar in which a new term, having a racial significance, was invented: he grouped all European languages, except Basque, Magyar, Turkish, and Finnish, as "Indo-Germanic". After the study of Sanskrit literature revealed, however, that the Aryans occupied but a small part of India when their sacred hymns, the Vedas, were composed, the cradle of the Aryan race was shifted to some uncertain area beyond the Himalayan mountains.

Max Müller, the distinguished Sanskrit authority, who in the words of an Indian scholar "devoted his lifetime to the elucidation of the learning, literature, and religion of ancient India",[1] abandoned Bopp's patriotic term "Indo-Germanic" and adopted Aryan, which he founded on the Sanskrit racial designation "Arya". At first he accepted the theory of an Aryan race and especially of an Aryan civilization which originated on the Central Asian plateau, but, as will be seen, he subsequently modified his views in this regard.

A new theory regarding the Aryans, who are now more commonly referred to as Indo-Europeans, was strongly advocated in 1851 and later by Dr. Robert Gordon Latham, who devoted many years to the study of ethnology and philology. He argued that as the major part of the peoples speaking Indo-European tongues was found in Europe, the cradle of the race might, after all, be transferred westward. This theory was supported by the fact (among others) that the Lithuanian language was no less archaic than Sanskrit.

The European hypothesis found in time many able supporters, and the advocates of rival Teutonic and Celtic claims waxed eloquent and heated over the exact location of the Aryan homeland. An industrious search was meanwhile conducted for words common to all Aryan languages which described the natural features of the racial "cradle". This work of reconstruction was certainly not lacking in picturesque results, for attractive visions were presented of Aryan Arcadias in which the simple and contemplative

[1] Romesh C. Dutt's *Ramáyana* dedication.

ancestors of many bitter controversialists dwelt together in exemplary unity and peace. The question of location might remain unsettled, but it was generally agreed that the ancient people were surrounded by cows, sheep, and goats; sometimes they rode their horses or yoked them in rough rumbling carts, and sometimes they ate them. No asses were admitted to the fold because of their decided partiality for Central Asian plains, which seemed quite reasonable. Trouble was occasionally caused by wolves and bears, or, mayhap, a stray lion, but these and other worries associated with the simple life might be compensated for by the fact that the primitive people, as one writer[1] put it, "understood the art of drinking". Mead, brewed from honey, was found to be "dear to the hearts of the ancient Aryans"; had the Brahman ever forgotten his "madhu", the Welshman his "medhu", or the Lithuanian his "medus"? Problems arose regarding the ancients' knowledge of trees: it was found that "bhaga" was applied indifferently by the family groups to the beech and the oak, and more than one ingenious explanation was suggested to account for this apparent discrepancy. Then, suddenly, Professor Max Müller swept into the background the rival Aryan homeland pictures, pointing out the while that it is "almost impossible to discover any animal or any plant that is peculiar to the north of Europe and is not found sporadically in Asia also". Destructive criticism proceeded apace, until now nothing has been left to us of the ancestral Arcadia but "air, water, heat and cold". In his review of the widely accepted philological "evidence" regarding the Aryan homeland, Max Müller declared it to be so pliant that it was possible "to make out a more or less plausible case for any part of the world". The advanced group of philologists held, indeed, that no racial

[1] Rydberg's *Teutonic Mythology.*

centre could be located. Ultimately "Delbrück went so far," says Professor Ripley, "as to deny that any single parent language ever existed in fact".[1]

Meanwhile ethnologists and archæologists were engaged accumulating important data. It was found that Europe had been invaded at the close of the Stone Age by a broad-headed (brachycephalic) people, who brought no culture and even retarded the growth of civilization in their areas of settlement. A new problem was thus presented: were the Aryans a brachycephalic (broad-headed) or a dolichocephalic (long-headed) people? Its solution was rendered all the more difficult when it was found that living representatives of both racial types were peoples of Aryan speech. The idea that skull shapes, which are associated with other distinct physical characteristics, were due to habits of life and the quality of food which had to be masticated, was in time advanced to discredit new methods of ethnic research, but it has since been thoroughly disproved. In many ancient graves are found skulls which do not differ from those of modern men and women, living under different conditions and eating different food.

Patriotic controversialists were not awanting again in dealing with the problem of varying skull shapes. French scientists, for instance, have identified the "broad heads", now generally known as the Alpine race, with the ubiquitous Celts, but as present-day Hindus are mainly "long heads", the Aryan racial connection here suggested remains obscure. A clue to the mystery was sought for in Asia Minor, but no satisfactory result could be obtained there to support philological theories, because the Armenians, who are "broad heads", and their enemies and neighbours the Kurds, who are "long heads", are

[1] *The Races of Europe*, W. Z. Ripley, p. 481.

both peoples of Aryan speech. A scornful scientist has dismissed as a "prehistoric romance", the theory that the fair Scandinavian "long heads" are identical with the brunet "long heads" of India. Both the Celtic (Alpine) and Indo-Germanic racial theories are as inconclusive as they are diametrically in opposition.

The science of philology, which, at its inception, "dazzled and silenced all", has been proved to be no safe guide in racial matters. We must avoid, as Professor Ripley says, "the error of confusing community of language with identity of race. Nationality may often follow linguistic boundaries, but race bears no necessary relation whatever to them."[1]

By way of illustration, it may be pointed out in this connection that English is spoken at the present day by, among others, the Hong Kong Chinamen, the American Red Indians and negroes, by the natives of Ireland, Wales, Cornwall, and the Scottish Highlands, besides the descendants of the ancient Britons, the Jutes, the Angles, the Saxons, the Norsemen, the Danes, and the Normans in England, but all these peoples cannot be classified in the racial sense simply as Englishmen. Similarly, the varied types of humanity who are Aryan in speech cannot all be regarded as representatives of the "Aryan race", that is, if we accept the theory of an "Aryan race", which Virchow, by the way, has characterized as "a pure fiction".

Max Müller, in his closing years, faced this aspect of the problem frankly and courageously. "Aryas", he wrote, "are those who speak Aryan languages, whatever their colour, whatever their blood. In calling them Aryas we predicate nothing of them except that the grammar of their language is Aryan. . . . I have declared again

[1] *The Races of Europe*, W. Z. Ripley, p. 17.

and again that if I say Aryas, I mean neither blood, nor bones, nor hair, nor skull; I mean simply those who speak an Aryan language. The same applies to Hindus, Greeks, Romans, Germans, Celts, and Slavs. When I speak of these I commit myself to no anatomical characteristics. The blue-eyed and fair-haired Scandinavians may have been conquerors or conquered, they may have adopted the language of their darker lords or their subjects, or vice versa. I assert nothing beyond their language when I call them Hindus, Greeks, Romans, Germans, Celts, and Slavs, and in that sense, and in that sense only, do I say that even the blackest Hindus represent an earlier stage of Aryan speech and thought than the fairest Scandinavians. . . . To me an ethnologist who speaks of an Aryan race, Aryan blood, Aryan eyes and hair, is as great a sinner as a linguist who speaks of a dolichocephalic dictionary or a brachycephalic grammar."[1]

Aryan, however, has been found to be a convenient term, and even ethnologists do not scorn its use, although it has been applied "in a confusing variety of signification by different philologists". One application of it is to the language group comprising Sanskrit, Persian, Afghan, &c. Some still prefer it to "Indo-European", which has found rivals in "Afro-European", among those who connect the Aryan languages with North Africa, and "Afro-Eurasian", which may be regarded as universal in its racial application, especially if we accept Darwin's theory that the Garden of Eden was located somewhere in Africa.[2] We may think of the Aryans as we do of the British when that term is used to include the peoples embraced by the British Empire.

[1] *Biographies of Words and the Home of the Aryas*, pp. 120 and 245.

[2] *The Descent of Man*, Charles Darwin, chap. vi, p. 155 (1889 ed.), and *The Ancient Egyptians*, G. Elliot Smith, pp. 63, 64 (1911).

In India the Aryans were from late Vedic times divided into four castes—Brahmans (priests), Kshatriyas (kings and warriors), Vaisyas (traders, &c.), and Sudras (aborigines).

Caste (Varna) signifies "colour", but it is not certain whether the reference is to be given a physical or mythological application. The first three castes were Aryans, the fairest people; the fourth caste, that comprising the dark-skinned aborigines, was non-Aryan. "Arya", however, was not always used in the sense that we have been accustomed to apply "Aryo-Indian". In one of the sacred books of the ancient people it is stated: "The colour of the Brahmans was white; that of the Kshatriyas red; that of the Vaisyas yellow; and that of the Sudras black".[1] This colour reference connects "caste" with the doctrine of yugas, or ages of the universe (Chapter VI).

Risley, dealing with "the leading castes and tribes in Northern India, from the Bay of Bengal to the frontiers of Afghanistan", concludes from the data obtained from census returns, that we are able "to distinguish two extreme types of feature and physique, which may be provisionally described as Aryan and Dravidian. A third type, which in some respects may be looked upon as intermediate between these two, while in other, and perhaps the most important, points it can hardly be deemed Indian at all, is found along the northern and eastern borders of Bengal. The most prominent characters are a relatively short (brachycephalic) head, a broad face, a short, wide nose, very low in the bridge, and in extreme cases almost bridgeless; high and projecting cheekbones and eyelids, peculiarly formed so as to give the impression that the eyes are obliquely set in the head. . . .

[1] Muir's *Original Sanskrit Texts*, vol. 1, p. 140.

This type . . . may be conveniently described as Mongoloid. . . ."[1]

According to Risley, the Aryan type is dolichocephalic (long-headed), "with straight, finely-cut (lepto-rhine) nose, a long, symmetrical narrow face, a well-developed forehead, regular features, and a high facial angle". The stature is "fairly high", and the body is "well proportioned, and slender rather than massive". The complexion is "a very light transparent brown—'wheat coloured' is the common vernacular description—noticeably fairer than the mass of the population".

The Dravidian head, the same authority states, "usually inclines to be dolichocephalic", but "all other characters present a marked contrast to the Aryan. The nose is thick and broad, and the formula expressing its proportionate dimensions is higher than in any known race, except the Negro. The facial angle is comparatively low; the lips are thick; the face wide and fleshy; the features coarse and irregular." The stature is lower than that of the Aryan type: "the figure is squat and the limbs sturdy. The colour of the skin varies from very dark brown to a shade closely approaching black. . . . Between these extreme types", adds Risley, "we find a large number of intermediate groups."[2]

Of late years ethnologists have inclined to regard the lower types represented by hill and jungle tribes, the Veddas of Ceylon, &c., as pre-Dravidians. The brunet and long-headed Dravidians may have entered India long before the Aryans: they resemble closely the Brahui of Baluchistan and the Man-tse of China.

India is thus mainly long-headed (dolichocephalic). We have already seen, however, that in northern and eastern Bengal there are traces of an infusion of Mon-

[1] *The Tribes and Castes of Bengal*, H. H. Risley, vol. I, xxxi. [2] *ibid.* xxxii–xxxiii.

golian "broad heads"; another brachycephalic element is pronounced in western India, but it is not Mongolian; possibly we have here evidences of a settlement of Alpine stock. According to Risley, these western broad heads are the descendants of invading Scythians,[1] but this theory is not generally accepted.

The Eur-Asian Alpine race of broad heads are a mountain people distributed from Hindu Kush westward to Brittany. On the land bridge of Asia Minor they are represented by the Armenians. Their eastern prehistoric migrations is by some ethnologists believed to be marked by the Ainus of Japan. They are mostly a grey-eyed folk, with dark hair and abundant moustache and beard, as contrasted with the Mongols, whose facial hair is scanty. There are short and long varieties of Alpine stock, and its representatives are usually sturdy and muscular. In Europe these broad-headed invaders overlaid a long-headed brunet population, as the early graves show, but in the process of time the broad heads have again retreated mainly to their immemorial upland habitat. At the present day the Alpine race separates the long-headed fair northern race from what is known as the long-headed dark Mediterranean race of the south.

A slighter and long-headed brunet type is found south of Hindu Kush. Ripley has condensed a mass of evidence to show that it is akin to the Mediterranean race.[2] He refers to it as the "eastern branch", which includes Afghans and Hindus. "We are all familiar with the type," he says, "especially as it is emphasized by inbreeding and selection among the Brahmans. . . . There can be no doubt of their (the Eastern Mediterraneans) racial affinities with our Berbers, Greeks, Italians, and

[1] *The People of India*, H. H. Risley, p. 59.
[2] *The Races of Europe*, W. Z. Ripley, 450 *et seq.*

Spaniards. They are all members of the same race, at once the widest in its geographical extension, the most populous and the most primitive of our three European types."[1]

Professor Elliot Smith supports Professor Ripley in this connection, and includes the Arabs with the southern Persians in the same group, but finding the terms "Hamitic" and "Mediterranean" insufficient, prefers to call this widespread family the "Brown race", tc distinguish its representatives from the fair Northerners, the "yellow" Mongolians, and the "black" negroes.

North of the Alpine racial area are found the nomadic Mongolians, who are also "broad heads", but with distinguishing facial characteristics which vary in localities. As we have seen, the Mongoloid features are traceable in India. Many settlers have migrated from Tibet, but among the high-caste Indians the Mongoloid eyes and high cheek bones occur in families, suggesting early crossment.

Another distinctive race has yet to be accounted for—the tall, fair, blue-eyed, long-headed Northerners, represented by the Scandinavians of the present day. Sergi and other ethnologists have classed this type as a variety of the Mediterranean race, which had its area of localization on the edge of the snow belt on lofty plateaus and in proximity to the Arctic circle. The theory that the distinctive blondness and great stature of the Northerners were acquired in isolation and perpetuated by artificial selection is, however, more suggestive than conclusive, unless we accept the theory that acquired characteristics can be inherited. How dark eyes became grey or blue, and dark hair red or sandy, is a problem yet to be solved.

The ancestors of this fair race are believed to have

[1] *The Races of Europe*, W. Z. Ripley, p. 451.

been originally distributed along the northern Eur-Asian plateaus; Keane's blonde long-headed Chudes[1] and the Wu-suns in Chinese Turkestan are classed as varieties of the ancient Northern stock. An interesting problem is presented in this connection by the fair types among the ancient Egyptians, the modern-day Berbers, and the blondes of the Atlas mountains in Morocco. Sergi is inclined to place the "cradle" of the Northerners on the edge of the Sahara.

The broad-headed Turki and Ugrians are usually referred to as a blend of the Alpine stock and the proto-Northerners, with, in places, Mongolian admixture.

As most of the early peoples were nomadic, or periodically nomadic, there must have been in localities a good deal of interracial and intertribal fusion, with the result that intermediate varieties were produced. It follows that the intellectual life of the mingling peoples would be strongly influenced by admixture as well as by contact with great civilizations.

It now remains for us to deal with the Aryan problem in India. Dr. Haddon considers that the invading Aryans were "perhaps associated with Turki tribes" when they settled in the Punjab.[2] Prior to this racial movement, the Kassites, whose origin is obscure, assisted by bands of Aryans, overthrew the Hammurabi dynasty in Babylon and established the Kassite dynasty between 2000 B.C. and 1700 B.C. At this period the domesticated horse was introduced, and its Babylonian name, "the ass of the East", is an indication whence it came. Another Aryan invasion farther west is marked by the establishment of the Mitanni kingdom between the area controlled by the Assyrians and the Hittites. Its kings had names

[1] *Man, Past and Present*, A. H. Keane, p. 270.

[2] *The Wanderings of Peoples*, A. C. Haddon, p. 21.

which are clearly Aryan. These included Saushatar, Artatatama, Sutarna, and Tushratta. The latter was the correspondent in the Tel-el-Amarna letters of his kinsmen the Egyptian Pharaohs, Amenhotep the Magnificent, and the famous Akhenaton. The two royal houses had intermarried after the wars of Thothmes III. It is impossible to fix the date of the rise of the Mitanni power, which held sway for a period over Assyria, but we know that it existed in 1500 B.C. The horse was introduced into Egypt before 1580 B.C.

It is generally believed that the Aryans were the tamers of the horse which revolutionized warfare in ancient days, and caused great empires to be overthrown and new empires to be formed. When the Aryans entered India they had chariots and swift steeds.

There is no general agreement as to the date of settlement in the Punjab. Some authorities favour 2000 B.C., others 1700 B.C.; Professor Macdonell still adheres to 1200 B.C.[1] It is possible that the infusion was at first a gradual one, and that it was propelled by successive folk-waves. The period from the earliest migrations until about 800 or 700 B.C. is usually referred to as the Vedic Age, during which the Vedas, or more particularly the invocatory hymns to the deities, were composed and compiled. At the close of this Age the area of Aryan control had extended eastward as far as the upper reaches of the Jumna and Ganges rivers. A number of tribal states or communities are referred to in the hymns.

It is of importance to note that the social and religious organization of the Vedic Aryans was based upon the principle of "father right", as contrasted with the principle of "mother right", recognized by representative communities of the Brown race.

[1] *Vedic Index of Names and Subjects* (1912), p. viii.

Like the Alpine and Mongoloid peoples, the Vedic Aryans were a patriarchal people, mainly pastoral but with some knowledge of agriculture. They worshipped gods chiefly: their goddesses were vague and shadowy: their earth goddess Prithivi was not a Great Mother in the Egyptian and early European sense; her husband was the sky-god Dyaus.

In Egypt the sky was symbolized as the goddess Nut, and the earth as the god Seb, but the Libyans had an earth-goddess Neith. The "Queen of Heaven" was a Babylonian and Assyrian deity. If the Brown race predominated in the Aryan blend during the Vedic Age, we should have found the Great Mother more in prominence.

The principal Aryan deities were Indra, god of thunder, and Agni, god of fire, to whom the greater number of hymns were addressed. From the earliest times, however, Aryan religion was of complex character. We can trace at least two sources of cultural influence from the earlier Iranian period.[1] The hymns bear evidence of the declining splendour of the sublime deities Varuna and Mitra (Mithra). It is possible that the conflicts to which references are made in some of the hymns were not unconnected with racial or tribal religious rivalries.

Indra, as we show (Chapter I), bears resemblances to other "hammer gods". He is the Indian Thor, the angry giant-killer, the god of war and conquests. That his name even did not originate in India is made evident by an inscription at Boghaz Koi, in Asia Minor, referring to a peace treaty between the kings of the Hittites and Mitanni. Professor Hugo Winckler has deciphered from this important survival of antiquity "In-da-ra" as a Mi-

[1] A convenient term to refer to the unknown area occupied by the Vedic Aryans before they invaded India.

tanni deity who was associated with Varuna, Mitra, and Nasatya.

No evidence has yet been forthcoming to indicate any connection between the Aryans in Mitanni and the early settlers in India. It would appear, however, that the two migrations represented by the widely separated areas of Aryan control, radiated from a centre where the gods Indra, Varuna, and Mitra were grouped in the official religion. The folk-wave which pressed towards the Punjab gave recognition to Agni, possibly as a result of contact, or, more probably, fusion with a tribe of specialized fire-worshippers.

If we separate the Indra from the Agni, cremating worshippers, it will be of interest to follow the ethnic clue which is thus suggested. Modern-day Hindus burn their dead in accordance with the religious practice of the Agni worshippers in the Vedic Age. It is doubtful, however, if all the Aryan invaders practised cremation. There are references to burial in the "house of clay", and Yama, god of the dead, was adored as the first man who explored the path to the "Land of the Pitris" (Fathers) which lay across the mountains. Professor Oldenberg considers that these burials referred to the disposal of the bones and ashes of the dead.

Professor Macdonell and Dr. Keith, however, do not share Professor Oldenberg's view in this connection.[1] They hold that the epithet *Agni-dagdhah*, "burnt with fire", "applies to the dead who were burned on the funeral pyre"; the other custom being burial—*An-agni-dagdhah*, "not burnt with fire". They also refer to *Paroptah*, "casting out", and *Uddhitah*, "Exposure of the dead", which are expressions of doubtful meaning

[1] *Vedic Index of Names and Subjects*, A. A. Macdonell and A. B. Keith, Vol. I, pp. 8, 9 (1912).

These authorities add: "Burial was clearly not rare in the Rigvedic period: a whole hymn (x, 18) describes the ritual attending it. The dead man was buried apparently in full attire, with his bow in his hand, and probably at one time his wife was immolated to accompany him. . . . But in the Vedic period both customs appear in a modified form: the son takes the bow from the hand of the dead man, and the widow is led away from her dead husband by his brother or nearest kinsman. A stone is set up between the dead and the living to separate them."

The Persian fire-worshippers, on the other hand, did not cremate their dead, but exposed them on "towers of silence" to be devoured by vultures, like their modern-day representatives the Parsees, who migrated into India after displacement by the Mohammedans. In Persia the sacred fire was called Atar,[1] and was identified with the supreme deity Ahura-Mazda (Ormuzd).

Agni of the Vedic Age is the messenger between gods and men; he conducts the deities to the sacrifice and the souls of the cremated dead to Paradise; he is also the twin brother of Indra.

Now, it is of interest to note, in considering the racial significance of burial rites, that cremation was not practised by the western representatives of the Brown race. In pre-Dynastic Egypt the dead were interred as in Babylon,[2] with food vessels, &c. Neolithic man in Europe also favoured crouched burials, and this practice obtained all through the Bronze Age.

The Buriats, who are Mongols dwelling in the vicinity of Lake Baikal, still perpetuate ancient customs, which

[1] Compared with the Latin *atrium*, "the room that contained the hearthfire". Agni is cognate with the Latin *ignis*, cf. Lithunian, *ugnis szwenta*, "holy fire"—*Early Religious Poetry of Persia*, Professor Moulton, pp. 38, 39.

[2] The theory that certain Babylonian graves show traces of cremation has been abandoned.—*A History of Sumer and Akkad*, L. W. King, pp. 20, 21 (1910).

resemble those of the Vedic Aryans, for they not only practise cremation but also sacrifice the horse (see Chap. V). In his important study of this remarkable people, Mr. Curtin says:[1] "The Buriats usually burn their dead; occasionally, however, there is what is called a 'Russian burial', that is, the body is placed in a coffin and the coffin is put in the ground. But generally if a man dies in the Autumn or the Winter his body is placed on a sled and drawn by the horse which he valued most to some secluded place in the forest. There a sort of house is built of fallen trees and boughs, the body is placed inside the house, and the building is then surrounded with two or three walls of logs so that no wolf or other animal can get into it." The horse is afterwards slain. "If other persons die during the winter their bodies are carried to the same house. In this lonely silent place in the forest they rest through the days and nights until the first cuckoo calls, about the ninth of May. Then relatives and friends assemble, and without opening the house burn it to the ground. Persons who die afterwards and during the Summer months are carried to the forest, placed on a funeral pile, and burned immediately. The horse is killed just as in the first instance."

When the dead are buried without being burned, the corpse is either carried on a wagon, or it is placed upright in front of a living man on horseback so as to ride to its last resting place. The saddle is broken up and laid at the bottom of the grave, while the body is turned to face the south-east. In this case they also sacrifice the horse which is believed to have "gone to his master, ready for use".

Cremation spread throughout Europe, as we have said,

[1] *A Journey in Southern Siberia*, Jeremiah Curtin, p. 101.

in the Bronze Age. It was not practised by the early folk-waves of the Alpine race which, according to Mosso,[1] began to arrive after copper came into use. The two European Bronze Age burial customs, associated with urns of the "food vessel" and "drinking cup" types, have no connection with the practice of burning the dead. The Archæological Ages have not necessarily an ethnic significance. Ripley is of opinion, however, that the practice of cremation indicates a definite racial infusion, but unfortunately it has destroyed the very evidence, of which we are most in need, to solve the problem. It is impossible to say whether the cremated dead were "broad heads" or "long heads".

"Dr. Sophus Müller of Copenhagen is of opinion that cremation was not practised long before the year 1000 B.C. though it appeared earlier in the south of Europe than in the north. On both points Professor Ridgeway of Cambridge agrees with him."[2]

The migration of the cremating people through Europe was westward and southward and northward; they even swept through the British Isles as far north as Orkney. They are usually referred to by archæologists as "Aryans"; some identify them with the mysterious Celts, whom the French, however, prefer to associate, as we have said, with the Alpine "broad heads" especially as this type bulks among the Bretons and the hillmen of France. We must be careful, however, to distinguish between the Aryans and Celts of the philologists and archæologists.

It may be that these invaders were not a race in the proper sense, but a military confederacy which maintained a religious organization formulated in some unknown area where they existed for a time as a nation. The Normans

[1] *The Dawn of Mediterranean Civilization*, A. Mosso, London Trans., 1910.
[2] British Museum *Guide to the Antiquities of the Bronze Age*, pp. 23, 24.

who invaded these islands were Scandinavians[1]; they settled in France, intermarried with the French, and found allies among the Breton chiefs. It is possible that the cremating people similarly formed military aristocracies when they settled in Hindustan, Mitanni, and in certain other European areas. "Nothing is commoner in the history of migratory peoples," says Professor Myres,[2] "than to find a very small leaven of energetic intruders ruling and organizing large native populations, without either learning their subjects' language or imposing their own till considerably later, if at all." The archæological evidence in this connection is of particular value. At a famous site near Salzburg, in upper Austria, over a thousand Bronze Age graves were discovered, just over half of which contained unburnt burials. Both methods of interment were contemporary in this district, "but it was noticed that the cremated burials were those of the wealthier class, or of the dominant race."[3] We find also that at Hallstatt "the bodies of the wealthier class were reduced to ashes".[4] In some districts the older people may have maintained their supremacy. At Watsch and St. Margaret in Carniola "a similar blending of the two rites was observed . . . the unburnt burials being the richer and more numerous".[5] The descent of the Achaens into Greece occurred at a date earlier than the rise of the great Hallstatt civilization. According to Homeric evidence they burned their dead; "though the body of Patroklos was cremated," however, "the lords of Mycenae were interred unburnt in richly furnished graves".[6] In Britain the cremating people mingled with their predecessors perhaps more intimately

[1] Associated, some authorities urge, with Germans from the mouth of the Elbe.
[2] *The Dawn of History*, J. L. Myres, p. 199.
[3] British Museum *Guide to the Antiquities of the Bronze Age*, p. 98.
[4] British Museum *Guide to the Antiquities of the Early Iron Age*, p. 8.
[5] *ibid.* p. 6. [6] *ibid.* p. 8.

than in other areas where there were large states to conquer. A characteristic find on Acklam Wold, Yorkshire, may be referred to. In this grave "a pile of burnt bones was in close contact with the legs of a skeleton buried in the usual contracted position, and they seemed to have been deposited while yet hot, for the knees of the skeleton were completely charred. It has been suggested in cases like this, or where an unburnt body is surrounded by a ring of urn burials, the entire skeleton may be those of chiefs or heads of families, and the burnt bones those of slaves, or even wives, sacrificed at the funeral. The practice of suttee (sati) in Europe rests indeed on the authority of Julius Cæsar, who represents such religious suicides as having, at no remote period from his own, formed a part of the funeral rites of the Gaulish chiefs; and also states that the relatives of a deceased chieftain accused his wives of being accessory to his death, and often tortured them to death on that account."[1] If this is the explanation, the cremating invaders constituted the lower classes in Gaul and Britain, which is doubtful. The practice of burning erring wives, however, apparently prevailed among the Mediterranean peoples. In an Egyptian folk-tale a Pharaoh ordered a faithless wife of a scribe to be burned at the stake.[2] One of the Ossianic folk tales of Scotland relates that Grainne, wife of Finn-mac-Coul, who eloped with Diarmid, was similarly dealt with.[3] The bulk of the archæological evidence seems to point to the invaders, who are usually referred to as "Aryans" having introduced the cremation ceremony into Europe. Whence came they? The problem is greatly complicated by the evidence from Palestine, where cremation was practised by the hewers of the great artificial caves which were constructed about

[1] British Museum *Guide to the Antiquities of the Bronze Age*, pp. 16, 17.

[2] *Egyptian Myth and Legend*, p. 143. [3] Campbell's *West Highland Tales*, vol. iii, p. 55.

3000 B.C.[1] As cremation did not begin in Crete, however, until the end of period referred to as "Late Minoan Third" (1450–1200 B.C.)[2] it may be that the Palestinian burials are much later than the construction of the caves.

It seems reasonable to suppose that the cremation rite originated among a nomadic people. The spirits of the dead were got rid of by burning the body: they departed, like the spirit of Patroklos, after they had received their "meed of fire". Burial sites were previously regarded as sacred because they were haunted by the spirits of ancestors (the Indian *Pitris* = "fathers"). A people who burned their dead, and were therefore not bound by attachment to a tribal holy place haunted by spirits, were certainly free to wander. The spirits were transferred by fire to an organized Hades, which appears to have been conceived of by a people who had already attained to a certain social organization and were therefore capable of governing the communities which they subdued. When they mingled with peoples practising other rites and professing different religious beliefs, however, the process of racial fusion must have been accompanied by a fusion of beliefs. Ultimately the burial customs of the subject race might prevail. At any rate, this appears to have been the case in Britain, where, prior to the Roman Age, the early people achieved apparently an intellectual conquest of their conquerors; the practice of the cremation rite entirely vanished.

We have gone far afield to find a clue to assist towards the solution of the Aryan problem in India. The evidence accumulated is certainly suggestive, and shows that the conclusions of the early philologists have been narrow in the extreme. If the long-headed Kurds are, as Ripley

[1] *A History of Civilization in Palestine*, R. A. S. Macalister.

[2] *The Discoveries in Crete*, Professor R. M. Burrows, p. 100. Dating according to *Crete the Forerunner of Greece*, C. H. and H. B. Hawes, p. xiv.

believes, the descendants of the Mitanni raiders, then the Aryans of history must be included in the Brown race. As, however, cremation was not practised by the Berbers, the Babylonians, the early Cretans, or other representatives of the ancient brunet dolichocephalic peoples, it may be that the custom, which still lingers among the Mongolian Buriats, was not in the narrow sense of Aryan origin. It may have been first practised among an unknown tribe of fire-worshippers, who came under the influence of a great teacher like Zoroaster. We cannot overlook in this connection the possibility of an individual origin for a new and revolutionary system of religious doctrines. Buddhism, for instance, originated with Buddha.

As we have said, the Vedic religion of the Aryans in India was characterized by the worship of male deities, the goddesses being of secondary and even slight importance. A religious revolution, however, occurred during the second or Brahmanical Age—the age of priestly ascendancy. Fresh invasions had taken place and the Aryans were divided into tribal groups of Westerners and Easterners, on either side of a central power in Madhyadesa, the "Middle Country" which extended between the upper reaches of the Saraswati and the Ganges and the Jumna rivers. The Westerners included the peoples of the Punjab and the north-western frontier, and the Easterners the kingdoms of Kasi (Benares) and Maghadha as well as Kosala and Videha, which figure prominently in the *Ramdyana* epic, where the kings are referred to as being of the "Solar race". The Middle Kingdom was the centre of Brahmanical culture and influence: it was controlled by those federated tribes, the Kuru Panchalas, with whom were fused the Bháratas of the "Lunar race". It is believed that the military aristocracy of the "Middle Country" were late comers who arrived by a new route and thrust themselves between the groups of early settlers.[1] The Bharatas worshipped a goddess Bharati who was associated with the Saraswati river on the banks of which the tribe had for a period been located. Saraswati became the wife of Brahma, the supreme god, and it would seem that she had a tribal significance.

If the Bharatas of the "Lunar race" worshipped the moon and rivers, it is possible that they belonged to the Brown race. The folk-religion of the tribe would be perpetuated by the people even although their priests became speculative thinkers like the unknown authors of the *Upanishads*. It is significant to note, therefore, that the goddesses ultimately came into as great prominence in India as in Egypt. This change took place during the obscure period prior to the revival of Brahmanism. In the sixth century before the Christian era Buddhism had origin, partly as a revolt of the Kshatriya (aristocratic) class against priestly ascendancy, and the new faith spread eastward where Brahmanic influence was least pronounced. When the influence of Buddhism declined, the Pantheon is found to have been revolutionized and rendered thoroughly Mediterranean in character. The Vedic gods had in the interval suffered eclipse; they were subject to the greater personal gods Brahma, with Vishnu and Shiva, each of whom had a goddess for wife. Brahma, as we have said, had associated with him the river deity Saraswati of the Bharatas; the earth goddess, Lakshmi, was the wife of Vishnu; she rose, however, from the Ocean of Milk. But the most distinctive and even most primitive goddesses were linked with Shiva, the Destroyer. The goddess Durga rivalled Indra as a deity of war. Kali, another form of Durga, was as vengeful and bloodthirsty

[1] *Vedic Index of Names and Subjects.*

2

KALI

From a bronze in the Calcutta Art Gallery

as the Scottish Cailleach, or the Egyptian Hathor, who, as the earlier Sekhet, rejoiced in accomplishing the slaughter of the enemies of Ra.[1] Kali, as we shall see (Chapter VIII) replaced the Vedic king of the gods as a successful demon slayer. As the Egyptian Ra went forth to restrain Hathor, so did Shiva hasten to the battlefield, flooded by gore, to prevail upon his spouse Kali to spare the remnant of her enemies.

The rise of the goddesses may have been due in part to the influence of Dravidian folk-religion. This does not, however, vitiate the theory that moon, water, and earth worship was not unconnected with the ascendancy of the Brown race in India. The Dravidian brunet long heads were, as we have said, probably represented in the pre-Aryan, as well as the post-Vedic folk-waves, which mingled with pre-Dravidian stocks. Mr. Crooke inclines to the view that the Aryan conquest was more moral and intellectual than racial.[2] The decline of the patriarchal religion of the Vedic military aristocracy may thus be accounted for; the religious practices of the earlier people might ultimately have attained prominence in fusion with imported ideas. If the Aryan racial type was distinctive, as it appears to have been, in colour at any rate, the predominant people who flourished when the hymns were composed, may have greatly declined in numbers owing to the ravages of disease which in every new country eliminates the unfit in the process of time. Even if Aryan conquest was more racial in character than Mr. Crooke will allow, the physical phenomena of the present day can be accounted for in this way, due allowance being made, of course, for the crossment of types. In all countries which have sustained the shock of invasion, the tendency to revert to the aboriginal type is very marked.

[1] See *Egyptian Myth and Legend.* [2] *The North-Western Provinces of India*, 1897, p. 60.

At any rate, this is the case in Egypt and Crete as present-day evidence shows. In Great Britain, which was invaded by the broad heads of the Bronze Age, the long-headed type is once again in the majority; a not inconsiderable proportion of our people show Stone Age (Mediterranean) physical characteristics.

In this connection it is of interest to refer to immemorial beliefs and customs which survive in representative districts in Britain and India where what may be called pre-Aryan influences are most pronounced. A people may change their weapons and their language time and again, and yet retain ancient modes of thought. In Devon, which the philologists claim to be largely Celtic like Cornwall, the folk-lore shows marked affinities with that of Ireland, Wales, and Scotland, suggesting the survival of ancient Mediterranean racial influence, for much of what we call Celtic links with what belongs to ancient Greece and the Egyptian Delta. Mr. Gomme has shown[1] in an interesting summary of recorded folk-practices that the "ram feast" of Devon resembles closely in essential details similar ceremonies in ancient Greece and modern India. At the beginning of May the people of Devon were wont to sacrifice a ram lamb to the deity of waters. The animal was tied to a pillar, its throat was cut, and young men scrambled to obtain pieces of its flesh for girls. The devourer was assured of good luck during the year. After the ceremony, dancing, wrestling, and drinking were indulged in. A comparison is drawn between this and similar rites among the ancient Semites and ancient Greeks. In India a Dravidian Paria acts as the temporary village priest. He uses a whip like the "gad whip" in Lincolnshire, and kills the lamb by tearing its throat with his teeth. A scramble takes place for the flesh, the people

[1] *Ethnology in Folklore*, George Laurence Gomme, p. 34 *et seq.*

circulate the village, as some communities in our own country still perpetuate the ceremony of "riding the marches" of ancient burghs; then universal licence prevails. Similarly law was suspended at the ancient Scottish Hallowe'en celebrations; in some districts even in our own day Hallowe'en and New Year practical jokes and rowdyism is still prevalent. Herodotus refers to the universal licence and debauchery which characterized the Isis festival in Egypt.

A remarkable feature of post-Vedic religion in ancient India is the prominence given to the doctrine of metempsychosis (transmigration of souls) and the conception of the yugas or ages of the universe.

In the *Rigveda* the soul of the dead proceeds at once, or at any rate after burial, towards the next world. In one passage only is it spoken of "as departing to the waters or the plants", and this reference, Professor Macdonell suggests,[1] "may contain the germs of the theory" of transmigration. In the speculative prose treatises, the *Upanishads*, which were composed in the Middle Country, the doctrine of metempsychosis is fully expounded. It does not follow, however, that it originated in India although it may have obtained there unrecognized by the priestly poets who composed the hymns to the deities, long before it became an essential tenet of orthodox or official religion. Other representative communities of the Brown race professed this doctrine which appears to have evolved from the vague belief shared by more than one primitive race, that the souls of the dead, and especially of dead children, were ever on the outlook for suitable mothers. Even in Central Australia a particular tribe has perpetuated "the germs of the theory", which may also be traced in the widespread custom of visiting standing

[1] *A History of Sanskrit Literature*, p. 115.

stones at a certain phase of the moon to perform a ceremony so that offspring may be obtained. The Upanishadic doctrine of metempsychosis is less likely to have been so much coincidental as racial when we find that it is restricted to those areas where definite racial influences must have been at work. The Greeks believed in transmigration. So did also a section of the Egyptian people as Herodotus has stated and as is proved by references in folk-tales, temple chants and inscriptions.[1] As we show (Chapter VI), the Irish conception closely resembled the Indian, and it also obtained among the Gauls. There is no trace, however, that the Teutonic peoples were acquainted with the fully developed doctrine of metempsychosis; the souls of the dead departed immediately to Valhal, Hela, or the loathsome Nifelhel.

The doctrine of the world's ages is common to the Indian, Greek, and Irish mythologies, but is not found in Teutonic mythology either.[2] There are indications that it may have at one time obtained in Egypt, for there was an Age of Ra, then a deluge, an Age of Osiris, an Age of Set, &c.; but the doctrine, like other conceptions in Egypt, probably suffered from the process of priestly transformation in the interests of sectarian propaganda.

In India the ages are called the yugas, and this term has a totally different meaning in Vedic and Upanishadic times. Evidently the Bharata invasion and the establishment of the middle country power of their allies, the Kuru-Panchalas, was not unconnected with the introduction of the doctrines of metempsychosis and the yugas, and the prominence subsequently given to the worship of female deities.

[1] See *Egyptian Myth and Legend*.

[2] The "Golden Age" of the gods, and the regeneration of the world after Ragnarok, do not refer to the doctrine of the world's ages as found in other mythologies.

If this theory can be established, we are confronted by an extremely interesting problem. It would appear that the mythology of the Vedic period bears a close resemblance to Teutonic, while that of the post-Vedic period connects more intimately with Greek, Celtic, and Egyptian. Assuming that the Vedic people were influenced by what we recognize as Teutonic modes of thought, do we find here proof that the Aryans came from Europe? In Chapter II it is shown that the Norse Heimdal displays points of resemblance to Agni. The former, however, has been developed almost beyond recognition as a fire god, and it is evident that we find him in northern Europe in his latest and most picturesque form. On the other hand, there is no dubiety about the origin of the Vedic Agni.

The evidence afforded by archæology is highly suggestive in this connection. Scandinavia received its culture from the south at a comparatively late period in the Bronze Age, and it certainly exercised no intellectual influence in Europe in earlier times. Bronze is, of course, of less ethnic significance than beliefs, but it is difficult to believe, at the same time, that an isolated and poorly armed people could have imposed its intellectual culture over a wide area without having received anything in return. It is more probable that the northern Germanic peoples were subjected to the same influences which are traceable in their mythology and in the Vedic hymns, from a common source, and there may be more than mere mythology in the persistent tradition that the ancestors of the Teutons immigrated from Asia led by Odin. We need not assume that the movement was so much a racial as a cultural one, which emanated from a particular area where religious conceptions were influenced by particular habits of life and "immemorial modes of thought". Among the settled and agricultural peoples of the Brown race, the development of religious ideas followed different lines, and were similarly controlled by early ideas which sprang from different habits and experiences.

In the opening chapters we present various phases of Aryan life and religion in India, beginning with the worship of Indra, and concluding with the early stages of modern Hinduism. From the ancient tribal struggles of the Middle Country accumulated the hero songs which received epic treatment in the *Mahábhárata*, while the traditions of the "Easterners" were enshrined in the *Rámáyana*. Although neither of these great works can be regarded as historical narratives, they contain a mass of historical matter which throws much light on the habits and customs and beliefs of the early peoples.

These epics were utilized by Brahmanical compilers for purposes of religious propaganda, and survive to us mainly as sacred books. In our pages we have given prominence to the heroic narrative which remains embedded in the mass of doctrinal treatises and mythological interpolations. The miraculous element is somewhat toned down in the accounts of conflicts, and the more dramatic phases of the heroic stories are presented in as full detail as space permits, so as to afford our readers glimpses of ancient life in northern India at a time when Vedic religion still held sway. This applies especially to the *Mahábhárata*, the kernel of which, no doubt, contains the hero songs of the Bharata and other tribes. The mythical conflicts of the *Rámáyana* appeal less to western minds than its purely human episodes. We cannot help being impressed by the chivalrous character of the leading heroes, the high sense of honour displayed by the princes, and the obedience shown by sons to their parents. We may weary of Rama's conflicts with giants and demons, but will long remember him as the child who pronounced his name as "'Ama" and cried for the moon, or sat on his father's knee at meetings of the State Council. Our interest will also abide with him as a lover and a faithful husband who suffered wrong. His brothers are noble and heroic characters, worthy of Shakespeare. But even the Bard of Avon never depicted more wonderful and fascinating women than the heroines of the *Mahábhárata* and *Rámáyana*. Our gallery includes, among others, the noble and self-sacrificing Savitri, who rescued her husband from the clutches of death by exercise of her strong love and devotion; the faithful and virtuous Sita, and the sorrowful and constant Damayantí, and beautiful Shakuntalá. In western literature romance usually ends with marriage; in India the devotion of wives is of more account than the yearnings of love-smitten Juliets on moonlight nights.

Another aspect of Sanskrit literature is the feeling of the poets for Nature. These voluminous writers revelled in the luxuriant loveliness and splendour of Indian forests, and the charms of gleaming valleys and serene, snow-capped mountains; even the gods loved to hear the hum of insects and the songs of melodious birds, and, like mortals, to gather flowers of sweet scents and brilliant colours. Hundreds of songs were sung in praise of the lotus blooms that gemmed the clear waters of lakes and ponds, and Paradise was pictured as a jungle of beauty, fanned by soft winds, radiant with blossoms, and ever vocal with music and song. To illustrate this phase of India's classic literature, we reproduce at length the representative story of Nala with much of its poetic details.

The civilization revealed by the narrative poems was of no mean order. The ancient Aryans were chivalrous knights. No such barbaric incident occurs in the *Mahábhárata* battles as when in the *Iliad* the victorious

Achilles drags behind his chariot the body of the slain Hector. When Arjuna, the Indian Achilles, slays Karna, the Indian Hector, he honours his fallen foe and performs those rites at the funeral pyre which assures the dead hero immortal bliss in Paradise. When, again, Arjuna mortally wounds Bhishma, he procures water to quench the thirst of his dying opponent. Even the villains are not without their redeeming qualities. Duryodhana of the *Mahábhárata*, who consents to the slaughter of his sleeping rivals, dies with grief because the innocent children of his enemies were slain. Rávana, the demon king of Ceylon, touches us in the *Rámáyana* by his grief for his son, who was slain fighting against Laksmana, brother of Rama.

To appreciate fully the sacred and romantic literature of India, we should follow the advice of Robert Louis Stevenson. "To learn aright from any teacher," he wrote, "we must first of all, like a historical artist, think ourselves into sympathy with his position." And if in endeavouring to understand the religious conceptions of the ancient forest sages, we, at times, find ourselves in difficulties, it may be that "if a saying is hard to understand, it is because we are thinking of something else"—we are looking on India with European eyes and with European prejudices. "There is always", said Stevenson, "a ruling spirit behind the code of rules, an attitude, a relation, a point of the compass, in virtue of which we conform or dissent."[1]

We are confident that our readers who peruse with sympathy and, we hope, with enjoyment, the chapters which follow, will feel themselves drawn closer than hitherto to the millions of our fellow subjects in the great dependency of the British Empire, by whom Rama and Yudhishthira are regarded as ideal types of strong manhood, and Savitri and Sita as perfect women and exemplary lovers and wives.

[1] *Lay Morals.*

3

A VYASA, OR PUBLIC READER, RECITING THE MAHABHARATA

INDIAN MYTH AND LEGEND

CHAPTER I

Indra, King of the Gods

Types of Hammer Gods—The Aryan Indra—Chinese World Shaper—Scottish Hunting Deity—Egyptian Artisan God—Greek and Roman Thunder Gods—Thor—Hittite, Assyrian, and other types—A Wail from Palestine—Babylonian Influence—Indra's Indian Character—A Nature Myth—Drought Demon slain—Gods and Demons in conflict—Origin of Indra's Thunderbolt—Demons' plot to destroy Universe—Babylonian Creation Myth—How Indra Shaped the World—Elfin Artisans in India, Egypt, and Germania—Babylonian Artisan God—Indra the Harvest God—The God of Battle—Comparison with Thor—Aryan Cattle Lifters—Indra's Queen and Attendants.

The ancient Eur-Asian "hammer god", bearing the tribal name of Indra, accompanied the earliest invading bands of hunting and pastoral Aryans, who hailed with joy the "fresh woods and pastures new" of the Punjab, the green country of "Five Rivers". This deity of wanderers and invaders was already of great antiquity and wide distribution; his attributes were in accord with the habits and ideals of his worshippers; they multiplied with the discoveries of man and were ever influenced by the conditions prevailing in new areas of localization. He was the Thunderer who brought rain to quicken dried-up pasture lands; he was the god of fertility, and he became the corn spirit; he was "the friend of man"; he was the artisan of the Universe which he shaped with his hammer, the dragon slayer, the giant killer, the slaughterer of enemies, the god of war. His racial significance must ever remain obscure. We cannot identify his original home, or even fix with certainty the archæological period in which he first took definite shape. It is possible that he may have been invoked and propitiated by Neolithic, or even by Palæolithic, flint knappers who struck fire from stone long ere they suspected the existence of metal; the primitive hunting and pastoral wanderers may have conceived of a thunder deity engaged in splintering the hills with his stone hammer, and fighting demons in the rude manner in which they themselves contended against beasts of prey. Memories of the Stone Age cling to the hammer god. Indra's bolt was "the all-dreaded thunder-stone" of Shakespeare's lyric; until recently Palæolithic and Neolithic artifacts were reputed to be "elf bolts" and "thunder bolts" which fell from the sky; in Scandinavian folklore "the flint hills" are the fragments of the weapon wielded by the thunder giant Hrungner. The bolt or hammer ultimately became an axe; and according to the modern Greeks, lightning flashes are caused by the blows of the "sky axe" (astropeléki); Scottish Gaelic retains an immemorial reference to the "thunder ball" (peleir-tarnainaich).

The hammer god's close association with hilly countries suggests that he was first worshipped on the steppes and then distributed by the nomads whose migrations were propelled by changing climatic conditions. He is found as far east as China, where, as P'an Ku, the dwarfish "first man", he smites primeval rocks with his thunder hammer while engaged in the work of shaping the hills;

he is found as far west as Scotland, where, as the hunting giant Finn-mac-Coul, "in height sixty feet", he strikes with his hammer, "Ord na Feinne", such mighty blows on his shield that he is heard by his followers in Lochlann (Scandinavia). From ancient Egypt come distant echoes of the world artisan Ptah, now a dwarf and anon a giant, who hammers out the copper sky, suggesting the presence in Memphis of early Asian settlers at the very dawn of history. In southern Europe the deity is Zeus-pater (Jupiter), the sublime wielder of the thunderbolt; in northern Europe he is lusty Thor, hurling Mjolner through the air against Jotuns, or cleaving valleys with it in the mountain range which he mistook for the giant Skrymer. We find the hammer god as Tarku among the Hittites; he is Indra in Mitanni as in the Punjab; he is Rammon, or Adad, who is carried aloft in triumph by the soldiers of Assur-banipal, the Assyrian Emperor; he is remembered in Palestine by the wail of Naaman, who cried: "When my master goeth into the house of Rimmon to worship there, and he leaneth on my hand, and I bow myself in the house of Rimmon: when I bow down myself in the house of Rimmon, the Lord pardon thy servant in this thing . . ."[1] The thunder god is also known in Babylon, which received many of its settlers from the hills of Elam and where Kassites, associated with Aryans, established a dynasty after successful invasion, prior to the discovery of the Punjab. The authorities are agreed that Aryan culture shows traces of Babylonian influence; it does not follow, however, that Indra is of Babylonian origin.

But although his name, which has been deciphered as "In-da-ra" at Boghaz-Köi in Asia Minor, may belong to the early Iranian period, the Vedic "King of the gods"

[1] *2 Kings*, v, 18.

assumed a distinctly Indian character after localization in the land of the "Five Rivers"; he ultimately stepped from his chariot, drawn by the steeds of the Aryan horse tamers, and mounted an elephant; his Heaven, called Swarga, which is situated on the summit of Mount Meru, eclipses Olympus and Valhal by reason of its dazzling Oriental splendour; his combats are reflections of the natural phenomena of Hindustan.

When the hot Indian summer draws to a close, the whole land is parched and athirst for rain; rivers are low and many hill streams have dried up; man and beast are weary and await release in the breathless enervating atmosphere; they are even threatened by famine. Then dense masses of cloud gather in the sky; the tempest bellows, lightnings flash and thunder peals angrily and loud; rain descends in a deluge; once again torrents pour down from the hills and rivers become swollen and turgid. Indra has waged his battle with the Drought Demons, broken down their fortress walls, and released the imprisoned cow-clouds which give nourishment to his human "friends"; the withered pastures become green with generous and rapid growth, and the rice harvest follows.

According to Vedic myth, Indra achieved his first great victory immediately after birth. Vritra, "the encompasser", the Demon of Drought, was holding captive in his mountain fortress the cloud-cattle which he had harried in the approved manner of the Aryan raiders.[1] Mankind entreated the aid of the gods, "the shining ones, the world guardians":

> Who will take pity? Who will bring refreshment?
> Who will come nigh to help us in distress?

[1] One of the sections of the epic *Mahabharata* is called "Go-Harran", which signifies "cattle harrying".

INDRA

From the Indra Temple, Ellora

> Counsels the thoughts within our hearts are counselling,
> Wishes are wished and soar towards the highest—
> O none but them, the shining ones, are merciful,
> My longing wings itself towards the Eternals.

Indra arose heroically to do battle for the sacrificers. Impulsively he seized the nectar of the gods, called Soma, and drank a deep draught of that intoxicating juice. Then he snatched up his thunderstone which had been fashioned by the divine artisan Twashtri, who resembles the Germanic Mimer, the "wonder smith". His "favourite bays", named the Bold and the Brown, were yoked in his golden chariot by his attendants and followers, the youthful Maruts.

Now, at the very beginning, Indra, the golden child, became the king of the three worlds. He it was who gave the air of life; he gave strength also. All the shining gods revered him and obeyed his commands. "His shadow is immortality; his shadow is death."

The Maruts, the sons of red Rudra, were the spirits of tempest and thunder. To each of their chariots were yoked two spotted deer and one swift-footed, never-wearying red deer as leader. They were stalwart and courageous youths, "full of terrible designs like to giants"; on their heads were golden helmets and they had golden breastplates, and wore bright skins on their shoulders; their ankles and arms were decked with golden bracelets. The Maruts were always strongly armed with bows and arrows and axes, and especially with gleaming spears. All beings feared those "cloud shakers" when they hastened forth with their lightning spears which "shattered cattle like the thunderstone"; they were wont to cleave cloud-rocks and drench the earth with quickening showers.

When Indra drove forth to attack the Drought

Demon, the "hastening Maruts" followed him, shouting with loud voices: in "a shower" were the Maruts "let loose"; they dashed towards the imprisoned cows of the clouds and "chased them aloft".

The dragon Vritra roared when Indra drew nigh; whereat heaven shook and the gods retreated. Mother Earth, the goddess Prithivi (prit'hi-vee), was troubled regarding her golden son. But Indra advanced boldly with the roaring Maruts; he was inspired by the hymns of the priests; he had drunken deeply of Soma; he was strengthened by the sacrifices offered on earth's altars; and he wielded the thunderstone.

The Drought Demon deemed itself invulnerable, but Indra cast his weapon and soon discovered the vulnerable parts of its writhing body. He slew the monster; it lay prone before him; the torrents burst forth and carried it away to the sea of eternal darkness. Then Indra rejoiced and cried out:

> I have slain Vritra, O ye hast'ning Maruts;
> I have grown mighty through my own great vigour;
> I am the hurler of the bolt of Thunder—
> For man flow freely now the gleaming waters.

On earth the worshippers of the god were made glad; the Rishi hymned his praises:

> I will extol the manly deeds of Indra:
> The first was when the Thunder stone he wielded
> And smote the Dragon; he released the waters,
> He oped the channels of the breasted mountains.
>
> He smote the dragon Vritra in its fortress—
> Twashtri had shaped for him the thunder weapon—
> Then rushing freely like to bellowing cattle
> The gladsome waters to the sea descended.

Bull-spirited did Indra choose the Soma,
He drank its juices from the triple ladles;
Then clutched the Bounteous One his thunder weapon,
And fiercely smote the first-born of the Dragons.

The smitten monster fell amidst the torrents,
That pause nor stay, for ever surging onward;
Then Vritra covered by the joyful billows
Was carried to the darksome deeps of Ocean.

—*Rigveda*, i. 32.

A post-Vedic version of the encounter between Indra and the demon Vritra is given in the "Vana Parva" section of *Mahābhārata*. Although it is coloured by the change which, in the process of time, passed over the religious beliefs of the Aryans, it retains some features of the original myth which are absent in the Vedic hymns. It should be understood that, at the period referred to, the belief obtained that the gods derived their powers from the saintly Rishis,[1] who fed them with sacrifices and underwent terrible penances, which enabled them to support or destroy the Universe at will.

It is related that in the Krita Age (the first Age of the Universe) a host of Dānāvas (giants and demons) were so strongly armed that they were invincible in battle. They selected the dragon Vritra as their leader, and waged war against the gods, whom they scattered in all directions.

Realizing that they could not regain their power until they accomplished the death of Vritra, the Celestials appeared before their Grandsire, the Supreme Being, Brahma, the incarnation of the Soul of the Universe. Brahma instructed them to obtain the bones of a Rishi named Dadhicha, from which to construct a demon-slaying weapon. So the gods visited the Rishi and bowed

[1] The deified poets and sages. See Chapter VIII.

down before him, and begged the boon according to Brahma's advice.

Said Dadhicha: "O ye gods, I will renounce my body for your benefit."

Then the Rishi gave up his life, and from his bones the artisan god, Twashtri, shaped Indra's great weapon, which is called Vajra.[1]

Twashtri spake to Indra and said: "With this, the best of weapons, O exalted one, reduce that fierce foe of the gods to ashes! And, having slain the foe, rule thou happily the entire domain of heaven, O chief of the celestials, with those that follow thee."[2]

Then Indra led the gods against the mighty host. They found that Vritra was surrounded by dreaded Danavas, who resembled mountain peaks. A terrible conflict was waged, but once again the gods were put to flight. Then Indra saw Vritra growing bolder, and he became dejected. But the Supreme Being protected him and the gods endowed him with their strength, so that he became mightier than before. Thereupon Vritra was enraged, and roared loudly and fiercely, so that the heavens shook and the earth trembled with fear. Deeply agitated, Indra flung his divine weapon, which slew the leader of the Danavas. But Indra, thinking the demon was still alive, fled from the field in terror to seek shelter in a lake. The Celestials, however, perceived that Vritra had been slain, and they rejoiced greatly and shouted the praises of Indra. Then, rallying once more, the gods attacked the panic-stricken Danavas, who turned and fled to the depths of ocean. There in the fathomless dark-

[1] Adolf Kaegi says: "Also Vadha or Vadhar", which he compares with German, *Wetter*; O.H. German, *Wetar*: Anglo-Saxon, *Weder*; English, *Weather*. The original word signifying the sudden change in atmospheric conditions caused by the thunderstorm was ultimately applied to all states of the air.

[2] Roy's translation of *Mahabharata*.

ness they assembled together, and began to plot how they would accomplish the destruction of the three worlds.[1]

At length the dread conspirators resolved to destroy all the Rishis who were possessed of knowledge and ascetic virtue, because the world was supported by them. So they made the ocean their abode, raising billows high as hills for their protection, and they began to issue forth from their fortress to make attacks on the mighty saints.

In the Babylonian Story of Creation the female dragon Tiawath (Tiamat), whose name signifies "the sea",[1] desired to possess the world, and plotted against the gods with her horde of giant serpents, "raging dogs, scorpion men, fish men, and other terrible beings". The gods then selected Belus (Bel-Merodach) as their leader, and proclaimed him their king. He slew Tiawath and covered the heavens with one part of her body, and fashioned the earth with the other half. Then he set the moon and the stars in the sky, and afterwards created man: "he divided the darkness, separated the heavens from the earth, and reduced the universe to order".[2] The sun was the offspring of the moon.

The Indian Vedic and Epic dragon-slaying stories have evidently no connection, however, with a lost Creation myth. It is possible that they are part of the floating material from which Babylonian mythology was framed. At the same time Babylonian influences may not have been absent in the post-Vedic Age. Indra bears points of resemblance to Bel-Merodach, but he is not a Creator in the sublime sense; he is rather an artisan god like the Chinese P'an Ku, the lonely hammerman, and

[1] Like the giants and demons of Teutonic mythology, who fought with the gods in the Last Battle.

[2] *The Religion of Babylonia and Assyria*, by T. G. Pinches, LL.D.

the Egyptian Ptah, who acquired a potter's wheel, in addition to his hammer, in the Nile valley.

Indra fashioned the universe in the simple manner that the early Aryans built their wooden houses.[1] How he obtained the requisite material puzzled the Vedic poets. It may be that there was a World Tree, however, like the great ash Ygdrasil of Teutonic mythology. After measuring space with the sun, Indra set up four corner posts and constructed the world walls; the roof was the cloud-thatched sky. The wide doors of the world opened to the east, and every morning they were opened to admit the sun, which Indra flung at evening into the darkness as a Neolithic man may have flung out a house torch. These doors are the "gates", celebrated in the Vedic hymns, through which the gods entered to partake of the sacrifices and libations. Indra, who is called "an accomplished artisan", is lauded as the god who "firmly secured the dominion of air in the frame of heaven and earth". In another hymn it is told: "Indra measured six broad spaces, from which no existing thing is excluded: he it is who made the wide expanse of earth and the lofty dome of the sky, even he". (V. i, 47. 3, 4.)

In the work of shaping the universe Indra is assisted by the shadowy deities Savitri, who merged with Surya, the sun god, Brihaspati, "Lord of Prayer", who merged with Agni, god of fire, and Vishnu, god of grace. He was also aided by the Ribhus, the artisans of the gods, who dwelt in the region of mid-air. Their number is given variously as three or the multiples of three; they were the sons of Sudhanvan, who was apparently identical with Indra, because "Indra is a Ribhu when he confers gifts"; indeed, the artisans are referred to as the children of the Thunder god. They make grass

[1] *Cosmology of Rigveda*, Wallis.

INTERIOR OF A TEMPLE TO VISHNU (BRINDABAN)

and herbs, and also channels for streams. In some respects they resemble the earth-gnomes, the Khnumu, "the modellers", the helpers of the Egyptian artisan god Ptah, who shaped the world. "Countless little figures of these gods are found in Egyptian tombs; for even as once the Khnumu had helped in the making of the world, so would they help to reconstruct in all its members the body of the dead man in whose tomb they were laid."[1] The Ribhus similarly renovated aged and decrepit parents; "they reunited the old cow to the calf"; they are also credited with having shaped the heavens and the earth,[2] and with having fashioned the "cow of plenty", and also a man named Vibhvan.[3]

According to the *Oxford Dictionary*, they are "the three genii of the seasons in Hindu mythology". The Sanskrit word "Ribhu" is sometimes compared with the Germanic word "Elf". Professor Macdonell considers it "likely that the Ribhus were originally terrestrial or aerial elves".[4] They are evidently of common origin with the Teutonic elfin artisans who are associated with Thor, the Germanic Indra.

The mother of the Ribhus was Saranyu, daughter of Twashtri, "the Hindu Vulcan", the "master workman". Twashtri forms the organism in maternal wombs and supports the races of man.[5] As we have seen, he was the fashioner of Indra's thunderbolt: similarly the Teutonic elfin artisan Sindre makes Thor's hammer.[6]

The two groups of Teutonic wonder-smiths were rivals; so were the Ribhus and Twashtri. The elfin artisans prove their skill in both cases by producing

[1] *Religion of the Ancient Egyptians*, Professor A. Wiedemann, p. 137.
[2] *Rigveda*, iv, 34. 9.
[3] *Cosmology of Rigveda*, Wallis.
[4] *A History of Sanskrit Literature*, pp. 106, 107.
[5] *Rigveda*, ii, 53; iii, 55.
[6] *Teutonic Myth and Legend*, pp. 35–9.

wonderful gifts for the gods. Loke acts as a mischief-making spy in Germanic myth, and Dadyak in Indian, and both lose their heads for wagers, but save them by cunning.

The Ribhus had provided the Celestials with horses and chariots, but Twashtri fashioned a wonderful bowl which filled itself with Soma for the gods. In the contest that ensued the Ribhus transformed the bowl into four cups. "This bowl", says Professor Macdonell, "perhaps represents the moon, the four cups being its phases." One of the Ribhus was a famous archer, like the elfin artisan Egil of Teutonic mythology.

The artisan of Babylonian mythology is Ea, father of Bel-Merodach. He is "King of the abyss, creator of everything, lord of all". He was the god of artisans in general, and is identified with the sea-deity of the Persian Gulf—half-fish, half-man—who landed "during the day to teach the inhabitants the building of houses and temples, the gathering of fruits, and also geometry, law and letters". His pupils included "potters, blacksmiths, sailors, stonecutters, gardeners, farmers, &c."[1]

The Ribhus and Twashtri were the artisans of nature, the spirits of growth, the genii of the seasons, the elves of earth and air. Indra's close association with them emphasizes his character as a god of fertility, who brought the quickening rain, and as the corn god, and the rice god. He was the son of Father Heaven and Mother Earth, two vague deities who were never completely individualized, but were never forgotten. Heaven was the sky-god Dyaus-pita (from div = to shine), the Zeus pater of the Greeks, Jupiter of the Romans, and Tivi[2] (later,

[1] *The Religion of Babylonia and Assyria*, T. G. Pinches, LL.D.

[2] An old Germanic name of Odin related to Divus. Odin's descendants were the "Tivar". (Pronounce *Dyaus* as one syllable rhiming with *mouse*.)

Odin) of the Germanic peoples, whose wife was the earth-goddess Jord, mother of Thor. The Hindu earth-mother (Terra mater) was Prithivi. Dyaus is sometimes referred to as a ruddy bull, whose bellowing is the thunder; as the Night heaven he is depicted as a black steed decked with pearls which are the stars; in one of the Vedic hymns reference is made to his "thunder-stone". Prithivi, who is sometimes symbolized as a cow, is the source of all vegetation, the supporter of earth, the female principle. She never assumes the importance of the Assyrian Ishtar, or the north Egyptian "earth-mother" Neith, or the "earth-mothers" of Europe. The Vedic Aryans were Great Father worshippers rather than Great Mother worshippers: their female deities were Night, Dawn, Earth, and the Rivers, but they were not sharply individualized until late; they are vague in the Vedas.

As the Greek Cronus (Roman Saturn) slew his father Urănus (Heaven), so did Indra slay his father Dyaus (Heaven). His earth-mother addresses him, saying: "Who has made thy mother a widow? Who has sought to slay the sleeping and the waking? What deity has been more gracious than thou, since thou hast slain thy father, having seized him by the foot?"[1]

The Indian father-slaying myth appears to be connected with the doctrine of reincarnation. In the *Laws of Manu* it is stated that "the husband, after conception by his wife, becomes an embryo and is born again of her; for that is the wifehood of a wife, that he is born again by her".[2] In the famous story of Shakuntălă, the husband is similarly referred to as the son of his wife, the son being a reincarnation of the father.[3] This belief

[1] *Rigveda*, iv, 18. Wilson, vol. iii, p. 153.
[2] *The Laws of Manu*, ix, 8; p. 329. (*Sacred Books of the East*, vol. xxv.)
[3] *Adi Parva*, sect. lxxiv of *Mahabharata*, Roy's translation.

resembles the Egyptian conception which is summed up in the phrase "husband of his mother".[1]

At the barley harvest in spring and the rice harvest in autumn offerings were made to the gods. A sacrificial cake of the new barley or rice was offered to Indra and Agni, a mess of old grain boiled and mixed with milk and water was given to the other gods, and a cake was also offered to Father Heaven and Mother Earth in which clarified butter was an important ingredient; or the offering might consist entirely of butter, because "clarified butter is manifestly the sap of these two, Heaven and Earth; . . . he (the offerer) therefore gladdens these two with their own sap or essence".

The reason for this harvest offering is explained as follows: The gods and the demons contended for supremacy. It chanced that the demons defiled, partly by magic and partly by poison, the plants used by men and beasts, hoping thus to overcome the gods. Men ceased to eat and the beasts stopped grazing; all creatures were about to perish because of the famine.

Said the gods: "Let us rid the plants of this."

Then they offered sacrifices and "accomplished all that they wanted to accomplish, and so did the Rishis".

A dispute then arose among the gods as to who should partake of the offerings of the firstfruits—that is, of the new plants which replaced those the demons had poisoned. It was decided to run a race to settle the matter. Indra and Agni won the race and were therefore awarded the cake. These two gods were divine Kshatriyas (noblemen), the others were "common people". Whatever Kshatriyas conquer, the commoners are permitted to share; therefore the other gods received the mess of old grain.

[1] See *Egyptian Myth and Legend.*

After the magic spell was removed from the plants by the gods, men ate food and cattle grazed once again. Ever afterwards, at the beginning of each harvest, the first fruits were offered up to Indra and Agni. The fee of the priest was the first-born calf "for that is, as it were, the firstfruits of the cattle".[1]

The popular Thunder god of the Vedic period bears a close resemblance to the hard-drinking, kindly, and impulsive Thor, the Teutonic god of few words and mighty deeds, the constant "friend of man" and the inveterate enemy of demons. In the hymns Indra is pictured as a burly man, with "handsome, prominent nose", "good lips", and "comely chin"; he is "long-necked, big-bellied, strongly armed", and has a weakness for ornaments. He is much addicted to drinking "sweet, intoxicating Soma"; he "fills his stomach"; he quaffs "thirty bowls" at a single draught ere he hastens to combat against "hostile air demons". Sometimes he is placed in a difficulty when two tribes of his worshippers are in conflict: both cry to him for victory, but—

> The god giveth victory unto him
> Who with generous heart pours out
> The draught he thirsts for—
> Nor feels regret in giving;
> Indra joins with him upon the battlefield.
>
> *Rigveda*, iv, 24. 2–6.

The Aryans, who were as notorious cattle lifters as the Gauls and the Scottish Highlanders, were wont to invoke the god ere they set out on a raid, chanting with loud voices:

> Indra, whose riches are boundless, O grant us
> Thousands of beautiful cows and horses:

[1] *The Satapatha Brahmana*, translated by Professor J. Eggeling, Part I, pp. 369, 373. (*Sacred Books of the East*, vol. xii.)

Destroy, thou mighty one, all who despise us,
Visit with death all those who would harm us, and
Indra, whose riches are boundless, O grant us,
Thousands of beautiful cows and horses.

Wilson's translation.

In other hymns the Thor-like character of Indra, the war god, is naively depicted. A sceptic is supposed to say: "Many men declare that there is no Indra. Who ever saw him? Why should we adore him?"

The god makes answer: "O singer, *I am*: behold me! I am here now, and I am greater than any living being. I delight in the performance of holy rites. I am also the Destroyer; I can hurl creation to ruin." *Rigveda*, viii, 89.

I never knew a man to speak so to me,
When all his enemies are safely conquered;
Yea, when they see how fierce the battle rages,
They even promise me a pair of bullocks.

When I am absent in far distant places,
Then all with open hands their gifts would bring me . . .
Lo! I will make the wealthy niggard needy,
Seize by the foot and on the hard rock dash him.

Rigveda, x, 27.

The lord of both the worlds hates all the haughty,
He cares for those who feel themselves but human.

Rigveda, vi, 47.[1]

These verses recall: "Silence, thou evil one," roared Thor, "or else with my hammer shall I strike thy head off and end thy life."

Then did Loke answer humbly: "Silent indeed I shall be now, O Thor, for I know full well thou wilt strike."[2]

[1] Arrowsmith's translation. [2] *Teutonic Myth and Legend*, p. 173.

6

THE PARADISE OF INDRA

From a Rock Sculpture at Mámallapuram

The human qualities of Indra are illustrated in epic narrative. Arjuna, the Indian Achilles, is his son, and pays a visit to the brilliant Celestial city on the summit of Mount Meru, where flowers are ever blooming, and pretty nymphs dance to pleasure battle-slain warriors.

Arjuna saluted his divine sire. "And Indra thereupon embraced him with his round and plump arms. And taking his hand, Shakra (Indra) made him sit on a portion of his own seat . . . And the lord of the Celestials—that slayer of hostile heroes—smelt the head of Arjuna, bending in humility, and even took him upon his lap . . . Moved by affection, the slayer of Vritra touched that beautiful face with his own perfumed hands. And the wielder of the thunderbolt, patting and rubbing gently again and again with his own hands, which bore the marks of the thunderbolt, the handsome and large arms of Arjuna, which resembled a couple of golden columns and were hard in consequence of drawing the bowstring and shooting arrows, began to console him. And the slayer of Vritra . . . eyeing his son of curling locks smilingly and with eyes expanded with delight, seemed scarcely to be gratified. The more he gazed, the more he liked to gaze on. And seated on one seat, the father and son enhanced the beauty of the assembly, like the sun and moon beautifying the firmament together."[1]

Indra was attended in his heaven by vague spirits, called Vasus, who appear to have acted as his counsellors. When Bhishma, a hero of the great Bhārata war, was slain in battle, he was given a place among the Vasus. The Thunder god's queen is a shadowy personality, and is called Indrani.

Indra was attended by a dog, as befitted a deity of

[1] *Vana Parva* section of *Mahâbhârata*, sect. xliii, Roy's translation.

primitive huntsmen. After the early Aryan period, he showed less favour for his bays and chariot, and seated himself upon a great white elephant, "the handsome and ever victorious", named Airavata; it "was furnished with four tusks" and "resembled the mountain of Kailasa with its summits".

CHAPTER II

The Great Vedic Deities

Agni the Fire God—Source of Life—The Divine Priest—Myths regarding his Origin—The Child God—Resemblances to Heimdal and Scyld—Messenger of the Gods—Martin Elginbrodde—Vayu or Vata, the Wind God—Teutonic Vate and Odin—The Hindu "Wild Huntsman"—Rudra the Howler—The Rain God—Sublime Varuna—The Omniscient One—Forgiver of Sins—Mitra, an ancient Deity—Babylonian Prototype—A Sun God—A Corn God—Mitanni Deities—Surya, the Sun God—The Adityas—Ushas, Goddess of Dawn—Ratri, Night—Chandra, the Moon—Identified with Soma—The Mead of the Gods—A Humorous Hymn—Sources of Life—Origin of Spitting Ceremonies.

AGNI, the fire god, was closely associated with Indra, and is sometimes called his twin brother. The pair were the most prominent deities in Vedic times: about 250 hymns are addressed to Indra and over 200 to Agni.

Indra gave the "air of life" to men; Agni symbolized the "vital spark", the principle of life in animate and inanimate Nature; he was in man, in beast, and fish; he was in plants and trees; he was in butter and in intoxicating Soma. The gods partook of the nature of Agni. In one of the post-Vedic Creation myths he is identified with the Universal soul; Brahma existed in the form of Agni ere the worlds were framed and gods and men came to be. Agni was made manifest in lightning, in celestial sun flames, in the sacred blaze rising from the altar and in homely household fires. The fire god was the divine priest as contrasted with Indra, the divine warrior.

In the Vedic invocations there are evidences that

several myths had gathered round the fascinating and wonderful fire god. One hymn refers to him as a child whose birth was kept a secret; his mother, the queen, concealed him from his sire; he was born in full vigour as a youth, and was seen sharpening his weapons at a distance from his home which he had forsaken.[1] Sometimes he is said to have devoured his parents at birth: this seems to signify that he consumed the fire sticks from which holy fire was produced by friction. Another hymn says that "Heaven and Earth (Dyaus and Prithivi) fled away in fear of (the incarnation of) Twashtri when he was born, but they returned to embrace the lion".[2]

Agni was also given ten mothers who were "twice five sisters",[3] but the reference is clearly explained in another passage: "The ten fingers have given him birth, the ancient, well-loved Agni, well born of his mothers".[4]

Dawn, with its darkness-consuming fires, and starry Night, are the sisters of Agni; "they celebrate his three births, one in the sea, one in the sky, one in the waters (clouds)". Typical of the Oriental mind is the mysterious reference to Agni's "mothers" owing their origin to him. The poet sings:

> Who among you hath understood the hidden (god)?
> The calf has by itself given birth to its mothers.

Professor Oldenberg, who suggests that the waters are the "mothers", reasons in Oriental mode: "Smoke is Agni, it goes to the clouds, the clouds become waters".[5]

In his early humanized form Agni bears some resemblance to Heimdal, the Teutonic sentinel god, who has

[1] *Rigveda*, v, 2. [2] *Rigveda*, i, 95.
[3] *Rigveda*, iv, 6. 8. [4] *Rigveda*, iii, 23. 3.
[5] *Rigveda*, i, 95. 4, and note, Oldenberg's *Vedic Hymns* (*Sacred Books of the East*, vol. xlvi).

7

AGNI, THE FIRE GOD

From a painting by Nanda Lall Bose

(By permission of the Indian Society of Oriental Art, Calcutta)

nine mothers, the daughters of sea-dwelling Ran, and is thus also a "son of the waters"; he is clad in silvern armour, and on his head is a burnished helmet with ram's horns. Horsed on his swift steed, Gulltop, he watches the demons who seek to attack the citadel of the gods. . . . His sight is so keen that he can see by night as well as by day. . . . Heimdal is loved both by gods and by men, and he is also called Gullintani because his teeth are of gold. There was a time when he went to Midgard (the earth) as a child; he grew up to be a teacher among men and was named Scef. Scef is identified as the patriarch Scyld in *Beowulf*, who came over the sea as a child and rose to be the king of a tribe. Mankind were descended from Heimdal-Scef: three sons were born to him of human mothers—Thrall, from whom thralls are descended; Churl, the sire of freemen, and Jarl from whom nobles have sprung.[1]

In *Mahabharata* there is a fragment of an old legend which relates the origin of Karna, the son of Queen Pritha and the sun god: the birth of the child is concealed, and he is placed in a basket which is set afloat on the river and is carried to a distant country.[2]

One of the Vedic references to Agni, as we have seen, suggests an origin similar to Karna of the epic period. He was connected with the introduction of agriculture like the Teutonic Scef, which signifies "Sheaf". Agni is stated to have been "carried in the waters. . . . The great one has grown up in the wide unbounded space. The waters (have made) Agni (grow)".[3] Agni is "sharp faced" (i, 95); he is "the bright, brilliant, and shining one" (iv, 1. 7); he is "gold toothed" (v, 22); he sees "even over the darkness of night" (i, 94. 7); he "makes

[1] *Teutonic Myth and Legend*, pp. 16 and 187–9.
[2] See Chapter X. [3] Oldenberg, *Rigveda*, iii, 1.

all things visible"; he conquers the godless, wicked wiles; he sharpens his two horns in order to pierce Rakshasas (giants) (v, 2). "O Agni, strike away with thy weapons those who curse us, the malicious ones, all ghouls, be they near or far" (i, 94. 9). Heimdal blows a trumpet in battle; Agni is "roaring like a bull" (i, 94. 10).

As Heimdal, in his Scef-child form, was sent to mankind by the gods, "Matarisvan[1] brought Agni to Bhrigu as a gift, precious like wealth, of double birth, the carrier, the famous, the beacon of the sacrifice, the ready, the immediately successful messenger. . . . The Bhrigus worshipping him in the abode of the waters have verily established him among the clans of Ayu. The people have established beloved Agni among the human clans as (people) going to settle (establish) Mitra" (i, 60). Oldenberg explains that people going anywhere secure safety by ceremonies addressed to Mitra, i.e. by concluding alliances under the protection of Mitra. Another reference reads, "Agni has been established among the tribes of men, the son of the waters, Mitra acting in the right way". Oldenberg notes that Mitra is here identified with Agni; Mitra also means "friend" or "ally" (iii, 5. 3, and note). Scyld in *Beowulf*, the mysterious child of the sea, became a king over men. Agni "indeed is king, leading all beings to gloriousness. As soon as born from here, he looks over the whole world. . . . Agni, who has been looked and longed for in Heaven, who has been looked for on earth—he who has been looked for has entered all herbs" (i, 98).[2] To Agni's love affairs upon earth there are epic references, and in the "Vishnu Purana" he is mentioned as the father of three human sons.

[1] A demi-god.

[2] *Vedic Hymns*, trans. by Oldenberg. (*Sacred Books of the East*, vol. xlvi.)

The reference to the Bhrigus, to whom Agni is carried, is of special interest. This tribe did not possess fire and were searching for it (*Rigveda*, x. 40. 2). In another poem the worshippers of Agni are "human people descended from Manush (Manu)" (vi, 48. 8). The Bhrigus were a priestly family descended from the patriarch Bhrigu: Manu was the first man. Two of the Teutonic patriarch names are Berchter and Mannus.

Agni was the messenger of the gods; he interceded with the gods on behalf of mankind and conducted the bright Celestials to the sacrifice. The priest chanted at the altar:

> Agni, the divine ministrant of the sacrifice, the greatest bestower of treasures; may one obtain through Agni wealth and welfare day by day, which may bring glory and high bliss of valiant offspring.
>
> Agni, whatever sacrifice and worship thou encompassest on every side, that indeed goes to the gods. Thou art King of all worship. . . . Conduct the gods hither in an easy-moving chariot.[1]

Like Indra, Agni was a heavy consumer of Soma; his intensely human side is not lost in mystic Vedic poetry.

> Agni, accept this log, conqueror of horses, thou who lovest songs and delightest in riches . . .
>
> Thou dost go wisely between these two creations (Heaven and Earth) like a friendly messenger between two hamlets . . .

His worshippers might address him with great familiarity, as in the following extracts:—

> If I were thee and thou wert me, thine aspirations should be fulfilled. *Rigveda*, xiii, 44. 23.

[1] *Rigveda*, i, 13 and i, 26 (Oldenberg).

If, O Agni, thou wert a mortal and I an immortal,
I would not abandon thee to wrong or to penury: my worshippers should not be poor, nor distressed, nor miserable. *Rigveda*, viii, 19.

These appeals are reminiscent of the quaint graveyard inscription:

Here lie I, Martin Elginbrodde.
Hae mercy on my soul, Lord God,
As I wad dae were I Lord God,
And ye were Martin Elginbrodde.

The growth of monotheistic thought is usually evinced in all mythologies by the tendency to invest a populai deity with the attributes of other gods. Agni is sometimes referred to as the sky god and the storm god. In one of the hymns he is entreated to slay demons and send rain as if he were Indra:

O Agni, overcome our enemies and our calamities;
Drive away all disease and the Rakshasas—
Send down abundance of waters
From the ocean of the sky. *Rigveda*, x, 98. 12.

Indra similarly absorbed, and was absorbed by, the wind god Vayu or Vata, who is also referred to as the father of the Maruts and the son-in-law of the artisan god Twashtri. The name Vata has been compared to Vate, the father of the Teutonic Volund or Wieland, the tribal deity of the Watlings or Vaetlings; in old English the Milky Way was "Watling Street". Comparisons have also been drawn with the wind god Odin—the Anglo-Saxon Woden, and ancient German Wuotan (pronounced Vuotan). "The etymological connection in this view", writes a critic, "is not free from difficulty."[1]

[1] Art. "Aryan Religion", Hastings' *Ency. Rel. and Ethics.*

Professor Macdonell favours the derivation from "va" = "to blow".

The Indian Vata is invoked, as Vayu, in a beautiful passage in one of the hymns which refers to his "two red horses yoked to the chariot": he had also, like the Maruts, a team of deer. The poet calls to the wind:

> Awake Purandhu (Morning) as a lover awakes a sleeping maid. . . . Reveal heaven and earth. . . .
> Brighten the dawn, yea, for glory, brighten the dawn. . . .

These lines recall Keats at his best:

> There is no light
> Save what from heaven is with the breezes blown . . .
> *Ode to the Nightingale.*

A stirring hymn to the wind god loses much of its vigour and beauty in translation:

> Sublime and shining is the car of Vata;
> It sweeps resounding, thundering and crashing;
> Athwart the sky it wakens ruddy flashes,
> Or o'er the earth it sets the dust-clouds whirling.
>
> The gusts arise and hasten unto Vata,
> Like women going to a royal banquet;
> In that bright car the mighty god is with them,
> For he is rajah of the earth's dominions.
>
> When Vata enters on the paths of heaven,
> All day he races on; he never falters;
> He is the firstborn and the friend of Ocean—
> Whence did he issue forth? Where is his birthplace?
>
> He is the breath[1] of gods: all life is Vata:
> He cometh, yea, he goeth as he listeth:
> His voice is heard; his form is unbeholden—
> O let us offer sacrifice to Vata. *Rigveda*, x, 168.

[1] The air of life = the spirit.

Another wind or storm god is Rudra, also the father of the Maruts, who are called "Rudras". He is the "Howler" and "the Ruddy One", and rides a wild boar. Saussaye calls him "the Wild Huntsman of Hindu Mythology". He is chiefly of historical interest because he developed into the prominent post-Vedic god Shiva, the "Destroyer", who is still worshipped in India. The poets invested him with good as well as evil qualities:

> Rudra, thou smiter of workers of evil,
> The doers of good all love and adore thee.
> Preserve me from injury and every affliction—
> Rudra, the nourisher.
>
> Give unto me of thy medicines, Rudra,
> So that my years may reach to a hundred;
> Drive away hatred, shatter oppression,
> Ward off calamity. *Rigveda*, ii, 33.

The rain cloud was personified in Parjanya, who links with Indra as the nourisher of earth, and with Agni as the quickener of seeds.

Indra's great rival, however, was Varuna, who symbolized the investing sky: he was "the all-enveloping one". The hymns impart to him a character of Hebraic grandeur. He was the sustainer of the universe, the lawgiver, the god of moral rectitude, and the sublime sovereign of gods and men. Men worshipped him with devoutness, admiration, and fear. "It is he who makes the sun to shine in heaven; the winds that blow are but his breath; he has hollowed out the channels of the rivers which flow at his command, and he has made the depths of the sea. His ordinances are fixed and unassailable; through their operation the moon walks in brightness, and the stars which appear in the nightly sky,

8

SHIVA'S DANCE OF DESTRUCTION, ELLORA (see pages 147–8)

vanish in daylight. The birds flying in the air, the rivers in their sleepless flow, cannot attain a knowledge of his power and wrath. But he knows the flight of the birds in the sky, the course of the far-travelling wind, the paths of ships on the ocean, and beholds all secret things that have been or shall be done. He witnesses men's truth and falsehood."[1]

He is the Omniscient One. Man prayed to him for forgiveness for sin, and to be spared from the consequences of evil-doing:

May I not yet, King Varuna,
Go down into the house of clay:
Have mercy, spare me, mighty Lord.

O Varuna, whatever the offence may be
That we as men commit against the heavenly folk,
When through our want of thought we violate thy laws,
Chastise us not, O god, for that iniquity.

Rigveda, vii, 89.[2]

His messengers descend
Countless from his abode—for ever traversing
This world and scanning with a thousand eyes its inmates.
Whate'er exists within this earth, and all within the sky,
Yea, all that is beyond, King Varuna perceives. . . .
May thy destroying snares, cast sevenfold round the wicked,
Entangle liars, but the truthful spare, O King!

Rigveda, iv, 16.[3]

In contrast to the devotional spirit pervading the Varuna hymns is the attitude adopted by Indra's worshippers; the following prayer to the god of battle is characteristic:—

O Indra, grant the highest, best of treasures,
A judging mind, prosperity abiding,

[1] Muir's *Original Sanscrit Texts*, v, 58, ff.
[2] Professor Macdonell's *A History of Sanskrit Literature*.
[3] *Indian Wisdom*, Sir Monier Williams.

Riches abundant, lasting health of body,
The grace of eloquence and days propitious.
Rigveda, ii, 21. 6.

The sinner's fear of Varuna prompted him to seek the aid of other gods. Rudra and the Moon are addressed:

O remove ye the sins we have sinned,
What evil may cling to us sever
With bolts and sharp weapons, kind friends,
And gracious be ever.
From the snare of Varuna deliver us, ward us,
Ye warm-hearted gods, O help us and guard us.

Associated with Varuna was the God Mitra (the Persian Mithra). These deities are invariably coupled and belong to the early Iranian period. Much controversy has been waged over their pre-Vedic significance. Some have regarded Mithra as the firmament by day with its blazing and fertilizing sun, and Varuna as the many-eyed firmament of night, in short, the twin forms of Dyaus. Prof. E. V. Arnold has shown, however, that in the Vedas, Mithra has no solar significance except in his association with Agni. The fire god, as we have seen, symbolized the principle of fertility in Nature: he was the "vital spark" which caused the growth of "all herbs", as well as the illuminating and warmth-giving flames of sun and household hearth.

Mitra as Mithra with Varuna, and a third vague god, Aryaman, belong to an early group of equal deities called the Adityas, or "Celestial deities". "It would seem that the worship of these deities", says Prof. Arnold, "was already decaying in the earliest Vedic period, and that many of them were then falling into oblivion. . . . In a late Vedic hymn we find that Indra boasts that he has dethroned Varuna, and invites Agni to enter his own service instead. We may justly infer from all these circumstances that the worship of the 'celestials' occupied at one time in the history of the race a position of greater importance than its place in the *Rigveda* directly suggests."[1]

The following extracts from a Mitra-Varuna hymn indicate the attitude of the early priests towards the "Celestial deities":—

> To the gods Mitra and Varuna let our praise go forth with power, with all reverence, to the two of mighty race.
> These did the gods establish in royal power over themselves, because they were wise and the children of wisdom, and because they excelled in power.
> They are protectors of hearth and home, of life and strength; Mitra and Varuna, prosper the mediations of your worshippers. . . .
> As the sun rises to-day do I salute Mitra and Varuna, and glorious Aryaman. . . . The blessings of heaven are our desire. . . . *Prof. Arnold's translation.*

In Babylonian mythology the sun is the offspring of the moon. The Semitic name of the sun god is Samas (Shamash), the Sumerian name is Utu; among other non-Semitic names was Mitra, "apparently the Persian Mithra". The bright deity also "bears the names of his attendants 'Truth' and 'Righteousness', who guided him upon his path as judge of the earth".[2]

It may be that the Indian Mitra was originally a sun god; the religion of the sun god Mithra spread into Europe. "Dedications to Mithra the Unconquered Sun have been found in abundance."[3] Vedic references suggest that Mitra had become a complex god in the pre-

[1] *The Rigveda*, by Professor E. Vernon Arnold, p. 16 (*Popular Studies in Mythology, Romance, and Folklore*).

[2] *The Religion of Babylonia and Assyria*, by Dr. T. G. Pinches, p. 68.

[3] Frazer's "Golden Bough" (*Adonis, Attis, Osiris*, p. 255, n., third edition).

Vedic Age, being probably associated with a group of abstract deities—his attributes symbolized—who are represented by the Adityas. The Mitra-Varuna group of Celestials were the source of all heavenly gifts; they regulated sun and moon, the winds and waters and the seasons. If we assume that they were of Babylonian or Sumerian origin—deities imported by a branch of Aryan settlers who had been in contact with Babylonian civilization—their rivalry with the older Aryan gods, Indra and Agni, can be understood. Ultimately they were superseded, but the influence exercised by their cult remained and left its impress upon later Aryan religious thought.

The Assyrian word "metru" signifies rain.[1] The quickening rain which caused the growth of vegetation was, of course, one of the gifts of the Celestials of the firmament. It is of interest to note, therefore, in this connection that Professor Frazer includes the western Mithra among the "corn gods". Dealing with Mithraic sculptures, which apparently depict Mithra as the sacrificer of the harvest bull offering, he says: "On certain of these monuments the tail of the bull ends in three stalks of corn, and in one of them cornstalks instead of blood are seen issuing from the wound inflicted by the knife".[2]

Commenting on the Assyrian "metru" Professor Moulton says: "If this is his (Mithra's) origin, we get a reasonable basis for the Avestan (Early Persian and Aryan) use of the word to denote a 'contract', as also for the fact that the deity is in the Avesta patron of Truth and in the Veda of Friendship. He is 'the Mediator' between Heaven and Earth, as the firmament was by

[1] Professor H. W. Hogg, in Professor Moulton's *Early Religious Poetry of Persia*, p. 37.

[2] "The Golden Bough" (*Spirits of the Corn and Wild*, vol. ii, p. 10).

its position, both in nature and mythology: an easy corollary is his function of regulating the relations of man and man."

The character of an imported deity is always influenced by localization and tribal habits. Pastoral nomads would therefore have emphasized the friendliness of Mithra, who sent rain to cause the growth of grass on sun-parched steppes. Both Mithra and Varuna had their dwelling-place in the sea of heaven, the waters "above the firmament" from which the rain descended. Ultimately the Indian Mitra vanished, being completely merged in Varuna, who became the god of ocean after the Aryans reached the sea coast. In post-Vedic sacred literature the priestly theorists, in the process of systematizing their religious beliefs, taught that a great conflict took place between the gods and demons. When order was restored, the various deities were redistributed. Indra remained the atmospheric god of battle, and Varuna became the god of ocean, where, as the stern judge and lawgiver and the punisher of wrongdoers, he kept watch over the demons. In the "Nala and Damayanti" epic narrative, the four "world guardians" are: Indra, king of the gods; Agni, god of fire; Varuna, god of waters; and Yama, judge of the dead.

It may be that the displacement of Varuna as supreme deity was due to the influence of the fire-worshipping cult of Agni, who was imported by certain unidentified Aryan tribes that entered India. Agni did not receive recognition, apparently, from the other Aryan "folk-wave", which established a military aristocracy at Mitanni in Mesopotamia, and held sway for a period over the Assyrians and some of the Hittite tribes. An important inscription, which is dated about 1400 B.C., has been deciphered at Boghaz-Köi in Asia Minor by Professor

Hugo Winckler, who gives the names of the following deities:

"Mi-it-ra, Uru-w-na, In-da-ra, and Na-sa-at-ti-ia"—

Mitra, Varuna, Indra, Nasatya. The latter is Nasatyau, the Vedic Aswins, twin gods of morning, who have been compared to the Greek Dioskouri (Castor and Pollux), sons of Zeus.

A Vedic triad, which suggests a rival cult to that of the worshippers of Varuna and other Adityas, is formed by Vayu (wind), Agni (fire), and Surya (the sun).

The Indian sun god Surya, like the Egyptian Ra, had three forms. The rising sun was Vivasvat; the setting sun was Savitri.

Vivasvat was the son-in-law of Twashtri, the artisan of Nature; he was an abstract deity, and apparently owed his origin to the group of Adityas.

Savitri, who had yellow hair, was of pre-Vedic origin. He was the "Stimulator". When he commanded Night to approach, men ceased their labours, birds sought their nests, and cattle their sheds.[1]

During the long centuries covered by the Vedic period many "schools of thought" must have struggled for supremacy. The Vivasvat myth belongs, it would appear, to the time before the elephant was tamed by the Aryans. Aditi, the mother of the Adityas, who is believed to be of later origin than her children, had eight sons. She cherished seven of them; the eighth, which was a shapeless lump, was thrown away, but was afterwards moulded into Vivasvat, the sun; the pieces of the lump which were cast away by the divine artisan fell upon the earth and gave origin to the elephant, therefore elephants should not be caught, because they partake of divine nature,

[1] *Rigveda*, ii, 38.

9

SURYA IN HIS CHARIOT

From the Kailāsa Temple, Ellora

Surya is an Aryanized sun god. He drives a golden chariot drawn by seven mares, or a mare with seven heads; he has golden hair and golden arms and hands. As he is alluded to as "the eye of Varuna and Mitra", and a son of Aditi, it is evident that if he did not originally belong to the group of Adityas, he was strongly influenced by them. In his Savitri character, which he possesses at morning as well as at evening, he stimulates all life and the mind of man. One of the most sacred and oldest mantras (texts) in the Vedas is still addressed by Brahmans to the rising sun. It runs:—

> Let us meditate on that excellent glory of the divine Vivifier.,
> May he enlighten (or stimulate) our understandings.[1]

The feeling for Nature pervades the ancient religion and literature of India. Priests were poets and singers in early Vedic times. A Rishi was a composer of hymns to the gods, and several are named in the collections. Every great family appears to have had its bardic priest, and its special poetic anthology which was handed down from generation to generation. Old poems might be rewritten and added to, but the ambition of the sacred poet was to sing a new song to the gods. The oldest Vedic hymns are referred to as "new songs", which suggests that others were already in existence.

These Rishis looked upon Nature with the poet's eye. They symbolized everything, but they revelled also in the gorgeous beauty of dawn and evening, the luxuriance of Indian trees and flowers, the serene majesty of Himalayan mountains, the cascades, the rivers, and the shining lakes. The wonder and mystery of the world inspired their hymns and their religion. Even the gods took delight in the songs of birds, the harping of forest

[1] *Indian Wisdom*, p. 20.

winds, the humming of bees, the blossoming trees, and the flower-decked sward. Heaven has its eternal summer and soft scented winds, its lotus-gemmed lakes and never-fading blooms.

The effulgence and silence of dawn inspired some of the most beautiful Vedic hymns. Dawn is Ushas, the daughter of Dyaus; she is the Indian Aurora:

> Hail, ruddy Ushas, golden goddess, borne
> Upon thy shining car, thou comest like
> A lovely maiden by her mother decked,
> Disclosing coyly all thy hidden graces
> To our admiring eyes; or like a wife
> Unveiling to her lord, with conscious pride,
> Beauties which, as he gazes lovingly,
> Seem fresher, fairer, each succeeding morn.
> Through years and years thou hast lived on, and yet
> Thou 'rt ever young. Thou art the breath of life
> Of all that breathes and lives, awaking day by day
> Myriads of prostrate sleepers, as from death,
> Causing the birds to flutter from their nests,
> And rousing men to ply with busy feet
> Their daily duties and appointed tasks,
> Toiling for wealth, or pleasure, or renown.[1]

The Vedic poets "looked before and after". One sang:

> In ages past did mortals gaze
> On Ushas veiled in gleaming gold.
> We who are living watch her rays,
> And men unborn will her behold.
>
> *Rigveda*, i, 113. 11.

Night, Ratri, is the sister of Dawn. The one robes herself in crimson and gold; the other adorns her dark raiment with gleaming stars. When benevolent Ratri draws nigh, men turn towards their homes to rest, birds

[1] *Indian Wisdom*, Sir Monier Williams.

seek their nests, cattle lie down; even the hawk reposes. The people pray to the goddess to be protected against robbers and fierce wolves, and to be taken safely across her shadow:

> She, the immortal goddess, throws her veil
> Over low valley, rising ground, and hill.
> But soon with bright effulgence dissipates
> The darkness she produces; soon advancing
> She calls her sister Morning to return,
> And then each darksome shadow melts away.
>
> *Rigveda*, x.[1]

The moon is the god Chandra, who became identified with Soma. Among ancient peoples the moon was regarded as the source of fertility and growth; it brought dew to nourish crops which ripened under the "harvest moon"; it filled all vegetation with sap; it swayed human life from birth till death; it influenced animate and inanimate Nature in its periods of increase and decline; ceremonies to secure offspring were performed during certain phases of the moon.

Soma was the intoxicating juice of the now unknown Soma plant, which inspired mortals and was the nectar of the gods. The whole ninth book of the *Rigveda* is devoted to the praises of Soma, who is exalted even as the chief god, the Father of all.

> This Soma is a god; he cures
> The sharpest ills that man endures.
> He heals the sick, the sad he cheers,
> He nerves the weak, dispels their fears;
> The faint with martial ardour fires,
> With lofty thought the bard inspires,
> The soul from earth to heaven he lifts,
> So great and wondrous are his gifts;

[1] *Indian Wisdom*, Sir Monier Williams.

Men feel the god within their veins,
And cry in loud exulting strains:
We 've quaffed the Soma bright
And are immortal grown:
We 've entered into light
And all the gods have known.
What mortal now can harm,
Or foeman vex us more?
Through thee beyond alarm,
Immortal god, we soar.[1]

"The sun", declared one of the poets, "has the nature of Agni, the moon of Soma." At the same time Agni was a great consumer of Soma; when it was poured on the altar, the fire god leapt up joyfully. The beverage was the "water of life" which was believed to sustain the Adityas and the earth, and to give immortality to all the gods; it was therefore called Amrita (ambrosia).

As in Teutonic mythology, the Hindu giants desired greatly to possess the "mead" to which the gods owed their power and supremacy. The association of Soma with the moon recalls the Germanic belief that the magic mead was kept for Odin, "the champion drinker", by Mani, the moon god, who snatched it from the mythical children who are the prototypes of "Jack and Jill" of the nursery rhyme.[2] Indra was the discoverer of the Soma plant and brought it from the mountains. The Persian mead (mada) was called Haoma.

The priests drank Soma when they made offerings and lauded the gods. A semi-humorous Rigvedic hymn compares them to the frogs which croak together when the rain comes after long drought.

Each (frog) with merry croak and loudly calling
Salutes the other, as a son his father;

[1] Muir's *Original Sanskrit Texts*, v, 130. [2] See *Teutonic Myth and Legend*.

What one calls out, another quickly answers,
Like boys at school their teacher's words repeating. . . .
They shout aloud like Brahmans drunk with Soma,
When they perform their annual devotions.

Rigveda, vii, 103.[1]

There are references in the *Rigveda* to the marriage of Soma, the moon, and Suryá, the maiden of the sun.

In Vedic religion many primitive beliefs were blended. We have seen, for instance, that life was identified with breath and wind; the "spirit" left the body as the last breath. Agni worshippers regarded fire as "the vital spark". Soma worship, on the other hand, appears to be connected with the belief that life was in the blood; it was literally "the life blood". The "blood of trees" was the name for sap; sap was water impregnated or vitalized by Soma, the essence of life. Water worship and Soma worship were probably identical, the moon, which was believed to be the source of growth and moisture, being the fountain head of "the water of life". In Teutonic mythology the "mead" is taken from a hidden mountain spring, which issued from "Mimer's well" in the Underworld. Odin drank from Mimer's well and obtained wisdom and long life. The "mead" was transported to the moon. The "mead" was also identified with saliva, the moisture of life, and spitting ceremonies resulted; these survive in the custom still practised in our rural districts of spitting on the hand to seal a bargain; "spitting stones" have not yet entirely disappeared. Vows are still taken in India before a fire. References to contracts signed in blood are common and widespread.

[1] Kaegi's *Rigveda*, Arrowsmith's translation. This was apparently a rain charm: its humour was of the unconscious order, of course.

CHAPTER III

Yama, the First Man, and King of the Dead

Burial Customs—Inhumation and Cremation—Yama the First Man—The Discoverer of Paradise—His Twin Sister—Persian Twin Deities—Yama and Mitra—Yama as Judge of the Dead—The "Man in the Eye"—Brahman's Deal with Dharma-Yama—Sacrifice for a Wife—Story of Princess Savitri—Her Husband's Fate—How she rescued his Soul from Yama—The Heavens of Yama, Indra, and Varuna—Teutonic, Greek, and Celtic Heavens—Paradise denied to Childless Men—Religious Need for a Son—Exposure of Female Infants—Infanticide in Modern India—A Touching Incident.

In early Vedic times the dead might be either buried or cremated. These two customs were obviously based upon divergent beliefs regarding the future state of existence. A Varuna hymn makes reference to the "house of clay", which suggests that among some of the Aryan tribes the belief originally obtained that the spirits of the dead hovered round the place of sepulture. Indeed, the dread of ghosts is still prevalent in India; they are supposed to haunt the living until the body is burned.

Those who practised the cremation ceremony in early times appear to have conceived of an organized Hades, to which souls were transferred through the medium of fire, which drove away all spirits and demons who threatened mankind. Homer makes the haunting ghost of Patroklos exclaim, "Never again will I return from Hades when I have received my meed of fire".[1] The Vedic worshippers

[1] *Iliad*, xxiii, 75.

of Agni burned their dead for the same reason as did the ancient Greeks. "When the remains of the deceased have been placed on the funeral pile, and the process of cremation has commenced, Agni, the god of fire, is prayed not to scorch or consume the departed, not to tear asunder his skin or his limbs, but, after the flames have done their work, to convey to the fathers the mortal who has been presented to him as an offering. Leaving behind on earth all that is evil and imperfect, and proceeding by the paths which the fathers trod, invested with a lustre like that of the gods, it soars to the realms of eternal light in a car, or on wings, and recovers there its ancient body in a complete and glorified form; meets with the forefathers who are living in festivity with Yama; obtains from him, when recognized by him as one of his own, a delectable abode, and enters upon more perfect life, which is crowned with the fulfilment of all desires, is passed in the presence of the gods, and employed in the fulfilment of their pleasure."[1]

Agni is the god who is invoked by the other deities, "Make straight the pathways that lead to the gods; be kind to us, and carry the sacrifice for us".[2]

In this connection, however, Professor Macdonell says, "Some passages of the *Rigveda* distinguish the path of the fathers or dead ancestors from the path of the gods, doubtless because cremation appeared as a different process from sacrifice".[3]

It would appear that prior to the practice of cremation a belief in Paradise ultimately obtained: the dead walked on foot towards it. Yama, King of the Dead, was the first man.[4] Like the Aryan pioneers who discovered the

[1] Muir, *Original Sanskrit Texts*, v. 302.
[2] *Rigveda*, x. 51 (Arnold's translation).
[3] *A History of Sanskrit Literature*, p. 117.
[4] As was also Manu of a different or later cult.

Punjab, he explored the hidden regions and discovered the road which became known as "the path of the fathers".

> To Yama, mighty king, be gifts and homage paid.
> He was the first of men that died, the first to brave
> Death's rapid rushing stream, the first to point the road
> To heaven, and welcome others to that bright abode.
>
> *Sir M. Monier Williams' translation.*[1]

Professor Macdonell gives a new rendering of a Vedic hymn[2] in which Yama is referred to as follows:

> Him who along the mighty heights departed,
> Him who searched and spied the path for many,
> Son of Vivasvat, gatherer of the people,
> Yama the king, with sacrifices worship.
>
> *Rigveda*, x, 14. 1.

Yama and his sister Yamí, the first human pair, are identical with the Persian Yima and Yimeh of Avestan literature; they are the primeval "twins", the children of Vivasvat, or Vivasvant, in the *Rigveda* and of Vivahvant in the *Avesta*. *Yama* signifies twin, and Dr. Rendel Harris, in his researches on the Greek Dioscuri cult, shows that among early peoples the belief obtained widely that one of each pair of twins was believed to be a child of the sky. "This conjecture is borne out by the name of Yama's father (Vivasvant), which may well be a cult-epithet of the bright sky, 'shining abroad' (from the root *vas*, 'to shine')". . . In the *Avesta* 'Yima, the bright' is referred to: he is the Jamshid of Fitzgerald's Omar.[3]

Yima, the Iranian ruler of Paradise, is also identical with Mitra (Mithra), whose cult "obtained from 200–400 A.D. a world-wide diffusion in the Roman Empire,

[1] From *Indian Wisdom*.

[2] *A History of Sanskrit Literature*, p. 117.

[3] *Early Religious Poetry of Persia*, Professor J. H. Moulton, p. 42.

10

THE KAILASA TEMPLE OF SHIVA, ELLORA

and came nearer to monotheism than the cult of any other god in paganism ".[1]

Professor Moulton wonders if the Yama myth "owed anything to Babylon?" It is possible that the worshippers of Agni represented early Iranian beliefs, and that the worshippers of Mitra, Varuna, and the twins (Yama and Yima and the twin Aswins) were influenced by Babylonian mythology as a result of contact, and that these opposing sects were rivals in India in early Vedic times.

In one of the hymns[2] Yami is the wooer of her brother Yama. She declares that they were at the beginning intended by the gods to be husband and wife, but Yama replies:

> "Who has sure knowledge of that earliest day? Who has seen it with his eyes and can tell of it? Lofty is the law of Mitra and Varuna; how canst thou dare to speak as a temptress?"
>
> *Arnold's translation.*

In the Vedic "land of the fathers", the shining Paradise, the two kings Varuna and Yama sit below a tree. Yama, a form of Mitra, plays on a flute and drinks Soma with the Celestials, because Soma gives immortality. He gathers his people to him as a shepherd gathers his flock: indeed he is called the "Noble Shepherd". He gives to the faithful the draught of Soma; apparently unbelievers were destroyed or committed to a hell called Put. Yama's messengers were the pigeon and the owl; he had also two brindled watch-dogs, each with four eyes. The dead who had faithfully fulfilled religious ordinances were addressed:

> Fear not to pass the guards—
> The four-eyed brindled dogs—that watch for the departed.

[1] *A History of Sanskrit Literature*, Professor Macdonell, p. 68.
[2] *Rigveda*, x, 10.

Return unto thy home, O soul! Thy sin and shame
Leave thou behind on earth; assume a shining form—
Thine ancient shape—refined and from all taint set free.
Sir M. Monier Williams' translation.[1]

Yama judged men as Dharma-rajah, "King of righteousness"; he was Pitripati, "lord of the fathers"; Samavurti, "the impartial judge"; Kritana, "the finisher"; Antaka, "he who ends life"; Samana, "the leveller", &c.

In post-Vedic times he presided over a complicated system of Hells; he was Dandadhara, "the wielder of the rod or mace". He had a noose with which to bind souls; he carried out the decrees of the gods, taking possession of souls at their appointed time.

In one of the *Brahmanas* death, or the soul which Death claims as his own, is "the man in the eye". The reflection of a face in the pupil of the eye was regarded with great awe by the early folk; it was the spirit looking forth. We read, "Now that man in yonder orb (of the sun) and that man in the right eye truly are no other than Death; his feet have stuck fast in the heart, and having pulled them out, he comes forth; and when he comes forth then that man dies; whence they say of him who has passed away, '*he has been cut off*' (life or life-string has been severed)".[2]

Yama might consent to prolong the life of one whose days had run out, on condition that another individual gave up part of his own life in compensation; he might even agree to restore a soul which he had bound to carry away, in response to the appeal of a mortal who had attained to great piety. The Vedic character of Yama survives sometimes in Epic narrative even after cremation

[1] From *Indian Wisdom*.

[2] *Satapatha Brahmana*, translated by Professor Eggeling, Part IV, 1897, p. 371 (*Sacred Books of the East*).

had become general. The following two touching and beautiful stories, preserved in *Mahabharata*, are probably very ancient Aryan folk tales which were cherished by the people and retold by the poets, who attached to them later religious beliefs and practices.

THE BRAHMAN AND HIS BRIDE

Once upon a time Menaka, the beautiful Apsara (celestial fairy), who is without shame or pity, left beside a hermitage her new-born babe, the daughter of the King of Gandharvas (celestial elves). A pious Rishi, named Sthula-kesha, found the child and reared her. She was called Pramadarva, and grew to be the most beautiful and most pious of all young women. Ruru, the great grandson of Bhrigu, looked upon her with eyes of love, and at the request of his sire, Pramati, the virgin was betrothed to the young Brahman.

It chanced that Pramadarva was playing with her companions a few days before the morning fixed for the nuptials. As her time had come, she trod upon a serpent, and the death-compelling reptile bit her, whereupon she fell down in a swoon and expired. She became more beautiful in death than she had been in life.

Brahmans assembled round the body of Pramadarva and sorrowed greatly. Ruru stole away alone and went to a solitary place in the forest where he wept aloud. "Alas!" he cried, "the fair one, whom I love more dearly than ever, lieth dead upon the bare ground. If I have performed penances and attained to great ascetic merit, let the power which I have achieved restore my beloved to life again."

Suddenly there appeared before Ruru an emissary from the Celestial regions, who spake and said: "Thy prayer is of no avail, O Ruru. That one whose days have been numbered can never get back her own life again. Thou shouldst not therefore abandon thine heart to grief. But the gods have decreed a means whereby thou canst receive back thy beloved."

Said Ruru: "Tell me how I can comply with the will of the Celestials, O messenger, so that I may be delivered from my grief."

The messenger said: "If thou wilt resign half of thine own life to this maiden, Pramadvara, she will rise up again."

Said Ruru: "I will resign half of my own life so that my beloved may be restored unto me."

Then the king of the Gandharvas and the Celestial emissary stood before Dharma-rajah (Yama) and said: "If it be thy will, O Mighty One, let Pramadarva rise up endowed with a part of Ruru's life."

Said the Judge of the Dead: "So be it."

When Dharma-rajah had spoken thus, the serpent-bitten maiden rose from the ground, and Ruru, whose life was curtailed for her sake, obtained the sweetest wife upon earth. The happy pair spent their days deeply devoted to each other, awaiting the call of Yama at the appointed time.[1]

STORY OF SAVITRI

There was once a fair princess in the country of Madra, and her name was Savitri. Be it told how she obtained the exalted merit of chaste women by winning a great boon from Yama.

Savitri was the gift of the goddess Gayatri,[2] wife of

[1] From *Adi Parva* section of *Mahabharata*.

[2] Saraswati's rival. Brahma took Gayatri, the milkmaid, as a second wife, because his chief wife, Saraswati, despite her wisdom, arrived late for a certain important ceremony, at which the spouse of the god was required.

Brahma, the self-created, who had heard the prayers and received the offerings of Aswapati, the childless king of Madra, when he practised austere penances so that he might have issue. The maiden grew to be beautiful and shapely like to a Celestial; her eyes had burning splendour, and were fair as lotus leaves; she resembled a golden image; she had exceeding sweetness and grace.

It came to pass that Savitri looked with eyes of love upon a youth named Satyavan "the Truthful". Although Satyavan dwelt in a hermitage, he was of royal birth. His father was a virtuous king, named Dyumatsena, who became blind, and was then deprived of his kingdom by an old enemy dwelling nigh to him. The dethroned monarch retired to the forest with his faithful wife and his only son, who in time grew up to be a comely youth.

When Savitri confessed her love to her sire, the great sage Narada, who sat beside him, spoke and said: "Alas! the princess hath done wrong in choosing for her husband this royal youth Satyavan. He is comely and courageous, he is truthful and magnanimous and forgiving, he is modest and patient and without malice; honour is seated upon his forehead; he is possessed of every virtue. But he hath one defect, and no other. He is endued with short life; within a year from this day he must die, for so hath it been decreed; within a year Yama, god of the dead, will come for him."

Said the king unto his daughter: "O Savitri, thou hast heard the words of Narada. Go forth, therefore, and choose for thyself another lord, for the days of Satyavan are numbered."

The beautiful maiden made answer unto her father the king, saying: "The die is cast; it can fall but once; once only can a daughter be given away by her sire; once only can a woman say, '*I am thine*'. I have chosen my lord; once have I chosen, nor can I make choice a second time. Let his life be brief or be long, I must now wed Satyavan."

Said Narada: "O king, the heart of thy daughter will not waver; she will not be turned aside from the path she hath selected. I therefore approve of the bestowal of Savitri upon Satyavan."

The king said: "As thou dost advise, so must I do ever, O Narada, because that thou art my preceptor. Thee I cannot disobey."

Then said Narada: "Peace be with Savitri! I must now depart. May blessings attend upon all of you!"

Thereafter Aswapati, the royal sire of Savitri, went to visit Dyumatsena, the blind sire of Satyavan, in the forest, and his daughter went with him.

Said Dyumatsena: "Why hast thou come hither?"

Aswapati said: "O royal sage, this is my beautiful daughter Savitri. Take thou her for thy daughter-in-law."

Said Dyumatsena: "I have lost my kingdom, and with my wife and my son dwell here in the woods. We live as ascetics and perform great penances. How will thy daughter endure the hardships of a forest life?"

Aswapati said: "My daughter knoweth well that joy and sorrow come and go and that nowhere is bliss assured. Accept her therefore from me."

Then Dyumatsena consented that his son should wed Savitri, whereat Satyavan was made glad because he was given a wife who had every accomplishment. Savitri rejoiced also because she obtained a husband after her own heart, and she put off her royal garments and ornaments and clad herself in bark and red cloth.

So Savitri became a hermit woman. She honoured Satyavan's father and mother, and she gave great joy to her husband with her sweet speeches, her skill at work, her subdued and even temper, and especially her love. She lived the life of the ascetics and practised every austerity. But she never forgot the dread prophecy of Narada the sage; his sorrowful words were always present in her secret heart, and she counted the days as they went past.

At length the time drew nigh when Satyavan must cast off his mortal body. When he had but four days to live, Savitri took the *Tritatra* vow of three nights of sleepless penance and fast.

Said the blind Dyumatsena: "My heart is grieved for thee, O my daughter, because the vow is exceedingly hard."

Savitri said: "Be not sorrowful, saintly father, I must observe my vow without fail."

Said Dyumatsena: "It is not meet that one like me should say, 'Break thy vow,' rather should I counsel, 'Observe thy vow.'"

Then Savitri began to fast, and she grew pale and was much wasted by reason of her rigid penance. Three days passed away, and then, believing that her husband would die on the morrow, Savitri spent a night of bitter anguish through all the dark and lonely hours.

The sun rose at length on the fateful morning, and she said to herself, "*To-day is the day.*" Her face was bloodless but brave; she prayed in silence and with fervour and offered oblations at the morning fire; then she stood before her father-in-law and her mother-in-law in reverent silence with joined hands, concentrating her senses. All the hermits of the forest blessed her and said: "Mayest thou never suffer widowhood."

Said Savitri in her secret heart: "So be it."

Dyumatsena spoke to her then, saying: "Now that

thy vow hath been completed thou mayest eat the morning meal."

Said Savitri: "I will eat when the sun goes down."

Hearing her words Satyavan rose, and taking his axe upon his shoulder, turned towards the distant jungle to procure fruits and herbs for his wife, whom he loved. He was strong and self-possessed and of noble seeming.

Savitri spoke to him sweetly and said: "Thou must not go forth alone, my husband. It is my heart's desire to go with thee. I cannot endure to-day to be parted from thee."

Said Satyavan: "It is not for thee to enter the darksome jungle; the way is long and difficult, and thou art weak on account of thy severe penance. How canst thou walk so far on foot?"

Savitri laid her head upon his bosom and said: "I have not been made weary by my fast. Indeed I am now stronger than before. I will not feel tired when thou art by my side. I have resolved to go with thee: do not therefore seek to thwart my wish—the wish and the longing of a faithful wife to be with her lord."

Said Satyavan: "If it is thy desire to accompany me I cannot but gratify it. But thou must ask permission of my parents lest they find fault with me for taking thee through the trackless jungle."

Then Savitri spoke to the blind sage and her husband's mother and said: "Satyavan is going towards the deep jungle to procure fruits and herbs for me, and also fuel for the sacrificial fires. It is my heart's wish to go also, for to-day I cannot endure to be parted from him. Fain, too, would I behold the blossoming woods."

Said Dyumatsena: "Since thou hast come to dwell with us in our hermitage thou hast not before asked anything of us. Have thy desire therefore in this matter, but do not delay thy husband in his duties."

Having thus received permission to depart from the hermitage, Savitri turned towards the jungle with Satyavan, her beloved lord. Smiles covered her face, but her heart was torn with secret sorrow.

Peacocks fluttered in the green woodland through which they walked together, and the sun shone in all its splendour in the blue heaven.

Said Satyavan with sweet voice: "How beautiful are the bright streams and the blossoming trees!"

The heart of Savitri was divided into two parts: with one she held converse with her husband while she watched his face and followed his moods; with the other she awaited the dread coming of Yama, but she never uttered her fears.

Birds sang sweetly in the forest, but sweeter to Savitri was the voice of her beloved. It was very dear to her to walk on in silence, listening to his words.

Satyavan gathered fruits and stored them in his basket. At length he began to cut down the branches of trees. The sun was hot and he perspired. Suddenly he felt weary and he said: "My head aches; my senses are confused, my limbs have grown weak, and my heart is afflicted sorely. O silent one, a sickness hath seized me. My body seems to be pierced by a hundred darts. I would fain lie down and rest, my beloved; I would fain sleep even now."

Speechless and terror-stricken, the gentle Savitri wound her arms about her husband's body; she sat upon the ground and she pillowed his head upon her lap. Remembering the words of Narada, she knew that the dread hour had come; the very moment of death was at hand. Gently she held her husband's head with caressing hands; she kissed his panting lips; her heart was beating fast and loud. Darker grew the forest and it was lonesome indeed.

Suddenly an awful Shape emerged from the shadows. He was of great stature and sable hue; his raiment was blood-red; on his head he wore a gleaming diadem; he had red eyes and was fearsome to look upon; he carried a noose. . . . The Shape was Yama, god of death. He stood in silence, and gazed upon slumbering Satyavan.

Savitri looked up, and when she perceived that a Celestial had come nigh, her heart trembled with sorrow and with fear. She laid her husband's head upon the green sward and rose up quickly: then she spake, saying, "Who art thou, O divine One, and what is thy mission to me?"

Said Yama: "Thou dost love thy husband; thou art endued also with ascetic merit. I will therefore hold converse with thee. Know thou that I am the Monarch of Death. The days of this man, thy husband, are now spent, and I have come to bind him and take him away."

Savitri said: "Wise sages have told me that thy messengers carry mortals away. Why, then, O mighty King, hast thou thyself come hither?"

Said Yama: "This prince is of spotless heart; his virtues are without number; he is, indeed, an ocean of accomplishments. It would not be fitting to send messengers for him, so I myself have come hither."

The face of Satyavan had grown ashen pale. Yama cast his noose and tore out from the prince's body the soul-form, which was no larger than a man's thumb; it was tightly bound and subdued.

So Satyavan lost his life; he ceased to breathe; his body became unsightly; it was robbed of its lustre and deprived of power to move.

Yama fettered the soul with tightness, and turned abruptly towards the south; silently and speedily he went upon his way. . . .

Savitri followed him. . . . Her heart was drowned in grief. She could not desert her beloved lord. . . . She followed Yama, the Monarch of Death.

Said Yama: "Turn back, O Savitri. Do not follow me. Perform the funeral rites of thy lord. . . . Thine allegiance to Satyavan hath now come to an end: thou art free from all wifely duties. Dare not to proceed farther on this path."

Savitri said: "I must follow my husband whither he is carried or whither he goeth of his own will. I have undergone great penance. I have observed my vow, and I cannot be turned back. . . . I have already walked with thee seven paces, and the sages have declared that one who walketh seven paces with another becometh a companion. Being thus made thy friend, I must hold converse with thee, I must speak and thou must listen. . . . I have attained the perfect life upon earth by performing my vows and by reason of my devotion unto my lord. It is not meet that thou shouldest part me from my husband now, and prevent me from attaining bliss by saying that my allegiance to him hath ended and another mode of life is opened to me."

Said Yama: "Turn back now. . . . Thy words are wise and pleasing indeed; therefore, ere thou goest, thou canst ask a boon of me and I will grant it. Except the soul of Satyavan, I will give thee whatsoever thou dost desire."

Savitri said: "Because my husband's sire became blind, he was deprived of his kingdom. Restore his eyesight, O mighty One."

Said Yama: "The boon is granted. I will restore the

vision of thy father-in-law. . . . But thou hast now grown faint on this toilsome journey. Turn back, therefore, and thy weariness will pass away."

Savitri said: "How can I be weary when I am with my husband? The fate of my husband will be my fate also; I will follow him even unto the place whither thou dost carry him. . . . Hear me, O mighty One, whose friendship I cherish! It is a blessed thing to behold a Celestial; still more blessed is it to hold converse with one; the friendship of a god must bear great fruit."

Said Yama: "Thy wisdom delighteth my heart. Therefore thou canst ask of me a second boon, except the life of thy husband, and it will be granted thee."

Savitri said: "May my wise and saintly father-in-law regain the kingdom he hath lost. May he become once again the protector of his people."

Said Yama: "The boon is granted. The king will return to his people and be their wise protector. . . . Turn back now, O princess; thy desire is fulfilled."

Savitri said: "All people must obey thy decrees; thou dost take away life in accordance with divine ordinances and not of thine own will. Therefore thou art called Yama—he that ruleth by decrees. Hear my words, O divine One. It is the duty of Celestials to love all creatures and to award them according to their merit. The wicked are without holiness and devotion, but the saintly protect all creatures and show mercy even unto their enemies."

Said Yama: "Thy wise words are like water to a thirsty soul. Ask of me therefore a third boon, except thy husband's life, and it will be granted unto thee."

Savitri said: "My sire, King Aswapati, hath no son. O grant that a hundred sons may be born unto him."

Said Yama: "A hundred sons will be born unto thy

11

YAMA AND SAVITRI

From a painting by Nanda Lall Bose

(By permission of the Indian Society of Oriental Art, Calcutta)

royal sire. Thy boon is granted. . . . Turn back, therefore, O princess; thou canst not come farther. Long is the path thou hast already travelled."

Savitri said: "I have followed my husband and the way hath not seemed long. Indeed, my heart desireth to go on much farther. Hear my words, O Yama, as thou dost proceed on thy journey. Thou art great and wise and powerful; thou dost deal equally with all human creatures; thou art the lord of justice. . . . One cannot trust oneself as one can trust a Celestial; therefore, one seeketh to win the friendship of a Celestial. It is meet that one who seeketh the friendship of a Celestial should make answer to his words."

Said Yama: "No mortal hath ever spoken unto me as thou hast spoken. Thy words are indeed pleasing, O princess. I will grant thee even a fourth boon, except thy husband's life, ere thou dost depart."

Savitri said: "May a century of sons be born unto my husband and me so that our race may endure. O grant me this, the fourth boon, thou Mighty One."

Said Yama: "I grant unto thee a century of sons, O princess; they will be wise and powerful and thy race will endure. . . . Be without weariness now, O lady, and turn back; thou hast come too far already."

Savitri said: "Those who are pious must practise eternal morality, O Yama. The pious uphold the universe. The pious hold communion with the pious only, and are never weary; the pious do good unto others nor ever expect any reward. A good deed done unto the righteous is never thrown away; such an act doth not entail loss of dignity nor is any interest impaired. Indeed, the doing of good is the chief office of the righteous, and the righteous therefore are the true protectors of all."

Said Yama: "The more thou dost speak, the more I respect thee, O princess. O thou who art so deeply devoted unto thy husband, thou canst now ask of me some incomparable boon."

Savitri said: "O mighty One, thou bestower of boons, thou hast already promised what cannot be fulfilled unless my husband is restored unto me; thou hast promised me a century of sons. Therefore, I ask thee, O Yama, to give me back Satyavan, my beloved, my lord. Without him, I am as one who is dead; without him, I have no desire for happiness; without him I have no longing even for Heaven; I will have no desire to prosper if my lord is snatched off; I cannot live without Satyavan. Thou hast promised me sons, O Yama, yet thou dost take away my husband from mine arms. Hear me and grant this boon: Let Satyavan be restored to life so that thy decree may be fulfilled."

Said Yama: "So be it. With cheerful heart I now unbind thy husband. He is free. . . . Disease cannot afflict him again and he will prosper. Together you will both have long life; you will live four hundred years; you will have a century of sons and they will be kings, and their sons will be kings also."

Having spoken thus, Yama, the lord of death, departed unto his own place. And Savitri returned to the forest where her husband's body lay cold and ashen-pale; she sat upon the ground and pillowed his head upon her lap. Then Satyavan was given back his life. . . . He looked upon Savitri with eyes of love; he was like to one who had returned from a long journey in a strange land.

Said Satyavan: "Long was my sleep; why didst thou not awaken me, my beloved? . . . Where is that dark One who dragged me away?"

Savitri said: "Yama hath come and gone, and thou hast slept long, resting thy head upon my lap, and art now refreshed, O blessed one. Sleep hath forsaken thee, O son of a king. If thou canst rise up, let us now depart hence for the night is already dark. . . ."

Satyavan rose up refreshed and strong. He looked round about and perceived that he was in the midst of the forest. Then he said: "O fair one, I came hither to gather fruit for thee, and while I cut down branches from the trees a pain afflicted me. I grew faint, I sank upon the ground, I laid my head upon thy lap and fell into a deep slumber even whilst thou didst embrace me. Then it seemed to me that I was enveloped in darkness, and that I beheld a sable One amidst great effulgence. . . . Was this a vision or a reality, O fairest and dearest?"

Savitri said: "The darkness deepens. . . . I will tell thee all on the morrow. . . . Let us now find our parents, O prince. The beasts of the night come forth; I hear their awesome voices; they tread the forest in glee; the howl of the jackal maketh my heart afraid."[1]

Said Satyavan: "Darkness hath covered the forest with fear; we cannot discover the path by which to return home."

Savitri said: "A withered tree burneth yonder. I will gather sticks and make a fire and we will wait here until day."

Said Satyavan: "My sickness hath departed and I would fain behold my parents again. Never before have I spent a night away from the hermitage. My mother is old and my father also, and I am their crutch. They will now be afflicted with sorrow because that we have not returned."

[1] Unfaithful wives were transformed into jackals after death.

Satyavan lifted up his arms and lamented aloud, but Savitri dried his tears and said: "I have performed penances, I have given away in charity, I have offered up sacrifices, I have never uttered a falsehood. May thy parents be protected by virtue of the power which I have obtained, and may thou, O my husband, be protected also."

Said Satyavan: "O beautiful one, let us now return to the hermitage."

Savitri raised up her despairing husband. She then placed his left arm upon her left shoulder and wound her right arm about his body, and they walked on together. . . . At length the fair moon came out and shone upon their path.

Meanwhile Dyumatsena, the sire of Satyavan, had regained his sight, and he went with his wife to search for his lost son, but had to return to the hermitage sorrowing and in despair. The sages comforted the weeping parents and said: "Savitri hath practised great austerities, and there can be no doubt that Satyavan is still alive."

In time Satyavan and Savitri reached the hermitage, and their own hearts and the hearts of their parents were freed from sorrow.

Then Savitri related all that had taken place, and the sages said: "O chaste and illustrious lady, thou hast rescued the race of Dyumatsena, the foremost of kings, from the ocean of darkness and calamity."

On the morning that followed messengers came to Dyumatsena and told that the monarch who had deprived him of his kingdom was dead, having fallen by the hand of his chief minister. All the people clamoured for their legitimate ruler. Said the messengers: "Chariots await thee, O king. Return, therefore, unto thy kingdom."

Great was their wonder to find that Dyumatsena was no longer blind.

So the king was restored to his kingdom, in accordance with the boon which Savitri had obtained from Yama. And sons were in time born unto her father. Thus did the gentle Savitri, by reason of her great piety, raise from misery to high fortune the family of her husband and her own father also. She was the rescuer of all; the bringer of happiness and prosperity. . . . He who heareth the story of Savitri will never endure misery again. . . .

The beauties of Yama's heaven are sung by the sage Narada in the great epic poem *Mahabharata*.[1] "Listen to me," he says. "In that fair domain it is neither too hot nor too cold. Life there is devoid of sorrow; age does not bring frailties, and none ever hunger or thirst; it is without wretchedness, or fatigue, or evil feelings. Everything, whether celestial or human, that the heart seeks after is found there. Sweet are the juicy fruits, delicious the fragrance of flowers and tree blossoms, and waters are there, both cold and hot, to give refreshment and comfort. Nymphs dance and sing to the piping of celestial elves, and merry laughter ever blends with the strains of alluring music.

"The Assembly House of Yama, which was made by Twashtri, hath splendour equal to the sun; it shines like burnished gold. There the servants of the Lord of Justice measure out the allotted days of mortals. Great rishis and ancestors await upon Yama, King of the Pitris (fathers), and adore him. Sanctified by holiness, their shining bodies are clad in swan-white garments, and decked with many-coloured bracelets and golden earrings. Sweet sounds, alluring perfumes, and brilliant

[1] *Lokapala-Sabhakhyana* section of *Sabha Parva*.

flower garlands make that building ever pleasant and supremely blest. Hundreds of thousands of saintly beings worship the illustrious King of the Pitris.

"The heaven of Indra was constructed by the great artisan-god himself. Like a chariot it can be moved anywhere at will. The Assembly House has many rooms and seats, and is adorned by celestial trees. Indra sits there with his beautiful queen, wearing his crown, with gleaming bracelets on his upper arms; he is decked with flowers, and attired in white garments. He is waited upon by brilliant Maruts, and all the gods and the rishis and saints, whose sins have been washed off their pure souls, which are resplendent as fire. There is no sorrow, or fear, or suffering in Indra's abode, which is inhabited by the spirits of wind and thunder, fire and water, plants and clouds, and planets and stars, and the spirits also of Prosperity, Religion, Joy, Faith, and Intelligence. Fairies and elves (Apsaras and Gandharvas) dance and sing there to sweet music; feats of skill are performed by celestial battle heroes, auspicious rites are also practised. Divine messengers come and go in celestial chariots, looking bright as Soma himself.

"The heaven of Varuna was constructed by Vishwakarman (Twashtri) within the sea. Its walls and arches are of pure white, and they are surrounded by celestial trees, made of sparkling jewels, which always blossom and always bear fruit. In the many-coloured bowers beautiful and variegated birds sing delightful melodies. In the Assembly House, which is also of pure white, there are many rooms and many seats. Varuna, richly decked with jewels and golden ornaments and flowers, is throned there with his queen. Adityas[1] wait upon the

[1] Sons of the goddess Aditi. They are attendants of Varuna, their chief, as the Maruts are attendants of Indra.

12

THE CITY OF THE GODS, PALITANA

lord of the waters, as also do hooded snakes (Nagas) with human heads and arms, and Daityas and Danavas (giants and demons) who have taken vows and have been rewarded with immortality. All the holy spirits of rivers and oceans are there, and the holy spirits of lakes and springs and pools, and the personified forms of the points of the heavens, the ends of the earth, and the great mountains. Music and dances provide entertainment, while sacred hymns are sung in praise of Varuna."

These heavens recall the Grecian "Islands of the Blest" and the Celtic Otherworld, where eternal summer reigns, trees bear blossoms and fruit continually, and there is no wasting with age. Indra's Assembly House is slightly reminiscent of the Teutonic Valhal, but is really more like the gardens of the underworld Hela. The Indian heroes do not feast on pork like those of Teutonic and Celtic myth; in the Assembly House of Kuvera, god of wealth, however, fat and flesh are eaten by fierce sentinel dwarfs. The fairy-like Apsaras are wooed by Indra's favoured warriors as well as by the gods.

One of the conditions which secured entry to the heaven of Yama was that a man should have offspring. A rishi, named Mandapala, devoted himself to religious vows and the observance of great austerities, but when he reached the region of the Pitris, he could not obtain "the fruit of his acts". He asked: "Why is this domain unattainable to me?"

Said the Celestials: "Because thou hast no children. . . . The Vedas have declared that the son rescueth the father from a hell called Put. O best of Brahmans, strive thou to beget offspring."[1]

A father could only reach Heaven if his son, after performing the cremation ceremony, poured forth the

[1] *Adi Parva* section of *Mahabharata*, Roy's trans., p. 635.

oblation and performed other necessary services to the dead. Consequently, all men showed great anxiety to have sons. In the Vedic period the exposure of female children was not unknown; indeed, this practice is referred to in the *Yajurveda*. "It is sorrowful to have a daughter," exclaims the writer of one of the *Brahmanas*.

One reason for infanticide in modern India is associated with the practice of exogamy (marriage outside of one's tribe). Raids took place for the purpose of obtaining wives and these were invariably the cause of much bloodshed. In 1842 members of the Kandhs tribe told Major Macpherson "that it was better to destroy girls in their infancy than to allow them to grow up and become causes of strife afterwards". Colonel Mac Culloch, Political Agent for Manipur, stamped out infanticide in the Naga country by assuring the people of a tribe that they would be protected against the wife-hunting parties of a stronger tribe. "Many years afterwards a troop of Naga girls from the weaker tribe paid a visit of ceremony to Colonel Mac Culloch, bearing presents of cloth of their own weaving in token of their gratitude to the man who had saved their lives."[1]

[1] The Tribes and Castes of Bengal. H. H. Risley (1892), vol. i, lxv, *et seq.*

CHAPTER IV

Demons and Giants and Fairies

Indian Asuras as Demons—Persian Ahura a God—Indian Gods as Persian Demons—Theory of Assyrian Influence—Indra's Battle with Asuras—Like Thor's Conflict with Giants—The Sun and Moon Devourer—Giants and Demons of Ocean—The Flying City—Destruction of World by Fire—Teutonic Parallel—Serpent Demigods—Man's Special Enemies—The Corpse Eaters—Demons of Disease, Unbelief, and Robbery—Elves and Fairies—The "Good People"—Celestial Musicians and Dancing Girls—Origin of Mythical Beings—Story of a Love-sick King—His Fairy Bride—The Echoing Forest Nymph—The "Language of Birds"—Birds as Spirits and Ghosts.

THE gods are the Suras and the demons the Asuras or "non-gods". This distinction, however, did not obtain in the early Vedic period. Originally the deities, and especially Varuna and Mitra, were called Asuras, but in the later part of the *Rigveda* the term is applied chiefly to the enemies of the gods. In the *Atharvaveda*, as in subsequent Epic literature, the Asuras are simply demons and giants and goblins.

No conclusive explanation can be offered as to how this remarkable change took place in the course of the centuries embraced by the Vedic period. It may have been due primarily to sectarian strife between the religious teachers of those tribes which had been influenced by Babylonian modes of thought and those which clung tenaciously to the forms of primitive Aryan nature worship, and perhaps also the worship of ancestors (Pitris). In the old Persian language, which, like Greek, places "h" before a vowel where "s" is used in Sanskrit, Ahura (= Asura) signifies "god". The Zoroastrian chief god is called Ahura-Mazda, "the wise Lord", as Varuna is addressed in early Rigvedic hymns, "wise Asura and King", and "the all-knowing Asura who established the heavens and fixed the limits of the earth". On the other hand "daeva" in the Iranian dialect, which is cognate with Sanskrit "deva", "god", came to mean "demon". "Asura" is derived from the root "asu", which signifies "the air of life", and "deva" from "div", "to shine", or "deiwo", "heavenly".

The view has been urged that the revolt against "Asura" in India was due to the hatred cherished towards the Persians who had become subject to the Assyrians, the worshippers of Ashur. It was originally based on the assumption that Assyrian aggression caused the migration of Aryan tribes towards India. Subsequent research, however, has tended to dispel this theory. It has been found, for instance, that Aryans were associated with the Kassites who overthrew the Hammurabi dynasty of Babylon prior to the invasion of the Punjab, and that the Assyrians were for a period vassals of the Mitanni kings, who had Aryan names and worshipped Indra, Varuna, and Mithra in Mesopotamia and Asia Minor. The weak point in the Ashur-Asura theory is that it throws no light on the process which caused the Persian "daeva" to be applied to demons instead of to gods. How the gods of the Indian Aryans became the lemons of Persia and the demons of Persia became the gods of India is a problem for which a solution has yet to be found.

The expository and speculative books of the priests—the *Brahmanas* and *Upanishads*—which are attached to the Vedic hymns, do not help us greatly in accounting for the change. We read that "the gods and Asuras contended together, and that the former, being less numerous than the latter, took some bricks, and placing them in a proper position to receive the sacrificial fire, with the formula, 'Thou art a multiplier', they became numerous".[1]

In one of the Brahmanas we are informed:

"The Asuras performed at the sacrifice all that the Devas performed. The Asuras became thus of equal power with the Devas, and did not yet yield to them. Thereupon the Devas had a vision of the 'silent praise'. The Asuras, not knowing it, did not perform the 'silent praise'. This 'silent praise' is the latent essence of the hymns. Till then, whatever weapons the Devas used against the Asuras, the Asuras used in revenge against them; but when the Devas had a vision of the 'silent praise' and raised it as a weapon, the Asuras did not comprehend it. With it the Devas aimed a blow at the Asuras, and defeated them, for they had no comprehension of this weapon. Thereupon the Devas became masters of the Asuras. He who has such a knowledge becomes master of his enemy, adversary, and hater."[2]

This explanation is but an echo of the Indra-Vritra combat. Another statement is to the effect that "the Devas gave up falsehood and adopted truth, while the Asuras gave up truth and adopted falsehood". Further, we learn that when a sacrifice was performed the Asuras put the offerings into their own mouths, while the Suras (gods) gave the offerings they received to one another.

The Asuras became completely identified with the demons and giants; they symbolized evil, darkness, and drought. In Epic literature we read that "in ancient times the gods and Asuras were very active in destroying one another. And the terrible Asuras always succeeded in defeating the gods." . . . Indra goes forth with

[1] Muir's *Original Sanskrit Texts*, v, 15.

[2] Professor E. Vernon Arnold's *The Rigveda*, p. 54.

his thunderbolt against Kesin, the leader of the Asuras, who wielded a great mace; this mace the demon hurled against the god, but Indra "cut it up in its course with his thunderbolt. Then Kesin, furious with rage, hurled a huge mass of rock at him." Indra "of a hundred sacrifices rent it asunder with his thunderbolt, and it fell down upon the ground. And Kesin himself was wounded by that falling mass of rock.[1] Thus sorely afflicted he fled". Indra rescues a beautiful lady who had been seized by the Asura, and she informs the god that her sister had previously fallen a victim to the demon. . . .[2]

The Asuras obstructed sacrifices; they were ever hovering round altars to discover if rites were properly performed; if a priest did not perform a ceremony in orthodox fashion, the sacrifice was of no avail, because the Asuras devoured it; if a man neglected a part of a ceremonial performance, a demon might take possession of him and accomplish his ruin.

One of the terrible Asuras is the demon Rahu, who causes eclipses by swallowing the sun and the moon, like the Chinese dragon, the wolf Managarm of Teutonic mythology, and the Grecian demons who devour Helena, the sun maiden, sister of the twin Dioscuri. In the Vedic period Rahu was represented by the demon Svarbhanu.

The Asuras of Ocean are the Daityas and Danavas, the descendants of the chaos hags Diti and Danu, and Kasyapa, a superhuman sage. These are the giants and demons who fought against the gods like the Titans, the Irish Fomorians, and the Norse Jotuns. Indra confined them in this region, which is called Patala, and they re-

[1] In the combat between Thor and the giant Hrungner, the thunder-hammer similarly cleaves a mass of flint hurled by the enemy.—*Teutonic Myth and Legend.*

[2] *Mahabharata*, *Vana Parva* section, pp. 679–80, Roy's trans.

13

DURGA SLAYING GIANTS AND DEMONS

From a sculpture at Mámallapuram

main there "afflicted by Time",[1] and subject to the sway of Varuna. Like the Norse giants, they will be let loose to take part in the "Last Battle". An "Asura fire" burns constantly in Patala, fed by water; it is "bound and confined", but cannot be extinguished; when the end of all comes, it will burst forth and burn up the three worlds.[2] In Teutonic mythology the Universe is similarly doomed to be consumed by fire at Ragnarok, "the Dusk of the Gods".

The abodes of these giants and demons are exceedingly beautiful; they are agleam with gold and precious stones; seats and beds are provided in the mansions, and there are also recreation grounds, and forests and mountains resembling clouds. Indeed, the Daityas and Danavas live pretty much in the same manner as the gods, for "the gods and Danavas are brothers, although ever hostile to one another".[3] The Danava women are of gigantic stature, and wear jewels as large as mountain boulders; when terrified by the attacks of the gods, they "bewail like unto cranes in Autumn". One of the Daitya tribes reside in the moving city named Hiranyapura, which they constructed for their protection; sometimes it sinks below the sea, or under the earth; at other times it soars across the heavens like the sun. Indra, as we have seen, has a similar aerial city.

In the Underworld dwell also the Nagas, the demoniac Cobras; they are of human form to the waist, the rest of their bodies being like those of serpents. Their king is Shesha, who is also named Vasuki and Karkotáka; he is sometimes represented with a thousand heads, and resembles Typhon, who fought with Zeus. In the *Ramayana* he is Ravana, the Demon of Ceylon. The

[1] "Overwhelmed by misfortune" (Roy).

[2] Heaven, Earth, and the Underworld.

[3] *Mahabharata.*

prototypes of Shesha and his hosts are the dragons Vritra, "the encompasser"; Ahi, "the confiner"; and fierce Kushna, "the scorcher", who spits out the sunset fires and burns up day.

When serpent worship became prevalent among the Aryans, the Nagas were regarded as demigods. They were occasionally "the friends of man", and to those they favoured they gave draughts of their nectar, which endowed them with great strength. Their city was the Paradise of serpent worshippers. The female Nagas were beautiful nymphs, who were sometimes wooed by mortals.

As the Asuras are the enemies of the gods, the Rakshas or Rakshasas are the enemies of man.[1] These demons are "night prowlers"; they have greatest power after "the first forty seconds of grey twilight preceding nightfall". They travel faster than the wind, and go through the air; they have also power to change their shape. Sometimes they appear in the guise of tigers, bears, or great monkeys; and their hues vary from yellow to red, and blue to green. In the *Ramayana* they are found associated with the Asuras of Ceylon; a spy enters a demon dwelling and sees them in all their shapes, some frightfully deformed, with small bodies and long arms; some as grotesque dwarfs, others as horrible giants with long projecting teeth; some with one eye, others with three eyes; some with one leg, two legs, or three, or even four; and some with heads of serpents, horses, or elephants. In the *Mahabharata* the Rakshasas are like gorillas; they have arrow-shaped ears, big red eyes, and red hair and beards, and mouths like caves; they feast on human beings and cattle. The heroic Bhima, like Siegfried Dietrich of Bern, Beowulf, and Finn-mac-Coul,

[1] Asuras are sometimes called Rakshasas also.

is a mighty slayer of these man-eating demons. They are impervious to weapons, but Bhima wrestles with them and breaks their backs or tears them asunder, after lively combats with trees and boulders. Female Rakshasas sometimes fall in love with human beings, and transform themselves into beautiful women. Bhima takes one for his bride, and she carries him through the air to a Celestial retreat among the mountains.

The most loathsome Rakshasas are the goblin-like Pisachas,[1] who are devourers of dead bodies in cemeteries, and are exceedingly vile and malignant fiends. They are the bringers of diseases and wasting fevers. In the *Atharvaveda* Agni is invoked by the priests, who mutter charms over suffering and "possessed" mortals, to take the Pisachas between his teeth and devour them. They are "those who hound us in our chambers, while shouting goes on in the night of the new moon . . . the flesh devourers, who plan to injure us, and whom I overcome". The priest declares: "I plague the Pisachas as the tiger the cattle owners. As dogs who have seen a lion, these do not find a refuge. . . . From villages I enter Pisachas fly away. . . . May Nirriti (a goddess of destruction) take hold of this one."[2]

Kali, a demon who holds friendly converse with the gods in the "Story of Nala", is attended by Dwápara, a flesh-eater like the Pisachas. The Panis are aerial demons, who are hated by bluff, honest Indra, because they are the inspirers of foolish actions, slander, and unbelief, and the imps who encourage men to neglect homage to deities. The black Dasyus are repulsive of aspect and jealous-hearted; they are the stealers of the cloud cows who are held captive for Vritra in the cave

[1] *Pron.* pe-shatch'as.

[2] Bloomfield's *Atharvaveda*, iv, 36 (*Sacred Books of the East*, vol. xlii).

of the demon Vala. The Darbas, "the tearers", are a variety of Pisachas. Reference is made in *Mahabharata* to "ugly Vartikas of dreadful sight, having one wing, one eye, and one leg"; when they "vomit blood, facing the sun", a dreadful happening is known to be at hand, because they are fiends of evil omen.

Among the supernatural beings who are sometimes the enemies, but in most cases the friends of mankind, are the Yakshas, the Gandharvas, and the Apsaras (Apsarasas).

The Yakshas are occasionally referred to as the Punyajanas, "the good people"; they may be of human stature, with big benevolent eyes, or powerful giants who can fight as fiercely as Rakshasas. They are guardians of hidden treasure, like the dwarfs and giants of Teutonic legend, being associated with Kuvera, god of wealth, whose abode is situated among the Himalayan mountains. In Kuvera's domain are found "multitudes of spirits" who do not visit the world of men as a rule, but remain near the treasure for purposes of defence; "some are of dwarfish stature, some of fierce visage, some hunchbacked, some of blood-red eyes, some of frightful yells; some are feeding upon fat and flesh, and some are terrible to behold; and all are armed with various weapons, and endued with the speed of the wind".[1]

The Gandharvas are grouped in tribes, and number over six thousand individuals. They are all of the male sex. They haunt the air, the forests, and the mountains, and, like the Rakshasas, have power to work illusions in the grey twilight before nightfall. References are made in the Epics to their combats with human beings. To warriors who overcome them they impart instruction in religious matters; those whom they conquer they carry

[1] *Mahabharata*, Roy's trans. (*Sabha Parva*, p. 32).

14

THE CELESTIAL FAIRIES (APSARAS)

away, like the Teutonic elves and dwarfs. The Gandharvas are renowned musicians and bards and singers. When they play on their divine instruments the fairy-like Apsaras, who are all females, dance merrily. In the various Aryan heavens these elves and fairies delight and allure with music and song and dance the gods, and the souls of those who have attained to a state of bliss. The Apsara dancing girls are "voluptuous and beautiful", and inspire love in Paradise as well as upon earth. Their lovers include gods, Gandharvas, and mortals. Arjuna, the human son of Indra, who was transported in a Celestial chariot to Swarga over Suravithi, "the Milky Way", was enchanted by the music and songs and dances of the Celestial elves and fairies. He followed bands of Gandharvas who were "skilled in music sacred and profane", and he saw the bewitching Apsaras, including the notorious Menaka, "with eyes like lotus blooms, employed in enticing hearts"; they had "fair round hips and slim waists", and "began to perform various evolutions, shaking their deep bosoms and casting their glances around, and exhibiting other attractive attitudes capable of stealing the hearts and resolutions and minds of the spectators".[1]

In the *Rigveda* there is a water-nymph, named Apsaras; she is the "spouse" of Gandharva, an atmospheric deity who prepares Soma for the gods and reveals divine truths to mortals. They vanish, however, in later times; the other Vedas deal with the spirit groups which figure so prominently in the Epics. No doubt the groups are older than Gandharva, the god, and Apsaras, the goddess, who may be simply the elf-king and the fairy-queen. The "black" Dasyus are sometimes referred to by modern-day writers as the dark aborigines who were displaced by the

[1] *Vana Parva* section of *Mahabharata*.

Aryans; a tribal significance is also given to the Rakshasas and the Gandharvas. But this tendency to identify the creatures of the spirit world with human beings may be carried too far. If "Dasyus" were really "dark folk",[1] it should be remembered that in Teutonic mythology there are "black dwarfs", who live in underground dwellings, and "white elves" associated with air and ocean; there are also black and white fairies in the Scottish Highlands, so that black and white spirits may simply belong to night and day spirit groups. It may be that the Indian aborigines were referred to contemptuously as Dasyus by the Aryans. The application of the names of repulsive imps to human enemies is not an unfamiliar habit even in our own day; in China the European is a "foreign devil", but Chinese "devils" existed long before Europeans secured a footing in the Celestial Kingdom. Those who seek for a rational explanation for the belief in the existence of mythical beings should remember that primitive man required no models for the creatures of his fancy. He symbolized everything—his ideals, his desires, his hopes and his fears, the howling wind, the low whispering breeze, the creaking tree, the torrent, the river, the lake, and the mountain; he heard the hammer or the trumpet of a mighty god in the thunderstorm, he believed that giants uprooted trees and cast boulders down mountain slopes, that demons raised ocean billows in tempest, and that the strife of the elements was a war between gods and giants; day and night, ever in conflict, were symbolized, as were also summer and winter, and growth and decay. If the fairies and elves of Europe are Lapps, or the small men of an interglacial period

[1] Dasyu and Dasa are "applied in many passages of the *Rigveda* to superhuman enemies". The colour reference in Dasa is probable, but it is also used in other senses. For a full discussion on conflicting views regarding Dasyu and Dasa see *Vedic Index of Names and Subjects*. Macdonell and Keith, vol. i, pp. 347–9 and 356–8.

in the Pleistocene Age, and if the Dasyus and Gandharvas of India are merely Dravidians and pre-Dravidians who resisted the Aryan invasion, who, then, it may be asked, were the prototypes of the giants "big as mountains", or the demons like "trees walking", the "tiger-headed" Rakshasas, "ugly Vartikas" with "one wing, one eye, and one leg"? and what animal suggested Vritra, or the fiery dragon that burned up daylight, or Rahu, the swallower of sun and moon? If the redhaired and red-bearded Rakshasas are to be given a racial significance, what of the blue Rakshasas and the green? The idea that primitive man conceived of giants because he occasionally unearthed the bones of prehistoric monsters, is certainly not supported by Scottish evidence; Scotland swarms with giants and hags of mountain, ocean, and river, although it has not yielded any great skeletons or even a single artifact of the Palæolithic Age. Giants and fairies are creations of fancy. Just as a highly imaginative child symbolizes his fears and peoples darkness with terrifying monsters, so, it may be inferred, did primitive man who crouched in his cave, or spent sleepless nights in tempest-stricken forests, conceive with childlike mind of demons thirsting for his blood and giants of wind and fire intent on destroying the Universe.

In India, as elsewhere, the folk of the spirit world might woo or be wooed by impressionable mortals. A Gandharva related to Arjuna, the Pandava prince, by whom he was defeated in single combat, the "charming story", as he called it, of King Samvarana and the fairy-like Tapati, a daughter of the sun god, Surya. Tapati was of all nymphs the most beautiful; she was "perfectly symmetrical" and "exquisitely attired"; she had "faultless features, and black, large eyes"; and, in contrast to an Apsara, she "was chaste and exceedingly well conducted". For a time the sun god considered that no husband could be found who was worthy of his daughter; and therefore "knew no peace of mind, always thinking of the person he should select". One day, however, King Samvarana worshipped the sun, and made offerings of flowers and sweet perfumes, and Surya resolved to bestow his daughter upon this ideal man.

It came to pass that Samvarana went a-hunting deer on the mountains. He rode swiftly in pursuit of a nimble-footed stag, leaving his companions behind, until his steed expired with exhaustion. Then he wandered about alone. In a secluded wood he beheld a maiden of exquisite beauty; he gazed at her steadfastly for a time, thinking she was a goddess or "the embodiment of the rays emanating from the sun". Her body was as radiant as fire and as spotless as the crescent moon; she stood motionless like to a golden statue. The flowers and the creepers round about partook of her beauty, and "seemed to be converted into gold". She was Tapati, daughter of the sun.

The king's eyes were captivated, his heart was wounded by the arrows of the love god Kama; he lost his peace of mind. At length he spoke and said: "Who art thou, O fair one? O maiden of sweet smiles, why dost thou linger in these lonely woods? I have never seen or heard of one so beautiful as thee. . . . The love god tortures me."

That lotus-eyed maiden made no answer; she vanished from sight like to lightning in the clouds.

The king hastened through the forest, lamenting for her: he searched in vain; he stood motionless in grief; he fell down on the earth and swooned.

Then, smiling sweetly, the maiden appeared again. In honeyed words she spoke, saying: "Arise, thou tiger among kings. It is not meet that thou shouldst lose thy reason in this manner."

Samvarana opened his eyes and beheld Tapati. Weak with emotion he spoke and said: "I am burning with love for thee, thou black-eyed beauty, O accept me. My life is ebbing away. . . . I have been bitten by Kama, who is even like a venomous snake. Have mercy on me. . . . O thou of handsome and faultless features, O thou of face like unto the lotus or the moon, O thou of voice sweet as that of singing Kinnaras, my life now depends on thee. Without thee, O timid one, I am unable to live. It behoveth thee not, O black-eyed maid, to cast me off; it behoveth thee to relieve me from this affliction by giving me thy love. At the first sight thou hast distracted my heart. My mind wandereth. Be merciful; I am thy obedient slave, thy adorer. O accept me. . . . O thou of lotus eyes, the flame of desire burneth within me. O extinguish that flame by throwing on it the water of thy love. . . ."[1]

Tapati replied: "I am not mistress of mine own self. I am a maiden ruled by my father. If thou dost love me, demand me of him. My heart hath been robbed by thee."

Then, revealing her identity, Tapati ascended to heaven, and once again Samvarana fell upon the earth and swooned.

The ministers and followers of the king came searching for him, and found him "lying forsaken on the ground like a rainbow dropped from the firmament". They sprinkled his face with cool and lotus-scented water. When he revived, the monarch sent away all his followers except one minister. For twelve days he worshipped the sun constantly on the mountain top. Then a great

[1] *Mahabharata*, Roy's translation (*Adi Parva*, section, pp. 495–6).

Rishi, whom he had sent for, came to him, and the Rishi ascended to the sun. Ere long he returned with Tapati, the sun god having declared that Samvarana would be a worthy husband for his daughter.

For twelve years the king lived with his fairy bride in the mountain forests, and a regent ruled over the kingdom.

But although the monarch enjoyed great bliss, living the life of a Celestial, the people of the kingdom suffered greatly. For twelve years no rain fell, "not even a drop of dew came from the skies, and no corn was grown". The people were afflicted with famine; men grew reckless, and deserted their wives and children; the capital became like to a city of the dead.

Then a great Rishi brought Samvarana back to his capital with his Celestial bride. And after that things became as they were before. Rain fell in abundance and corn was grown. "Revived by that foremost of monarchs of virtuous soul, the capital and the country became glad with exceeding joy."[1] A son was born to the king, and his name was Kuru.

There are many other uncatalogued Celestial beings like Tapati in Indian fairyland. In the *Atharva-veda* there are numerous named and nameless spirits of good and evil, and throughout the Epics references are made to semi-divine beings who haunt streams, lakes, forests, and plains. A *Rigveda* hymn is addressed to the forest nymph Aranyani. She echoes the voices of man and beast and creates illusions:

> She mimics kine that crop the grass,
> She rumbles like a cart at even,

[1] Like an Egyptian Pharaoh, the rajah is here a god among men. His presence was necessary to ensure the success of rain-bringing ceremonies.

> She calls a cow, she hews down wood,
> The man who lingers says, "Who calleth?"
>
> O Aranyani will not harm
> If one will not invade her dwelling,
> When, having eaten luscious fruit,
> At her sweet will she turns to slumber.

The singing birds are all singing spirits in India as in Europe. The "language of birds" is the language of spirits. When Siegfried, after eating of the dragon's heart, understood the "language of birds", he heard them warning him regarding his enemies. Our seafarers whistle when they invoke the spirit of the wind. Sir Walter Scott drew attention, in his *Minstrelsy of the Scottish Border*, to the belief that the speech of spirits was a kind of whistling. As we have seen, the wives of Danavas had voices like Cranes; Homer's ghosts twittered like bats; Egyptian ghosts were hooting owls. In India the croaking raven is still a bird of evil omen, as it is also in the West. In the Scottish Highlands the spirits of the dead sometimes appear as birds; so do fairies. The Irish gods and the Celestial Rishis of India take the form of swans, like the "swan maidens", when they visit mankind. In the Assyrian legend of Ishtar the souls of the dead in Hades "are like birds covered with feathers". Numerous instances could be quoted to illustrate the widespread association of birds with the spirit world.

CHAPTER V

Social and Religious Developments of the Vedic Age

Aryan Civilization—Tribes and Clans—Villages and Trade—Divisions of Society — Origin of Castes — Rise of the Priestly Cult — Brahmanic Ideals of Life—Brahmanic Students—The Source of Algebra—Samaveda and Yajurveda —Atharva-veda Charms and Invocations—The "Middle Country" the Centre of Brahmanic Culture—Sacred Prose Books—Bold Pantheism of the Upanishads—Human Sacrifice and its Symbolism—Chaos Giant Myth in India, Babylonia, and China, and in Teutonic Mythology—Horse Sacrifices in India, Siberia, Greece, Rome, &c.—Creation the Result of Sacrifice—Death as the Creator and Devourer.

During the Vedic Age, which came to a close in the eighth century B.C., the Aryan settlers spread gradually eastward and southward. At first they occupied the Punjab, but ere the Rigvedic period was ended they had reached the banks of the Jumna and the Ganges in the "Middle Country". In the early hymns the great Himalayan mountains dominate fertile river valleys, but the greater part of northern India is covered by vast and dense forests. No mention is made of the sea.

The Aryans were a pastoral and hunting people, with some knowledge of agriculture. They possessed large herds of cattle, and had also sheep, goats, and asses; they were, besides, famous breeders and tamers of horses; the faithful dog, man's earliest friend, followed both herdsman and hunter. The plough was in use, and bullocks were yoked to it; grain was thrashed in primitive manner and ground between "pounding stones". Barley and wheaten cakes, milk, curds, butter, and cheese, and wild fruits were the chief articles of diet; the products of the chase were also eaten, but there appears to have been at the earliest period a restriction in the consumption of certain foods. Beef was not eaten at meals. Bulls were sacrificed to the gods. Two kinds of intoxicating liquors were brewed—the mysterious Soma, beloved by deities, and a mead or ale called "sura", the Avestan "hura", prepared probably from grain, which had ever an evil reputation as a cause of peace-breaking, like dice, and of wrongdoing generally.

Metals were in use, for the earliest Aryan invasion took place in the Bronze Age, during which there were great race movements and invasions and conquests in Asia and in Europe. It is doubtful whether or not iron was known by the earliest Aryan settlers in India; it was probably not worked, but may have been utilized for charms, as in those countries in which meteoric iron was called "the metal of heaven". The knowledge of the mechanical arts had advanced beyond the primitive stage. Warriors fought not only on foot but also in chariots, and they wore breastplates; their chief weapons were bows and horn or metal-tipped arrows, maces, battleaxes, swords, and spears. Smiths roused their fires with feather fans; carpenters are mentioned in the hymns, and even barbers who used razors.

The father was the head of the family, and the family was the tribal unit. War was waged by a loose federation of small clans, each of which was distinguished by the name of a patriarch. The necessity of having to conduct frequent campaigns in a new country, peopled by hostile aliens, no doubt tended to weld tribal units into small kingdoms and to promote the monarchic system. But intertribal feuds were frequent and bitter. The Aryans of the Punjab, like the Gauls who settled in northern Italy, and the clans of the Scottish Highlands in the Middle Ages, were continually divided among themselves, and greatly occupied in subduing rivals and in harrying their cattle.

Villages were protected by stockades or earthworks against the attacks of enemies and wild beasts, or they contained strongholds. They were governed by headsmen, who were, no doubt, military leaders also; disputes were settled by a judge. Land, especially grazing land, appears to have been held in common by communities, but there are indications that cultivated plots and houses were owned by families and ultimately by individuals, the father in such cases being the supreme authority. Village communities, however, might be migratory, and certain of them may have had seasonal areas of settlement.

Permanent villages existed in groups and also at some distance from one another, and were connected by roads, and one clan might embrace several separate communities. Trade was conducted by barter, the cow being the standard of value, but in time jewels and gold ornaments were used like money for purchases; "nishka", a necklet, afterwards signified a coin. Foreign traders were not unknown at an early period. The use of alphabetic signs appears to have been introduced by Semites before the close of the Vedic period; from these evolved ultimately the scientific Sanskrit alphabet and grammar.

In the Iranian period[1] there were social divisions of the people, but the hereditary system does not appear to have obtained until the close of Rigvedic times. Kings might be elected, or a military aristocracy might impose its sway over an area; a priest was originally a poet or

[1] A convenient term as explained in our Introduction.

leader of thought, or a man of elevated character, like the Scottish Highland *duine-usual*, the "upwardly man", who might be the son of a chief or of the humblest member of a community.

The earliest Aryan divisions of society were apparently marked by occupations. At first there were three grades: warriors, priests, and traders, but all classes might engage in agricultural pursuits; even in the Epic period princes counted and branded cattle. In the later Vedic age, however, a rigid system of castes came into existence, the result, apparently, of having to distinguish between Aryans and aborigines at first, and subsequently between the various degrees of Aryans who had intermarried with aliens. Caste (Varna) signifies colour, and its relation to occupation is apparent in the four divisions—Brahmans, priests; Kshatriyas, the military aristocracy; Vaisyas, commoners, workers, and traders, who were freemen; and Sudras, slaves and aborigines. In the *Yajurveda*, the third Veda, the caste system is found established on a hereditary basis. The three upper castes, which were composed of Aryans only, partook in all religious ceremonials, but the members of the Sudra caste were hedged about by severe restrictions. The knowledge of the Vedas was denied to them, and they were not allowed to partake of Soma offerings, and although in the process of time their position improved somewhat in the religious life of the mingled people, their social inferiority was ever emphasized; they might become traders, but never Kshatriyas or Brahmans.

The most renowned of early Brahmans were the Rishis, the poets[1] who composed the "new songs" to the

[1] "A Rishi, 'seer', is primarily a composer of hymns. . . . The Rishis ultimately become the representatives of a sacred past." *Vedic Index of Names and Subjects*, vol. i, pp. 115–117 (1912).

gods. They were regarded as divinely inspired men and their fame was perpetuated after death. Several renowned poets are referred to in sacred literature and invested with great sanctity. The hymns or mantras were committed to memory and then handed down from generation to generation. At religious ceremonies these were chanted by reciters, the Hotri priests. There were also priests who were skilled in the correct performance of sacrificial rites, and family priests, the Purohitas, who were the guides, philosophers, and friends of kings and noblemen. A Rishi might be a Purohita and a seer, who ensured by the performance of mystic ceremonies a monarch's success in battle and afterwards celebrated his achievements in song.

In the process of time an organized priesthood came into existence, and a clan or kingdom had its chief priest. The production of new hymns came to an end; those which existed were considered sufficient for all purposes; religious beliefs were systematized, and an arbitrary ritual became more and more complicated.

There are indications that at an early period a chief or king might offer up a sacrifice, but when the profession of the Brahman became hereditary, no rite could be performed unless presided over by holy men. A sacrifice might be rendered futile by an error in the construction of an altar, or in the order of ceremonial practices, or by failure to select appropriate chants. The Asuras and Rakshasas and other demons were ever hovering round the altar, endeavouring to obstruct ceremonies and to take advantage of ritualistic errors to intercept offerings intended for the gods. It was by making sacrifices that man was believed to obtain power over the gods, or magical control over the forces of nature.

For the performance of some sacrifices a day of pre-

15 Photo. Frith

GROUP OF PRESENT-DAY BRAHMANS

paration might be required. Altars had to be erected with mathematical exactness; the stones were blessed and anointed; offerings were made at every stage of the work so that the various deities might give protection in their various spheres. The following extract from one of the Brahmanas affords a glimpse of the preparatory rites:—

> Thrice he (the priest) perambulates it (the altar); for thrice he walks round it (whilst sprinkling); thus as many times as he walks round it, so many times does he perambulate it. . . .
>
> Having thereupon put that stone into the water pitcher, (he) throws it in that (south-westerly) direction, for that is Nirriti's region; he thus consigns pain to Nirriti's region. . . .
>
> Outside the fire altars he throws it, &c.[1]

Human failings may be imputed to Brahmans, but it must be recognized that the ideals of their caste were of a high order. They were supposed to be born with "spiritual lustre", and their lives were consecrated to the instruction and uplifting of mankind and the attainment of salvation. A Brahman's life was divided into four periods. The first was the period of childhood, and the second was the period of probation, when he went to live in a forest hermitage, where he acted as the servant of a revered old sage, his spiritual father, and received instruction in Brahmanic knowledge for a number of years. During the third period the Brahman lived the worldly life; he married and reared a family and performed the duties pertaining to his caste. Hospitality was one of the chief worldly duties; if a stranger, even although he might be an enemy, came and asked for food he received it, although the Brahman family should have to fast to supply him. In the fourth period the Brahman, having proved himself a faithful husband and exemplary father,

[1] *Satapatha Brahmana*, trans. by Prof. Eggeling (*Sacred Books of the East*, No. XLIII, p. 170).

divided his worldly possessions between his grown-up sons and daughters; then he abandoned his comfortable home and, assuming the deerskin clothing of hermits, went to live in a lonely forest, or among the Himalayan mountains, to prepare for the coming of death, far away from the shadows cast by sin and sorrow. In solitude he performed rigid penances and addressed himself with single-minded devotion to the contemplation of spiritual problems. Subduing the five senses, he attained to the state of Yoga (concentration). Placing his mind entirely upon the contemplation of the soul, he became united ultimately with the World Soul (God), thus obtaining the release which was Salvation. Some Brahmans were teachers who instructed pupils and composed the sacred writings. The forest hermitages were the universities of ancient India.

The profession of the priesthood had certainly its mercenary aspect; sacrificial fees were fixed as well as sacrificial rites, and a not unimportant part of a ceremony was the offering of generous gifts to the Brahmans, who presided at the altar. But on the whole the riches thus expended were not given in vain. As in Egypt, the rise and endowment of the priestly cult was due to the accumulation of wealth which enabled a section of society to find leisure for study and the promotion of culture. Aryan civilization in India owed much to the Brahmans. They introduced and elaborated alphabetic signs; the devoted scholars among them compiled the first Sanskrit grammar and studied the art of composition. Among the hermits there were great and original thinkers who laid the basis of Indian metaphysical thought, and rose from the materialism of the early Vedic hymns to the idealism of the speculative prose works, which included the *Forest Books*, a name redolent of leafy solitude and of simple

16

SADHUS (RELIGIOUS MENDICANTS) AT BENARES

and contemplative lives on the banks of sweetly-flowing waters. Even their devotion to the mysteries of sacrificial ritual, which became more and more complicated, was not unproductive of permanent benefits to mankind. The necessity for the exact construction of altars, and the observance of ceremonies in due season, promoted the study of mathematical science. These Brahmans invented the numerical figures which have attained universal usage, and in time they gave the world Algebra. The influence of their culture may be traced in other directions. At the present day it has indirectly brought into existence the science of Comparative Religion.

At the close of the Rigvedic period the Aryans had extended their sway to the district known as Madhyadesa, the "middle country", between the "Five Rivers" of the Punjab and the upper reaches of the Jumna and Ganges. Pioneers were meantime pressing southward and eastward towards the sea. Migrations were, no doubt, due to propulsion as well as attraction; fresh folk-waves probably poured in periodically from the north-west, while the settled population must have increased rapidly in the fertile land controlled by the invaders, to whom the aborigines offered but slight resistance.

The second Vedic book, the *Samaveda*, does not contain much fresh material: it is mainly a compilation of the Rigvedic hymns which the priests chanted at the Soma sacrifice. Its sole interest, from a historical point of view, is the evidence it affords of the steady growth of ritualistic tendencies. A new era of Aryan civilization is revealed, however, by the third Veda, the *Yajurveda*. In this book the tribes are found to have extended their area of control down the Ganges valley, and southward along the banks of the Indus. It is of interest to note here that the word "Samudra", first applied to the broadening Indus where it receives its tributaries, and signifying "collected waters", became in the *Brahmanas* the name of the world-encircling ocean, across which in due time loomed the ships which "once in three years" carried to Solomon's order "gold, and silver, ivory (or elephants' tusks), and apes, and peacocks".[1]

In the *Yajurveda* we find that Aryan civilization has developed greatly in the course of three or four centuries. Powerful tribes have established kingdoms, and small states are being subjected to the larger. The hardened system of social organization is reflected by the references to the four distinct castes. Hitherto the Kshatriyas have controlled the destinies of the people, but now the Brahmans achieve an intellectual conquest and impose their sway over kings and nobles. The holy men are no longer the humble servants of generous patrons; they are the human representatives of the all-controlling deities. "Verily, there are two kinds of gods; for the gods themselves, assuredly, are gods, and those priests who have studied and teach Vedic lore, are the human gods."

The offerings to the deities are "consecrated by the feeding of priests".[2]

Even the gods become dependent upon the priests, who provided them by offering sacrifices with the "food" they required, and also with the Soma which gave them length of years. Indra could not combat against the Asuras without the assistance of the priests who chanted formulas to ensure victory; it was, therefore, due to the power exercised, in the first place, by the priests that the drought demon was overcome and rain fell in abundance.

Priests might also accumulate in heaven credit balances

[1] 1 *Kings*, x, 22.

[2] *Satapatha Brahmana*, translated by Professor Eggeling, Part I, p. 374 (*Sacred Books of the East*).

17

A YOGI ON A BED OF SPIKES

An example of present-day austerities

of Celestial power by undergoing penances for long periods. A heavy debt was also due to them by the gods for their sacrificial offerings. When a Brahman desired to exercise his accumulated power, he might even depose the deities, who were therefore placed under compulsion to fulfil his demands; his Celestial credit might exceed the "paying" possibilities of the supreme Powers. In the sacred tales Brahmans were credited with performing rigid penances for centuries.

In the fourth Veda, the *Atharva-veda*, the revival of belief in formulas is emphasized. This book, which did not receive recognition as an inspired work at first, is in the main a collection of metrical charms of great antiquity. Many resemble closely those which have been collected by folk-lorists during late years in the Scottish Highlands and elsewhere throughout Europe. The Rigveda hymns reveal the religious beliefs and aspirations of the advanced thinkers of their age; the *Atharva-veda* contains the germs of folk religion—the magical formulas chanted to dispel or invoke the vague spirits who helped or thwarted mankind. It teaches that the Universe is upheld by sacrifice and the spiritual exaltation of Brahmans, and that Brahmanic power may be exercised by the use of appropriate charms. Human beings might also be influenced by the spirits invoked by means of formulas.

Primitive man believed that all emotions were caused by spirits. When the poet sang, he was "inspired"—he drew in a spirit; ecstasy was "a standing outside of oneself", the soul having escaped temporarily from the body. Wrath was caused by a demon, and "battle fury" by the spirit of war which possessed the warrior. When a human being was "seized" by a fit, his convulsions were believed to be caused by the demon who had entered his body. Love was inspiration in the literal sense, and an

Indian lover might compel a heedless lady to regard him with favour by reciting an Atharva-vedic spell. Apparently the love spirit had a weakness for honey. The lover chanted:

> Honey be mine at the tip of my tongue,
> May sweetness of honey pervade my speech,
> So that my love may come under my spell—
> So that my lady may yield to my will.
>
> *Atharva-veda*, i, 34.

> As the grass is shorn from earth by the wind,
> So may thy soul be shorn to my will,
> And then, O lady, thou'lt give me thy love,
> Nor be averse to me as thou wert.
>
> *Atharva-veda*, ii, 30.

A lover, we find, can invoke the lady to embrace him "as the creeper embraces a tree"; if she clings to his arm he can cause her to cling to his heart; his influence over her mind is like the influence of a wing-beating eagle over the wind. It may be, too, that a neglected girl finds it necessary to prepare a love potion with "salve, sweet wood, and spikenard", and to cause the heart of an ungallant swain to suffer from "a parching heart", which "languishes for love", and experiences the "yearning of the Apsaras".

Warriors were charmed against spells, cattle and sheep were charmed against wild beasts, a house was charmed against evil spirits and demons.[1] Greedy demons of disease, who devoured the flesh of patients, were greatly feared: Brahmans performed ceremonies of riddance and

[1] There are formulas in Gaelic for blessing a house, &c. The customs of nailing horse-shoes upon doors and hanging up holly at Christmas for protection against evil spirits indicate the persistence of ceremonial practices long after ancient beliefs have been forgotten.

"plagued them as the tiger plagues the cattle owners". The following is a charm against cough:

As the soul with the soul's desires swiftly to a distance flies,
Thus do thou, O cough, fly forth along the soul's course of flight.
As a well-sharpened arrow swiftly to a distance flies,
Thus do thou, O cough, fly forth along the expanse of the earth.
As the rays of the sun swiftly to a distance fly,
Thus do thou, O cough, fly forth along the flood of the sea.
Atharva-veda, vi, 105.[1]

A Scottish Highland charm similarly invokes the Powers, or the "King of the Elements":

To cause the wrath of men to ebb,
Like to a wave from the sea to the floodtide,
And a wave from the floodtide to the ebb.

Occasionally a mantra is infused with high religious fervour. A Brahman might pray:

From the sins which knowingly or unknowingly we have committed, do ye, all gods, of one accord release us.

If awake or asleep, to sin inclined, I have committed a sin, may what has been, and what shall be, as if from a wooden post, release me. *Atharva-veda*, vi, 115. 1–2.[2]

Another hymn of this character concludes:

In heaven, where our righteous friends are blessed,
Having cast off diseases from their bodies,
From lameness free and not deformed in members,
There may we see our parents and our children.
Atharva-veda, vi, 120.[3]

While the tribes were spreading southward and east-

[1] Bloomfield's *Atharva-veda* (*Sacred Books of the East*, vol. xlii).
[2] Bloomfield's translation.
[3] *A History of Sanskrit Literature*, Professor Macdonell, p. 199.

ward, Madhyadesa, the "middle country", remained the centre of Brahmanic culture. In that district came into existence the earliest sacred prose works which constitute the basis of classic Hinduism. The first were the oldest *Brahmanas*; these comment on and expound the doctrines of the Vedic hymns, especially in their relation to the ritual of sacrifices. To the *Brahmanas* were added the *Aran'yakas*, "forest books", which are more speculative in tendency. The expository appendices to the *Aran'yakas* are called the *Upanishads*, "the sittings down", or "the sessions"—the pupil sat at his master's feet—and in these a high level of thought is attained. "For the first time", says Professor Macdonell, "we find the Absolute grasped and proclaimed."

All the tribes were not infused with the same degree of culture. In the *Yajur-veda* period there were various schools of thought, and these continued to exercise their influence into historic times, even after Upanishadic doctrines became widespread.

Ere we deal, however, with the new theological doctrines of the Brahmanic teachers, we should follow the development of sacrificial practices, because from these evolved the bold Pantheism which characterized the conception of the World Soul, Brahmă.

The two greatest sacrifices were the *purusha-medha*, the human sacrifice, and *aswa-medha*, the sacrifice of the horse. Both were prevalent in early times, and in simpler form than they survive to us in the doctrinal works and the Epics. A human sacrifice was believed to be of highest potency, but it became extremely rare, as in Egypt, among the ruling and cultured classes. It was perpetuated in India, however, until about half a century ago, by the Dravidian Khonds in Bengal and Madras, and had to be suppressed by British officers.

Human sacrifices, in historic times, were "offered to the earth goddess, Tari Pennu or Bera Pennu, and were believed to ensure good crops, and immunity from all diseases and accidents". One official record states that the victim, after being stabbed by the priest, was "literally cut to pieces". Each person who was "so fortunate as to procure it carried away a morsel of the flesh, and presented it to the idol of his own village".[1]

From the practice of sacrificing human beings arose the conception that the first act of Creation was, if not human sacrifice, at least the sacrifice of the first being with human attributes. The Universe is the giant Purusha ("man"); he is "all that hath been and shall be". In a Rigvedic hymn, which is regarded as being of later composition than the Rigvedic period, it is set forth:

> "When the gods performed a sacrifice with Purusha as the oblation, the Spring was its butter, the Summer its fuel, and the Autumn its (accompanying) offering. This victim, Purusha, born in the beginning, they immolated on the sacrificial grass."

From this universal sacrifice issued forth all that exists. The Brahman rose from Purusha's mouth, the Rajanya (Kshatriya) from his arms, the Vaisya from his thighs, and the Sudra sprang from his feet. Indra and Agni came from his mouth, and Vayu from his breath.

> "When the gods, performing sacrifice, bound Purusha as a victim, there were seven sticks (stuck up) for it (around the fire). . . . With sacrifice the gods performed the sacrifice. These were the earliest rites."[2]

"From his (Purusha's) navel arose the air, from his head the sky, from his ears the four quarters; in this

[1] *Omens and Superstitions of Southern India*, by Edgar Thurston, p. 199 *et seq.*, 1912.

[2] Muir's *Original Sanskrit Texts*, vol. i, pp. 9–10.

manner (the gods) formed the worlds." This conception resembles closely the story in Teutonic mythology of the cutting up by the gods of the body of the chaos giant Ymer; his skull became the sky, his bones the rocks, his blood the sea, and so on. One of the Chinese P'an Ku[1] myths is of similar character; the world is composed of different parts of his body. The Babylonian Merodach also divided the body of the chaos demon, Tiawath or Tiamat; her head became the sky, her body the earth, and her blood the rivers which fill the sea. Purusha, the chaos giant of India, had "a thousand heads, a thousand eyes, and a thousand feet"; the earth was equal to the space covered by ten of his fingers; he was "the whole universe".

The horse sacrifice was also infused, like the human sacrifice, with symbolic significance. It was probably practised in the early Iranian period by the Aryan horse tamers, who may have substituted man's fleet-footed friend for human beings. The Mongolian Buriats in the vicinity of Lake Baikal, Siberia, are the latest surviving sacrificers of the domesticated animal. Their horse sacrifice (Tailgan) was held on 2 August on a sacred hill inhabited by their gods, the Burkans, "the masters". The horse was bound, thrown upon its back and held tightly by ropes, while the officiating person cut open its breast and pulled out the pulsating heart like the sacrificers of human beings in Ancient Mexico. The animal's bones were burned on the altars, and the flesh was cooked and devoured by the worshippers. Portions of the flesh, and some of the broth prepared, were given to the flames, which also received libations of the liquor called *tarasun*, distilled from sour milk. *Tarasun* was

[1] P'an Ku in his giant form. Like the Egyptian Ptah, he is now a dwarf and anon a giant.

the Soma of the Buriats, and their fire spirit was, like the Indian Agni, a ready drinker of it. Bits of food were also flung to aerial spirits, while oblations were poured on the hill, the belief prevailing that these offerings multiplied sufficiently to permit of the gods feeding sumptuously. As each of the worshippers of the spirits of nature accepted a portion of sacrificial food, a prayer was chanted, entreating the gods to cause increase of all things.

"Let our villages be one verst longer," they said; "create cattle in our enclosures; under our blankets create a son; send down rain from high heaven to us; cause much grass to grow; create so much grain that the sickle cannot raise it, and so much grass that the scythe cannot cut it."

After the sacrifice, the food was divided and the fragments that remained were carefully burned, "for none of it must be eaten by dogs; that would be desecration, and misfortune would follow in its wake".[1]

The purpose of this annual sacrifice was evidently to secure fertility and prosperity generally, and we refer to it here so fully because of the light it throws on the Indian ceremonial which it resembles closely in some of its details.

There are two direct references to the horse sacrifice in the *Rigveda*.[2] The animal is "covered with rich trappings" and led thrice round the altar. It is accompanied by a goat, which is killed first to "announce the sacrifice to the gods". A goat was also slain at a burial to inform the gods that the soul was about to enter Heaven.

In the *Story of Nala* and in the *Ramáyana*, the horse

[1] *A Journey in Southern Siberia*, by Jeremiah Curtin, pp. 44–8.

[2] *Rigveda*, i, 162, and i, 163.

sacrifice is performed to secure human offspring. A second *Ramáyana* horse sacrifice is offered as an atonement after the slaying of the demon Ravana. An elaborate account of this great ceremonial is also given in the *Mahábhárata*. It was performed after "the great war" on the advice of the sage Vyasa to atone for the slaying of kinsmen. The horse was let loose and an army followed it. Whichever country the animal entered had to be conquered for the owner of the horse, so that only a powerful monarch could fulfil the conditions of the sacrifice. A hundred such sacrifices might enable a king to depose Indra.

It is significant, however, that the animal was released to wander from kingdom to kingdom on the night of the full moon in the spring month of Choitro, and that it returned in the following year at the close of the winter season. When the ground was prepared by being ploughed by the king, the queen followed him, sowing the seeds of every kind of vegetable and curative herb which grew in the kingdom. A countless number of representative animals were sacrificed before the sacred horse was slain, the rain drum and trumpet were sounded, and the king and queen were drenched with holy water.

The flesh of the horse was cooked and eaten, and Indra and the other gods appeared and partook of their portions. Pieces were also flung in the fire, and the fire received also its meed of Soma. When the sacrifice was completed, the king divided the herb offerings among the people; what remained over was burned.

In the *Mahábhárata* a white horse is sacrificed, but in the *Ramáyana* a black victim is offered up. White horses were sacrificed to Mars by the Romans; the Greeks sacrificed white horses to the sun by throwing them in the sea; the Spartans offered up their horses, like the Buriats, on a hilltop.

There can be little doubt that the Greek and Roman horse sacrifices were also intended to ensure fertility. A horse was offered up to Diana at the August harvest festival, and we know that that popular goddess gave plentiful crops and was the guardian of flocks and herds and wild animals of the chase; she also presided at birth, and women invoked her aid. Virgins and youths took a prominent part at this harvest festival. The Roman horse sacrifice took place on 15 October. The animal was offered to Mars; the head was conveyed to the king's house[1] and decorated with loaves, and the blood was preserved until April, when it was mixed by virgins with the blood of calves; this mixture was given to shepherds to ensure the increase of flocks which were fumigated. In the *Mahábhárata* the king and the princes stand for a time in the smoke belching from the altar, to be cleansed of their sins.

The Persians, and other peoples of Aryan speech and custom, sacrificed horses regularly. But the custom was not confined to Indo-Europeans. The Scythians,[2] who were probably Mongols, not only offered horses to the Spirit of Fertility, but also, like the Buriats, to the dead. The Patagonians sacrificed horses to tree spirits. In this connection it may be noted that some European horse sacrifices took place in sacred groves; the Buriats tied their horse to a birch tree, which was carried to the mountain top and fixed to a stake; the Indian sacrificial posts were probably substitutes for trees.

In the *Upanishads* the sacrifice of the horse is infused, as we have indicated, with mystic symbolism. We read:

[1] That is, the so-called "royal house", or house of the "king of the sacred rites".
[2] A broad-headed people.

"The dawn in truth is the head of the sacrificial horse. The sun is the eye; the wind the breath . . . the year the body, the heaven is the back . . . the constellations the bones; the sky the muscles; the rivers, arteries and veins; the liver and spleen, the mountains; the herbs and trees, the various kinds of hair." The horse is also identified with the sun: "The sun, as long as he rises is the fore part of the body; the sun, as long as he descends is the hind part of the body, &c." The horse is also day and night in turn, and its birthplace is the sea; it carries the gods and the Asuras; it is the symbol of Death, "who is voracity", from whom all things came. "There was not anything here before." Death first "created this mind, desiring, *May I have a soul.* He went forth worshipping. From him, when worshipping, the waters were produced. . . . The froth of the waters which was there became consistent. This became the earth. . . . He made himself threefold. His eastern quarter is the head . . . his western quarter is the tail, &c."

The work of Creation proceeds, and then "he (Death as the Creator) resolved to devour all that he had created; for he eats all. . . . He is the eater of the whole universe; this whole universe is his food."

After a year of purification the Creator slaughtered his horse body. "He gave up the animal to the gods. Therefore they (the gods) slaughter the purified animal, representing in its nature, as Prajápati, all deities. He (the Creator) is the Ashwameda[1] who shines."

The gods performed the sacrifice to overcome the demons, the representatives of sin. Therefore the horse sacrifice removes all sin.

After much fantastic symbolism the following lesson

[1] Horse sacrifice.

in the form of a mantra is extracted from the parable of Creation:—

> "From the unreal lead me to the real, from darkness lead me to light, from death lead me to immortality."

The Upanishadic treatment of the Purusha myth differs somewhat from the Vedic, and is intended to strengthen the Monotheistic tendencies displayed in some of the hymns.

When the Universal soul, according to this later doctrine, took at the beginning "the shape of a man" . . . he "beheld nothing but himself".

> "He said first *This, I am.* Hence the name of 'I' was produced. Therefore, even now a man, when called, says first, 'It is I', and tells afterwards any other name that belongs to him. And, because He, as the first of all of them consumed by fire all the sins, therefore he is called Purusha. . . .
>
> He was afraid; therefore man, when alone, is afraid. He then looked round. Since nothing but myself exists, of whom should I be afraid? Hence his fear departed; for whom should he fear, since fear arises from another.
>
> He did not feel delight. Therefore nobody, when alone, feels delight. He was desirous of a second. He was in the same state as husband (Pati) and wife (Patni). . . . He divided this self twofold. Hence were husband and wife produced. Therefore was this only a half of himself, as a split pea is of the whole. . . . This void is thus completed by woman. He approached her. Hence men were born."

The first two "mortals" then assumed the forms of all creatures, male and female in turn. They were, in order, the first cattle, the first horses, the first asses, the first goats, the first sheep, and so on. "In this manner He created every living pair whatsoever down to the ants." Then he reflected and said: "I am verily this creation, for I created this all."

The lesson then follows. Men say, "Sacrifice to this, sacrifice to this, sacrifice to one or the other god?" But these words are "not proper", because "He is really this creation; for he verily is all the gods".

Thus the first Being, as a commentator remarked, "whose nature comprehended all elements, who is eternal, who is not conceived by thought, sprang forth by himself. . . . He consumed all sins, for unless one is in a worldly state he cannot consume sins. . . . Being mortal he created immortals."[1]

From the myth of the chaos-giant Purusha we pass to the higher pantheistic conception of Brahmă, the soul of the Universe.

[1] *The Brihad Aranyaka Upanishad.*

CHAPTER VI

Mysteries of Creation, the World's Ages, and Soul Wandering

The World Soul—Vedic Hymn of Creation—Brahmă the only Reality—Doctrine of the Upanishads—Creation Myths—The Chaos Egg in India and Egypt—Ancestor Worship—Celestial Rishis and Manus—Influence of Folk Religion—Imported Doctrines—The Yugas or Ages of the Universe—Ape God's Revelations—The Ages in Greek and Celtic Mythologies—Universal Destruction—A Deathless Sage—His Account of the Mysteries—Narayana the Creator and Destroyer—Transmigration of Souls—Beliefs in India, Egypt, Greece, and among the Celts.

Before the Vedic Age had come to a close an unknown poet, who was one of the world's great thinkers, had risen above the popular materialistic ideas concerning the hammer god and the humanized spirits of Nature, towards the conception of the World Soul and the First Cause—the "Unknown God". He sang of the mysterious beginning of all things:

> There was neither existence, nor non-existence,
> The kingdom of air, nor the sky beyond.
>
> What was there to contain, to cover in—
> Was it but vast, unfathomed depths of water?
>
> There was no death there, nor Immortality.
> No sun was there, dividing day from night.
>
> Then was there only THAT, resting within itself.
> Apart from it, there was not anything.

At first within the darkness veiled in darkness,
Chaos unknowable, the All lay hid.

Till straightway from the formless void made manifest
By the great power of heat was born that germ.
Rigveda, x, 129 (Griffith's trans.).

The poet goes on to say that wise men had discovered in their hearts that the germ of Being existed in Not Being. But who, he asked, could tell how Being first originated? The gods came later, and are unable to reveal how Creation began. He who guards the Universe knows, or mayhap he does not know.

Other late Rigvedic poets summed up the eternal question regarding the Great Unknown in the interrogative pronoun "What?" (Ka). Men's minds were confronted by an inspiring and insoluble problem. In our own day the Agnostics say, "I do not know"; but this hackneyed phrase does not reflect the spirit of enquiry like the arresting "What?" of the pondering old forest hermits of ancient India.

The priests who systematized religious beliefs and practices in the *Brahmanas* identified "Ka" with Pra-ja'pati, the Creator, and with Brahma, another name of the Creator.

In the Vedas the word "brahma" signifies "devotion" or "the highest religious knowledge". Later Brahmă (neuter) was applied to the World Soul, the All in All, the primary substance from which all that exists has issued forth, the Eternal Being "of which all are phases"; Brahmă was the Universal Self, the Self in the various Vedic gods, the Self in man, bird, beast, and fish, the Life of Life, the only reality, the unchangeable. This one essence or Self (Atman) permeates the whole Universe. Brahmă is the invisible force in the seed, as he is the "vital spark" in mobile creatures. In the *Khandogya Upanishad* a young Brahman receives instruction from his father. The sage asks if his pupil has ever endeavoured to find out how he can hear what cannot be heard, how he can see what cannot be seen, and how he can know what cannot be known? He then asks for the fruit of the Nyagrodha tree.

"Here is one, sir."

"Break it."

"It is broken, sir."

"What do you see there?"

"Not anything, sir."

"My son," said the father, "that subtile essence which you do not perceive there, of that very essence this great Nyagrodha tree exists. Believe it, my son. That which is the subtile essence, in it all that exists has itself. It is the True. It is the Self; and thou, my son, art it."

In *Katha Upanishad* a sage declares:

> The whole universe trembles within the life (Brahmă); emanating from it (Brahmă) the universe moves on. It is a great fear, like an uplifted thunderbolt. Those who know it become immortal. . . .
>
> As one is reflected in a looking-glass, so the soul is in the body; as in a dream, so in the world of the forefathers; as in water, so in the world of the Gandharvas; as in a picture and in the sunshine, so in the world of Brahmă. . . .
>
> The soul's being (nature) is not placed in what is visible; none beholds it by the eye. . . . Through thinking it gets manifest Immortal become those who know it. . . .
>
> The soul is not to be gained by word, not by the mind, not by the eye, how could it be perceived by any other than him who declares it exists?
>
> When all the desires cease that are cherished in his heart (intellect) then the mortal becomes immortal.

When all the bonds of the heart are broken in this life, then the mortal becomes immortal. . . .[1]

The salvation of the soul is secured by union with Brahmă, the supreme and eternal Atman (Self), "the power which receives back to itself again all worlds. . . . The identity of the Brahmă and the Atman, of God and the Soul, is the fundamental thought of the entire doctrine of the Upanishads."[2]

Various creation myths were framed by teachers to satisfy the desire for knowledge regarding the beginning of things. The divine incarnation of Brahmă is known as Brahma (masculine) Prajapati, and Nărăyana.

In one account we read: "At first the Universe was not anything. There was neither sky, nor earth, nor air. Being non-existent it resolved, 'Let me be'. It became fervent. From that fervour smoke was produced. It again became fervent. From that fervour fire was produced." Afterwards the fire became "rays" and the rays condensed like a cloud, producing the sea. A magical formula (Dásahotri) was next created. "Prajapati is the Dásahotri."

Eminently Brahmanic in character is the comment inserted here: "That man succeeds who, thus knowing the power of austere abstraction (or fervour), practises it."

When Prajapati arose from the primordial waters he "wept, exclaiming, 'For what purpose have I been born if (I have been born) from this which forms no support? . . .' That (the tears) which fell into the water became the earth. That which he wiped away became the air. That which he wiped away, upwards, became the sky. From the circumstance that he wept (*arodit*), these two regions have the name of *rodasí* (worlds) . . ."

[1] Dr. E. Röer's translation (Calcutta).
[2] Deussen's *Philosophy of the Upanishads*, p. 39.

18

THE BIRTH OF BRAHMA: SPRINGING FROM A LOTUS ISSUING FROM VISHNU (see page 124)

From an original Indian painting

Prajapati afterwards created Asuras and cast off his body, which became darkness; he created men and cast off his body, which became moonlight; he created seasons and cast off his body, which became twilight; he created gods and cast off his body, which became day. The Asuras received milk in an earthen dish, men in a wooden dish, the seasons in a silver dish, and the gods were given Soma in a golden dish. In the end Prajapati created Death, "a devourer of creatures".

"Mind (or soul, *manas*) was created from the non-existent", adds a priestly commentator. "Mind created Prajapati. Prajapati created offspring. All this, whatever exists, rests absolutely on mind."[1]

In another mythical account of Creation, Prajapati emerges, like the Egyptian Horus, from a lotus bloom floating on the primordial waters.

The most elaborate story of Creation is found in the *Laws of Manu*, the eponymous ancestor of mankind and the first lawgiver.

It relates that in the beginning the Self-Existent Being desired to create living creatures. He first created the waters, which he called "narah", and then a seed; he flung the seed into the waters, and it became a golden egg which had the splendour of the sun. From the egg came forth Brahma, Father of All. Because Brahma came from the "waters", and they were his first home or path (ayana), he is called Narayana.

The Egyptian sun god Ra similarly rose from the primordial waters as the sun-egg. Ptah came from the egg which, according to one myth, was laid by the chaos goose, and to another issued from the mouth of Khnumu.[2] This conception may have had origin in the story of the

[1] Muir's *Original Sanskrit Texts*, vol. i, pp. 29–30.
[2] See *Egyptian Myth and Legend*.

giant of the folk tales who concealed his soul in the egg, in the tree, and in various animal forms. There are references in Indian literature to Brahma's tree, and Brahma is identified with Purusha, who became in turn a cow, a goat, a horse, &c., to produce living creatures.

In Manu's account of Creation we meet for the first time with the Maha-rishis or Deva-rishis, the Celestial priest poets. These are the mind-born sons of Brahma, who came into existence before the gods and the demons. Indeed, they are credited with some acts of creation. The seven or fourteen Manus were also created at the beginning. Originally there was but a single Manu, "the father of men".

The inclusion of the Rishis and the Manus among the deities is a late development of orthodox Brahmanism. They appear to represent the Fathers (Pitris) who were adored by ancestor worshippers. The tribal patriarch Bhrigu, for instance, was a Celestial Rishi.

It must be borne in mind that more than one current of thought was operating during the course of the centuries, and over a wide area, in shaping the complex religion which culminated in modern Hinduism. The history of Hinduism is the history of a continual struggle between the devotees of folk religion and the expounders of the Forest Books produced by the speculative sages who, in their quest for Truth, used primitive myths to illustrate profound doctrinal teachings. By the common people these myths were given literal interpretation. Among the priests there were also "schools of thought". One class of Brahmans, it has been alleged, was concerned chiefly regarding ritual, the mercenary results of their teachings, and the achievement of political power: men of this type appear to have been too ready to effect compromises by making concession to popular opinion.

Just as the *Atharva-veda* came into existence as a book after the *Rigveda* had been compiled, so did many traditional beliefs of animistic character receive recognition by Brahmanic "schools" after the period of the early *Upanishads*. It may be, however, that we should also recognize in these "innovations" the influence of races which imported their own modes of thought, or of Aryan tribes that had been in contact for long periods with other civilizations known and unknown.

In endeavouring to trace the sources of foreign influences, we should not always expect to find clues in the mythologies of great civilizations like Babylonia, Assyria, or Egypt alone. The example of the Hebrews, a people who never invented anything, and yet produced the greatest sacred literature of the world, is highly suggestive in this connection. It is possible that an intellectual influence was exercised in early times over great conquering races by humble forgotten peoples whose artifacts give no indication of their mental activity.

In Indian Aryan mythology we are suddenly confronted at a comparatively late period, at any rate some time after tribal settlements were effected all over Hindustan from the Bay of Bengal to the Arabian Sea, with fully developed conceptions regarding the World's Ages and Transmigration of Souls, which, it is quite evident, did not originate after the Aryan conquest of Hindustan. Both doctrines can be traced in Greek and Celtic (Irish) mythologies, but they are absent from Teutonic mythology. From what centre and what race they originally emanated we are unable to discover. The problem presented is a familiar one. At the beginnings of all ancient religious systems and great civilizations we catch glimpses of unknown and vanishing peoples who had sowed the seeds for the harvests which their conquerors reaped in season.

The World's Ages are the "Yugas" of Brahmanism. "Of this elaborate system . . . no traces are found in the hymns of the *Rigveda*. Their authors were, indeed, familiar with the word 'yuga', which frequently occurs in the sense of age, generation, or tribe. . . . The first passage of the *Rigveda* in which there is any indication of a considerable mundane period being noted is where 'a first' or an earlier age (yuga) of the gods is mentioned when 'the existent sprang from the non-existent'. . . . In one verse of the *Atharva-veda*, however, the word 'yuga' is so employed as to lead to the supposition that a period of very long duration is intended. It is there said: 'We allot to thee a hundred, ten thousand years, two, three, four ages (yugas)'."[1]

Professor Muir traced references in the *Brahmanas* to the belief in "Yugas" as "Ages", but showed that these were isolated ideas with which, however, the authors of these books were becoming familiar.

When the system of Yugas was developed by the Indian priestly mathematicians, the result was as follows:—

> One year of mortals is equal to one day of the gods. 12,000 divine years are equal to a period of four Yugas, which is thus made up, viz.:

Krita Yuga,	with its mornings and evenings,				4,800	divine years.
Treta Yuga,	"	"	"	"	3,600	"
Dwāpara Yuga,	"	"	"	"	2,400	"
Kali Yuga,	"	"	"	"	1,200	"
				Making	12,000	"

These 12,000 divine years equal 4,320,000 years of

[1] Muir's *Original Sanskrit Texts*, vol. i, p. 46.

mortals, each human year being composed of 360 days. A thousand of these periods of 4,320,000 years equals one day (Kalpa) of Brahma. During "the day of Brahma" fourteen Manus reign: each Manu period is a Manvantara. A year of Brahma is composed of 360 Kalpas, and he endures for 100 of these years. One half of Brahma's existence has now expired.

At the end of each "day" (Kalpa) Brahma sleeps for a night of equal length, and before falling asleep the Universe becomes water as at the beginning. He creates anew when he wakes on the morning of the next Kalpa.[1]

One of the most interesting accounts of the Yugas is given in the *Mahábhárata*. It is embedded in a narrative which reflects a phase of the character of that great epic.

Bhima of the Pan'davas, the human son of the wind god Vayu, once went forth to obtain for his beloved queen the flowers of Paradise—those Celestial lotuses of a thousand petals with sun-like splendour and unearthly fragrance, which prolong life and renew beauty: they grow in the demon-guarded woodland lake in the region of Kuvera, god of treasure. Bhima hastened towards the north-east, facing the wind, armed with a golden bow and snake-like arrows; like an angry lion he went, nor ever felt weary. Having climbed a great mountain he entered a forest which is the haunt of demons, and he saw stately and beautiful trees, blossoming creepers, flowers of various hues, and birds with gorgeous plumage. A soft wind blew in his face; it was anointed with the perfume of Celestial lotus; it was as refreshing as the touch of a father's hand. Beautiful was that sacred retreat. The great clouds spread out like wings and the mountain seemed to dance; shining streams adorned it like to a necklace of pearls.

[1] Abridged from Muir's *Original Sanskrit Texts*, pp. 43, 44, and Wilson's *Manu*, p. 50.

Bhima went speedily through the forest; stags, with grass in their mouths, looked up at him unafraid; invisible Yakshas and Gandharvas watched him as he went on swifter than the wind, and ever wondering how he could obtain the flowers of Paradise without delay. . . .

At length he hastened like to a hurricane, making the earth tremble under his feet, and lions and tigers and elephants and bears arose and took flight from before him. Terrible was then the roaring of Bhima. Birds fluttered terror-stricken and flew away; in confusion arose the geese and the ducks and the herons and the kokilas.[1] . . . Bhima tore down branches; he struck trees and overthrew them; he smote and slew elephants and lions and tigers that crossed his path. He blew on his war-shell and the heavens trembled; the forest was stricken with fear· mountain caves echoed the clamour; elephants trumpeted in terror and lions howled dismally.

The ape god Hanuman[2] was awakened; drowsily he yawned and he lashed his long tail with tempest fury until it stretched forth like a mighty pole and obstructed the path of Bhima. Thus the ape god, who was also a son of Vayu, the wind, made Bhima to pause. Opening his red sleepy eyes, he said: "Sick am I, but I was slumbering sweetly; why hast thou awakened me so rudely? Whither art thou going? Yonder mountains are closed against thee: thou art treading the path of the gods. Therefore pause and repose here: do not hasten to destruction."

Said Bhima: "Who art thou? I am a Kshatriya, the son of Vayu. . . . Arise and let me pass, or else thou wilt perish."

Hanuman said: "I am sickly and cannot move; leap over me."

[1] Indian cuckoo. [2] In his character as the Typhoon.

19

HANUMAN

From a bronze in the Victoria and Albert Museum

Said Bhima: "I cannot leap over thee. It is forbidden by the Supreme Soul, else would I bound as Hanuman bounded over the ocean, for I am his brother."

Hanuman said: "Then move my tail and go past."

Then Bhima endeavoured to lift the tail of the ape god, but failed, and he said: "Who art thou that hath assumed the form of an ape; art thou a god, or a spirit, or a demon?"

Hanuman said: "I am the son of Vayu, even Hanuman. Thou art my elder brother."

Said Bhima: "I would fain behold the incomparable form thou didst assume to leap over the ocean."

Hanuman said: "At that Age the universe was not as it is now. Thou canst not behold the form I erstwhile had. . . . In Krita Yuga there was one state of things and in the Treta Yuga another; greater change came with Dwāpara Yuga, and in the present Yuga there is lessening, and I am not what I have been. The gods, the saints, and all things that are have changed. I have conformed with the tendency of the present age and the influence of Time."

Said Bhima: "I would fain learn of thee regarding the various Yugas. Speak and tell what thou dost know, O Hanuman."

The ape god then spake and said: "The Krita Yuga (Perfect Age) was so named because there was but one religion, and all men were saintly: therefore they were not required to perform religious ceremonies. Holiness never grew less, and the people did not decrease. There were no gods in the Krita Yuga, and there were no demons or Yakshas, and no Rakshasas or Nagas. Men neither bought nor sold; there were no poor and no rich; there was no need to labour, because all that men required was obtained by the power of will; the chief virtue was the abandonment of all worldly desires. The Krita Yuga was without disease; there was no lessening with the years; there was no hatred, or vanity, or evil thought whatsoever; no sorrow, no fear. All mankind could attain to supreme blessedness. The universal soul was Narayana: he was *White*; he was the refuge of all and was sought for by all; the identification of self with the universal soul was the whole religion of the Perfect Age.

"In the Treta Yuga sacrifices began, and the World Soul became *Red*; virtue lessened a quarter. Mankind sought truth and performed religious ceremonies; they obtained what they desired by giving and by doing.

"In the Dwāpara Yuga the aspect of the World Soul was *Yellow*: religion lessened one-half. The Veda, which was one (the *Rigveda*) in the Krita Yuga, was divided into four parts, and although some had knowledge of the four Vedas, others knew but three or one. Mind lessened, Truth declined, and there came desire and diseases and calamities; because of these men had to undergo penances. It was a decadent Age by reason of the prevalence of sin.

"In the Kali Yuga[1] the World Soul is *Black* in hue: it is the Iron Age; only one quarter of virtue remaineth. The world is afflicted, men turn to wickedness; disease cometh; all creatures degenerate; contrary effects are obtained by performing holy rites; change passeth over all things, and even those who live through many Yugas must change also."

Having spoken thus, Hanuman bade Bhima to turn back, but Bhima said: "I cannot leave thee until I have gazed upon thy former shape."

Then Hanuman favoured his brother, and assumed

[1] The present Age, according to Hindu belief.

his vast body; he grew till he was high as the Vindhya mountain: he was like to a great golden peak with splendour equal to the sun, and he said: "I can assume even greater height and bulk by reason of mine own power."

Having spoken thus, Hanuman permitted Bhima to proceed on his way under the protection of Vayu, god of wind. He went towards the flowery steeps of the sacred mountain, and at length he reached the Celestial lotus lake of Kuvera, which was shaded by trees and surrounded by lilies; the surface of the waters was covered with golden lotuses which had stalks of lapis lazuli. Yakshas, with big eyes, came out against Bhima, but he slew many, and those that remained were put to flight. He drank the waters of the lake, which renewed his strength. Then he gathered the Celestial lotuses for his queen.

In this tale we discover the ancient Indo-European myth regarding the earth's primitive races. The first age is the White Age, the second is the Red Age, the third the Yellow Age, and the fourth, the present Kali Yuga, is the Black or Iron Age.

Hesiod, the Greek poet, in his *Works and Days*, divided the mythical history of Greece similarly, but the order of the Ages was different; the first was the Golden Age (yellow); the second was the Silver Age (white); the third was the Bronze Age (red); the fourth was the Age of the Heroes; and the fifth was the Age in which Hesiod lived—the Iron (black) Age. The fourth Age is evidently a late interpolation. Authorities consider that the Heroic Age did not belong to the original scheme.

In the Greek Golden Age men lived like the gods under the rule of Kronos; they never suffered the ills of old age, nor lost their strength; they feasted continually, and enjoyed peace and security. The whole world prospered. When this race passed away they became beneficent spirits who watched over mankind and distributed riches.

In the Silver Age mankind were inferior; children were reared up for a century, and died soon afterwards; sacrifice and worship was neglected. In the end Zeus, son of Kronos, destroyed the Silver Race.

In the Bronze Age mankind sprang from the ash. They were endowed with great strength, and worked in bronze and had bronze houses: iron was unknown. But Bronze Age men were takers of life, and at length Black Death removed them all to Hades.

Zeus created the fourth race, which was represented by the semi-divine heroes of a former generation; when they fell in battle on the plain of Troy and elsewhere, Zeus consigned them to the Islands of the Blest, where they were ruled over by Kronos. The fifth Age may originally have been the fourth. As much is suggested by another Hesiodic legend which sets forth that all mankind are descended from two survivors of the Flood at the close of the Bronze Age.

In *Le Cycle Mythologique Irlandais et la Mythologie Celtique*, the late Professor D'Arbois de Jubainville has shown that these Ages are also a feature of Celtic (Irish) mythology. Their order, however, differs from those in Greek, but it is of special interest to note that they are arranged in exactly the same colour order as those given in the *Mahábhárata*. The first Celtic Age is that of Partholon, which de Jubainville identified with the Silver Age (white); the second is Nemed's, the Bronze Age (red); the third is the Tuatha de Danann, the Golden Age (yellow); and the fourth is the Age of the dark Milesians, called after their divine ancestor Mile, son of

Beli, the god of night and death. The Irish claim descent from the Milesians.

Professor D'Arbois de Jubainville considered that the differences between the Irish and Greek versions of the ancient doctrine were due in part to the developments which Irish legend received after the introduction of Christianity. There are, however, he showed, striking affinities. The Tuatha de Danann, for instance, like the "Golden Race" of the Greeks, became invisible, and shared the dominion of the world with men, "sometimes coming to help them, sometimes disputing with them the pleasures of life".

Like the early Christian annalists of Ireland, the Indian Brahmans appear to have utilized the legends which were afloat among the people. Both in the Greek and Celtic (Irish) myths the people of the Silver Age are distinguished for their folly; in the Indian Silver or White Age the people were so perfect and holy that it was not necessary for them to perform religious ceremonies; they simply uttered the mystic word "Om".[1]

There are many interesting points of resemblance between certain of the Irish and Indian legends. We are informed, for instance, of the Celtic St. Finnen, who fasted like a Brahman, so to compel a pagan sage, Tuan MacCarell, to reveal the ancient history of Ireland. Tuan had lived all through the various mythical Ages; his father was the brother of Partholon, king of the "Silver Race". At the end of the First Age, Tuan was a "long-haired, grey, naked, and miserable old man". One evening he fell asleep, and when he woke up he rejoiced to find that he had become a young stag. He saw the people of Nemed (the Bronze or Red Race) arriving in Ireland; he saw them passing away. Then he was trans-

[1] "Om" originally referred to the three Vedas; afterwards it signified the Trinity.

formed into a black boar; afterwards he was a vulture, and in the end he became a fish. When he had existed as a fish for twenty years he was caught by a fisherman. The queen had Tuan for herself, and ate his fish form, with the result that she gave birth to the sage as her son.

In similar manner Bata of the Egyptian Anpu-Bata story,[1] after existing as a blossom, a bull, and a tree, became the son of his unfaithful wife, who swallowed a chip of wood.

Tuan MacCarell assured St. Finnen, "in the presence of witnesses", as we are naively informed, that he remembered all that happened in Ireland during the period of 1500 years covered by his various incarnations.

Another, and apparently a later version of the legend, credits the Irish sage, the fair Fintan, son of Bochra, with having lived for 5550 years before the Deluge, and 5500 years after it. He fled to Ireland with the followers of Cesara, granddaughter of Noah, to escape the flood. Fintan, however, was the only survivor, and, according to Irish chronology, he did not die until the sixth century of the present era.

One of the long-lived Indian sages was named Markandeya. In the *Vana Parva* section of the *Mahábhárata* he visits the exiled Pandava brethren in a forest, and is addressed as "the great Muni, who has seen many thousands of ages passing away. In this world", says the chief exile, "there is no man who hath lived so long as thou hast. . . . Thou didst adore the Supreme Deity when the Universe was dissolved, and the world was without a firmament, and there were no gods and no demons. Thou didst behold the re-creation of the four orders of beings when the winds were restored to their places and the waters were consigned to their proper

[1] See *Egyptian Myth and Legend.*

place. . . . Neither death nor old age which causeth the body to decay have any power over thee."

Markandeya, who has full knowledge of the Past, the Present, and the Future, informs the exiles that the Supreme Being is "great, incomprehensible, wonderful, and immaculate, without beginning and without end. . . . He is the Creator of all, but is himself Increate, and is the cause of all power."[1]

After the Universe is dissolved, all Creation is renewed, and the cycle of the four Ages begins again with Krita Yuga. "A cycle of the Yugas comprises twelve thousand divine years. A full thousand of such cycles constitutes a Day of Brahma." At the end of each Day of Brahma comes "Universal Destruction".

Markandeya goes on to say that the world grows extremely sinful at the close of the last Kali Yuga of the Day of Brahma. Brahmans abstain from prayer and meditation, and Sudras take their place. Kshatriyas and Vaisyas forget the duties of their castes; all men degenerate and beasts of prey increase. The earth is ravaged by fire, cows give little milk, fruit trees no longer blossom, Indra sends no rain; the world of men becomes filled with sin and immorality. . . . Then the earth is swept by fire, and heavy rains fall until the forests and mountains are covered over by the rising flood. All the winds pass away; they are absorbed by the Lotus floating on the breast of the waters, in which the Creator sleeps; the whole Universe is a dark expanse of water.

Although even the gods and demons have been destroyed at the eventide of the last Yuga, Markandeya survives. He wanders over the face of the desolate waters and becomes weary, but is unable to find a resting-place. At length he perceives a banyan tree; on one of

[1] Roy's translation.

its boughs is a Celestial bed, and sitting on the bed is a beautiful boy whose face is as fair as a full-blown lotus. The boy speaks and says; "O Markandeya, I know that thou art weary. . . . Enter my body and secure repose. I am well pleased with thee."

Markandeya enters the boy's mouth and is swallowed. In the stomach of the Divine One the sage beholds the whole earth (that is, India) with its cities and kingdoms, its rivers and forests, and its mountains and plains; he sees also the gods and demons, mankind and the beasts of prey, birds and fishes and insects. . . .

The sage related that he shook with fear when he beheld these wonders, and desired the protection of the Supreme Being, whereat he was ejected from the boy's mouth, and found himself once again on the branch of the banyan tree in the midst of the wide expanse of dark waters.

Markandeya was then informed by the Lord of All regarding the mysteries which he had beheld. The Divine One spoke saying: "I have called the waters 'Nara', and because they were my 'Ayana', or home, I am Narayana, the source of all things, the Eternal, the Unchangeable. I am the Creator of all things, and the Destroyer of all things. . . . I am all the gods. . . . Fire is my mouth, the earth is my feet, and the sun and the moon are my eyes; the Heaven is the crown of my head, and the cardinal points are my ears; the waters are born of my sweat. Space with the cardinal points are my body, and the Air is in my mind."[1]

The Creator continues, addressing Markandeya: "I am the wind, I am the Sun, I am Fire. The stars are the pores of my skin, the ocean is my robe, my bed and

[1] Roy's translation. This conception of the World God resembles the Egyptian Ptah and Ra. See *Egyptian Myth and Legend*.

my dwelling-place. . . . " The Divine One is the source of good and evil: "Lust, wrath, joy, fear, and the overclouding of the intellect, are all different forms of me. . . . Men wander within my body, their senses are overwhelmed by me. . . . They move not according to their own will, but as they are moved by me."

Markandeya then related that the Divine Being said: "I create myself into new forms. I take my birth in the families of virtuous men. . . . I create gods and men, and Gandharvas and Rakshas and all immobile beings, and then destroy them all myself (when the time cometh) For the preservation of rectitude and morality, I assume a human form; and when the season for action cometh, I again assume forms that are inconceivable. In the Krita Age I become white, in the Treta Age I become yellow, in the Dwāpara I become red, and in the Kali Age I become dark in hue. . . . And when the end cometh, assuming the fierce form of Death, alone I destroy all the three worlds with their mobile and immobile existences. . . . Alone do I set agoing the wheel of Time: I am formless: I am the Destroyer of all creatures: and I am the cause of all efforts of all my creatures."[1]

Markandeya afterwards witnessed "the varied and wondrous creation starting into life".

The theory of Metempsychosis, or Transmigration of Souls, is generally regarded as being of post-Vedic growth in India as an orthodox doctrine. Still, it remains an open question whether it was not professed from the earliest times by a section of the various peoples who entered the Punjab at different periods and in various stages of culture. We have already seen that the burial customs differed. Some consigned the dead hero to the "House of Clay", invoking the earth to shroud him as a mother

[1] *Mahabharata*, *Vana Parva*, section clxxxix, P. C. Roy's translation.

who covers her son with her robe, and the belief ultimately prevailed that Yama, the first man, had discovered the path leading to Paradise, which became known as the "Land of the Fathers" (Pitris). The fire worshippers, who identified Agni with the "vital spark", cremated the dead, believing that the soul passed to heaven like the burnt offering, which was the food of the gods. It is apparent, therefore, that in early times sharp differences of opinion existed among the tribes regarding the destiny of the soul. Other unsung beliefs may have obtained ere the Brahmans grew powerful and systematized an orthodox creed. The doctrine of Metempsychosis may have had its ancient adherents, although these were not at first very numerous. In one passage of the *Rigveda* "the soul is spoken of as departing to the waters or the plants", and it "may", says Professor Macdonell, "contain the germs of the theory" of Transmigration of Souls.[1]

The doctrine of Metempsychosis was believed in by the Greeks and the Celts. According to Herodotus the former borrowed it from Egypt, and although some have cast doubt on the existence of the theory in Egypt, there are evidences that it obtained there as in early Aryanized India among sections of the people.[2] It is possible that the doctrine is traceable to a remote racial influence regarding which no direct evidence survives.

All that we know definitely regarding the definite acceptance of the theory in India is that in *Satapatha Brahmana* it is pointedly referred to as a necessary element of orthodox religion. The teacher declares that those who perform sacrificial rites are born again and attain to immortality, while those who neglect to sacrifice pass through successive existences until Death ultimately claims them.

[1] *History of Sanskrit Literature*, p. 115.
[2] See *Egyptian Myth and Legend*.

According to Upanishadic belief the successive rebirths in the world are forms of punishment for sins committed, or a course of preparation for the highest state of existence.

In the code of Manu it is laid down, for instance, that he who steals gold becomes a rat, he who steals uncooked food a hedgehog, he who steals honey a stinging insect; a murderer may become a tiger, or have to pass through successive states of existence as a camel, a dog, a pig, a goat, &c.; other wrongdoers may have to exist as grass, trees, worms, snails, &c. As soon as a man died, it was believed that he was reborn as a child, or a reptile, as the case might be. Sufferings endured by the living were believed to be retribution for sins committed in a former life.

Another form of this belief had evidently some connection with lunar worship, or, at any rate, with the recognition of the influence exercised by the moon over life in all its phases; it is declared in the *Upanishads* that "all who leave this world go directly to the moon. By their lives its waxing crescent is increased, and by means of its waning it brings them to a second birth. But the moon is also the gate of the heavenly world, and he who can answer the questions of the moon is allowed to pass beyond it. He who can give no answer is turned to rain by the moon and rained down upon the earth. He is born again here below, as worm or fly, or fish or bird, or lion, or boar or animal with teeth, or tiger, or man, or anything else in one or another place, according to his works and his knowledge."[1]

Belief in Metempsychosis ultimately prevailed all over India, and it is fully accepted by Hinduism in our own day. Brahmans now teach that the destiny of the soul depends on the mental attitude of the dying person: if

[1] Paul Deussen's translation.

his thoughts are centred on Brahma he enters the state of everlasting bliss, being absorbed in the World Soul; if, however, he should happen to think of a favourite animal or a human friend, the soul will be reborn as a cow, a horse, or a dog, or it may enter the body of a newly-born child and be destined to endure once again the ills that flesh is heir to.

In Egypt, according to Herodotus, the adherents of the Transmigration theory believed that the soul passed through many states of existence, until after a period of about three thousand years it once again reanimated the mummy. The Greeks similarly taught that "the soul continues its journey, alternating between a separate, unrestrained existence and fresh reincarnation, round the wide circle of necessity, as the companion of many bodies of men and animals".[1] According to Cæsar, the Gauls professed the doctrine of Metempsychosis quite freely.[2]

Both in India and in Egypt the ancient doctrine of Metempsychosis was coloured by the theologies of the various cults which had accepted it. It has survived, however, in primitive form in the folk tales. Apparently the early exponents of the doctrine took no account of beginning or end; they simply recognized "the wide circle of necessity" round which the soul wandered, just as the worshippers of primitive nature gods and goddesses recognized the eternity of matter by symbolizing earth, air, and heaven as deities long ere they had conceived of a single act of creation.

[1] *Psyche*, Erwin Rhode. [2] *De Bello Gallico*, vi, xiv, 4.

CHAPTER VII

New Faiths: Vishnu Religion, Buddhism, and Jainism

Religious Ages—Influence of the Upanishads—The Inspiration of Great Teachers—Conception of a Supreme Personal God—Rise of Vishnu and Shiva Cults—Krishna a Human Incarnation of Vishnu—The Bhagavad-gita—Salvation by Knowledge—Buddha's Revolt against Brahmanism—His Gloomy Message to Mankind—Spread of Buddhism—Jainism—Revival of Brahmanism—The Puranas—Incarnations of Vishnu—Creator as a Boar—Egyptian and European Conceptions and Customs—Jagganath—Kalki.

MODERN-DAY Brahman pundits, the cultured apostles of the ancient forest sages, acknowledge a Trinity composed of Brahma the Creator, Vishnu the Preserver, and Shiva the Destroyer. A rock carving at Elephanta, which depicts the supreme god with three heads, indicates that the conception is of considerable antiquity. To what particular period it must be assigned, however, we cannot yet definitely decide.

The religious history of India is divided into four Ages: (1) the Vedic Age; (2) the Brahmanical Age; (3) the Buddhist Age; and (4) the Age of the reform and revival of Brahmanism.

As we have seen, many gods were worshipped in the Vedic Age, but ere it had ended Pantheistic ideas found expression in the hymns. Two distinct currents of thought characterize the Brahmanical Age. On the one hand there was the growth of priestly influence which is the feature of the *Brahmanas*, and on the other the development of the bold Pantheism of the *Upanishads*, which are permeated with a catholicity of spirit directly opposed to narrow and pedantic ritualism. Towards the close of this Age, Vishnu and Shiva were deities of growing ascendancy.

The Buddhist Age began in the sixth century before Christ, and Buddhism gradually supplanted Brahmanism as a national religion. In the tenth century of our era, however, Brahmanism was revived, drawing its inspiration mainly from the *Upanishads*, and purified by the teachings of Buddha and other reformers.

These religious movements of the post-Vedic times, which have exercised a cumulative influence in shaping modern-day Hinduism, were due directly and indirectly to the speculative reasonings of the unknown authors of the *Upanishads*. The Pantheistic doctrines of these ancient philosophers, however, hardly constituted a religion: they were rather an esoteric system of belief devoid of popular appeal. But they have been the inspiration of a succession of profound thinkers and eloquent teachers of revered memory in India, who infused ancient modes of thought with high philosophic doctrines, and utilized archaic myths to develop a religion which in its purest form permeates the acts of everyday life and requires the whole-hearted devotion and service of pious Hindus to the will of the Supreme Being.

In the Brahmanical Age Upanishadic teachings made limited appeal, but evidences are not awanting that knowledge of them was not confined to the Brahmans, because the revolts which gave India Buddhism and Jainism originated among the Kshatriyas. Meanwhile the gods of the *Vedas* continued their hold upon the allegiance of the great masses of the people, although the ancient Vedic

20

THE HINDU TRINITY AT ELEPHANTA (see page 119)

religion had been divested of its simplicity and directness by the ritualistic priesthood. Gods and men depended upon the Brahmans for their prosperity and even for their continued existence. It was taught that "the gods lived in fear of death, the strong Ender", but were supported and fed by penance and sacrifice. The priests achieved spiritual dominion over their rivals, the Kshatriyas.

There was, however, more than one "school of thought" among the Brahmans. The sages who memorized and repeated the older Upanishads, and composed new ones, could not have failed to pass unrecorded judgments on the superstitious practices of their ritualistic brethren. Account must also be taken of the example and teachings of the bands of wandering devotees, the Bhiksus, who neither performed penances nor offered up sacrifices, and of the influence exercised by the independent thinkers among the Kshatriyas, who regarded with disfavour the pretensions of the powerful priesthood. The elements of revolt could never have been absent during the two centuries of the Brahmanical Age. Upanishadic teachings had stirred the minds of thinking men, but they had one marked defect; they left unsatisfied the religious sense which could find no repose in a jungle of abstract thought. It was impossible, however, for the leaders of thought to return to the polytheism of the Vedic Age, or to worship deities controlled by human beings. A new and higher religion became a necessity for those who, like the Hebrew Psalmist, appear to have cried:

> "O Lord . . . thou desirest not sacrifice, else would I give it; thou delightest not in burnt offering. The sacrifices of God are a broken spirit."—*Psalms*, li, 16, 17.

At any rate, we find that, before the Brahmanical Age

had ended, the conception was becoming more prevalent of a supreme personal god, greater than Indra or Agni, and worthy of minds influenced by the *Upanishads*—a god who was the embodiment of the First Cause, an Infinite Being uncontrolled by the priesthood. One section of the people appears to have worshipped Vishnu as the Celestial incarnation of the World Soul, while another gave recognition to Shiva. In the absence of records, however, it is impossible to ascertain to what extent monotheistic ideas were developed by unorthodox teachers. The new doctrines may have degenerated, like Buddhism, as they became widespread. It is evident, however, that the priesthood were unable to ignore them, for they are referred to in their "books".

Although the political prominence of Vishnu and Shiva belong to the Age of reformed Brahmanism, it is undoubted that both deities were worshipped throughout the long period of Buddhistic ascendancy. The Greek ambassador Megasthenes, who resided in India between B.C. 311 and 302, and wrote *Ta Indika*, furnishes interesting evidence in this connection. "By his description of the god Dionysus, whom they worshipped in the mountains, Shiva", says Professor Macdonell, "must be intended, and by Herakles, adored in the plains . . . no other can be meant than Vishnu and his incarnation Krishna. . . . These statements seem to justify the conclusion that Shiva and Vishnu were already prominent as highest gods, the former in the mountains, the latter in the Ganges valley. . . . We also learn from Megasthenes that the doctrine of the four Ages of the World (Yugas) was fully developed in India by this time."[1]

In the *Rigveda* Vishnu is a god of grace. He is, however, a secondary deity—an attribute of the sun and

[1] *A History of Sanskrit Literature*, p. 411.

a phase of Agni. From the earliest times, it is significant to note, his benevolent character is emphasized. In one of the hymns[1] he is called "the Kinsman"; he welcomed to his heaven of bliss the faithful worshippers of the gods. An interesting reference is made to his "highest step". As detailed in later writings, the myth involved is to the effect that the demon Bali, one of the dreaded Danavas (Titans), had, in the Treta Yuga, secured temporary ascendancy over the gods. Vishnu appeared before him in the form of the dwarf Vamana, and requested as much territory as he could measure out by taking three strides. The demon granted this request, and Vishnu immediately assumed the form of a giant; his first step covered the heavens, the second crossed the entire earth, and the third and highest reached the abode of the gods. So was the Universe won back from the Asuras. It is believed that the myth refers to the progress of the conquering sun by day and by night.

In *Yajurveda* Vishnu is more prominent than in the *Rigveda*, and in the *Brahmanas* "there is a growing tendency", remarks Professor Barnett, "to regard him as a blessed Cosmic Spirit".[2] He is fully identified with Brahma in the *Mahábhárata*. In some of the myths he is the source of Indra's strength and valour, and he appears to have absorbed the sublime character of Varuna, the god of sinners; he is similarly associated with the sea, but the Sea of Milk.

Shiva is a development of the Vedic storm god Rudra, who was not only dreaded, but also revered as a destroyer of evil-doers, hatred, evil, and disease, and as a nourisher who gave long life.[3]

Both deities inspired love and reverential fear; they

[1] *Rigveda*, i, 154, 155. [2] *Hinduism*, by L. D. Barnett.
[3] *Rigveda*, ii, 33.

won the affections of human hearts and were worshipped emotionally. Their cults have had independent doctrinal development, however, and they divide Hinduism to-day into two great churches, one of which recognizes Vishnu, and the other Shiva, as the greatest god. Their union in the Trinity has not yet obliterated sectarian differences.

Many myths have collected round Vishnu, originally a purely abstract deity, because the faith which he represents had to be imparted to the masses in "parables". These "parables" were, of course, given literal interpretation by the people. The majority of the myths belong to the post-Buddhist Age—the Age of Brahmanical revival, during which came into existence the sacred poems called the *Puranas*. Many were also incorporated in the great epics, the *Mahábhárata* and the *Ramáyana*, which existed in part, at least, before the rise of Buddhism and Jainism.

When Vishnu, the god of mercy and goodness, received recognition as Narayana in the Brahmanical Age, he was worshipped as the "unconquerable preserver" who at the dawn of each Yuga (Age) awoke as the child of the primordial waters. In one myth he rises from a lotus bloom; in another he is supposed to sleep, as Brahma, on the coils of the world-serpent Shesha, which is "a part of a part of Vishnu". This serpent rests on the tortoise, Kurma, another form of Vishnu. When the tortoise moves its limbs, Shesha is roused to yawn; thus are earthquakes caused. A creation myth which teaches the absolute supremacy of Vishnu tells that at the beginning Brahma sprang from a lotus issuing from the navel of the Preserver, while Shiva came from his forehead.

Vishnu is a dark god with four arms; in one of his right hands he holds a warshell, and in the other a

21

VISHNU UPHOLDING THE UNIVERSE

From a sculpture at Māmallapuram

flaming discus, which destroys enemies and returns after it is flung; in one left hand he holds a mace, and in the other a lotus bloom.

The belief that the Supreme Being from time to time "assumes a human form . . . for the preservation of rectitude and morality" is an outstanding feature of Vishnuite religion, which teaches that Vishnu was born among men as Ramachandra, Krishna, Balarama, and Buddha. These are the Avataras of the Preserver. Avatara means literally "a descent", but is used in the sense of an "Incarnation".

Rama Chandra is the hero of the *Ramâyana* epic, which is summarized in our closing chapters; he is the human ideal of devotion, righteousness, and manliness, the slayer of the demon Ravana, who oppressed and persecuted mankind.

Krishna and his brother Balarama figure as princes of Dwaraka in the *Mahâbhârata*. Krishna is represented as the teacher of the Vishnuite faith, the devotional religion which displaced the Vedic ceremonies and links Upanishadic doctrines with modern Hinduism. It recognizes that all men are sinful, and preaches salvation by Knowledge which embraces Works. Sinners must surrender themselves to Krishna, the human incarnation (Avatara) of Vishnu, the Preserver, the God of Love.

This faith is unfolded in the famous *Bhagavad-gita*[1] in the *Bhishma Parva* section of the *Mahâbhârata* epic. Krishna is acting as the counsellor and charioteer of the Pandava warrior Arjuna. Ere the first day's battle of the Great War begins, the human Avatara of Vishnu reveals himself to his friend as the Divine Being, and gives instruction as to how men may obtain salvation.

Krishna teaches that the soul is "unborn, un-

[1] The "Divine Song".

changeable, eternal, and ancient"; it is one with the Supreme Soul, Vishnu, the First Cause, the Source of All. The soul "is not slain when the body is slain"; it enters new bodies after each death, or else it secures emancipation from sin and suffering by being absorbed in the World Soul. . . . All souls have to go through a round of births. "On attaining to Me, however," says Krishna, "there is no rebirth."

Krishna gives Salvation to those who obtain "Knowledge of self or Brahma". . . . He says: "The one who hath devoted his Self (Soul) to abstraction, casting an equal eye everywhere, beholdeth his Self in all creatures, and all creatures in his Self. Unto him that beholdeth Me in everything and beholdeth everything in Me, I am never lost and he also is never lost in Me. He that worshippeth Me as abiding in all creatures, holding yet that All is One, is a devotee, and whatever mode of life he may lead, he liveth in Me. . . .

"Even if thou art the greatest sinner among all that are sinful, thou shalt yet cross over all transgressions by the raft of Knowledge". . . . Knowledge destroys all sins. It is obtained by devotees who, "casting off attachment, perform actions for attaining purity of Self, with the body, the mind, the understanding, and even the senses, free from desire". To such men "a sod, a stone, and gold are alike".

Krishna, as Vishnu, is thus revealed: "I am the productive cause of the entire Universe and also its destroyer. There is nothing else that is higher than myself. . . . I am Om (the Trinity) in all the Vedas, the sound in space, the manliness in man. I am the fragrant odour in earth, the splendour in fire, the life in all creatures, and penance in ascetics. . . . I am the thing to be known, the means by which everything is cleansed. . . . I am the soul (self) seated in the heart of every being. I am the beginning, the middle, and the end of all beings. . . . I am the letter A (in the Sanskrit alphabet). . . . I am Death that seizeth all, and the source of all that is to be. . . . He that knoweth me as the Supreme Lord of the worlds, without birth and beginning . . . is free from all sins. . . . He who doeth everything for me, who hath me for his supreme object, who is freed from attachment, who is without enmity towards all beings, even he cometh to me. . . . He through whom the world is not troubled, and who is not troubled by the world, who is free from joy, wrath, fear, and anxieties, even he is dear to me."

To Arjuna Krishna says: "Exceedingly dear art thou to me. Therefore I will declare what is for thy benefit. Set thy heart on Me, become my devotee, sacrifice to me, bow down to me. Then shalt thou come to me. . . . Forsaking all (religious) duties, come to me as thy sole refuge. I will deliver thee from all sins. Do not grieve."

It is, however, added: "This is not to be declared by thee to one who practiseth no austerities, to one who is not a devotee, to one who never waiteth on a preceptor, nor yet to one who calumniateth Me."

Unbelievers are those who are devoid of knowledge. Krishna says: "One who hath no knowledge and no faith, whose mind is full of doubt, is lost. . . . Doers of evil, ignorant men, the worst of their species . . . do not resort to Me." . . . Such men "return to the path of the world that is subject to destruction". He denounces "persons of demoniac natures" because they are devoid of "purity, good conduct, and truth. . . . They say that the Universe is void of truth, of guiding principle and of ruler. . . . Depending on this view these men of lost souls, of little intelligence and fierce deeds, these enemies of the world, are born for the destruction of the Universe." They "cherish boundless hopes, limited by death alone", and "covet to obtain unfairly hoards of wealth for the gratification of their desires"; they say, "This foe hath been slain by me—I will slay others. . . . I am lord, I am the enjoyer. . . . I am rich and of noble birth—who else is there that is like me? . . . I will make gifts, I will be merry. . . . Thus deluded by ignorance, tossed about by numerous thoughts, enveloped in the meshes of delusion, attached to the enjoyment of objects of desire, they sink into foul hell. . . Threefold is the way to hell, ruinous to the Self (Soul), namely, lust, wrath, likewise avarice. . . . Freed from these three gates of darkness, a man works out his own welfare, and then repairs to the highest goal."[1]

Balarama is an incarnation of the world serpent Shesha. According to the legend, he and Krishna are the sons of Vasudeva and Devakí. It was revealed to Kansa, King of Mat'hurā[2], who was a worshipper of Shiva, that a son of Devakí would slay him. His majesty therefore commanded that Devakí's children should be slain as soon as they were born. Balarama, who was fair, was carried safely away. Krishna, the dark son, performed miracles soon after birth. The king had his father and mother fettered, and the doors of the houses were secured with locks. But the chains fell from Vasudeva, and the doors flew open when he stole out into the night to conceal the babe. As he crossed the river Jumna, carrying Krishna on his head in a basket, the waters rose high and threatened to drown him, but the child put out a foot and the river immediately fell and

[1] Extracts from Roy's translation of *Mahábhárata*.

[2] Or Muttra.

22

KRISHNA AND THE GOPIS (HERDSMAIDS)

From a modern sculpture

became shallow. In Mathura the two brothers performed miraculous feats during their youth. Indeed, the myths connected with them suggest that their prototypes were voluptuous pastoral gods. Krishna, the flute-player and dancer, is the shepherd lover of the Gopis or herdsmaids, his favourite being Radhá. He was opposed to the worship of Indra, and taught the people to make offerings to a sacred mountain.

King Kansa had resort to many stratagems to accomplish the death of Krishna, but his own doom could not be set aside; ultimately he was slain by the two brothers. The *Harivamsa*, an appendix to the *Mahábhárata*, which is as long as the Iliad and the Odyssey together, is devoted to the life and adventures of Krishna, who also figures in the *Puranas*.

Vishnu's Buddha Avatara was assumed, according to orthodox teaching, to bring about the destruction of demons and wicked men who refused to acknowledge the inspiration of the Vedas and the existence of deities, and were opposed to the caste system. This attitude was assumed by the Brahmans because Buddhism was a serious lay revolt against Brahmanical doctrines and ceremonial practices.

Buddha, "the Enlightened", was Prince Siddartha of the royal family Gautama, which, as elsewhere told, ruled over a Sakya tribe. At his birth marvellous signs foretold his greatness. Reared in luxury, he was kept apart from the common people; but when the time of his awakening came, he was greatly saddened to behold human beings suffering from disease, sorrow, and old age. One night he left his wife and child, and went away to live the life of a contemplative hermit in the forest, with purpose to find a solution for the great problem of human sin and suffering. He came under the influence of Upanishadic doctrines, and at the end of six years he returned and began his mission.

Buddha, the great psychologist, was one of the world's influential teachers, because his doctrines have been embraced in varying degrees of purity by about a third of the human race. Yet they are cold and unsatisfying and gloomy. The "Enlightener's" outlook on life was intensely timid and pessimistic; he was an "enemy of society" in the sense that he made no attempt to effect social reforms so as to minimize human suffering, which touched him with deepest sympathy, but unfortunately filled him with despair; his solution for all problems was Death; he was the apostle of benevolent Nihilism and Idealistic Atheism.

There is no supreme personal god in Buddhism and no hope of immortality. Gods and demons and human beings are "living creatures"; gods have no power over the Universe, and need not be worshipped or sacrificed to, because they are governed by laws, and men have nothing to fear from them.

Buddha denied the existence of the Self-Soul of the *Upanishads*. Self is not God, in the sense that it is a phase of the World Soul. The "self-state" is, according to the "Enlightener", a combination of five elements—matter, feeling, imagination, will, and consciousness; these are united by Kamma,[1] the influence which causes life to repeat itself. Buddha had accepted, in a limited sense, the theory of Transmigration of Souls. He taught, however, that rebirth was the result of actions and desire. "It is the yearning for existence", he said, "which leads from new birth to new birth, which finds its desire in different directions, the desire for pleasure, the desire for existence, the desire for power." Death occurs when

[1] Karma, "works" and their consequences.

23

BUDDHA EXPOUNDING THE LAW

the five elements which constitute life are divided; after death nothing remains but the consequences of actions and thoughts. Rebirth follows because "the yearning", the essence of "works", brings the elements together again. The individual exists happily, or the reverse, according to his conduct in a former life; sorrow and disease are results of wrong living and wrong thinking in previous states of existence.

The aim of the Buddhist is to become the "master of his fate". Life to him is hateful because, as the Enlightener taught, "birth is suffering, death is suffering; to be joined to one thou dost not love is suffering, to be divided from thy love is suffering, to fail in thy desire is suffering; in short, the fivefold bonds that unite us to earth—those of the five elements—are suffering". As there can be no life without suffering in various degrees, it behoves the believer to secure complete emancipation from the fate of being reborn. Life is a dismal and tragic failure. The Buddhist must therefore destroy the influence which unites the five elements and forms another life. He must achieve the complete elimination of inclination—of the yearning for existence. Buddha's "sacred truth", which secures the desired end, is eightfold—"right belief, right resolve, right speech, right action, right life, right desire, right thought, and right self-absorption". The reward of the faithful, who attains to perfect knowledge, unsullied by works, is eternal emancipation by Nirvana, undisturbed repose or blissful extinction[1], which is the Supreme Good. If there had been no belief in rebirth, the solution would have been found in suicide.

[1] Buddha's negative attitude towards immortality and the conception of a Supreme Being was departed from by those of his followers who have taught that Nirvana is a conscious state of eternal bliss.

Buddha taught that the four Noble Verities are: (1) pain, (2) desire, the cause of pain, (3) pain is extinguished by Nirvana, (4) the way which leads to Nirvana. The obliteration of Desire is the first aim of the Buddhist. This involves the renunciation of the world and of all evil passions; the believer must live a perfect life according to the Buddhist moral code, which is as strict as it is idealistic in the extreme. "It does not express friendship, or the feeling of particular affection which a man has for one or more of his fellow creatures, but that universal feeling which inspires us with goodwill towards all men and constant willingness to help them."[1]

Belief in the sanctity of life is a prevailing note in Buddhism. The teacher forbade the sacrifice of animals, as did Isaiah in Judah.

> "To what purpose is the multitude of your sacrifices unto me? saith the Lord: I am full of the burnt offerings of rams, and the fat of fed beasts; and I delight not in the blood of bullocks, or of lambs, or of he goats." *Isaiah*, i, 11.

Brahmanism was influenced in this regard, for offerings to Vishnu were confined to cakes, curds, sweetmeats, flowers, oblations, &c.

Buddha, the enemy of the priesthood, was of the Kshatriya caste, and his religion appears to have appealed to aristocrats satiated with a luxurious and idle life, who felt like the Preacher that "all is vanity"; it also found numerous adherents among the wandering bands of unorthodox devotees. The perfect Buddhist had to live apart from the world, and engage for long intervals in introspective contemplation so as to cultivate by a stern analytic process that frame of mind which enabled him to obliterate Desire blankly and coldly. Familiar statues of Buddha

[1] Burnouf, quoted by Max Muller, *Chips from a German Workshop*, i, 222.

show the posture which must be assumed; the legs are crossed and twisted, and the hands arranged to suggest inaction; the eyes gaze on the bridge of the nose.

Monastic orders came into existence for men and women, but the status of women was not raised. From these orders were excluded all officials and the victims of infectious and incurable diseases. A lower class of Buddhists engaged in worldly duties. Although Buddha recognized the caste system, his teaching removed its worst features, for Kshatriyas and converted Brahmans could accept food from the Sudras without fear of contamination. Kings embraced the new religion, which ultimately assumed a national character.

Missionaries were from the earliest times sent abroad, and Buddhism spread into Burma, Siam, Anam, Tibet, Mongolia, China, Java, and Japan. The view is suggested that its influence can be traced in Egypt. "From some source," writes Professor Flinders Petrie, "perhaps the Buddhist mission of Asoka, the ascetic life of recluses was established in the Ptolemaic times, and monks of the Serapeum illustrated an ideal to man which had been as yet unknown in the West. This system of monasticism continued until Pachomios, a monk of Serapis in Upper Egypt, became the first Christian monk in the reign of Constantine."[1]

Jainism, like Buddhism, was also a revolt against Brahmanic orthodoxy, and drew its teachers and disciples chiefly from the aristocratic class. It was similarly influenced in its origin by the *Upanishads*. Jainites believe, however, in soul and the world soul; they recognize the Hindu deities, but only as exalted souls in a state of temporary bliss achieved by their virtues; they also worship a number of "conquerors" or "openers of the way",

[1] Petrie, *The Religion of Egypt*, pp. 92–3.

as Buddhism, in debased form, recognizes Buddha and his disciples as gods, and allows the worship here of a tooth and there of a hair of the Enlightener, as well as sacred mounds connected with his pilgrimages. In the gloomy creed of the Jainites it is taught that "emancipation" may be hastened by rigid austerities which entail systematic starvation. Many Jainites have in their holy places given up their lives in this manner, but the practice is now obsolete.

In the Age which witnessed the decline of Buddhism in India, and the rise of reformed Brahmanism, the religious struggle was productive of the long poems called the *Puranas* (old tales) to which we have referred. In these productions some of the ancient myths about the gods were preserved and new myths were formulated. They were meant for popular instruction, and especially to make converts among the unlettered masses. Their authors were chiefly of the Vishnu cult, which had perpetuated the teachings of the unknown sages who at the close of the Brahmanical Age revolted against impersonal Pantheism, the ritualistic practices of the priesthood, and the popular conceptions regarding the Vedic deities who ensured worldly prosperity, but exercised little influence on the character of the individual.

Indra and Agni and other popular deities were not, however, excluded from the Pantheon, but were divested of their ancient splendour and shown to be subject to the sway of Brahma, their Lord and Creator, whose attributes they symbolized in their various spheres of activity. Vishnuites taught that Vishnu was Brahma, and Shivaites that Shiva was the supreme deity.

In this way, it would appear, the authors of the *Puranas* effected a compromise between immemorial beliefs and practices and the higher religious conceptions towards which the people were being gradually elevated. A similar policy was adopted by Pope Gregory the Great, who in the year 601 caused the Archbishop of Canterbury to be instructed to infuse Pagan ceremonials with Christian symbolism. It was decreed that heathen temples should be changed into churches, and days consecrated to sacrificial ceremonies to be observed as Christian festivals. The Anglo-Saxons were not to be permitted to "sacrifice animals to the Devil", but to kill them for human consumption "to the praise of God", so that "while they retained some outward joys they might give more ready response to inward joys". The Pope added: "It is not possible to cut off everything at once from obdurate minds; he who endeavours to climb to the highest place must rise not by bounds, but by degrees or steps."[1]

It is necessary for us, therefore, in dealing with Puranic beliefs, and the movement which culminated in modern-day Hinduism, to make a distinction between the popular faith and the beliefs of the most enlightened Brahmans, and also between the process of mythology-making and the development of religious ideas.

In early Puranic times, when Brahmanism was revived, Vishnu's benevolent character was exalted to so high a degree that, it was taught, even demons might secure salvation through his grace. Prahlada, son of the King of the Danavas, worshipped Vishnu. As a consequence, terrible punishments were inflicted upon him by his angry father. At length Vishnu appeared in the Danava palace as the Nrisinha incarnation (half man, half lion), and slew the presumptuous giant king who had aspired to control the Universe.

Another incarnation of Vishnu was the boar, Varáha. A demon named Hiranyaksha had claimed the earth,

[1] Bede, *Historia Ecclesiastica*, lib. i, chap. xxx.

when at the beginning of one of the Yugas it was raised from the primordial deep by the Creator in the form of a boar. Vishnu slew the demon for the benefit of the human race. Earlier forms of this myth recognize Brahma, or Prajapati, as the boar. In *Taittiriya Brahmana* it is set forth: "This Universe was formerly water, fluid; with that (water) Prajapati practised arduous devotions (saying), 'How shall this universe be (developed)?' He beheld a lotus leaf standing. He thought, 'There is something on which this rests.' He as a boar—having assumed that form—plunged beneath towards it. He found the earth down below. Breaking off (a portion of) her, he rose to the surface."

This treatment of the boar is of special interest. In Egypt the boar was the demon Set, and the "black pig" is the devil in Wales and Scotland, and also in a "layer" of Irish mythology. Hatred of pork prevailed in Egypt and its vicinity, and still lingers in parts of Ireland and Wales, but especially in the Scottish Highlands. The Gauls, like the Aryans of India, did not regard the boar as a demon, and they ate pork freely, as did also the Achæans and the Germanic peoples. Roast pig is provided in Valhal and in the Irish Danann Paradise, but the Irish "devil", Balor, who resembles the Asura king of India, had a herd of black pigs.

The struggle between Kshatriyas and Brahmans is reflected in Vishnu's incarnation as Parasu-rama (Rama with the axe). He clears the earth twenty-one times of the visible Kshatriyas, but on each occasion a few survive to perpetuate the caste.

Jagannath[1] is also regarded as a form of Vishnu, although apparently not of Brahmanic origin. He is represented by three forms, representing the dark Krishna,

[1] Juggernaut.

24

THE BOAR INCARNATION OF VISHNU RAISING THE EARTH FROM THE DEEP

From a rock sculpture at Udayagiri

the fair Balarama, and their sister, Subhadra. Once a year the idol is bathed and afterwards taken forth in a great car, which is dragged by pious worshippers. Some have considered it a meritorious act to commit suicide by being crushed under its wheels.

It is believed that Vishnu will yet appear as Kalki, riding on a white horse and grasping a flaming sword. He will slay the enemies of evil and re-establish pure religion. Many pious Vishnuites in our own day look forward to the coming of their supreme deity with fear and trembling, but not without inflexible faith.

CHAPTER VIII

Divinities of the Epic Period

The Great Indian Epics—Utilized by the Brahmans—The Story of Manu—Universal Cataclysm—How Amrita (Ambrosia) was obtained—Churning of the Ocean—The Demon Devourer of Sun and Moon—Garuda, the Man Eagle—Attributes of the God Shiva—Comparison with Irish Balor—Rise of the Goddesses—Saraswati and Lakshmi or Sri—Fierce Durga and Kali—Sati, the Ideal Hindu Wife—Legend of the Ganges—The Celestial Rishis—Vishwamitra and Vasishtha—History in the Vedas—Wars between Aryan Tribes—Kernel of Mahábhárata Epic.

THE history of Brahmanism during the Buddhist Age is enshrined in the great epics *Mahábhárata* and *Ramáyana*, which had their origin before B.C. 500, and continued to grow through the centuries.

The *Mahabharata*, which deals with the Great War for ascendancy between two families descended from King Bharata, has been aptly referred to as "the Iliad of India". It appears to have evolved from a cycle of popular hero songs, but after assuming epic form it was utilized by the Brahmans for purposes of religious propaganda. The warriors were represented as sons of gods or allies of demons, and the action of the original narrative was greatly hampered by inserting long speeches and discussions regarding Brahmanic conceptions and beliefs. An excellent example of this process is afforded by the famous *Bhagavad-gita*, from which we have quoted in the previous chapter. The narrative of the first day's battle is interrupted to allow Krishna to expound the doctrines of the Vaishnava faith, with purpose to make converts to the cult of Vishnu. Almost every incident in the poem is utilized in a similar manner. In fact the epic, as we are informed in the opening section, "furnisheth the means of arriving at the knowledge of Brahma". The priests, with this aim in view, loaded the chariots of heroes with religious treatises, and transformed a tribal struggle for supremacy into a great holy war. If the *Iliad* survived to us only in Pope's translation, and our theologians had scattered through it, say, metrical renderings of Bunyan's *Pilgrim's Progress*, the Thirty-nine Articles of the Church of England, the *Westminster Confession of Faith*, Fox's *Book of Martyrs*, and a few representative theological works of rival sects, a fate similar to that which has befallen the *Mahabharata* would now overshadow the great Homeric masterpiece. The "Iliad of India" is a part of what may be called the Hindu Bible, which embraces the *Ramayana*, the *Vedas*, the *Upanishads*, the *Puranas*, &c.

The *Ramáyana*, which is called "the Odyssey of India", because it deals with the wanderings and adventures of the exiled prince Rama, was utilized mainly by the cult of Vishnu, but both Vishnu and Shiva figure as great gods in the *Mahábhárata*, and now one and anon the other is given first place.

If the documentary material, which is available in India for dealing with its ancient religious beliefs, were as scanty as those which survive to us from Ancient Egypt, comparisons might have been drawn between the Brahmanic cults and the priestly theorists of Heliopolis, Memphis, Sais, &c., and it might have been remarked of the one nation as of the other that its people clung to archaic beliefs long after new and higher religious conceptions obtained as tenets of orthodox religion. In India the process of change and development can, however, be not only traced, but partially accounted for, as we have shown. Old myths were embraced in the epics and the *Puranas* for the purpose of educating the people by effecting a compromise between folk religion and the profound doctrines of the ancient forest sages.

"Father Manu" of the *Vedas*, who appears to have been worshipped as a patriarchal ancestor, was, for instance, embraced in the *Mahábhárata* by the cult of Vishnu. He had been exalted by the ritualists as one who was greater than the gods, because he had been the first to inaugurate sacrificial rites, and he was afterwards associated with Brahma in performing some of the acts of Creation at the beginning of one of the Yugas (Ages). It was necessary, therefore, to show that he owed his power and opportunities to Vishnu.

In the *Mahábhárata* the sage Markandeya refers to Manu as the great Rishi, who was equal unto Brahma in glory. He had practised rigid austerities in a forest for ten thousand years, standing on one leg with uplifted hand. One day while he brooded in wet clothes, a fish rose from a stream and asked for his protection against the greater fish which desired to swallow it, at the same time promising to reward him. Manu placed the fish in an earthen jar and tended it carefully till it increased in size; then he put it in a tank. The fish continued to grow until the tank became small for it, and Manu heard it pleading to be transferred to the Ganges, "the favourite spouse of Ocean". He carried it to the river, and in time the fish spoke to him, saying: "I cannot move about in the river on account of my great length and bulk. Take me quickly to the Ocean." Manu was enabled to carry the fish from the Ganges to the sea, and then it spoke with a smile and said:

25

INTERIOR OF A ROCK-HEWN BUDDHIST TEMPLE (AJANTA)

"Know thou, O worshipful one, my protector, that the dissolution of the Universe is at hand. The time is ripe for purging the world. I will therefore advise thee what thou shouldst do, so that it may be well with thee. Build a strong and massive ark, and furnish it with a long rope; thou wilt ascend in it with the seven Rishis (the Celestial Rishis), and take with thee all the different seeds enumerated by Brahmans in days of yore, and preserve them carefully. Wait for me and I will appear as a horned animal. Act according to my instructions, for without mine aid thou canst not save thyself from the terrible deluge."

Manu gathered together all the different seeds and "set sail in an excellent vessel on the surging sea". He thought of the fish, and it arose out of the waters like an island; he cast a noose which he fastened to the horns on its head, and the fish towed the ark over the roaring sea; tossed by the billows the vessel reeled about like one who is drunk. No land was in sight. "There was water everywhere, and the waters covered the heaven and the firmament also. . . . When the world was thus flooded none but Manu, the seven Rishis, and the fish could be seen."

After many long years the vessel was towed to the highest peak of the Himavat, which is still called Naubandhana (the harbour), and it was made fast there. The fish then spoke and said: "I am Brahma, the Lord of all Creatures; there is none greater than me. I have saved thee from this cataclysm. Manu will create again all beings—gods, Asuras, and men, and all those divisions of creation which have the power of locomotion and which have it not. By practising severe austerities he will acquire this power. . . ."

Then Manu set about creating all beings in proper and exact order.[1]

Markandeya elsewhere described the universal cata-

[1] Condensed from *Vana Parva* section of *Mahâbhârata*, sec. clxxxvii, Roy's trans.

clysm with more detail. After a drought lasting for many years, seven blazing suns will appear in the firmament; they will drink up all the waters. Then wind-driven fire will sweep over the earth, consuming all things; penetrating to the nether world it will destroy what is there in a moment; it will burn up the Universe. Afterwards many-coloured and brilliant clouds will collect in the sky, looking like herds of elephants decked with wreaths of lightning. Suddenly they will burst asunder, and rain will fall incessantly for twelve years until the whole world with its mountains and forests is covered with water. The clouds will vanish. Then the Self-created Lord, the First Cause of everything, will absorb the winds and go to sleep. The Universe will become one dread expanse of water.

Account has to be taken of the persistent legend regarding the ambrosia which gave strength to the gods and prolonged their existence. In "Teutonic mythology" it is snatched by Odin from the giants of the Underworld, and is concealed in the moon, which is ever pursued by the demon wolf Managarm, who seeks to devour it.

The development of the Indian form of the myth is found in the story of "The Churning of the Ocean", which is dealt with in the *Mahábhárata*, the *Ramáyana*, and several of the *Puranas*.

According to the epics, the ambrosia, the Indian name of which is amrita (both words implying immortality), was required by the gods so as to enable them to overcome the demons. In *Vishnu Purva*, however, a Brahmanic addition to the myth was made so as to exalt a sage and illustrate the power he could exercise over the old Vedic deities. It is related that Durvásas obtained from a merry nymph a sweet-scented, inspiring garland which made him dance. He presented it to Indra, who placed it on the head of his elephant. The elephant then began to prance about, and grew so excited that it cast the garland on the ground. Durvásas was enraged because that his gift was slighted in this manner, and cursed Indra and foretold the ruin of his kingdom. Thereafter the king of the gods began to suffer loss of power, whereat the other deities became alarmed, fearing that the demons would overcome him in battle. Appeal was made to Brahma, who referred the gods to Vishnu, the Preserver. That supreme being commanded that the ocean should be churned for amrita.

In the epics the gods allied themselves with the demons to procure amrita from Vishnu's Sea of Milk. The "churning stick" was the mountain Mandara, and the "churning rope" the serpent Vasuka[1] (Ananta or Shesha). Vishnu said: "The demons must share in the work of churning, but I will prevent them from tasting of the amrita, which must be kept for Indra and the gods only."

The gods carried the mountain Mandara to the ocean, and placed it on the back of Kurma, the king of tortoises, who was an incarnation of Vishnu.[2] Round the mountain they twisted the serpent, which was "a part of a part of Vishnu", the Asuras holding its hood and the gods its tail. As a result of the friction caused by the churning, masses of vapour issued from the serpent's mouth which, becoming clouds charged with lightning, poured down refreshing rains on the weary workers. Fire darted forth and enwrapped the mountain, burning its trees and destroying many birds, and the lions and elephants that crouched on its slopes. In time the Sea of Milk produced butter flavoured by the gums and juices which dropped from

[1] Va'suki.

[2] Brahma, as Prajapati, assumes, in one of the myths, the form of a tortoise to "create offspring".

the mountain. The gods grew weary, but Vishnu gave them fresh strength to proceed with the work. At length the moon emerged from the ocean; then arose the Apsaras, who became nymphs in Indra's heaven; they were followed by the goddess Lakshmi, Vishnu's white steed, and the gleaming gem which the god wears on his breast. Then came Dhanwantari, the physician of the gods, who carried a golden cup brimming with amrita. Beholding him, the Asuras cried out: "The gods have taken all else; the physician must be ours."

Next arose the great elephant Airávata, which Indra took for himself. The churning still went on until the blue, devastating poison appeared and began to flow over the earth, blazing like a flame mixed with fumes. To save the world from destruction, Shiva swallowed the poison and held it in his throat. From that time he was called Nilakantha, "the blue-throated".

Meanwhile the demons desired to combat against the gods for the possession of the beautiful goddess Lakshmi and the amrita. But Vishnu assumed a bewitching female form, and so charmed the Asuras that they presented the amrita to that fair woman.

Vishnu immediately gave the amrita to the gods, but soon it was discovered that a demon named Rahu had assumed Celestial form with purpose to drink it. The amrita had only reached his throat when the sun and moon discovered him and informed Vishnu. The divine Preserver then flung his discus and cut off Rahu's huge head, which resembled a mountain peak. Rendered immortal by the amrita the head soared to the sky, roaring loud and long. From that day Rahu's head, with mouth agape, has followed sun and moon, and when he swallows one or the other he causes the eclipses.

Meanwhile the demons fought against the gods, but

26

LAKSHMI ARISING FROM THE SEA OF MILK

From a sculpture at Mâmallapuram

were defeated, although they flung rocks and mountains. Thousands were slain by the sky-scouring discus of Vishnu, and those who survived concealed themselves in the bowels of the earth and the depths of the ocean of salt waters.

Once upon a time the ambrosia was robbed from the gods by Gar′uda, half giant and half eagle, the enemy of serpents. This "lord of birds" was hatched from an enormous egg five hundred years after it had been laid by Diti, mother of giants; his father was Kas′yapa, a Brahman identified with the Pole Star, who had sacrificed with desire for offspring. It happened that Diti, having lost a wager, was put under bondage by the demons, and could not be released until she caused the amrita to be taken from a Celestial mountain where it was surrounded by terrible flames, moved by violent winds, which leapt up to the sky. Assuming a golden body, bright as the sun, Garuda drank up many rivers and extinguished the fire. A fiercely revolving wheel, sharp-edged and brilliant, protected the amrita, but Garuda diminished his body and entered between the spokes. Two fire-spitting snakes had next to be overcome. Garuda blinded them with dust and cut them to pieces. Then, having broken the revolving wheel, that bright sky-ranger flew forth with the amrita which was contained in the moon goblet.

The gods went in pursuit of Garuda. Indra flung his thunderbolt, but the bird suffered no pain and dropped but a single feather. When he delivered the amrita to the demons his mother was released, but ere the demons could drink Indra snatched up the golden moon-goblet and wended back to the heavens. The demon snakes licked the grass where the goblet had been placed by Garuda, and their tongues were divided. From that day all the snakes have had divided tongues. . . . Garuda became afterwards the vehicle of Vishnu; he has ever "mocked the wind with his fleetness".

Shiva, as we have indicated, developed from Rudra, the storm god. He is first mentioned as Mahadeva, "the great god", in the *Yajurveda*, and in the *Mahábhárata* he is sometimes exalted above Vishnu. In one part he is worshipped by Krishna. He is the "blue-necked, three-eyed trident-bearing lord of all creatures". The trident is a lightning symbol which appears to have developed from the three wriggling flashes held in the left hand of hammer-gods like Tarku and Rammon. Shiva's third eye was on his forehead, and from it issued on occasion a flame of fire which could consume an enemy; once he slew Kamadeva, the love god, who wounded him with flowery arrows, by causing the flame to spring forth.

Balor, the night god of Irish mythology, had similarly a destroying eye; "its gaze withered all who stood before it";[1] he was the god of lightning and death, the "eye-flame" being the thunderbolt.

Shiva's dwelling is on the Himalayan mount Kaila'sa[2]. He is Girisha, "the lord of the hills", and Chandra-Shekara, "the moon crested", Bhuteswara, "lord of goblins", and Sri Kanta, "beautiful throated". When he is depicted with five heads, he is regarded as the source of the five sacred rivers flowing from the mountains. As the god with snow-white face, he is the spirit of asceticism (Maha-Yogi) adored by Brahmans performing penances. In the *Mahábhárata* Arjuna, the warrior, invoked him by engaging in austerities until smoke issued from the earth. Then Shiva, "the illustrious Hara", appeared in huge and stalwart form and wrestled with him. Arjuna's limbs were bruised and he was deprived of his senses. When he recovered he hailed the god, saying: "Thou art

[1] *Celtic Myth and Legend*, p. 49. [2] Or Kailása.

Shiva in the form of Vishnu and Vishnu in the form of Shiva . . . .[1] O Hari, O Rudra, I bow to thee. Thou hast a (red) eye on thy forehead. . . . Thou art the source of universal blessing, the cause of the cause of the Universe. . . . Thou art worshipped of all the worlds. I worship thee to obtain thy grace. . . . This combat in which I was engaged with thee (arose) from ignorance. . . . I seek thy protection. Pardon me all I have done."

Shiva, whose sign is the bull, embraced Arjuna and said, "I have pardoned thee."

The god was invoked by another warrior, Ashwattaman, son of Drona. Having naught else to sacrifice, the worshipper flung himself upon the altar fire; Shiva accepted him and entered his body so as to assist him in slaughtering his sleeping enemies. Bloody rites were at one time associated with Shiva worship. As the Destroyer of the Hindu Trinity, he is armed with a discus, a sword, a bow, and a club; but his most terrible weapon is the trident. Sometimes he is clad in the skin of an elephant and sometimes in that of a leopard, the tail dangling behind. A serpent, coiled on his head, rears itself to strike; another serpent darts from his right shoulder against an enemy.

The bull symbol, Nandi, the moon crescent on his forehead, and the serpent girdle, indicate that Shiva is a god of fertility. A phallic symbol is associated with his worship. In localities he is adored at the present day in the form of a great boulder painted red which usually stands below a tree. Offerings are made to this stone, and women visit it during the period of the moon's increase to pray for offspring.

As Natesa, the dancer, Shiva dances triumphantly on the body of a slain Asura. A fine bronze in the Madras

[1] Combined with Vishnu he is Hari-hara.

Museum depicts him with four arms, and a beaming, benevolent face, wearing a tiara, and surrounded by a halo of fire; he absorbed the attributes of Agni as well as those of Rudra. He is the destroyer of evil and disease, the giver of long life and the god of medicine, and is accordingly invoked to cure sickness. Victims of epilepsy are believed to be possessed by Shiva.

In early Puranic times, when Brahmanism was revived and reformed, the worship of goddesses came into prominence. This was one of the most pronounced features of the anti-Buddhist movement, and was due probably to the influence of Great Mother worshippers. In the Vedic Age, as we have seen, the goddesses were vague and shadowy; as wives of the gods they were strictly subordinate, reflecting, no doubt, the social customs which prevailed among the Aryans. Ushas, the dawn, and Ratri, the night, were mainly poetic conceptions. Even Prithivi, the Earth Mother, who was symbolized as a cow, played no prominent part in Vedic religion: a magical influence was exercised by water goddesses. The male origin of life appears to have been an accepted tenet of Vedic belief. Aditi, mother of the Adityas, is believed to be of more recent origin than her sons. Indra seems to have similarly had existence before his mother, like the other hammer gods, and especially P'an Ku and Ptah.

Female water spirits are invariably regarded as givers of boons, inspiration and wisdom; holy wells have from remote times been regarded as sources of luck; by performing ceremonial acts those who visit them obtain what they wish for in silence; their waters have, withal, curative properties, or they may be used for purposes of divination. The name of the goddess Saraswati signifies "waters"; she was originally the spirit of the Saraswati river, and was probably identical with Bharati, the goddess

27

SHIVA DANCING ON TRIPURA

From a bronze in the Madras Museum

of the Vedic Bharata tribe. In Puranic times she became the wife of Brahma and the Minerva of the Hindu Pantheon. She is identical with Vach, "Mother of the Vedas", the goddess of poetry and eloquence, and Viraj, the female form of Purusha, who divided himself to give origin to the gods and demons and all living creatures. When Brahma took for a second wife Gayatri, the milk-maid, she cursed him so that he could only be worshipped once a year.

Saranyu, who may have developed from Ushas, the Dawn, is the bride of Surya, the sun god, and mother of the twin Aswins; she fashioned the trident of Shiva and the discus of Vishnu, and other weapons besides.

Lakshmi, or Sri, who had her origin at the Churning of the Ocean, became the wife of Vishnu, and the goddess of beauty, love, and prosperity. She has had several human incarnations, and in each case was loved by the incarnation of Vishnu. She is Sita in the *Ramáyana*, and the beautiful herdswoman beloved by Krishna. Lakshmi is "the world-mother, eternal, imperishable; as Vishnu is all-pervading, she is omnipresent. Vishnu is meaning, she is speech; Vishnu is righteousness, she is devotion; Sri is the earth, and Vishnu is the support of the earth." This benevolent goddess is usually depicted as a golden lady with four arms, seated on a lotus.

Shiva's complex character is reflected in the various forms assumed by his bride. As the Destroyer he is associated with Durga, who has great beauty and is also a war goddess. As Kali she is the black earth-mother, and as Jagadgauri, the yellow woman, the harvest bride. Armed with Celestial weapons, Durga is a renowned slayer of demons. In her Kali form she is of hideous aspect. Sculptors and painters have depicted her standing on the prostrate form of Shiva and grinning with outstretched tongue. Her body is smeared with blood because she has waged a ferocious and successful war against the giants. Like Shiva, she has a flaming third eye on her forehead. Her body is naked save for a girdle of giants' hands suspended from her waist; round her neck she wears a long necklace of giants' skulls: like the Egyptian Isis, Kali can conceal herself in her long and abundant hair. She has four arms: in one she holds a weapon, and in another the dripping head of a giant; two empty hands are raised to bless her worshippers. Like the Egyptian Hathor or Sekhet, the "Eye of Ra", she goes forth to slay the enemies of the gods, rejoicing in slaughter. Like Hathor, too, she is asked to desist, but heeds not. Then Shiva approaches her and lies down among her victims. Kali dances over the battlefield and leaps on her husband's body. When she observes, however, what she has done, she ejects her tongue with shame.

As Sati, Shiva's wife is the ideal of a true and virtuous Hindu woman. When Sati's husband was slighted by her father, the Deva-rishi, Daksha, she cast herself on the sacrificial fire. Widows who died on the funeral pyres of their husbands were called Sati[1], because in performing this rite they imitated the faithful goddess.

Sati was reborn as Uma, "Light", the impersonation of divine wisdom; as Amvika the same goddess was a sister of Rudra, or his female counterpart, Rudra taking the place of Purusha, the first man. Par′vati was another form of the many-sided goddess. Shiva taunted her for being black, and she went away for a time and engaged in austerities, with the result that she assumed a golden complexion.

A trinity of goddesses is formed by Saraswati, the white one, Lakshmi, the red one, and Par′vati, the black one. The three were originally one—a goddess who

[1] Often spelled *Suttee*.

GANESA (see page 151)

From a sculpture in the Victoria and Albert Museum

came into existence when Brahma, Vishnu, and Shiva spoke of the dreaded Asura, Andhaka (Darkness) and looked one at another. The goddess was coloured white, red, and black, and divided herself, according to the Varaha Purana, into three forms representing the Past, Present, and Future.

It was after Sati burned herself that the sorrowing Shiva was wounded by Kamadeva, the love god, whom he slew by causing a flame of fire to dart from his third eye. This god is the son of Vishnu and Lakshmi. He is usually depicted as a comely youth like the Egyptian Khonsu; he shoots flowery arrows from his bow; his wife Rati symbolizes Spring, the cuckoo, the humming bee, and soft winds. As Manmatha he is the "mind-disturber"; as Mara, "the wounder"; as Madan, "he who makes one love-drunk"; and as Pradyumna he is the "all-conqueror".

Gane′sa[1], the four-armed, elephant-headed god of wisdom, is the son of Shiva and Parvati. He is the general of Shiva's army, the patron of learning and the giver of good fortune. At the beginning of books he is invoked by poets, his image is placed on the ground when a new house is built, and he is honoured before a journey is begun or any business is undertaken. The elephant's head is an emblem of sagacity. A myth in one of the Puranas relates that the planet Saturn, being under a curse, decapitated Ganesa simply by looking at him. Vishnu mounted on the back of the man-eagle Garuda and came to the child's aid. He cut off the head of Indra's elephant and placed it on Ganesa's neck. In a conflict with a Deva-rishi Ganesa lost one of his tusks. Several myths have gathered round this popular, elephant-headed deity, who is also identified with the wise rat.

[1] A familiar Bengali rendering is "Gonesh", which is often given as a pet name to an exemplary boy.

Another son of Shiva and Parvati is Kartikeya, the Celestial general and slayer of demons. He is also regarded as the son of Agni and the Ganges.

The goddess of the Ganges is Gangá. This most sacred of all Indian rivers, the cleanser of sins and the giver of immortality, was originally confined to the Celestial regions, where it flowed from a toe of Vishnu. How it came to earth is related in the following myth: Sag'ara, a King of Ayodha (Oude), had great desire for offspring. He performed penance, with the result that one wife became the mother of a single son and the other of sixty thousand sons. He prepared to perform a horse sacrifice, but Indra stole the sacred animal. All the sons went in search of it by digging each for the depth of a league towards the centre of the earth. They were, however, consumed by the fire of Kapila, a form of Vishnu, who protected the earth goddess, his bride. Sagara was informed that his sons would come to life again and rise to heaven when the Ganges flowed down to the earth. His grandson went through rigid penances, and at length Brahma consented to grant the prayer that the sacred river should descend from the Himalayas. Shiva broke the fall of the waters by allowing them to flow through his hair, and they were divided into seven streams. When the waters reached the ashes of the slain princes, their spirits rose to heaven and secured eternal bliss. Sagra island, at the mouth of the Ganges, is invested with great sanctity, on account of its association with the King of Ayodha of this legend. All the Indian rivers are female, with the exception of the Sona and Brahmaputra, the spirits of which are male.

Other goddesses include Man'asa, sister of Vasuka, King of the Nagas, who gives protection against snake bites, and is invoked by the serpent worshippers: Sasti,

29

KARTIKEYA, THE WAR GOD

From a painting by Surendra Nath Gangoly

(By permission of the Indian Society of Oriental Art, Calcutta)

the feline goddess of maternity and protectress of children, who rides on a cat; and Shitala, the Bengali goddess of smallpox, who is mounted on an ass, carries a bundle of reeds in her hand, and is clad in red; she is propitiated on behalf of victims of the dreaded disease.

A prominent part is played in the Brahmanic mythology of the Restoration period by the Deva-rishis, the deified Vedic poets, sages, and priests, who stand between the Vedic gods and the Trinity of Brahma, Vishnu, and Shiva.

Originally there were seven Deva-rishis, and these were identified with the seven stars of the Great Bear, their wives being represented by the Pleiades. Their number was, however, increased in time.[1] Sometimes they visit the earth in the form of swans, but more often they are brooding sages who curse gods and mortals on receiving the slightest provocation.

One of the most prominent of these Rishis is Na'rada[2], who cursed and was cursed by Brahma. In the *Mahábhárata* he is a renowned teacher and a counsellor of kings, and also a messenger between Indra and heroes. He is a patron of music, and invented the Vina (lute) on which he loves to play. His great rival is Parvata, who also acts as a Celestial messenger.

Daksha is the father of Sati, the peerless wife of Shiva. It was on account of this rishi's quarrel with her husband, who was not invited to a great feast, that she flung herself upon the sacrificial fire. Shiva cut off Daksha's head and replaced it with the head of a goat.

Bhrigu was the patriarch of a Vedic priestly family. He married a daughter of Daksha, and was the father of

[1] In *Vishnu Purana* the Rishis are divided as follows: 1, Brahmarishis, sons of Brahma; 2, Devarishis, semi-divine saints; 3, Rajarishis, royal saints who had practised austerities. There are variants in other sacred books which refer to Maharishis, Paramarishis, &c.

[2] Or Nārada.

Lakshmi, wife of Vishnu, who rose from the ocean of milk. Bhrigu once cursed Agni, whom he compelled to consume everything. Angiras, Kratu, and Pulaha were Deva-rishis who also married daughters of Daksha. Pulastya was a famous slayer of Rakshasas. He once cursed a king who refused to make way for him on a narrow forest path, and the king became a Rakshasa.

Marichi was the grandfather of the dwarf incarnation of Vishnu, and Atri was the father of the irascible sage Durvasas, a master curser.

Vasishtha is sometimes referred to as identical with Vyasa, the reputed arranger of the Vedas, and author of the *Mahâbhârata*. He possessed a wonderful cow which granted whatever he wished for. A king named Vishwamitra desired to possess this wonderful animal, and when he found that he was unable to obtain it by force, he determined to raise himself from the Kshatriya to the Brahman caste by performing prolonged austerities. When Vishwamitra secured this elevation he fought with his rival.

Some Vedic scholars regard Vishwamitra and Vasishtha as actual historical personages. They argue that Vishwamitra was originally a Purohita (family priest) in the service of Sudas, the king of an Aryan tribe called the Tritsus. References are found in the *Rigveda* to the wars of Sudas, who once defeated a coalition of ten kings. Vishwamitra is believed to have been deposed by Sudas in favour of Vasishtha, and to have allied himself afterwards with the enemies of the Tritsus.[1]

Professor Oldenberg, the German Sanskrit scholar, is convinced, however, that there is no evidence in the *Rigveda* of the legendary rivalry between Vishwamitra and Vasishtha. He regards the Vasishthas as the family priests of the Bharata tribe and identical with the Tritsus.

[1] *Rigveda*, viii, 53. 9–11, and vii, 18.

30

PARVATI, WIFE OF SHIVA (see page 150)

From a South Indian temple

Among the tribes which opposed the advance of the conquering King Sudas, who appears to have been a late comer, was the Puru people on the banks of the Saraswati river. We find that the early authors suddenly cease to refer to them, and the problem is presented: What fate had befallen the Purus? Professor Oldenberg, whose view is accepted by Professor Macdonell, Oxford, explains that the Purus merged in the Kuru coalition. The Kurus gave their name to Kuru-kshetra, the famous battlefield of the epic *Mahábhárata*; they had already fused with the Panchala tribe and formed the Kuru-Panchala nation in Madhyadesa, the "Middle Country", the home of Brahmanic culture, the birthplace of the famous old *Upanishads*.

The Bharatas, and their priestly aristocracy of Tritsus, the Vasishthas, appear to have joined the Kuru-Panchala confederacy about the time that the *Brahmanas* were being composed, and these were probably influenced by the ritualistic practices of the Vasishthas. There are references to Agni of the Bharatas, and a goddess Bharati is mentioned in connection with the Saraswati river.

It appears highly probable that the Bharatas and the Kuru-Panchalas represent late invasions of peoples who displaced the earlier Aryan settlers in Hindustan. Among the enemies of the invaders were the Kasis, a tribe which became associated with Benares. It is not possible to prove the theory that this people had any connection with the Kassites who established a Dynasty at Babylon. The Kassites are believed to be identical with the Cossæi of later times, who were settled between Babylon and the Median highlands. Some think the Kassites came from Asia Minor after the Hittite raid on Babylon, if the Kassites, as Hittite allies, were not the actual raiders. The fact that the Maltese cross, which is found on

Elamite neolithic pottery, first appears on Babylonian seals during the Kassite Dynasty, suggests, however, that the Kassites came from the east and not the west, with the horse, called in Babylon "the ass of the east".

The great epic *Mahábhárata*, "the Iliad of India", may have been founded on the hero songs which celebrated the Aryan tribal wars in India. Its action is centred in Kuru-kshetra, "the country of the Kurus", in which the Bharatas had settled. Two rival families contend for supremacy; these are the Kauravas (the Kurus) and the Pandavas who are supported by the Panchalas and others. The Pandavas and Kauravas are cousins and the descendants of the eponymous King Bharata. In the royal family tree the tribal names of Kuru and Puru appear as names of kings.

A popular rendering is given in several chapters which follow of the epic narrative embedded in the *Mahábhárata*, which is about eight times as long as the *Iliad* and *Odyssey* combined. This monumental work is divided into eighteen books; a supplementary nineteenth book alone exceeds in length the two famous Greek epics.

As we have stated, the *Mahábhárata* had its origin as an epic prior to B.C. 500. It was added to from time to time until it assumed its present great bulk. The kernel of the narrative, however, which appears to have dealt with the early wars between the Kurus and Panchalas, must be placed beyond B.C. 1000.

Our narrative begins with the romantic stories which gathered round the names of the legendary ancestors of the Kauravas and the Pandavas. The sympathies of the Brahmanic compilers are with the latter, who are symbolized as "a vast tree formed of religion and virtue", while their opponents are "a great tree formed of passion".

CHAPTER IX

Prelude to the Great Bharata War

Dushyanta and Shakuntala—Romantic Wooing—Birth of Bharata—Shakuntala's Appeal—Her Claim vindicated—King Bharata's Reign—King Hastin and King Kuru—King Shantanu's Bride a Goddess—Seven Babes drowned—Story of Satyavati—Vyasa, Poet and Sage—Bhishma's Terrible Vow—Fisher Girl becomes Queen—Marriage by Capture—A Childless King—Origin of Dhritarashtra, Pandu, and Vidura.

Now the sire of the great King Bharata[1] was royal Dushyanta of the lunar race, the descendant of Atri, the Deva-rishi, and of Soma, the moon; his mother was beautiful Shakuntala, the hermit maiden, and daughter of a nymph from the celestial regions. And first be it told of the wooing of Shakuntala and the strange childhood of her mighty son.

One day King Dushyanta, that tiger among men, went forth from his stately palace to go a-hunting with a great host and many horses and elephants. He entered a deep jungle and there slew numerous wild animals; his arrows wounded tigers at a distance; he felled those that came near with his great sword. Lions fled from before him, wild elephants stampeded in terror, deer sought to escape hastily, and birds rose in the air uttering cries of distress.

The king, attended by a single follower, pursued a deer across a desert plain, and entered a beautiful forest

[1] *Pron.* bah'ra-ta or bhah'ra-ta.

which delighted his heart, for it was deep and shady, and was cooled by soft winds; sweet-throated birds sang in the branches, and all round about there were blossoming trees and blushing flowers; he heard the soft notes of the kokila[1], and beheld many a green bower carpeted with grass and canopied by many-coloured creepers.

Dushyanta, abandoning the chase, wandered on until he came to a delightful and secluded hermitage, where he saw the sacred fire of that austere and high-souled Brahman, the saintly Kanva. It was a scene of peace and beauty. Blossoms from the trees covered the ground; tall were the trunks, and the branches were far-sweeping. A silvery stream went past, breaking on the banks in milk-white foam; it was the sacred River Malini, studded with green islands, loved by water fowl, and abounding with fish.

Then the king was taken with desire to visit the holy sage, Kanva, he who is without darkness. So he divested himself of his royal insignia and entered the sacred grove alone. Bees were humming; birds trilled their many melodies; he heard the low chanting voices of Brahmans among the trees—those holy men who can take captive all human hearts. . . .

When he reached the abode of Kanva, he wondered to find that it was empty, and called out: "Who is here?" and the forest echoed his voice.

Then came towards him a beautiful black-eyed virgin, clad in a robe of bark. She reverenced the king and said: "What seekest thou? I am thy servant."

Said the royal Dushyanta to the maiden of faultless form and gentle voice: "I have come to honour the wise and blessed Kanva. Tell me, O fair and amiable one, whither he hath gone?"

[1] The Indian cuckoo.

The maiden answered: "My illustrious sire is gathering herbs, but if thou wilt tarry he will return ere long."

Dushyanta was entranced by the beauty and sweet smiles of the gentle girl, and his heart was moved towards her, for she was in the bloom of youth. So he spake, saying: "Who art thou, O fairest one? Whence comest thou, and why dost thou wander alone in the woods? O comely maiden, thou hast taken captive my heart."

The bright-eyed one made answer: "I am the daughter of the holy and high-souled Kanva, the ever-wise and ever-constant."

Said the king: "But Kanva is chaste and austere and hath ever been a celibate, nor can he have broken his rigid vow. How came it that thou wert born the daughter of such a one?"

Then the maiden, who was named Shakuntala, because that the birds (shakunta) had nursed her, revealed unto the king the secret of her birth. Her real sire was Vishwamitra[1], the holy sage who had been a Kshatriya and was made a Brahman in reward for his austerities. It came to pass that Indra became alarmed at his growing power, and he feared that the mighty sage of blazing energy would, by reason of his penances, cast down even him, the king of the gods, from his heavenly seat. So Indra commanded Menaka, the beauteous Ap'sara, to disturb the holy meditations of the sage, for he had already achieved such power that he created a second world and many stars. The nymph called on the wind god and on the god of love, and they went with her towards Vishwamitra.

Menaka danced before the brooding sage; then the

[1] *Pron.* vish-wah-mit'ra.

wind god snatched away her moon-white garments, and the love god shot his arrows at Vishwamitra, whereupon that saintly man was stricken with love for the nymph of peerless beauty, and he wooed her and won her as his bride. So was he diverted from his austerities. In time Menaka became the mother of a girl babe, whom she cast away on the river bank.

Now the forest was full of lions and tigers, but vultures gathered round the infant and protected her from harm. Then Kanva found and took pity on the child; he said: "She will be mine own daughter."

Said Shakuntala: "O king, I was that child who was abandoned by the nymph, and now thou dost know how Kanva came to be my sire."

The king said: "Blessed are thy words, O princess. Thou art of royal birth. Be thou my bride, O beautiful maid, and thou wilt have garlands of gold and golden ear-rings and white pearls and rich robes; my kingdom also will be thine, O timid one; wed thou me in Gandharva mode, which of all marriages is the best."[1]

Then Shakuntala promised to be the king's bride, on condition that he would choose her son as the heir to his throne.

"As thou desirest, so let it be," said Dushyanta. And the fair one became his bride.

Ere Dushyanta went away he promised Shakuntala that he would send a mighty host to escort her to his palace.

When Kanva returned, the maiden did not leave her hiding-place to greet him; but he searched out and found her, and he read her heart. "Thou hast not broken the law," he said. "Dushyanta, thine husband, is noble and

[1] The Gandharva marriage was legalized by Manu, but only for members of the Kshatriya (kings and warriors) caste.

true, and a son will be born unto thee who will achieve great renown."

In time fair Shakuntala became the mother of a comely boy, and the wheel mark[1] was on his hands. He grew to be strong and brave, and when but six years old he sported with young lions, for he was suckled by a lioness; he rode on the backs of lions and tigers and wild boars in the midst of the forest. He was called All-tamer, because that he tamed everything.

Now when Kanva perceived that the boy was of unequalled prowess, he spake to Shakuntala and said: "The time hath come when he must be anointed as heir to the throne." So he bade his disciples to escort mother and son unto the city of Gajasahvaya[2], where Dushyanta had his royal palace.

So it came that Shakuntala once again stood before the king, and she said unto him: "Lo! I have brought unto thee this thy son, O Dushyanta. Fulfil the promise thou didst make aforetime, and let him be anointed as thine heir."

Dushyanta had no pleasure in her words, and made answer: "I have no memory of thee. Who are thou and whence cometh thou, O wicked hermit woman? I never took thee for wife, nor care I whether thou art to linger here or to depart speedily."

Stunned by his cold answer, the sorrowing Shakuntala stood there like a log. . . . Soon her eyes became red as copper and her lips trembled; she cast burning glances at the monarch. For a time she was silent; then she exclaimed with fervour: "O king without shame, well dost thou know who I am. Why wilt thou deny knowledge of me as if thou wert but an inferior person? Thy heart is a witness against thee. Be not a robber of thine

[1] A sign of martial and royal origin.

[2] *Pron.* Gaj-as-ah-va'ya.

own affections. . . . The gods behold everything: naught is hidden from them; verily, they will not bless one who doth degrade himself by speaking falsely regarding himself. Spurn not the mother of thy son; spurn not thy faithful wife. A true wife beareth a son; she is the first of friends and the source of salvation; she enables her husband to perform religious acts, her sweet speeches bring him joy; she is a solace and a comforter in sickness and in sorrow; she is a companion in this world and the next. If a husband dies, a wife follows soon afterwards; if she is gone before, she waiteth for her husband in heaven. She is the mother of the son who performs the funeral rite to secure everlasting bliss for his sire, rescuing him from the hell called Put. Therefore a man should reverence the mother of his son, and look upon his son as if he beheld his own self in a mirror, rejoicing the while as if he had found heaven. . . . Why, O king, dost thou spurn thine own child? Even the ants will protect their eggs; strangers far from home take the children of others on their knees to be made happy, but thou hast no compassion for this child, although he is thy son, thine own image. . . . Alas! what sin did I commit in my former state that I should have been deserted by my parents and now by thee! . . . If I must go hence, take thou thy son to thy bosom, O king."

Said Dushyanta: "It has been well said that all women are liars. Who will believe thee? I know naught regarding thee or thy son. . . . Begone! O wicked woman, for thou art without shame."

Shakuntala made answer, speaking boldly and without fear: "O king, thou canst perceive the shortcomings of others, although they may be as small as mustard seeds; thou art blind to thine own sins, although they may be big as Vilwa fruit. As the swine loveth dirt even in a flower garden, so do the wicked perceive evil in all that the good relate. Honest men refrain from speaking ill of others: the wicked rejoice in scandal. O king! truth is the chief of all virtues. Truth is God himself. Do not break thy vow of truth: let truth be ever a part of thee. But if thou wouldst rather be false, I must needs depart, for, verily, such a one as thee should be avoided. . . . Yet know now, O Dushyanta, that when thou art gone, my son will be king of this world, which is surrounded by the four seas and adorned by the monarch of mountains."

Shakuntala then turned from the king, but a voice out of heaven spoke softly down the wind, saying:

"*Shakuntala hath uttered what is true. Therefore, O Dushyanta, cherish thy son, and because thou wilt cherish him by command of the gods, let his name be Bharata ('the cherished').*"

When the king heard these words, he spoke to his counsellors and said: "The celestial messenger hath spoken. . . . Had I welcomed this my son by pledge of Shakuntala alone, men would suspect the truth of her words and doubt his royal birth."

Thereafter Dushyanta embraced his son and kissed him, and he honoured Shakuntala as his chief rani[1]; he said to her, soothingly: "From all men have I concealed our union; and for the sake of thine own good name I hesitated to acknowledge thee. Forgive my harsh words, as I forgive thine. Thou didst speak passionately because thou lovest me well, O great-eyed and fair one, whom I love also."

The son of Shakuntala was then anointed as heir to the throne, and he was named Bharata.[2]

[1] Queen.

[2] This story is the plot of "Shakuntala", the Sanskrit drama of the poet Kalidasa,

When Dushyanta died, Bharata became king. Great was his fame, as befitted a descendant of Chandra.[1] He was a mighty warrior, and none could withstand him in battle; he made great conquests, and extended his kingdom all over Hindustan, which was called Bharatavarsha.[2]

King Bharata was the sire of King Hastin, who built the great city of Hastinapur; King Hastin begot King Kuru, and King Kuru begot King Shantanu.

Be it told of the King Shantanu that he was pious and just and all-powerful, as was meet for the great grandson of King Bharata. His first wife was the goddess Ganga of the Ganges river, and she was divinely beautiful like to her kind. Ere she assumed human form for a time, there came to her the eight Vasus, the attendants of Indra. It chanced that when the Brahman Vasishtha was engaged in his holy meditations the Vasus flew between him and the sun, whereupon the angered sage cursed them, saying: "Be born among men!" Nor could they escape this fate, so great was the Rishi's power over celestial beings. So they hastened to Ganga, and she consented to become their human mother, promising that she would cast them one by one into the Ganges soon after birth, so that they might return speedily to their celestial state. For this service Ganga made each of the Vasus promise to confer an eighth part of his power on her son, who, according to her desire, should remain among men for many years, but would never marry or have offspring.

who lived in the fifth century A.D. He makes the king give the heroine a ring, which she loses while bathing. A fish swallows the ring, and it is found by a fisherman, who delivers it to the king. Then suddenly His Majesty remembers his bride, whom he had forgotten and already denied. The misfortunes of the monarch and maid resulted from the curse of the sage Durvasas. *Pron.* Sha-koon'-ta-lah.

[1] *Pron.* chun'dra ("ch" as in "change"). Also Soma, the moon god.

[2] Subsequently the name for India as a whole.

2

SHANTANU MEETS THE GODDESS GANGA

From the painting by Warwick Goble

A day came thereafter when King Shantanu walked beside the Ganges. Suddenly there appeared before him a maiden of surpassing beauty. She was Ganga in human form. Her celestial garments had the splendour of lotus blooms; she was adorned with rare ornaments, and her teeth were radiant as pearls. The king was silenced by her charms, and gazed upon her steadfastly . . . In time he perceived that the maiden regarded him with love-lorn eyes, as if she sought to look upon him for ever, and he spoke to her, saying: "O slender-waisted and fair one, art thou one of the Danavas, or art thou of the race of Gandharvas, or art thou of the Apsaras; art thou one of the Yakshas or Nagas,[1] or art thou of human kind, O peerless and faultless one? Be thou my bride."

The goddess made answer that she would wed the king, but said she must needs at once depart from him if he spoke harshly to her at any time, or attempted to thwart her in doing as she willed. Shantanu consented to her terms, and Ganga became his bride.

In time the goddess gave birth to a son, but soon afterwards she cast him into the Ganges, saying: "This for thy welfare."

The king was stricken with horror, but he spake not a word to his beautiful bride lest she should leave him.

So were seven babes, one after another, destroyed by their mother in like manner. When the eighth was born, the goddess sought to drown him also; but the king's pent-up wrath broke forth in a torrent of speech, and he upbraided his heartless wife. Thus was his marriage vow broken, and Ganga given power to depart unto her own place. But ere she went she revealed unto the king who she was, and also why she had cast the Vasus, her children, into the Ganges. Then she

[1] Art thou a demon or nymph or fairy or dwarf or demi-god?

suddenly vanished from before his eyes, taking the last babe with her.

Ere long the fair goddess returned to Shantanu for a brief space, and she brought with her for the king a fair and noble son, who was endowed with the virtues of the Vasus. Then she departed never to come again. The heart of Shantanu was moved towards the child, who became a comely and powerful youth, and was named Satanava.[1]

When Shantanu had grown old, he sought to marry a young and beautiful bride whom he loved. For one day as he walked beside the Jumna river he was attracted by a sweet and alluring perfume, which drew him through the trees until he beheld a maiden of celestial beauty with luminous black eyes.[2] The king spake to her and said: "Who art thou, and whose daughter, O timid one? What doest thou here?"

Said the maiden, blessing Shantanu: "I am the daughter of a fisherman, and I ferry passengers across the river in my boat."

Now, the name of this fair maiden was Satyavati.[3] Like Shakuntala, she was of miraculous origin, and had been adopted by her reputed sire. It chanced that a fish once carried away in its stomach two unborn babes, a girl and a boy, whose father was a great rajah. This fish was caught by a fisherman, who opened it and found the children. He sent the manchild unto the rajah and kept the girl, who was reared as his own daughter. She grew to be comely and fair, but a fishy odour ever clung to her.

[1] His other names are Deva-bratta and Ganga-bratta, and he was ultimately known as Bhishma.

[2] The Pharaoh of the Anpu-Bata Egyptian story was similarly attracted by a perfume which issued from a lock of hair. See *Egyptian Myth and Legend*.

[3] *Pron.* sat'ya-vat-ee.

One day, as she ferried pilgrims across the Jumna, there entered her boat alone the high and pious Brahman Parashara, who was moved by the maiden's great beauty. He desired that she should become the mother of his son, and promised that ever afterwards an alluring perfume would emanate from her body. He then caused a cloud to fall upon the boat, and it vanished from sight.

When the fisher girl became the mother of a son, he grew suddenly before her eyes, and in a brief space was a man. His name was Vyasa[1]; he bade his mother farewell, and hastened to the depths of a forest to spend his days in holy meditation. Ere he departed he said unto Satyavati: "If ever thou hast need of me, think of me, and I shall come to thine aid."

When this wonder had been accomplished, Satyavati became a virgin again through the power of the great sage Parashara, and a delicious odour lingered about her ever afterwards.

On this maiden King Shantanu gazed with love. Then he sought the fisherman, and said he desired the maiden to be his bride. But the man refused to give his daughter to the king in marriage until he promised that her son should be chosen as heir to the throne. Shantanu could not consent to disinherit Satanava, son of Ganga, and went away with a heavy heart.

Greatly the king sorrowed in his heart because of his love for the dark-eyed maiden, and at length Satanava was given his secret. Then that noble son of Ganga went to search for the beautiful daughter of the fisherman, and he found her. The fisherman said unto him, when he had made known his mission: "If Satyavati bears sons, they will not inherit the kingdom, for the king hath already a son, and he will succeed him."

[1] *Pron.* vyas'a (two syllables). The reputed author of the *Mahá-bhárata.*

Satanava thereupon made a vow renouncing his claim to the throne, and said: "If thou wilt give thy daughter unto my sire to be his queen, I, who am his heir, will never accept the throne, nor marry a wife, or be the father of children. If, then, Satyavati will become the mother of a son, he will surely be chosen rajah." When he had spoken thus, the gods and Apsaras, the mist fairies, caused flowers to fall out of heaven upon the prince's head, and a voice came down the wind, saying: "*This one is Bhishma.*"

So from that day the son of Ganga was called Bhishma, which signifies the "Terrible", for the vow that he had taken was terrible indeed.

Then was Satyavati given in marriage to the king, and she bore him two sons, who were named Chitrangada and Vichitra-virya.[1]

In time Santanu sank under the burden of his years, and his soul departed from his body. Unto Bhishma was left the care of the queen-mother, Satyavati, and the two princes.

When the days of mourning went past, Bhishma renounced the throne in accordance with his vow, and Chitrangada was proclaimed king. This youth was a haughty ruler, and his reign was brief. He waged war against the Gandhari of the hills[2] for three years, and was slain in battle by their rajah. Then Bhishma placed Vichitra-virya on the throne, and, as he was but a boy, Bhishma ruled as regent for some years.

At length the time came for the young king to marry, and Bhishma set out to find wives for him. It chanced

[1] *Pron.* chit-ran'gad-a ("ch" as in "change") *and* vi-cheet'ra-veer-ya.

[2] An Aryan tribe in the north-west of India. Part of their territory was included in the Persian empire. Keith identifies them with the Gandarians who accompanied Xerxes in his campaign against the Greeks.

that the King of Kasi (Benares) had three fair daughters whose swayamvara[1] was being proclaimed. When Bhishma was told of this he at once entered his chariot and drove from Hastinapur[2] to Kasi to discover if the girls were worthy of the monarch of Bharatavarsha. He found that they had great beauty, and he was well pleased thereat. The great city was thronged with rajahs who had gathered from far and near to woo the maidens, but Bhishma would not tarry until the day of the swayamvara. He immediately seized the king's fair daughters and placed them in his chariot. Then he challenged the assembled rajahs and sons of rajahs in a voice like thunder, saying:

"The sages have decreed that a king may give his daughter with many gifts unto one he has invited when she hath chosen him. Others may barter their daughters for two kine, and some may give them in exchange for gold. But maidens may also be taken captive. They may be married by consent, or forced to consent, or be obtained by sanction of their sires. Some are given wives as reward for performing sacrifices, a form approved by the sages. Kings ever favour the swayamvara, and obtain wives according to its rules. But learned men have declared that the wife who is to be most highly esteemed is she who is taken captive after battle with the royal guests who attend a swayamvara. Hear and know, then, ye mighty rajahs, I will carry off these fair daughters of the king of Kasi, and I challenge all who are here to overcome me or else be overcome themselves by me in battle."

The royal guests who were there accepted the chal-

[1] A festival at which a princess selected a husband from among the kings and warriors assembled together.

[2] A drive of about 500 miles. Indian poets, however, have never troubled about geographical difficulties.

lenge, and Bhishma fought against them with great fury. Bows were bent and ten thousand arrows were discharged against him, but he broke their flight with innumerable darts from his own mighty bow. Strong and brave was he indeed; there was none who could overcome him; he fought and conquered all, until not a rajah was left to contend against him.[1]

Thus did Bhishma, the terrible son of the ocean-going Ganga, take captive after battle the three fair daughters of the King of Kasi; and he drove away with them in his chariot towards Hastinapur.[2]

When he reached the royal palace he presented the maidens unto Queen Satyavati, who was well pleased, and at once gave many costly gifts to Bhishma. She decided that the captives should become the wives of her son, King Vichitra-virya.

Ere the wedding ceremony was held, the eldest maiden, whose name was Amba, pleaded with the queen to be set free, saying:

"I have been betrothed already by my sire unto the Rajah of Sanva. Oh, send me unto him now, for I cannot marry a second time."

Her prayer was granted, and Bhishma sent her with an escort unto the Rajah of Sanva. Then the fair Amba related unto him how she had been taken captive; but the rajah exclaimed, with anger: "Thou hast already dwelt in the house of a strange man, and I cannot take thee for my wife."

The maiden wept bitterly, and she knelt before the monarch and said: "No man hath wronged me, O

[1] The Kasi tribe was Aryan but was disliked by the eastern Aryans because its beliefs were not according to the standards imposed by the Brahmans. Conflicts were frequent.

[2] *Pron.* has-teen'a-poor. Marriage by capture was called a Rákshas marriage, and was sanctioned by Manu.

mighty rajah. Bhishma hath taken a terrible vow of celibacy which he cannot break. If thou wilt not have me for wife, I pray thee to take me as thy concubine, so that I may dwell safely in thy palace."

But the rajah spurned the beautiful maiden, and his servants drove her from the palace and out of the city. So was she compelled to seek refuge in the lonely forest, and there she practised great austerities with purpose to secure power to slay Bhishma, who had wronged her. In the end she threw herself upon a pyre, so that she might attain her desire in the next life.[1]

Her two sisters, Amvika and Amvalika, became the wives of Vitchitra-virya, who loved them well; but his days were brief, and he wasted away with sickness until at length he died. No children were born to the king, and his two widows mourned for him.

The heart of Queen Satyavati was stricken with grief because that her two sons were dead, and there was left no heir to the throne of King Bharata.

Now it was the custom in those days that a kinsman should become the father of children to succeed the dead king.[2] So Queen Satyavati spake unto Bhishma, saying: "Take thou the widows of my son and raise up sons who will be as sons of the king."

But Bhishma said: "That I cannot do, for have I not vowed never to be the sire of any children."

In her despair Satyavati then thought of her son Vyasa, and he immediately appeared before her and consented to do as was her desire.[3]

Now Vyasa was a mighty sage, but, by reason of his

[1] She helps to kill Bhishma in the great war, having changed her sex with a Yaksha.

[2] A similar practice is referred to in Genesis xxxviii; it was a regular institution among the ancient Hebrews.

[3] This custom is called "niyoga", and was legalized by Manu, but only for the lower castes.

austerities in his lonely jungle dwelling, he had grown gaunt and repulsive of aspect so that women shrank from before him; fearsome was he, indeed, to look upon.

Amvika closed her eyes with horror when she beheld the sage, and she had a son who was born blind: he was named Dhritarashtra. Amvalika turned pale with fear: she had a son who was named Pandu, "the pale one".

Satyavati desired that Vyasa should be the father of a son who had no defect; but Amvika sent her handmaiden unto him, and she bore a son who was called Vidura. As it happened, Dharma, god of justice, was put under the spell of a Rishi at this time, to be born among men, and he chose Vidura to be his human incarnation.

The three children were reared by Bhishma, who was regent over the kingdom, and was yet subject to Queen Satyavati. He taught them the laws and trained them as warriors. When the time came to select a king, Dhritarashtra[1] was passed over because that he was blind, and Vidura because of his humble birth, and Pandu, "the pale one", was set upon the throne.

[1] *Pron.* dreet'a-rash"tra, Pan'doo, *and* Ve-dur'a ("u" as "oo").

CHAPTER X

Royal Rivals: the Pandavas and Kauravas[1]

King Pandu's Two Wives—Pritha and the Sun God—Birth of Karna—The Indian Moses—Babe rescued from Floating Cradle—Pandu slays Brahman in Deer Guise—His Doom pronounced—Queen burned on King's Pyre—Blind Brother becomes Rajah—The Rival Princes—Attempt to kill Bhima—His Visit to the Underworld—The Draught of Strength—Drona, Preceptor of Princes—His Royal Rival Draupada—Training of Young Warriors—The Faithful Bhil Prince—His Sacrifice.

King Pandu became a mighty monarch, and was renowned as a warrior and a just ruler of his kingdom. He married two wives: Pritha, who was chief rani, and Madri[2], whom he loved best.

Now Pritha was of celestial origin, for her mother was a nymph; her father was a holy Brahman, and her brother, Vasudeva, was the father of Krishna.[3] When but a babe she had been adopted by the Rajah of Shurasena, whose kingdom was among the Vindhya mountains. She was of pious heart, and ever showed reverence towards holy men. Once there came to the palace the great Rishi Durvasas, and she ministered unto him faithfully by serving food at any hour he desired, and by kindling the sacred fire in the sacrificial chamber. After his stay, which was in length a full year, Durvasas, in reward for her services, imparted to Pritha a powerful charm[4], by

[1] *Pron.* pan'davas *and* kow'ravas.

[2] *Pron.* pree'tha *and* ma-dree'.

[3] Krishna of the Yadavas was descended from the moon through Yadu: Bharata was descended through Puru, Yadu's brother.

[4] A *mantra.*

virtue of which she could compel the love of a celestial being. One day she had a vision of Surya, god of the sun; she muttered the charm, and received him when he drew nigh in the attire of a rajah, wearing the celestial ear-rings. In secret she became in time the mother of his son, Karna, who was equipped at birth with celestial ear-rings and an invulnerable coat of mail, which had power to grow as the wearer increased in stature. The child had the eyes of a lion and the shoulders of a bull.

In her maidenly shame Pritha resolved to conceal her new-born babe. So she wrapped him in soft sheets and, laying under his head a costly pillow, placed him in a basket of wicker-work which she had smeared over with wax. Then, weeping bitterly, she set the basket afloat on the river, saying: "O my babe, be thou protected by all who are on land, and in the water, and in the sky, and in the celestial regions! May all who see thee love thee! May Varuna, god of the waters, shield thee from harm: May thy father, the sun, give thee warmth! . . . I shall know thee in days to come, wherever thou mayst be, by thy coat of golden mail. . . . She who will find thee and adopt thee will be surely blessed. . . . O my son, she who will cherish thee will behold thee in youthful prime like to a maned lion in Himalayan forests."

The basket drifted down the River Aswa until it was no longer seen by that lotus-eyed damsel, and at length it reached the Jumna; the Jumna gave it to the Ganges, and by that great and holy river it was borne unto the country of Anga. . . . The child, lying in soft slumber, was kept alive by reason of the virtues possessed by the celestial armour and the ear-rings.

Now there was a woman of Anga who was named Radha, and she had peerless beauty. Her husband was Shatananda, the charioteer. Both husband and wife had for long sorrowed greatly because that they could not obtain a son. One day, however, their wish was gratified. It chanced that Radha went down to the river bank, and she beheld the basket drifting on the waves. She caused it to be brought ashore; and when it was uncovered, she gazed with wonder upon a sleeping babe who was as fair as the morning sun. Her heart was immediately filled with great gladness, and she cried out: "The gods have heard me at length, and they have sent unto me a son." So she adopted the babe and cherished him. And the years went past, and Karna grew up and became a powerful youth and a mighty bowman.

Pritha, who was comely to behold, chose King Pandu at her swayamvara. Trembling with love, she placed the flower garland upon his shoulders.

Madri came from the country of Madra[1], and was black-eyed and dusky-complexioned. She had been purchased by Bhishma for the king with much gold, many jewels and elephants and horses, as was the marriage custom among her people.

The glories of King Bharata's reign were revived by Pandu, who achieved great conquests and extended his territory. He loved well to go a-hunting, and at length he retired to the Himalaya mountains with his two wives to pursue and slay deer. There, as fate had decreed, he met with dire misfortune. One day he shot arrows at two deer which he beheld sporting together; but they were, as he discovered to his sorrow, a holy Brahman and his wife in animal guise. The sage was wounded mortally, and ere he died he assumed his wonted form, and foretold that Pandu, whom he cursed, would die in the arms of one of his wives.

The king was stricken with fear; he immediately took

[1] Identified with Cashmere by some of the authorities.

vows of celibacy, and gave all his possessions to Brahmans; then he went away to live in a solitary place with his two wives.

Some have told that Pandu never had children of his own, and that the gods were the fathers of his wives' great sons. Pritha was mother of Yudhishthira[1], son of Dharma, god of justice, and of Bhima, son of Vayu, the wind god, and also of Arjuna[2], son of mighty Indra, monarch of heaven. Madri received from Pritha the charm which Durvasas had given her, and she became the mother of Nakula and Sahadeva, whose sires were the twin Aswins, sons of Surya, the sun god. These five princes were known as the Pandava brothers.

King Pandu was followed by his doom. One day, as it chanced, he met with Madri, his favourite wife; they wandered together in a forest, and when he clasped her in his arms he immediately fell dead as the Brahman had foretold.

His sons, the Pandava brothers, built his funeral pyre, so that his soul might pass to heaven. Both Pritha and Madri desired to be burned with him, and they debated together which of them should follow her lord to the region of the dead.

Said Pritha: "I must go hence with my lord. I was his first wife and chief rani. O Madri, yield me his body and rear our children together. O let me achieve what must be achieved."

Madri said: "Speak not so, for I should be the chosen one. I was King Pandu's favourite wife, and he died because that he loved me. O sister, if I survived thee I should not be able to rear our children as thou canst rear them. Do not refuse thy sanction to this which is dear unto my heart."

[1] *Pron.* yoo-dish'thi-ra (*h* sounded after *t*). [2] *Pron.* arjoo'na".

So they held dispute, nor could agree; but the Brahmans, who heard them, said that Madri must be burned with King Pandu, having been his favourite wife. And so it came to pass that Madri laid herself on the pyre, and she passed in flames with her beloved lord, that bull among men.

Meanwhile King Pandu's blind brother, Dhritarashtra, had ascended the throne to reign over the kingdom of Bharatavarsha, with Bhishma as his regent, until the elder of the young princes should come of age.

Dhritarashtra had taken for wife fair Gándhári, daughter of the Rajah of Gándhára. When she was betrothed she went unto the king with eyes blindfolded, and ever afterwards she so appeared in his presence. She became the mother of a hundred sons, the eldest of whom was Duryodhana. These were the princes who were named the Kauravas, after the country of Kuru-jangala.[1]

The widowed Pritha returned to Hastinapur with her three sons and the two sons of Madri also. When she told unto Dhritarashtra that Pandu his brother had died, he wept and mourned greatly; then he bathed in holy waters and poured forth the funeral oblation. The blind king gave his protection to the five princes who were Pandu's heirs.

So the Pandavas and Kauravas were reared together in the royal palace at Hastinapur. Nor was favour shown to one cousin more than another. The young princes were trained to throw the stone and to cast the noose, and they engaged lustily in wrestling bouts and practised

[1] The upper part of the Punjab, which was ruled over ultimately by the sons of Duryodhana. Another explanation is that the Kauravas, or Kuru brothers, were called after their eponymous ancestor, King Kuru. The Kuru people are believed to be a group of the tribes mentioned in the *Rigveda*. The Kurus may have been latecomers who formed a military aristocracy, and displaced earlier settlers who opposed their rule.

boxing. As they grew up they shared work with the king's men; they marked the young calves, and every three years they counted and branded the cattle. Yet, despite all that could be done, the two families lived at enmity. Of all the young men Bhima[1], of the Pandavas[2], was the most powerful, and Duryodhana[3], the leader of the Kauravas, was jealous of him. Bhima was ever the victor in sports and contests. The Kauravas could ill endure his triumphs, and at length they plotted among themselves to accomplish his death.

It chanced that the young men had gone to dwell in a royal palace on the banks of the Ganges. One day, when they feasted together in the manner of warriors, Duryodhana put poison in the food of Bhima, who soon afterwards fell into a deep swoon and seemed to be dead. Then Duryodhana bound him hand and foot and cast him into the Ganges; his body was swallowed by the waters.

But it was not fated that Bhima should thus perish. As his body sank down, the fierce snakes, which are called Nagas, attacked him; but their poison counteracted the poison he had already swallowed, so that he regained consciousness. Then, bursting his bonds, he scattered the reptiles before him, and they fled in terror.

Bhima found that he had sunk down to the city of serpents, which is in the underworld. Vasuki, king of the Nagas, having heard of his prowess, hastened towards the young warrior, whom he desired greatly to behold.

Bhima was welcomed by Aryaka, the great grandsire of Pritha, who was a dweller in the underworld. He

[1] *Pron.* bhee'ma. [2] The *Mahá-bhárata* favours the Pandavas from the outset.
[3] *Pron.* door-yo'dhan-a.

was loved by Vasuki, who, for Aryaka's sake, offered great gifts to fearless Bhima. But Aryaka chose rather that the lad should be given a draught of strength which contained the virtues of a thousand Nagas. By the king of serpents was this great boon granted, and Bhima was permitted to drain the bowl eight times. He immediately fell into a deep slumber, which continued for the space of eight days. Then he awoke, and the Nagas feasted him ere he returned again unto his mother and his brethren, who were mourning for him the while. Thus it fell that Bhima triumphed over Duryodhana, for ever afterwards he possessed the strength of a mighty giant. He related unto his brothers all that had befallen him, but they counselled him not to reveal his secret unto the Kauravas, his cousins.

About this time the prudent Bhishma deemed that the young men should be trained to bear arms; so he searched far and wide for a preceptor who was at once a warrior and a scholar, a pious and lofty-minded man, and a lover of truth. Such was Drona, the brave and god-adoring son of Bharadwaja. He was well pleased to have care of the princes, and to give them instruction worthy of their rank and martial origin.

Drona had no mother: his miraculous birth was accomplished by a beautiful nymph, and his sire was Bharadwaja, a most pious Brahman. Of similar origin was Drupada[1], son of a rajah named Prishata[2]. Drona and Drupada were reared together like brothers by the wise Bharadwaja, and it was the hope of both sires that their sons would repeat their own lifelong friendship. But when, after happy youth, they grew into manhood, fate parted them. The rajah retired from the throne, and

[1] *Pron.* droo'pa-da. [2] *Pron.* prish'ata.

Drupada ruled the kingdom of Panchala[1]. Bharadwaja died soon afterwards, and Drona married a wife named Kripa, who became the mother of his son Ashwatthama[2]. The child was so named because at birth he uttered a cry like to the neighing of a horse. Drona devoted himself to rearing his son, while he accumulated the wisdom of the sages and performed sacred rites with pious mind like to his holy sire.

When the sage Jamadagni, son of Bhrigu, closed his career, he bestowed his great wealth on the sons of Brahmans. Drona received heavenly weapons and power to wield them. Then he bethought him to visit Drupada, the friend of his youth, and share his inheritance with him.[3]

Drona stood before the rajah and exclaimed: "Behold thy friend."

But Drupada frowned; his eyes reddened with anger, and for a while he sat in silence. At length he spoke haughtily and said:

"Brahman, it is nor wise nor fitting that thou shouldst call me friend. What friendship can there be between a luckless beggar and a mighty rajah? . . . I grant that in youth such a bond united us, one to another, but it has wasted away with the years. Do not think that the friendship of youth endures for ever in human hearts; it is weakened by time, and pride plucks it from one's bosom. Friendship can exist only between equals as we two once were, but no longer chance to be. Hear and know! Rich and poor, wise and ignorant, warriors and cowards, can never be friends; it is for those who are of equal station to exercise mutual esteem. . . . Say, can a

[1] *Pron.* pan-chal'a.

[2] *Pron.* ash-wat-tha'ma. *Aswa*, a horse; *sthama*, sound or strength.

[3] Apparently Drona had a claim to part of the kingdom ruled over by Drupada.

Brahman respect one who is ignorant of the Vedas? Can a warrior do other than despise one who cannot go forth to battle in his rumbling chariot? Say, can a monarch condescend to one who is far beneath him? . . . Begone, then, thou dreamer! Forget the days and the thoughts of the past. . . . I know thee not. . . ."

Drona heard the harsh words of his old friend with mute amaze. For a moment he paused. Then abruptly he turned away, nor spake he in reply. His heart burned with indignation as he hastened out of the city.

In time he reached the city of Hastinapur, and Bhishma bade him welcome. When Drona undertook the training of the princes he said: "I will do as is thy desire, O Bhishma, but on condition that when the young men are become complete warriors they will help me to fight against mine enemy, Drupada, the Rajah of Panchala."

Bhishma gave willing consent to this condition. Thereafter Drona abode with his wife in the royal palace, and his son Ashwatthama was trained with the Pandavas and Kauravas. He became the family priest as well as the instructor of the princes. And ere long the young men were accomplished warriors, and deeply learned in wisdom and in goodness.

Drona took most delight in the Pandavas. Yudhishthira was trained as a spearman, but he was more renowned as a scholar than for feats of arms. Arjuna surpassed all others in warrior skill; he was of noble bearing, and none like him could ride the steed, guide the elephant, or drive the rattling chariot, nor could any other prince withstand his battle charge or oppose him in single combat. He was unequalled with javelin or dart, with battleaxe or mace, and he became the most famous archer of his day. Strong Bhima learned to wield the club, Nakula acquired the secret of taming steeds, and Sahadeva became a mighty swordsman, and acquired great knowledge of astronomy.

Drona trained the Kauravas with diligence also, as well as his own son, who was wise and brave; but among all his pupils he loved Arjuna best, for he was the most modest and the most perfect, the most fearless, and yet the most obedient to his preceptor.

Duryodhana of the Kauravas was jealous of all the Pandavas, and especially of Arjuna.

The fame of Drona as a preceptor was spread far and wide, and the sons of many rajahs and warriors hastened to Hastinapur to be instructed by him. All were welcomed save one, and he was the son of the rajah of the robber Bhils. This young man pleaded that he might be trained as an archer, but without avail. Drona said: "Are not the Bhils highwaymen and cattle-lifters? It would be a sin, indeed, to impart unto one of them great knowledge in the use of weapons."

When he heard these words, the rajah's son was stricken with grief, and he turned homeward. But he resolved to become an accomplished warrior. So he fashioned a clay image of Drona and worshipped it, and wielded the bow before it until his fame as an archer was noised abroad.

One day Drona went forth with the princes to hunt in the Bhil kingdom. Their dog ran through the woods, and it beheld the dark son of the rajah of the Bhils and barked at him. Desiring to display his skill, the young man shot seven arrows into the dog's mouth ere it could be closed, and, moaning and bleeding, the animal returned thus to the princes.

Wondering greatly, the princes searched for the greatly-skilled archer, and found him busy with his bow. They spoke, saying: "Who art thou?" And the Bhil made answer: "I am a pupil of Drona."

When Drona was brought to the place, the young man kissed his feet.

Said the wise preceptor: "If thou art my pupil, I must receive my reward."

The young man made answer: "Command me, and I will give thee whatsoever thou dost desire."

Said Drona: "I should like to have the thumb of thy right hand."

The faithful prince of the Bhils did not hesitate to obey his preceptor; with a cheerful face he severed his thumb from his right hand and gave it to Drona.

After his wound had healed, the young man began to draw his bow with his middle fingers, but found that he had lost his surpassing skill, whereat Arjuna was made happy.

All the other Bhil warriors who trained in archery followed the prince's example and drew the bow with their middle fingers, and this custom prevailed ever afterwards amongst the tribe.

Now when all the Hastinapur princes had become expert warriors, Drona addressed the blind king, as he sat among his counsellors, and said: "O mighty rajah, thy sons and the sons of thy brother Pandu have now attained surpassing skill in arms, and they are fit to enter the battlefield."

Said the king, who was well pleased: "So thy task is finished, O noble son of Bharadwaja? Let now a place be made ready, in accordance with thy desire, so that the princes may display their martial skill in the presence of their peers and the common people."

Then Drona, accompanied by Vidura, the king's

brother, made choice of a wide and level plain on which the Pandavas and Kauravas might perform their mighty feats.

So be it next told of the great tournament on the plain, and of the coming of illustrious Karna.

CHAPTER XI

The Tournament

A Brilliant Assembly—Princes display Feats of Arms—Mimic Warfare —Duryodhana and Bhima—A Fierce Struggle—Arjuna's Wonderful Skill— Despondency of Kauravas—The Coming of Karna—He proves Himself equal to Arjuna—Challenge to Single Combat—The Gods intervene—Queen Pritha's Emotion—Karna taunted with Low Birth—Kauravas make him a King—Joy of his Foster Father—Bitter and Angry Rivals.

On the day of the great tournament, vast multitudes of people from all parts of the kingdom assembled round the barriers on the wide plain. A scene of great splendour was unfolded to their eyes. At dawn many flags and garlands of flowers had been distributed round the enclosure; they adorned the stately royal pavilion, which was agleam with gold and jewels and hung with trophies of war; they fluttered above the side galleries for the lords and the ladies, and even among the clustering trees. White tents for the warriors occupied a broad green space. A great altar had been erected by Drona beside a cool, transparent stream, on which to offer up sacrifices to the gods.

From early morn the murmurous throng awaited the coming of king and counsellors, and royal ladies, and especially the mighty princes who were to display their feats of arms and engage in mimic warfare. The bright sun shone in beauty on that festal day.

The clarion notes of the instruments of war proclaimed the coming of the king. Then entered the royal procession, and blind Dhritarashtra was led towards his throne in the gleaming pavilion. With him came the fair queen Gandhari, mother of the Kauravas, and stately Pritha, widow of King Pandu, the mother of the Pandavas. There followed in their train many high-born dames and numerous sweet maidens renowned for their beauty. When all these ladies, attired in many-coloured robes and glittering with jewels and bright flowers, were mounting the decorated galleries, they seemed like to goddesses and heavenly nymphs ascending to the golden summit of the mountain of Meru. . . . The trumpets were sounding loud, and the clamour which arose from the surging multitude of people of every caste and every age and every tribe was like the voice of heaving ocean in sublime tempest.

Next came venerable and white-haired Drona, robed in white, with white sacrificial cord; his sandals were white, and the garlands he wore were white also. His valiant son, Aswatthama, followed him as the red planet Mars follows the white moon in cloudless heaven. The saintly preceptor advanced to the altar where the priestly choir gathered, and offered up sacrifices to the gods and chanted holy texts.

Then heralds sounded their trumpets as the youthful princes entered in bright array, bejewelled and lightly girded for exercise, their left arms bound with leather. They were wearing breastplates; their quivers were slung from their shoulders, and they carried stately bows and gleaming swords. The princes filed in according to their years, and Yudhishthira came first of all. Each saluted Drona in turn and awaited his commands.

One by one the youthful warriors displayed their skill at arms, while the vast crowd shouted their plaudits. The regent Bhishma, sitting on the right side of the throne, looked down with delight, and Vidura, sitting on the left side, informed the sightless king of all that took place.

The princes shot arrows at targets, first on foot and then mounted on rapid steeds,[1] displaying great skill; they also rode on elephants and in chariots, and their arrows ever flew with unerring aim.

Next they engaged in mimic warfare, charging with chariots and on elephants: swords clamoured on shields, ponderous maces were wielded, and falchions shimmered like to the flashes of lightning. The movements of the princes, mounted and on foot, were rapid and graceful; they were fearless in action and firm-footed, and greatly skilled in thrust and parry.

But ere long the conflict was waged with more than mimic fury. Proud Duryodhana and powerful Bhima had sought one another and were drawn apart from their peers. They towered on the plain with uplifted maces, and they seemed like two rival elephants about to fight for a mate. Then they charged with whirling weapons, and the combat was terrible to behold.

Vidura pictured the conflict to blind Dhritarashtra, as did Pritha also to the blindfolded Queen Gandhari. Round the barriers the multitudes swayed and clamoured, some favouring Duryodhana and others mighty Bhima.

The princes fought on, and their fury increased until at length it seemed that one or the other would be slain. But while yet the issue hung doubtful, Drona, whose brow was troubled, marked with concern the menacing crowd, which was suspended with hope and fear, and seemed like an ocean shaken by fitful gusts of changing wind. Then he interposed, bidding his son to separate the angry combatants so that the turmoil might have end.

[1] Like the Parthians, the ancient Hindus were expert archers on horseback.

The princes heard and obeyed, and they retired slowly like ocean billows, tempest-swollen, falling apart.

To allay excitement, trumpet and drum were sounded aloud. Then white-haired Drona stepped forward, and in a voice like thunder summoned brave Arjuna to come forth.

First of all the valiant hero performed a sacred rite. Thereafter he came before the multitude in all his splendour, clad in golden armour, like to a glorious evening cloud. Modestly he strode, while trumpets blared and the drums bellowed, and he seemed a very god. He was girdled with jewels, and he carried a mighty bow. As the people applauded and shouted his praises, Pritha, his mother, looked down, and tears dropped from her eyes. The blind king spake to Vidura, saying: "Why are the multitudes shouting now like to the tumultuous sea?"

Said Vidura: "The valiant son of Pritha hath come forth in golden armour, and the people hail him with joy."

The blind monarch said: "I am well pleased. The sons of Pritha sanctify the kingdom like to sacrificial fires."

Silence fell upon the people, and Drona bade his favourite pupil to display his skill. Arjuna performed wonders with magic arms; he created fire by the *Agneya* weapon, water by the *Varuna* weapon, wind by the *Vayavya* weapon, clouds by the *Paryanya* weapon, land by the *Bhanma* weapon, and he caused mountains to appear by the *Parvatya* weapon. Then by the *Antardhyana* weapon he caused all these to vanish.[1]

Arjuna then set up for his target an iron image of

[1] This is a notable example of the characteristic exaggerations of late Brahmanical compilers. Other exaggerations are of milder form.

a great boar, and at one bending of the bow he shot five arrows into its gaping jaws. Wondrous was his skill. Next he suspended a cow horn, which swayed constantly in the wind, and discharged into its hollow with unerring aim twenty rapid arrows. Heaven and earth resounded with the plaudits of the people when he leapt into his chariot and discharged clouds of arrows as he was driven speedily round the grounds. Having thus displayed his accomplishments as an archer, he drew his sword, which he wielded so rapidly round and about that the people thought they beheld lightning and heard thunder. Ere he left the field he cast the noose with exceeding great skill, capturing horses and cows and scampering deer at a single throw. Then Drona embraced him, and the people shouted his praises.

Great was the joy of the Pandavas as they rested around Drona like to the stars that gather about the white moon in heaven. The Kauravas were grouped around Aswatthama as the gods gather beside Indra when the giant Daityas threaten to assail high heaven. Duryodhana's heart burned with jealous anger because of the triumph achieved by Arjuna.

Evening came on, and it seemed that the tournament was ended; the crowds began to melt away. Then, of a sudden, a mighty tumult of plaudits broke forth, and the loud din of weapons and clank of armour was heard all over the place. Every eye immediately turned towards the gate, and the warriors and the people beheld approaching an unknown warrior, who shook his weapons so that they rattled loudly.

So came mighty Karna, son of Surya, the sun god, and of Pritha, the mother of the three Pandavas—Arjuna, Bhima, and wise Yudhishthira. He was comely as a shining god, clad in golden armour, and wearing celestial ear-rings. In his right hand he carried a great many-coloured bow; his gleaming falchion was on his thigh. Tall as a cliff he strode forward; he was an elephant in his fury, a lion in his wrath; stately as a palm tree was that tamer of foemen, so fearless and so proud, so dauntless and so self-possessed.

He paused in the centre of the plain and surveyed the people with pride. Stiffly he paid homage to Drona and Kripa. Then he, the eldest son of Pritha, spake to Pritha's youngest son, Arjuna, the brothers being unknown one to another, and he said: "Whatever feats thou hast performed this day with vain boast, Arjuna, these will I accomplish and surpass, if Drona will permit me."

His voice was like to thunder in heaven, and the multitude of people sprang up and uttered cries of wonder. Duryodhana and the other sons of Kuru heard the challenge with glad hearts, but Arjuna remained silent, while his eyes flashed fire.

Then Drona gave the warrior permission to display his skill. Karna was well pleased, and he performed every feat which had given Arjuna fame on that great day.

Duryodhana proclaimed his joy with beaming countenance, and he embraced Karna, whom he hailed as "brother", saying: "I bid thee welcome, thou mighty warrior. Thou hast won the honours of the field. Demand from me whatsoever thou dost desire in this kingdom, and it will be given unto thee."

Said Karna: "Thy word is thy bond, O prince. All I seek is to combat against Arjuna, whom I have equalled so far. Fain would I win the victor's renown."

Duryodhana said: "Thou dost ask for a worthy boon indeed. Be our ally, and let the enemy fear thee."

Arjuna was moved to great wrath, and cried out: "Uninvited chief! Boasting thus, thou wouldst fain be regarded as mine equal, but I will so deal with thee that thou wilt die the death of a braggart who cometh here an unbidden guest, speaking boastfully ere thou art spoken to."

Said Karna, answering proudly and calm: "Waste not words, Arjuna, nor taunt me with coming hither uninvited. The field of combat is free to all warriors; they enter by their valour, and do not await until thou dost call them; they win their places by strength and skill, and their warrant is the sword. Wrathful speech is the weapon of a coward. Do not boast of thy pastimes or be vain of thy bloodless feats. Speak with thine arrows, O Arjuna, until, in Drona's presence, mine will cause all men to wonder, flying towards thee."

Drona was stirred to wrath, and spake to Arjuna, saying: "Canst thou hear him boast in this manner? I give thee leave to fight him here and now."

Arjuna at once strode forward, fully armed, and he was supported by Drona and Bhishma. Duryodhana and his band stood by Karna. Then the two warriors prepared for single combat, but not in mimic warfare.

Thick clouds gathered in the sky; lightning flashed and thunder pealed; the mighty Indra guarded his son Arjuna, who stood in shadow. Surya, the sun god, cast a shaft of light athwart the darkening plain, and Karna's golden armour gleamed bright and fair.

The noble dames looked on, and some praised Arjuna and others praised Karna. Pritha, the mother of both heroes, was alone divided in her love. She knew her firstborn by his voice and noble bearing and by his armour, and her heart was torn with grief to behold the two brothers ready to slay each other. A cloud blinded her eyes, and, uttering a low cry, she swooned where she sat. Vidura sprinkled water on her face, and she was revived. Then she wept bitterly because that she could not reveal the secret of Karna's birth.

Kripa,[1] the foster-brother of Bhishma, performed the duties of herald, and as Arjuna strode forth to combat he proclaimed: "Behold! this is mighty Arjuna, of Bharata's great line, son of Pandu and of Pritha, a prince of valour and worth who will not shrink from battle. Unknown and long-armed chief," he said unto Karna, "declare now thy name and lineage, the royal house thou dost adorn, and the names of thy sire and thy mother. Know thou that by the rules of single combat the sons of kings cannot contend against low-born or nameless rivals."

Karna heard, but was silent. He hung his head like the dew-laden lotus bloom; he could claim nor lineage or high rank, as he believed, for he regarded the charioteer of Anga as his sire.

Duryodhana, perceiving his discomfiture, cried out to Kripa, saying: "Valour is not reckoned by birth but by deeds. Karna hath already shown himself to be the peer of princes. I now proclaim him the Rajah of Anga."

Having spoken thus, the elder of the Kauravas led Karna by the hand and placed him upon a throne, and the red umbrella was held above his head. Brahmans chanted the texts for the ceremony and anointed Karna as a king. Then the fan was waved and the royal umbrella raised on high, while the Kauravas shouted: "The rajah is crowned; blessings on the rajah; honour to the valorous warrior!"

Robed in royal attire, Karna then spake to Duryodhana and said: "With generous heart thou hast conferred upon

[1] Kripa, like Drona, was of miraculous birth. He and his sister were found in a forest, and were adopted by King Shantanu.

me, a kingdom. O prince, speak and say what service thou wouldst have me to render unto thee."

Said Duryodhana: "But one boon do I ask of thee, O king. Be my comrade and, O valiant warrior, be my helper also."

Karna said: "As thou desirest, so be it."

Then Duryodhana and Karna embraced one another to confirm their loyal friendship.

Lo! now a charioteer drew nigh; he was a scantily-clad and wearied old man, and he stooped, leaning heavily upon his staff. He was the aged sire of Karna, and rejoiced in his heart to see his son so highly honoured among princes. Karna cast aside his weapons, knelt down, and kissed the old man's feet. The happy sire embraced the crowned head of the warrior and wept tears of love.

The Pandava brothers gazed upon father and son, amused and scornful. . . . Bhima spake to Karna, saying: "So thou, with such a sire, hast presumed to seek combat with a Pandava! . . . Son of a charioteer, what hast thou to do with weapons of war? Better were it that thou shouldst find thee a goad and drive a bullock-cart behind thy sire."

Karna grew pale with wrath; his lips quivered, but he answered not a word. He heaved a deep sigh and looked towards the sun.

Then Duryodhana arose like a proud elephant and spake to Bhima, saying: "Seek not with insults to give sorrow unto a mighty hero. Taunts come ill from thee, thou tiger-like chief. The proudest warrior may contend against the most humble: a hero is known by his deeds. Of Karna's birth we care naught. Hath Drona other than humble lineage? 'Tis said, too, that thou and thy brethren are not sons of Pandu, but of certain amorous deities. . . . Look upon Karna, adorned with jewels and in golden armour! Do hinds bring forth tigers? . . . Karna was born to be a king; he hath come to rule by reason of his valour and his worth. If any prince or warrior among you will deny my words, hear and know, now, that I will meet him in deadly combat."

The assembled multitude heard these mighty words with joy and shouted loud applause.

But darkness came on, and lamps were lit upon the plain. . . . Drona and the sons of Pandu made offerings at the altar, and the king and his counsellors, the noble dames and the high-born maids, departed in silence to their homes. . . . Then all the people deserted the barriers, some shouting, "Arjuna hath triumphed;" others, "Karna is victor;" and some also, "Duryodhana hath won."

Pritha had rejoiced in her heart to behold her noble son crowned king. . . .

Duryodhana walked by Karna's side and took him away to his own palace, glad of heart, for he no longer feared Arjuna's valour and skill at arms.

Even Yudhishthira doubted Arjuna's worth; he feared that Karna was the greatest hero in the world of men.

CHAPTER XII

First Exile of the Pandavas

Princes' First Campaign—Kauravas driven back—Pandavas achieve Victory—Drupada humbled by Drona—Panchala Kingdom divided—Pandava Prince made "Little Rajah"—Duryodhana's Plot—Pandavas' First Exile—Their New Home—Escape in the Night—Wanderings in the Jungle—Bhima slays a Rakshasa—The Demon Bride—Sojourn in Ekachakra—Story of the Brahman Family—Bhima overcomes the Asura King—Miraculous Birth of Drupada's Children—Swayamvara proclaimed—Pandavas depart to Panchala.

THE Pandavas and Kauravas had now become accomplished warriors, and Drona, their preceptor, claimed his reward. So he spoke unto his pupils and said: "Go forth against Drupada, Rajah of Panchala; smite him in battle and bring him to me."

The cousins could not agree to wage war together by reason of their jealousies. So the Kauravas, led by Duryodhana, were first to attack Drupada; they rode in their chariots and invaded the hostile capital, and slaked their thirst for battle. The warriors of Panchala arose to fight; their shouting was like the roaring of lions, and their arrows were showered as thickly as rain dropping from the clouds. The Kauravas were defeated, and they retired in disorder, uttering cries of despair.

The Pandavas then rushed against the enemies of Drona. Arjuna swept forward in his chariot like to the fire which consumeth all things at the end of time, and he destroyed horses and cars and warriors. The battle-roar of Bhima was like to the roar of ocean stricken by a tempest; wielding his mace, he struck down elephants big as mountains, and many horses and charioteers also, and he covered the ground with rivers of blood; as a herdsman driveth his cattle before him, so did Bhima drive before him with his mace the terror-stricken hosts of Panchala.

Drupada endeavoured to turn the tide of battle; surrounded by his mightiest men, he opposed Arjuna. Then a great uproar arose among the Panchala forces, for as the lion leaps upon the leader of a herd of elephants, so did Arjuna rush against Drupada. A boastful warrior intervened, but the strong Pandava overcame him, and at length, after fierce fighting, Arjuna seized Drupada as Garuda, king of birds,[1] seizeth a mighty snake after disturbing the waters of the ocean.

The remnant of the Panchala host then broke and fled, and the Pandavas began to lay waste the capital. Arjuna, however, cried unto Bhima: "Remember that Drupada is the kinsman of the Kauravas; therefore cease slaying his warriors."[2]

Drupada was led before Drona, who, remembering the proud words of the fallen rajah, spoke and said: "At last I have conquered thy kingdom, and thy life is in my hands. Is it thy desire now to revive our friendship?"

Drona smiled a little and continued thus: "Brahmans are full of forgiveness; therefore have no fear for thy life, O king. I have not forgotten that we were children together. So once again I ask for thy friendship, and I grant thee, unasked, the half of the kingdom; the other half will be mine, and if it pleaseth thee we will be friends."

[1] Half man and half eagle, and enemy of the serpent race.

[2] The Kurus and Panchalas were allies.

Said Drupada: "Thou art indeed noble and great. I thank thee, and desire to be thy friend."

So Drona took possession of half of the kingdom. Drupada, who sorrowed greatly, went to rule the southern Panchalas; he was convinced that he could not defeat Drona by Kshatriya power alone, which is inferior to Brahman power, and he resolved to discover means whereby he might obtain a son who could overcome his Brahman enemy.

Thereafterwards the Pandavas waged war against neighbouring kings, and they extended the territory over which the blind maharajah held sway.

The Kauravas were rendered more jealous than ever by the successes achieved by the Pandavas, and also because the people favoured them. Now Duryodhana desired to become heir to the throne, but the elder prince of the conquering Pandavas could not be set aside. In the end Yudhishthira was chosen, although unwillingly, by the blind king, and he became Yuva-rajah, "Little Rajah", supplanting Bhishma, who had been regent during the minority. Yudhishthira, accordingly, ruled over the kingdom, and he was honoured and beloved by the people; for although he was not a mighty warrior like Arjuna, or powerful like to Bhima, he had great wisdom, and he was ever just and merciful, and a lover of truth.[1]

Duryodhana remonstrated with his blind father, the maharajah, and he spoke to him, saying: "Why, O my father, hast thou thus favoured the Pandavas and forgotten thine own sons? Thou wert Pandu's elder brother, and should have reigned before him. Now the children of thy younger brother are to succeed thee. The kingdom is thine own by right of birth, and thy sons are thine

[1] The modern-day Hindu regards Yudhishthira as an ideal man.

heirs. Why, then, hast thou lowered us in the eyes of thy subjects?"

Said the blind Dhritarashtra: "Duryodhana, my son, know thou that Pandu, my brother, was the mightiest ruler in the world. Could I, who have ever been blind, have set him aside? His sons have great wisdom and worth, and are loved by the people. How, then, could I pass them over? Yudhishthira hath greater accomplishments for governing than thou dost possess, my son. How could I turn against him and banish him from my council?"

Duryodhana said: "I do not acknowledge Yudhishthira's superiority as a ruler of men. And this I know full well, I could combat against half a score of Yudhishthiras on the field of battle. . . . If, my father, thou wilt set me aside and deny me my right to a share of government in the kingdom, I will take mine own life and thus end my sorrow."

Said Dhritarashtra: "Be patient, O my son, nor give way to thy vexation. If such is thy desire, I will divide the kingdom between thee and Yudhishthira, so that no jealousy may exist between you both."

Duryodhana was well pleased, hearing these words, and he said: "I agree, O my father, and will accept thine offer. Let the Pandavas take their own land and rule over it, and I and my brethren will remain at Hastinapur with thee. If the Kauravas and Pandavas continue to dwell here together, there will be conflicts and much shedding of blood."

Said Dhritarashtra: "Neither Bhishma, the head of our family, nor Vidura, my brother, nor Drona, thy preceptor, will consent to the Pandavas being sent hence."

Duryodhana made answer: "Consult them not; they are beneath thee, my sire. Command the Pandavas to depart unto the city of Varanavartha[1] and dwell there; when they have gone no one will speak to thee regarding this matter."

Dhritarashtra listened to his son and followed his counsel. He commanded Yudhishthira to depart with his brethren to the city of Varanavartha, rich in jewels and gold, to dwell there until he recalled them. Accordingly the Pandava brethren bade farewell to Dhritarashtra and left Hastinapur, taking with them their mother, the widowed queen Pritha, and went towards the city of Varanavartha. The people of Hastinapur mourned for them greatly.

Ere they departed, Vidura spoke to them in secret, bidding them to be aware of the perils of fire. He repeated a verse to Yudhishthira and said: "Put thy trust in the man who will recite these words unto thee; he will be thy deliverer."

Now Duryodhana had plotted with Shakuni, the brother of Queen Gandhari, to accomplish the destruction of his kinsmen. Then their ally, Kanika the Brahman, said in secret to Dhritarashtra: "When thine enemy is in thy power, destroy him by whatever means is at thy disposal, in secret or openly. Show him no mercy, nor give him thy protection. If thy son, or brother, or kinsman, or thy father even, should become thine enemy, do not hesitate to slay if thou wouldst have prosperity. Let him be overcome either by spells, or by curses, or by deception, or by payment of money. Do not forget thine enemy, even although thou mayst disdain him."

The maharajah lent a willing ear thereafter to the counsel of his son, whom, in his secret heart, he favoured most.

[1] Allahabad, then probably a frontier town of the area of Aryan control, pronounced Var'an-a-vart"ha.

Ere the Pandavas had left Hastinapur, Duryodhana sent unto Varanavartha his secret agent, Purochana, to erect a commodious new dwelling for them. This was accomplished with all speed, and it became known as the "house of lac". It was built of combustible material: much hemp and resin were packed in the walls and between the floors, and it was plastered over with mortar well mixed with pitch and clarified butter.

Purochana welcomed the Pandavas when they arrived at Varanavartha, and they wondered at the splendour of the great new dwelling. But Yudhishthira smelt the mortar, and he went over the whole house examining it closely; then he said unto Bhima: "The enemy hath caused this mansion to be erected for us, and their trusted workers have done well for them, for it is full of hemp and straw, resin and bamboo, and the mortar is mixed with pitch and clarified butter."

In due time a stranger visited the Pandavas, and he repeated the secret verse which Vidura had communicated to Yudhishthira. He said: "I will construct for you a secret passage underground which will lead to a place of safety, lest you should have to escape from this house when the doors are made secure and it is set on fire."

So the man set to work in secret, and ere long the underground passage was ready. Then Bhima resolved to deal with Purochana in the very manner that he had undertaken to deal with the princes.

One evening Pritha gave a feast in the new dwelling to all the poor people in Varanavartha. When the guests had taken their departure, there remained behind a poor Bhil woman and her five sons, who had drunken heavily, as was the custom of their people, and were unable to rise up. They slumbered on the floor.

A great windstorm had arisen, and the night was dark. So Bhima deemed that the time had come to accomplish his purpose. He went outside and secured the doors of the dwelling of Purochana, which stood beside that of the Pandavas; then he set it on fire. Soon the flames spread towards the new mansion which had been erected according to Duryodhana's desire, and it burned fiercely and speedily. Pritha and her sons made swift escape by the underground passage and took refuge in the jungle. In the morning the people discovered among the embers of Purochana's house the blackened remains of his body and the bodies of his servants. In the ruins of the Pandavas' dwelling they found that a woman and five men had perished, and they lamented, believing that Pritha and her sons were dead. There was great sorrow in Hastinapur when the tidings were borne thither. All the people bewailed the fate of the Pandavas. Bhishma and Vidura wept, and blind Dhritarashtra was moved to tears also. But Duryodhana rejoiced in secret, believing that his enemies had all been destroyed.

The Pandavas, having escaped through the subterranean passage, hastened southwards and entered the forest, which abounded with reptiles and wild animals and with ferocious man-eating Asuras and Rakshasas of gigantic stature. Weary and footsore were they all, and greatly oppressed with sleepiness and fear. At length the mighty Bhima lifted up all the others and hastened on through the darkness: he took his mother on his back, and Madri's sons on his shoulders, and Yudhishthira and Arjuna under his arms. He went swifter than the wind, breaking down trees by his breast and furrowing the ground that he stamped upon. The whole forest was shaken as with fear.

At length the Pandavas, fatigued and athirst and heavy with sleep, found a place to rest in safety; and they all lay down to slumber below a great and beautiful Banyan tree except mighty Bhima, who kept watch over them.

Now there lived in the forest on a Shala tree a ferocious Rakshasa named Hidimva. He was of grim visage and terrible to behold; his eyes were red, and he was red-haired and red-bearded; his cheeks were of cloud colour and his mouth was large, with long, sharp-pointed teeth, which gleamed in darkness; his ears were shaped like to arrows; his neck was broad as a tree, his belly was large, and his legs were of great length.

The monster was exceedingly hungry on that fateful night. Scenting human flesh in the forest, he yawned and scratched his grizzly beard, and spoke to his sister, saying: "I smell excellent food, and my mouth waters; to-night I will devour warm flesh and drink hot, frothy blood. Hasten, now, and bring the sleeping men unto me; we will eat them together, and afterwards dance merrily in the wood."

Then the Rakshasa woman went towards the place where the Pandavas slept. When she beheld Bhima, the long-armed one, clad in royal garments and wearing his jewels, she immediately fell in love with him, and she said to herself: "This man with the shoulders of a lion and eyes like to lotus blooms is worthy to be my husband. I will not slay him for my evil brother."

Now a Rakshasa woman has power to transform herself, and this one at once assumed the shape of a beautiful woman; her face became as fair as the full moon; on her head was a garland of flowers, her hair hung in ringlets; delicate was the hue of her skin, and she wore rich ornaments of gold with many gems. Timidly she approached

Bhima and spoke to him, saying: "O bull among men, who art thou and whence comest thou? Who are these fair ones lying in slumber there? Hear and know that this forest is the abode of the wicked chieftain of the Rakshasas. He is my brother, and hath sent me hither to kill you all for food, but I desire to save thee, O long-armed one. Be thou my husband. I will take thee to a secret place among the mountains, for I can speed through the air at will."

Said Bhima: "I cannot leave my mother and my brethren to become food for a Rakshasa."

The woman said: "Let me be thy servant. Awaken thy mother and thy brethren and I will rescue you all from my fierce brother."

Said Bhima: "I will not awaken them from pleasant and needful slumber, because I do not fear a Rakshasa. O fair one, thou canst go as it pleaseth thee, and I care not if thou dost send thy brother unto me."

Meantime the Rakshasa chieftain had grown impatient. He descended from his tree and hastened after his sister, with gaping mouth and head thrown back. Darkly blue was his body, like to a raincloud.

The Rakshasa woman said to Bhima: "He cometh hither in wrath. Awaken thy kinsfolk, and I will carry you all through the air to escape him."

Said Bhima: "Look on my arms, which are strong as the trunks of elephants; my legs are like iron maces, and my chest is indeed powerful and broad. I will slay this man-eater, thy brother."

The Rakshasa chieftain heard the boast of Bhima, and he fumed with rage when he beheld his sister in comely human guise, and said to her: "I will slay thee and those whom thou wouldst fain help against me." Then he rushed against her, but Bhima cried: "Thou wilt not kill a woman while I am near. I challenge thee to single combat now. This night will thy sister behold thee slain by me as an elephant is slain by a lion."

Said the Rakshasa: "Boast not until thou art the victor. I will kill thee first of all, then thy friends, and last of all my treacherous sister."

Having spoken thus, he rushed towards Bhima, who nimbly seized the monster's outstretched arms and, wrestling violently, cast him on the ground. Then as a lion drags off his prey, Bhima dragged the struggling Rakshasa into the depths of the forest, lest his yells should awaken the sleepers. There they fought together like furious bull elephants, tearing down branches and overthrowing trees.

At length the dread clamour awoke the Pandavas, and they gazed with wonder on the beautiful woman who kept watch in Bhima's place.

Said Pritha: "O celestial being, who art thou? If thou art the goddess of woods or an Apsara, tell me why thou dost linger here?"

The fair demon said: "I am the sister of the chieftain of the Rakshasas, and I was sent hither to slay you all; but when I beheld thy mighty son the love god wounded me, and I chose him for my husband. Then my brother followed angrily, and thy son is fighting with him, and they are filling the forest with their shouting."

All the brethren rushed to Bhima's aid, and they saw the two wrestlers struggling in a cloud of dust, and they appeared like two high cliffs shrouded in mist.

Arjuna cried out: "O Bhima, I am here to help thee. Let me slay the monster."

Bhima answered: "Fear not, but look on. The Rakshasa will not escape from my hands."

Said Arjuna: "Do not keep him alive too long. We

must hasten hence. The dawn is near, and Rakshasas become stronger at daybreak; they exercise their powers of deception during the two twilights. Do not play with him, therefore, but kill him speedily."

At these words Bhima became strong as Vayu, his sire, when he is angered,[1] and, raising aloft the Rakshasa, he whirled him round and round, crying: "In vain hast thou gorged on unholy food. I will rid the forest of thee. No longer wilt thou devour human beings."

Then, dashing the monster to the ground, Bhima seized him by the hair and by the waist, laid him over a knee, and broke his back. So was the Rakshasa slain.

Day was breaking, and Pritha and her sons immediately turned away to leave the forest. The Rakshasa woman followed them, and Bhima cried to her: "Begone! or I will send thee after thy brother."

Said Yudhishthira: "It is unseemly to slay a woman. Besides, she is the sister of that Rakshasa, and even although she became angry, what harm can she do us?"

Kneeling at Pritha's feet, the demon wailed: "O illustrious and blessed lady, thou knowest the sufferings women endure when the love god wounds them. Have pity upon me now, and command thy son to take me for his bride. If he continues to scorn me, I will slay myself. Let me be thy slave, and I will carry you all wheresoever you desire and protect you from perils."

Pritha heard her with compassion, and prevailed upon Bhima to take her for his bride. So the two were married by Yudhishthira; then the Rakshasa took Bhima upon her back and sped through the air to a lonely place among the mountains which is sacred to the gods. They lived together beside silvery streams and lakes sparkling with

[1] The god of wind.

lotus blooms; they wandered through woods of blossoming trees where birds sang sweetly, and by celestial sea-beaches covered with pearls and nuggets of gold. The demon bride had assumed celestial beauty, and ofttimes played sweet music, and she made Bhima happy.

In time the woman became the mother of a mighty son; his eyes were fiercely bright, like arrows were his ears, and his mouth was large; he had copper-brown lips and long, sharp teeth. He grew to be a youth an hour after he was born, but, still remaining bald, his mother named him Ghatotkacha, which signifies "pot-headed".[1]

Bhima then returned to his mother and his brethren with his demon bride and her son. They abode together for a time in the forest; then the Rakshasa bade all the Pandavas farewell and departed with Ghatotkacha, who promised to come to aid the Pandavas whenever they called upon him.

One day thereafter Vyasa appeared before the Pandavas and counselled them to go towards the city of Eka-chakra[2] and to live there for a time in the house of a Brahman. Then he vanished from sight, promising to come again.

The Pandavas went therefore to Eka-chakra and lived with a Brahman who had a wife and a daughter and an infant son. Disguised as holy men, the brethren begged for food as alms. Every evening they brought home what they had obtained, and Pritha divided the whole into two portions; the one half she gave to wolf-bellied Bhima, and the rest she kept for his brethren and herself.

Now the city of Eka-chakra was protected against every enemy by a forest-dwelling Rakshasa named Vaka,

[1] Bald as a pot. *Pron.* gat-ot-katch'a.
[2] *Pron.* eka-chak'ra.

who was king of the Asuras.[1] Each day the people had to supply him with food, which consisted of a cartload of rice, two bullocks, and the man who conveyed the meal to him.

One morning a great wailing broke forth in the Brahman's house because that the holy man was required to supply the demon's feast. He was too poor to purchase a slave, and he said he would deliver himself unto Vaka. "Although I reach Heaven," he cried, "I will have no joy, for my family will perish when I am gone." His wife and his daughter pleaded in turn to take his place, and the three wept together. Then the little boy of tender years plucked a long spear of grass, and with glowing eyes he spoke sweetly and said: "Do not weep, Father; do not weep, Mother; do not weep, Sister. With this spear I will slay the demon who devours human beings."

As they wept there they heard him, nor could forbear smiling.

Pritha was deeply moved by the lamentations of the Brahman family, and she said: "Sorrow not. I will send forth my son Bhima to slay the Asura king."

The Brahman made answer, saying: "That cannot be. Thy sons are Brahmans and are under my protection. If I go forth, I will but obey the rajah; if I send thy son, I will be sin-guilty of his death, for the gods abhor the man who causeth a guest to be slain, or permits a Brahman to perish."

Said Pritha: "Bhima is strong and mighty, nor can a demon do him any harm. He will slay this bloodthirsty Rakshasa and return again in safety. But, O Brahman, thou must not reveal unto anyone who hath performed

[1] As a rule the Asuras are the enemies of the gods and the Rakshasas the enemies of mankind. See Chapter IV.

this mighty deed, lest the people should trouble my son and desire to obtain the secret of his power, for he is skilled in mantras."[1]

Then was the household made happy, and Bhima prepared to go forth. That mighty hero collected the rice and drove the bullocks towards the forest. When he drew nigh to the appointed place, he began to eat the food himself, and called the Rakshasa by name over and over again. Vaka heard and came through the trees towards Bhima. Red were his eyes, and his hair and his beard were red also; his ears were pointed like arrows; he had a mouth like a cave, and his forehead was puckered in three lines. Terrible was he to look upon; his body was huge, indeed.[2]

The Rakshasa saw Bhima eating his meal, and approached angrily, biting his lower lip. "Fool," he cried, "wouldst thou devour my food before my very eyes?"

Bhima smiled, and continued eating with face averted. The demon smote him, but the hero only glanced round as if one had touched his shoulder, and he went on eating as before.

Raging furiously, the Rakshasa tore up a tree, and Bhima rose leisurely and waited until it was flung at him. When that was done, he caught the trunk nimbly and hurled it back. Many trees were uprooted and flung by one at the other. Then Vaka sprung forward to wrestle, but the Pandava overthrew him and dragged

[1] Charms.

[2] A man-devouring demon was supposed to sit under a bridge in Caithness every night. When a late wayfarer began to walk over, the monster growled, "Tramp, tramp, tramp", so as to terrify him and obtain him for food. According to local belief, the demon "had eyes like a saucer, a nose like a poker, and a mouth like a cave". The Egyptian demon Set was red like the Indian Rakshasa. Red-haired people are disliked in India still; a native girl with auburn locks is not cared for as a bride.

him round and round until the demon gasped with fatigue. The earth shook; trees were splintered in pieces. Then Bhima began to strike the monster with his iron fists, and at length he broke Vaka's back across his knee. Terrible were the loud screams of the Rakshasa while Bhima was bending him double. He died howling.

A mighty clamour was then awakened in the forest. All the other Asuras were terror-stricken, and, bellowing horribly, they hastened towards Bhima and made obeisance before him. Then Bhima made them take vows never again to eat human flesh or to oppress the people of the city. They promised willing obedience, and he allowed them to depart.

Thereafter Pritha's son dragged the monster's body to the main gate of Eka-chakra. He entered the city secretly and hastened to the Brahman's house, and he told Yudhishthira all that had taken place.

When the people of the city discovered that the Asura king had been slain, they rejoiced greatly, and hastened towards the house of the Brahman. But that holy man made evasive answer to them, and said that his deliverer was a certain high-souled Brahman who had offered to supply food to the demon. Thereafter the people established a festival in honour of Brahmans.

The Pandavas remained a time in the city, and they studied the Vedas. One day there came to their dwelling a saintly man of rigid vows, and he told the story of the miraculous births of Drupada's son and daughter from sacrificial fire.

When Drupada had lost half of his kingdom, he paid pilgrimages to holy places. He promised great rewards to superior Brahmans, so that he might have offspring, ever desiring greatly to be avenged upon Drona. He offered the austere Upayája a million cows if he would procure a son for him, and that sage sent him unto his brother Yája. Now Yája was reluctant to aid the rajah thus; but at length he consented to perform the sacrificial rite, and prevailed upon Upayája to help him.

So the rite was performed, and when the vital moment came, the Brahmans called for the queen to partake in it. But Drupada's wife was not prepared, and said: "My mouth is still filled with saffron and my body is scented. I am not fit to receive the libation which will bring offspring. Tarry a little time for me."

But the Brahmans could not delay the consummation of the sacrificial rite. Ere the queen came, a son sprang forth from the flames: he was clad in full armour, and carried a falchion and bow, and a diadem gleamed brightly upon his head. A voice out of the heavens said: "*This prince hath come to destroy Drona and to increase the fame of the Panchalas*".

Next arose from the ashes on the altar a daughter of great beauty. She was exceedingly dark, with long curling locks and lotus eyes, and she was deep-bosomed and slender-waisted. A sweet odour clung to her body.

A voice out of heaven said: "*This dusky girl will become the chief of all women. Many Kshatriyas must die because of her, and the Kauravas will suffer from her. She will accomplish the decrees of the gods.*"

Then the son was called Dhrishta-dyumna[1] and the daughter Draupadi.[2] Drona thereafter took the Panchala prince to his palace, and instructed him to become an accomplished warrior. He knew that he could not thwart destiny, and he desired to perpetuate his own mighty deeds.

[1] *Pron.* dhrish-ta-dyum'na. [2] *Pron.* drow'pa-dee"

Having heard these words, Pritha desired to journey towards Panchala, and she and her sons took leave of their host. Ere they went away, the high-souled ascetic said that Draupadi had been destined to become a Pandava queen.

Pritha and her sons wandered from the banks of the Ganges and went northwards, and soon they fell in with great numbers of people all going the same way. Yudhishthira spake to a troop of Brahmans, and asked them whither they were bound, and they answered saying that Drupada of Panchala was observing a great festival, and that all the princes of the land were hastening to the swayamvara of his peerless and slender-waisted daughter, the beautiful Draupadi.

In that great and increasing company were Brahmans who were to perform the sacred rites, and youths who were to take part in joyous revelry—dancers and jugglers, boxers and wrestlers, and those who displayed feats of strength and skill at arms; there were also bards there and singers to chant the praises of heroes.

The Brahmans praised the beauty of Draupadi, and said to the Pandava brethren: "Come with us to the festival and the sports and the swayamvara; you will be feasted and will receive gifts. You are all as comely as princes and as fair as the bright gods; mayhap Draupadi may choose from among ye this stalwart and noble youth, strongly armed and of fearless bearing, and if he should perform mighty feats, the garland may be thrown upon his shoulders."

Said Yudhishthira: "So be it. We will hasten with you to the swayamvara and share banquet and bounty."

So the Pandavas went towards Panchala with the troop of Brahmans. When they reached the city they took up their abode in the humble dwelling of a potter, still disguised as Brahmans, and they went out and begged food from the people.

In their secret hearts the brethren desired greatly to win the fair bride whose fame had been bruited abroad.

CHAPTER XIII

The Choice of Draupadi

Drupada's Hope—Conditions for winning his Daughter—The Great Bow and Whirling Target—The Swayamvara—Pandavas in Disguise—Love-sick Rajahs put to Shame—Karna strings the Bow—Rejected as a Base-born Suitor—Arjuna's Triumph—Chosen by Princess—An Angry Scene—Rajahs seek Vengeance—Warriors attack Supposed Brahmans—Karna and Salya overcome—Princess taken to Potter's House—Pritha's Command—An Evening Meal—The Royal Spy.

Now Drupada had long cherished the hope that Arjuna would become his daughter's husband. He never revealed his wish to any man, but ere he proclaimed the swayamvara of Draupadi, he thought of the great Pandava archer, and caused to be made a powerful bow which only a strong man could bend and string. For a target he had constructed a strange and curious device: a high pole was erected, and it was surmounted by a golden fish, which was poised above a swiftly-revolving wheel. Then Drupada issued a proclamation far and wide summoning the regents and princes of the world to the swayamvara. He said: "The man who will bend the bow and shoot an arrow through the wheel which will strike and bring down the golden fish shall obtain my daughter in marriage." None but a mighty archer who was Arjuna's equal could hope to win the beautiful Draupadi, for five arrows only were allowed to each competitor, and the fish must needs be struck on an eye to be brought down.

A great field was enclosed for the swayamvara. It was surrounded by a fosse and barrier and swan-white pavilions, with domes and turrets that were agleam with gold and jewels, festoons and streamers and bright garlands. The turrets of the royal mansion were lofty and golden like Himalayan mountain peaks.

For sixteen days there were sports and banquets, and everyone within the city made merry. Then came the great and festal day. At dawn trumpets and drums awakened the people, and flags and flowers decorated every street. The whole populace gathered on the plain and massed around the barriers. The rajah's soldiers kept order, and wrestlers and jugglers and dancers and musicians performed merrily until the appointed hour drew nigh.

At length the people roared their welcome to the king and the high-born ladies and all the royal guests, who thronged the galleries and pavilions. The mighty rajahs, frowning defiance one upon another, were ranged on lofty seats round the throne of King Drupada. Multitudes had gathered to gaze on the glittering scene, pressing against the barriers, or clustering on trees and scaffolds, while others looked down from lofty lattice and high house roofs. . . . A thousand trumpets clamoured; and the murmuring of the swaying people was like the voice of the heaving main.

Among others came in all her beauty the Princess Draupadi, stepping gently and sweet, bearing in a delicate hand the golden bridal garland, which was adorned with sparkling gems. Tardily she made approach, blushing with increasing loveliness, and appeared in the presence of the princes. Mighty and high-born men were there. The Pandavas beheld in the galleries their enemies Duryodhana, Karna, and all the great Kauravas, and they saw also Krishna, the amorous and powerful one, and his brother, the wine-drinking Balarama[1], the Yádava princes, the Rajah of Sindhu and his sons, the Rajah of Chedi, the Rajah of Kosala, the Rajah of Madra, and many more. Now the Pandavas were still disguised as Brahmans, and stood among the holy men.

An aged and white-haired Brahman, clad in white, approached the high altar, chanting mantras. He spread the holy grass and poured out oil; then he kindled the sacred fire, and the offering to the gods was blessed.

Thereafter the thousand trumpets were sounded, and a tense silence fell upon the buzzing crowd. In the solemn hush all eyes were turned towards the royal mansion as Drupada's valiant son, Dhrishta-dyumna, led forth his sister Draupadi, and in a voice like thunder proclaimed his father's will, saying:

"Here stands the noble princess, my sister. Whosoever can bend this bow, and strike with an arrow yonder whirling target set on high, may, if his lineage is noble, claim Draupadi for his bride. My words are truth!"

Having spoken thus, the prince recited to his sister the names of the royal guests, their lineage and their deeds of fame, and bade her award the golden garland to the successful archer.

The rajahs then descended from their gorgeous thrones and gathered around Draupadi as the bright gods gather around Párvati, the mountain bride of Shiva. Their hearts were filled with love for the maiden and with hate for one another. Rivals frowned upon rivals. Those who had been close friends became of a sudden angry enemies because that Draupadi was so beautiful. Krishna

[1] *Pron.* bal-a-rah'ma.

and Balarama alone remained aloof; calmly and self-restrained they stood apart, while rajah opposed rajah like to angry elephants.

Each of the love-sick monarchs gazed upon the mighty bow and upon the whirling target on high, and for a time no man sought to lift the bow lest he should be unable to bend it and then be put to shame. At length a rajah, more bold than the others, picked it up and tried his strength without avail; another followed and another, but failed to string it. Soon many rajahs strained their arms in vain, and some fell upon the ground and groaned, while the laughter of the people pealed around the barriers. . . . The gods had assembled in mid-air and looked down with steadfast eyes.

At length proud Karna strode forward; he took the bow and bent it and fixed the bowstring. Then he seized an arrow. Drupada and his son were alarmed, fearing he might succeed and claim the bride. Suddenly Draupadi intervened, for she would not have the son of a charioteer for her lord. She said, speaking loudly: "I am a king's daughter, and will not wed with the base-born. . . ."

Karna smiled bitterly, his face aflame. He cast down the bow and walked away, gazing towards the sun. He said: "O sun! be my witness that I cast aside the bow, not because I am unable to hit the mark, but because Draupadi scorns me."

Others sought to perform the feat, but in vain, and many rajahs feared to make attempt lest they should compel the laughter of the people. A buzz of merry voices arose from beyond the barriers.

Meanwhile the Pandava brethren, disguised as Brahmans, looked on with the others.

Then suddenly silence fell upon everyone, for Arjuna

advanced from the priestly band to lift the bow. The Brahmans applauded him, shaking their deerskins.

Said the rajahs: "Can a weakly Brahman, who is a mere stripling, accomplish a feat which is beyond the strength of mighty warriors."

Others said: "The Brahman knoweth best his own skill. He would not go forward if he were not confident of success."

An aged priest endeavoured to restrain Arjuna, lest he should by his failure bring ridicule upon the Brahmans; but the hero would not be thwarted. He strode forward like to a stately elephant and bared his broad shoulders and ample chest. He was nimble as a lion, and calm and self-possessed.

Ere he lifted the bow, he walked round it; then he addressed a prayer to the gods. . . . He stood up unmoved and serene as a mountain peak, and he bent the bow and fixed an arrow in it. . . .

All eyes watched him. He drew the cord, and the arrow flew upwards with a hissing sound; it hit the target eye, and the golden fish fell over and clashed upon the ground.

Like distant thunder arose the plaudits of the multitude; hundreds of Brahmans shouted in ecstasy and waved their scarfs; a thousand trumpets clamoured in triumph, and the drums were beaten loud. . . .

The heart of Draupadi was filled with joy, and, smiling coyly, she advanced towards Arjuna and flung the golden bridal garland over his shoulders. Celestial blossoms fluttered, descending through the air, and the sound of celestial music was heard.

Drupada was well pleased, because he had already recognized the hero in his Brahman guise; but the jealous rajahs stormed in fury, and each said unto the other:

"Behold! the king goeth to greet this youth. To him we are as worthless as jungle grass; he tramples upon us in his pride. . . . Are we to be humbled by a Brahman and denied the fruit of our nourished hopes? The daughter of a rajah must even choose a Kshatriya for her husband. . . . Verily, the life of a priest is sacred, but the rajah who scorns his peers must die—he and his son together. Let us seize also this shameless woman who honours the Brahman—that trespasser of our birthright—so that she may be burned at the stake!"

Shouting with anger one to another, the rajahs poured from the galleries with drawn swords and rushed towards Arjuna and the princess. Like ponderous wild elephants they advanced; but the Pandavas rose against them. Arjuna bent the great bow, and Bhima, having no weapon, uprooted a tree and stood defying them like to hell's stern judge wielding his mighty club. Yudhishthira and the younger brothers were soon beside them, and the Brahmans hastened also to give their aid.

For a moment the rajahs paused, wondering at the daring of the priestly band; but impatient Karna and angry Salya, Rajah of Madra, dashed forward like to infuriated elephants against Arjuna and Bhima. The brothers sustained the shock, and when Karna had been struck by Arjuna, he faltered in amaze and said: "Brahman, who art thou? Art thou a god in human guise? No Brahman could thus attack me, nor dost there live a man who can thwart me with defiance as thou hast done even now, save Arjuna alone."

Said Arjuna, "I am nor god nor hero, but a humble Brahman who hath been trained to use of arms. I have come hither to tame thy pride, thou haughty youth; therefore be firm."

But Karna fell back, deeming it vain to oppose the power of a holy man.

Meanwhile Madra's king fought against peerless Bhima. Both were long-armed and of gigantic strength. Sharp and fierce was their conflict. When their clubs were splintered, they leapt one upon the other and wrestled fiercely, struggling with all their might. Then, of a sudden, Bhima stopped and swung aloft the mighty rajah and threw him heavily upon the ground, where he lay unconscious and bleeding before the eyes of the multitude.

The rajahs drew back, humbled because of Karna's flight and Salya's downfall.

"Brave, indeed, are the Brahmans," they said. "Who can they be? What is their lineage? and whence come they?"

The Pandavas scorned to make answer. But Krishna had knowledge of who they were, and he interposed with gentle words to soothe the angry rajahs. The monarchs heard him and withdrew, and the tumult was appeased.

Then Arjuna took Draupadi by the hand and led her away in peace from that scene of angry strife. So ended the swayamvara, and Krishna declared that the bride had been fairly won.

The Pandava brethren went towards the house of the potter, and they entered and addressed their mother Pritha, saying: "A great gift have we obtained this day."

Said Pritha: "Then share the gift between you, as becomes brethren."

Yudhishthira said: "What hast thou said, O mother? The gift is the Princess Draupadi whom Arjuna hath won at the swayamvara."

Said Pritha: "Alas! what have I said? I have sinned deeply in saying, 'Then share the gift between you, as becomes brethren.' But, O Yudhishthira, my son, the fatal words have been spoken; you must devise how they can be obeyed without involving one another in wrong."

Yudhishthira pondered a time and then spake to Arjuna, saying: "My brother, thou hast won Draupadi by thine own merit. She must therefore be thy bride."

Said Arjuna: "Thou, Yudhishthira, art our elder brother and we are thy servants. The princess is for thee."

Yudhishthira said: "Let this matter be arranged in accordance with the will of the gods. It is for Drupada to say unto which of us his daughter will be given."

Now, as hath already been told, each one of the Pandavas yearned in his secret heart to have Draupadi for his bride. . . .

Meanwhile the evening meal had been prepared, and Pritha desired that the princess should at once take her place, and serve out the portions to the brethren. So she said unto Draupadi: "Divide the food, and first set aside a share for the poor; then cut what is left into two parts, one part for Bhima, and the rest for my other sons and for thee and me."

The princess smiled when she beheld the great meal which Bhima devoured.

When they had all eaten they retired to rest. Draupadi slept with Pritha, and the brethren lay at their feet.

King Drupada was sore troubled in heart after his daughter had been led away to the potter's house, and he sent his valiant son to watch her. Dhrishta-dyumna went forth in disguise, and, listening at the window, he discovered to his joy that the Brahmans were no other than the Pandava brethren. He returned to his royal sire and related all that had happened, and what had been spoken at the evening meal. The king was well pleased because that the brethren were Kshatriyas and not Brahmans.

In the morning Drupada sent a priest to the potter's house to ask how it fared with all the brethren.

Said Yudhishthira: "Inform thou the rajah that his daughter hath been won by a family who will not bring shame or disgrace upon his royal name. None but a man of high birth could have shot down the fish of gold."

Drupada, ere this message was delivered unto him, sent a second messenger bidding the brethren to come to the palace because that the nuptial feast was ready. . . . Two chariots awaited them. Then Pritha and Draupadi entered one of the chariots together, and the five brethren entered the other, and they were all driven towards the royal palace.

When the people beheld the Pandavas and marked their comely bearing and royal gait, they knew that they were not Brahmans, but high-born Kshatriyas.

The Pandava guests were made welcome, and the king and his son and all his counsellors sat down to feast with them.

Said the rajah at length unto Yudhishthira: "I perceive that you are men of high birth. Tell me, therefore, I pray thee, who ye are—your names and your lineage."

Yudhishthira said: "We are of humble birth. Do now with us as is thy desire."

Said Drupada: "In Indra's name, I adjure thee to reveal yourselves unto me now."

Yudhishthira said: "Know, then, that we are the Pandava princes. . . . Our brother Arjuna was the winner of Draupadi. Thy daughter, like to a lotus, hath been but transferred from one lake to another. I have spoken what is true."

Drupada glowed with joy and satisfaction. He prevailed upon the brethren to remain at the palace, and entertained them for many days.

At length Yudhishthira was addressed by Drupada, who said: "Thou art the elder brother. Speak and say if it is thy desire that Arjuna be given Draupadi for his bride."

Said Yudhishthira: "I would fain speak with Vyasa, the great Rishi, regarding this matter."

Now Vyasa was in the city of Panchala at that time, and he was brought before the rajah, who spake to him regarding Draupadi.

The Rishi said: "The gods have already declared that she will become the wife of all the five Pandava brethren."

Drupada's son spoke and said: "With reverence I have heard thy words, O Vyasa, but to me it appears that Draupadi hath been betrothed unto Arjuna alone."

Said Yudhishthira: "Thou hast spoken truly, but there is wisdom in the words of Vyasa which in my heart I cannot condemn. Besides, our mother hath already commanded us to share our gift together."

Then Vyasa told that Draupadi was the re-incarnation of a pious woman who once prayed unto the god Shiva for a husband: five times she prayed, and the god rewarded her with the promise of five husbands in her next existence. Vyasa also revealed that the Pandava brethren were five incarnations of Indra, and thus were but as one.

Drupada then gave consent for his daughter to become the bride of all the brethren, and it was arranged that she should be married unto them all, one after the other, according to their ages. So on five successive days she was led round the holy fire by each of the five Pandava princes.

Drupada thereafter conferred great gifts upon his sons-in-law; he gave them much gold and many jewels, and he gave them numerous horses and chariots and elephants, and also a hundred female servants clad in many-coloured robes, and adorned with gems and bright garlands. Unto the Pandavas Krishna gave much raiment and ornaments of gold, and rare vessels sparkling with jewels, besides female servants from various kingdoms.

Now when Duryodhana came to know that the Pandava brethren were still alive, and had formed a powerful alliance with Drupada, he was moved to jealous wrath. A great council was held, at which the young men clamoured for war and the grave elders spoke in favour of peace. At length it was agreed that the Pandava princes should be invited to return to Hastinapur so that the raj might be divided between them and the sons of Dhritarashtra. Then Vidura was sent to Panchala to speak with the Rajah Drupada and his sons-in-law regarding this matter.

CHAPTER XIV

Triumph of the Pandavas

Pandavas visit Drupada's Palace—Their Identity revealed—Draupadi's Five Husbands—Kingdom assigned to Pandavas—Building of Indra-prastha—Arjuna goes into Exile—His Serpent Bride—Marriage in Manipur—An Heir to a Throne—Meeting with Krishna—Abduction of Princess—Miraculous Origin of Jarasandhu—His Two Mothers—Slain by Bhima—The Imperial Sacrifice—Krishna kills Shishupala—Yudhishthira's Triumph—Jealousy of Duryodhana.

The Pandava brethren returned to Hastinapur with Vidura. They took with them their mother, Queen Pritha, and their wife, Draupadi, and the people went forth in great multitudes and bade them glad welcome. Then there was much rejoicing and many banquets.

At length Dhritarashtra spake unto Yudhishthira and his brethren and said: "I will now divide the raj between you and my sons. Your share will be the south-western country of Khandava-prastha."

Said Bhishma: "The maharajah hath spoken wisely. It is meet that you should depart unto the country of Khandava-prastha as he hath decreed."

So the Pandava princes bade farewell to all their kinsmen and to wise Drona, and they went towards their own country. On the banks of the Jumna they built a strong fort, and in time they made a great clearance in the forest. When they had gathered together the people who were subject unto them, they erected a great and wonderful city like unto the city of Indra, and it was called Indra-prastha.[1] High walls, which resembled the Mandara mountains, were built round about, and these were surrounded by a deep moat wide as the sea.

In time the fame of Rajah Yudhishthira went far and wide. He ruled with wisdom and with power, and he had great piety. Forest robbers were pursued constantly and put to death, and wrongdoers were ever brought to justice; indeed, the people who suffered from evildoing went before the rajah as children go before a father seeking redress.

The brethren lived happily together. In accordance with the advice of a Rishi, they made a compact that when one of them was sitting beside Draupadi, none of the others should enter, and that if one of them should be guilty of intrusion, he must needs go into exile for the space of twelve years.

As it chanced, Yudhishthira was sitting with Draupadi one day when a Brahman, whose cattle had been carried off, hastened to Arjuna and entreated him to pursue the band of robbers. The weapons of the prince were in the king's palace, and to obtain them Arjuna entered the room in which Yudhishthira and Draupadi sat, thus breaking the compact made by the brethren. He hastened after the robbers and recovered the stolen cattle, which he brought back unto the Brahman.

On his return to the palace, Arjuna said unto his brother that he must needs become an exile for twelve years to expiate his offence. Yudhishthira, however, sought to prevail upon him not to depart. But Arjuna made answer that he had pledged his oath to fulfil the terms of the compact. "I cannot waver from truth," he said; "truth is my weapon." So when he had bidden farewell to Pritha and Draupadi and his four brethren,

[1] *Pron.* indra-praat'ha.

he took his departure from the city of Indra-prastha. And a band of Brahmans went with him.

Arjuna wandered through the jungle, and he visited many holy places. One day he went unto Hurdwar, where the Ganges flows upon the plain, and he bathed in the holy waters. There he met with Ulúpí, daughter of Vásuka, king of the Nagas, who had great beauty. She loved him, and she led him to her father's palace, where he abode a time, and she gave him the power to render himself invisible in water. A child was born unto them, and he was named Iravat.

Thereafterwards Arjuna went southwards until he came to the Mahendra mountain.[1] He was received there by Parasu Rama, the Brahman hero, who gave him gifts of powerful weapons, and imparted to him the secret of using them.

So he wandered from holy place to holy place until he reached Manipur. Now the rajah of that place had a beautiful daughter whose name was Chitrángadá. Arjuna loved her, and sought her for his bride. The rajah said: "I have no other child, and if I give her unto thee, her son must remain here to become my heir, for the god Shiva hath decreed that the rajahs of this realm can have each but one child." Arjuna married the maiden, and he dwelt for three years at Manipur. A son was born, and he was named Chitrangada. Thereafter Arjuna set out on his wanderings once more.

He passed through many strange lands, travelling westward, and at length he reached the city of Prabhása[2], which is nigh to Dwáraká, on the southern sea, the capital of his kinsman Krishna, rajah of the Yádhavas.

Krishna welcomed Arjuna, and took the Pandava hero to dwell in his palace. Then he gave a great feast on

[1] In Ganjam district, Madras.

[2] *Pron.* pra-bha'sa.

ARJUNA AND THE RIVER NYMPH

From the painting by Warwick Goble

the holy mountain of Raivataka, which lasted for two days. Arjuna looked with love upon Krishna's fair sister, Subhadra[1], a girl of sweet smiles, and desired her for a bride.

Now it was the wish of Balarama that Subhadra should be given unto Duryodhana, whom, indeed, she would have chosen had a swayamvara been held. So Krishna advised Arjuna to carry her away by force, in accordance with the advice of the sages, who had said aforetime: "Men applaud the Kshatriyas who win brides by abducting them."

When the feast was over, Arjuna drove his chariot from the holy mountain towards Dwaraka until he came nigh to Subhadra. Nimbly he leapt down and took her by the hand and lifted her into his chariot; then he drove hastily towards the city of Indra-prastha.

Balarama was greatly angered, and desired to pursue Arjuna; and he spoke to Krishna, saying: "Thou art calm, and I can perceive that Arjuna has done this thing with thy knowledge. Thou shouldst not have given our sister unto him without my consent. But let the deed be upon his own head, for I will pursue him and slay him and his brethren, one and all."

Said Krishna: "Arjuna is our kinsman[2] and of noble birth, and is a worthy husband for Subhadra. If thou wilt pursue him and bring back our sister, no one else will marry her now because that she hath been in the house of another. Better were it that we should send messengers after Arjuna and invite him to return here, so that the marriage may be held according to our rites."

Balarama said: "So be it, seeing that thou art well pleased with this matter."

[1] *Pron.* soo-bhad'ra.

[2] Krishna's father, Vasudeva, was the brother of Pritha, mother of Arjuna.

Thus it came to pass that messengers followed Arjuna and prevailed upon him to return with Subhadra to Dwaraka. A great feast was then held, and they were married with pomp and in state. And Arjuna abode at the court of Krishna for many months, until the time of his exile came to an end.

When Arjuna returned to Indra-prastha with Subhadra, he was received with great rejoicing by his brethren. He went unto Draupadi and greeted her; but she said coldly: "Why come hither? Where is the sister of Krishna?"

Arjuna soothed her with gentle words; and then Subhadra approached Draupadi, attired in red silk, but in the simple fashion of a keeper of cows, and made obeisance before her, saying: "I am thy handmaiden."

Draupadi embraced the sister of Krishna and said. "Let thy husband be without an enemy."

The heart of Subhadra was filled with joy at these words; she said: "So be it."

Thus was peace made; the two women thereafter loved one another, and to Pritha both were very dear.

Now Draupadi became the mother of five sons to her five husbands; and Subhadra had one son only, and his name was Abhimanyu[1], who in the years that followed was an illustrious warrior.

As time went on, the Pandavas grew more and more powerful. They waged great wars, until many rajahs owed them allegiance; and at length Yudhishthira deemed that the time had come to hold his great Rajasúya sacrifice to celebrate the supremacy of his power over all.

Krishna came to Indra-prastha at this time and said: "There is now but one rajah who must needs be over-

[1] *Pron.* ab-hi-mun'yoo ("u" as in "bun").

come ere the Imperial sacrifice can be performed: his name is Jarasandha, monarch of Magadha. He hath already conquered six-and-eighty kings, and he hath slaughtered those who were our kinsmen dear."

Now this rajah was of great valour and matchless strength. His body was invulnerable against weapons; not even the gods could wound him with mace or sword or with arrow. He was also of miraculous birth, for he was born of two mothers[1] who had eaten of a mantra-charmed mango which fell into the lap of his sire when that he was childless and was undergoing penances to obtain offspring. Nor did the babe come to life after birth until he was united by a Rakshasa woman, named Jara, the goddess of the household, who, because she was worshipped in the palace, performed some good each day in return.[2] So the child was called Jarasandha[3], which signifies "united by Jara", and he increased daily like to the moon in its first phase.

Krishna said unto Yudhishthira: "This monarch of Magadha cannot be vanquished in battle even by gods or by demons. But he may be overcome in a conflict, fighting with bare arms. Now I am 'Policy', Bhima is 'Strength', and Arjuna is 'Protector'. Together, O king, we will surely accomplish the death of Jarasandha, who is arrogant and covetous and proud."

Said Yudhishthira: "Do as it seemeth best unto thee, O lord of the universe; thou art our wise counsellor and guide."

Then Krishna, Arjuna, and Bhima disguised themselves as Brahmans and went towards the city of Mathura, which was Jarasandha's capital. When they arrived there

[1] In one of the Egyptian temple chants Osiris is called "the progeny of the two cows Isis and Nepthys".

[2] Like the Europran household elves and fairies.

[3] *Pron.* ja-ra-sund'ha.

they entered the palace of the mighty rajah like to mountain lions eyeing cattle-folds. They went boldly before the king decked with flowers, and the king said: "Ye are welcome."

Arjuna and Bhima were silent, but Krishna spake to Jarasandha, saying: "These two men are observing vows, and will not open their mouths until midnight; after that hour they will speak."

The king provided for his guests in the sacrificial chamber, and after midnight he visited them, and discovering that they were warriors, he asked: "Tell me truly who ye are, and why ye have come hither."

Said Krishna: "We are decked with flowers to achieve prosperity, and we have entered the abode of our enemy to fulfil the vows of Kshatriyas."

Jarasandha said: "I have never done you an injury. Why, therefore, do ye regard me as your enemy?"

Then Krishna revealed himself, and upbraided the king because that he was wont to offer up in sacrifice to Shiva the rajahs whom he took captive in battle. He said: "Thou hast slaughtered our kinsmen in this manner because thou dost imagine there liveth no man who is so powerful as thou. For thy sins thou art doomed to go to Yama's kingdom, there to be tortured a time. But thou canst attain to the Heaven of Indra by dying the death of a Kshatriya in battle with thy peers. Now, O king, we challenge thee to combat. Set free the rajahs who are in thy dungeons, or die at our hands!"

Said the king: "I have taken captive in battle these royal prisoners of mine, whom I shall offer in sacrifice to Shiva, according to my vow. Let us therefore meet in battle, army against army, or in single combat."

Krishna said: "Meet thou one of us in single combat. With whom dost thou desire to fight?"

Then Jarasandha expressed his wish to meet Bhima in battle. Bhima was made glad thereat, for, in truth, he thirsted for the conflict; but he desired that they should fight without weapons, and the king consented, and made ready for the fray.

Now Jarasandha was of lofty stature and great strength, and he fought so fiercely that the combat lasted for thirteen days in presence of great multitudes of the people. In the end the king was swung aloft, and his back was broken over Bhima's knee. Then a mighty tumult arose, which caused all who were there to quake with fear, for the roar of the Pandavas mingled with the shrieks of Jarasandha ere death silenced him.

Krishna went boldly into the palace and set free all the rajahs who were in captivity. And one by one they took vows to attend the Imperial sacrifice. Then Krishna received Sahadeva, son of Jarasandha, and installed him as Rajah of Magadha.

When the great Yudhishthira came to know that Jarasandha had been slain, he sent forth his four brethren with great armies to collect tribute from every rajah in the world.[1] Some there were among the kings who welcomed them; others had to be conquered in battle. But when they had sworn allegiance to Yudhishthira, they joined the Pandava force and assisted in achieving further victories. A whole year went past ere the brethren returned again unto Indra-prastha.

Krishna came from Dwaraka to aid Yudhishthira at the ceremony, and he brought with him much wealth and a mighty army.

Stately pavilions were erected for the kings who came

[1] That is, in Northern India.

to attend the great sacrifice: their turrets were high, and they were swan-white and flecked with radiant gold. Silver and gold adorned the walls of the rooms, which were richly perfumed and carpeted and furnished to befit the royal guests.

Then the rajahs came to Indra-prastha in all their splendour and greeted mighty Yudhishthira. Those who were friends brought gifts, and those who had been subdued in battle brought tribute. White-haired and blind old Dhritarashtra came, and with him were Kripa and Bhishma and Vidura. Proud Duryodhana and his brethren came also, professing friendship, and Karna came with bow and spear and mace. Drona and his son, and their enemies Drupada and his son, were there also, and Balarama, Krishna's brother, and their father Vasudeva. And among many others were jealous Sishupala[1], King of Chedi[2], and his son, and both wore bright golden armour.

Many Brahmans assembled at Indra-prastha, and Krishna honoured them and washed their feet. The gifts that were given to these holy sages were beyond computation. In great numbers came men of every caste also; and all were feasted at banquets, so that the words "Take ye and eat" were heard continuously on every hand.

Now there were deep and smouldering jealousies among the assembled rajahs, and when the time came to honour him who was regarded as the greatest among them by presenting the Arghya[3], their passions were set ablaze. First Bhishma spake forth and said that the honour was due to Krishna, the pious one, who was the noblest and greatest among them all. "Krishna," he

[1] *Pron.* sish-oo-pah'la. [2] *Pron.* chay'dee.

[3] A gift of fruit or flowers, like an offering to the image of a god.

said, "is the origin of all things; the universe came into being for him alone. He is the incarnation of the Creator, the everlasting one, who is beyond man's comprehension."

When the Arghya was given unto Krishna, Sishupala, the Rajah of Chedi, arose in wrath and said: "It ill becomes thee, O Yudhishthira, to honour thus an uncrowned chieftain. Gathered about thee are ruling kings of highest fame. If the honour be due to age, then Vasudeva can claim it before his son; if it is due to the foremost rajah, then Drupada should be honoured; if it is due to wisdom, Drona is the most worthy; if it is due to holiness, Vyasa is the greatest. Drona's son hath more knowledge than Krishna, Duryodhana is peerless among younger men, Kripa is the worthiest priest, and Karna the greatest archer. For what reason should homage be paid unto Krishna, who is neither the holiest priest, the wisest preceptor, the greatest warrior, nor the foremost chieftain? To the shame of this assembly be it said that it doth honour the murderer of his own rajah, this cowherd of low birth."

So spake Sishupala, the tiger-hearted one, and terrible was his wrath. He hated Krishna, because that he had carried away by force the beautiful Rukmini, who had been betrothed unto himself, the mighty Rajah of Chedi.

Krishna then spoke. Calm was he of voice and demeanour, but his eyes were bright. Unto the rajahs he said: "Hear me, O ye princes and kings! The evil-tongued Sishupala is descended from a daughter of our race, and in my heart I have never sought to work ill against a kinsman. But once, when I went eastward, he sacked my sea-swept Dwaraka and laid low its temple; once he broke faith with a rajah and cast him into prison; once he seized the consort of a king by force; and once he disguised himself as the husband of a chaste princess and deceived her. And I have suffered because of his sins, nor sought vengeance, because that he was of our own race. He hath even come after my consort Rukmini, and is worthy of death."

As he spoke, the faces of many rajahs grew red with shame and anger, but Sishupala laughed aloud and made answer: "I seek no mercy from Krishna, nor do I fear him."

Then Krishna thought of his bright, resistless discus, and immediately it was in his hand. In anger he spake forth and said: "Hear me, ye lords of earth! I have promised the pious mother of Sishupala to pardon a hundred sins committed by her son. And I have fulfilled my vow. But now the number is more than full, and I will slay him, O ye mighty rajahs, before your eyes."

Having spoken thus, Krishna flung the discus, and it struck Sishupala on the neck, so that his head was severed from his body. He fell down like to a cliff struck by the thunderbolt. Then the assembled rajahs beheld a great wonder, for the passion-cleansed soul of Sishupala issued from his body, beautiful as the sun in heaven, and went towards Krishna. Its eyes were like to lotus blooms, and its form like to a flame; and it adored Krishna and entered into his body.[1]

The rajahs all looked on, silent and amazed, while thunder bellowed out of heaven, and lightning flashed, and rain poured down in torrents. Some grew angry, and laid hands on their weapons to avenge the death of Sishupala; others rejoiced that he had been slain; the Brahmans chanted the praises of Krishna.

[1] Krishna represented the worshippers of Vishnu, of whom he was an incarnation. Sishupala, who was reputed to have been born with three eyes, was an incarnation of Shiva. Rukmini was an incarnation of Lakshmi.

Yudhishthira commanded his brothers to perform the funeral rites over the dead with every honour. So the body of Sishupala was burned and the oblation poured forth. Then his son was proclaimed Rajah of Chedi.

Thereafter the great sacrifice was performed with solemnity and in peace. Krishna, who had maintained the supremacy of Yudhishthira by slaying a dangerous and jealous rival, looked on benignly.

Holy water was sprinkled by the Brahmans, and all the monarchs made obeisance and honoured Yudhishthira, saying: "Thou hast extended the fame of thy mighty sire, Pandu, and thou art become even greater than he was. Thou hast graced with this sacrifice thine high station and fulfilled all our hopes. Now, O emperor over all, permit us to depart to our own homes, and bestow thy blessing upon us."

So one by one they took leave of Yudhishthira and went away, and the four Pandavas accompanied the greatest of them to the confines of their kingdoms. Krishna was the last to bid farewell.

Said Yudhishthira: "Unto thee I owe all things. Because thou wert here, O valorous one, I was able to perform the great sacrifice."

Krishna said: "Monarch of all! rule thou over thy people with a father's wisdom and care. Be unto them like rain which nourisheth the parched fields; be a shade in hot sunshine; be a cloudless heaven bending over all. Be thou ever free from pride and passion; ever rule with power and justice and holiness, O Yudhishthira."

So he spake from his chariot and then went his way, and Yudhishthira turned homeward with tear-dimmed eyes.

Now when Duryodhana had witnessed the triumph

of the Pandavas, his heart burned with jealous rage. He envied the splendour of the palaces at Indra-prastha; he envied the glory achieved by Yudhishthira. Well he knew that he could not overcome the Pandavas in open conflict, so he plotted with his brethren to accomplish their fall by artifice and by wrong.

As in after-time the wise Sanjaya said: "The gods first deprive of his reason that man unto whom they ultimately send disgrace and defeat".

But Duryodhana had to work the will of the Creator under the influence of fate, and it was doomed that the Pandavas should suffer for a time at his hands.

CHAPTER XV

The Great Gambling Match

Duryodhana's Plot—Shakuni the Gambler—Loaded Dice—Challenge to Yudhishthira—An Unequal Contest—Pandavas lose Kingdom and become Slaves—Draupadi Staked and Lost—How Duhsasana humbled her—Pandava Queen's Appeals—Treated as a Menial—Attempt to Disrobe her—Taunted by Karna — Bhima's Terrible Vows — Alarming Omens — Pandavas regain Liberty—Second Gambling Match—Pandavas go into Exile.

Now Shakuni, Prince of Gandhara,[1] and brother of Dhritarashtra's queen, was renowned for his skill as a gambler. He always enjoyed good fortune because that he played with loaded dice. Duryodhana plotted with him, desiring greatly to subjugate the Pandavas, and Shakuni said: "Be advised by me. Yudhishthira loves the dice, although he knows not how to play. Ask him to throw dice with me, for there is no gambler who is my equal in the three worlds. I will put him to shame. I will win from him his kingdom, O bull among men."

Duryodhana was well pleased at this proposal, and he went before his blind father, the maharajah, and prevailed upon him to invite the Pandavas to Hastinapur for a friendly gambling match, despite the warnings of the royal counsellors.

Said Dhritarashtra: "If the gods are merciful, my sons will cause no dispute. Let it be as fate hath ordained. No evil can happen so long as I am near,

[1] Candahar

and Bhishma and Drona are near also. Therefore, let the Pandavas be invited hither as my son desireth."

So Vidura, who feared trouble, was sent unto Indraprastha to say: "The maharajah is about to hold a great festival at Hastinapur, and he desires that Yudhishthira and his brethren, their mother Pritha and their joint wife Draupadi, should be present. A great gambling match will be played."

When Yudhishthira heard these words, he sorrowed greatly, for well he knew that dice-throwing was ofttimes the cause of bitter strife. Besides, he was unwilling to play Prince Shakuni, that desperate and terrible gambler. . . . But he could not refuse the invitation of Dhritarashtra, or, like a true Kshatriya, disdain a challenge either to fight or to play with his peers.

So it came to pass that the Pandava brethren, with Pritha, their mother, and their joint wife Draupadi, journeyed to Hastinapur in all their splendour. Dhritarashtra welcomed them in the presence of Bhishma and Drona and Duryodhana and Karna; then they were received by Queen Gandhari, and the wives of the Kaurava princes; and all the daughters-in-law of the blind maharajah became sad because that they were jealous of the beauty of Draupadi and the splendour of her attire.

The Pandava lords and ladies went unto the dwelling which had been prepared for them, and there they were visited in turn by the lords and ladies of Hastinapur.

On the day that followed, Yudhishthira and his brethren went together to the gambling match, which was held in a gorgeous pavilion, roofed with arching crystal and decorated with gold and lapis lazuli: it had a hundred doors and a thousand great columns, and it was richly carpeted. All the princes and great chieftains and warriors of the kingdom were gathered there. And

Prince Shakuni of Gandhari was there also with his false dice.

When salutations had passed, and the great company were seated, Shakuni invited Yudhishthira to play.

Said Yudhishthira: "I will play if mine opponent will promise to throw fairly, without trickery and deceit. Deceitful gambling is sinful, and unworthy a Kshatriya; there is no prowess in it. Wise men do not applaud a player who winneth by foul means."

Shakuni said: "A skilled gambler ever playeth with purpose to vanquish his opponent, as one warrior fighteth another less skilled than himself to accomplish his overthrow. Such is the practise in all contests; a man plays or fights to achieve victory. . . . But if thou art in dread of me, O Yudhishthira, and afraid that thou wilt lose, 'twere better if thou didst not play at all."

Said Yudhishthira: "Having been challenged, I cannot withdraw. I fear not to fight or to play with any man. . . . But first say who doth challenge and who is to lay stakes equally with me."

Then Duryodhana spoke, saying: "O rajah, I will supply jewels and gold and any stakes thou wilt of as great value as thou canst set down. It is for me that Shakuni, my uncle, is to throw the dice."

Said Yudhishthira: "This is indeed a strange challenge. One man is to throw the dice and another is to lay the stakes. Such is contrary to all practice. If, however, thou art determined to play in this fashion, let the game begin."

Well did the Rajah of Indra-prastha know then that the match would not be played fairly. But he sat down, notwithstanding, to throw dice with Shakuni.

At the first throw Yudhishthira lost; indeed, he lost at every throw on that fatal day. He gambled away all his money and all his jewels, his jewelled chariot with golden bells, and all his cattle; still he played on, and he lost his thousand war elephants, his slaves and beautiful slave girls, and the remainder of his goods; and next, he staked and lost the whole kingdom of the Pandavas, save the lands which he had gifted to the Brahmans. Nor did he cease to play then, despite the advice offered him by the chieftains who were there. One by one he staked and lost his brethren; and he staked himself and lost also.

Said Shakuni: "You have done ill, Yudhishthira, in staking thine own self, for now thou hast become a slave; but if thou wilt stake Draupadi now and win, all that thou hast lost will be restored unto thee."

Yudhishthira said: "So be it. I will stake Draupadi."

At these words the whole company was stricken with horror. Vidura swooned, and the faces of Bhishma and Drona grew pallid; many groaned; but Duryodhana and his brethren rejoiced openly before all men.

Shakuni threw the dice, and Yudhishthira lost this the last throw. In this manner was Draupadi won by Duryodhana.

Then all the onlookers gazed one upon another in silence and wide-eyed. Karna and Duhsasana[1] and other young princes laughed aloud.

Duryodhana rose proudly and spake unto Vidura, saying: "Now hasten unto Draupadi and bid her to come hither to sweep the chambers with the other bondswomen."

Vidura was made angry, and answered him: "Thy words are wicked, O Duryodhana. Thou canst not command a lady of royal birth to become a household slave. Besides, she is not thy slave, because Yudhishthira

[1] *Pron.* doo-sas'a-na.

did stake his own freedom before he staked Draupadi. Thou couldst not win aught from a slave who had no power to stake the princess."

But Duryodhana cursed Vidura, and bade one of his servants to bring Draupadi before him.

Said Vidura: "Duryodhana is this day deprived of his reason. Dishonesty is one of the doors to hell. By practising dishonesty Duryodhana will accomplish yet the ruin of the Kauravas."

The beautiful Draupadi was sitting at peace within the fair dwelling set apart for the Pandavas on the banks of the Ganges; its walls and towers were mirrored on the broad clear waters. Then suddenly, as a jackal enters stealthily the den of a lion, the menial sent by Duryodhana entered the palace and stood before high-born Draupadi.

Said this man: "O queen, the mighty son of Pandu hath played and lost; he hath lost all, even his reason, and he hath staked thee, and thou hast been won by Duryodhana. And now Duryodhana bids me to say that thou art become his slave, and must obey him like to other female slaves. So come thou with me, for thou must henceforth engage in menial work."

Draupadi was astounded when he spake these words, and in her anguish she cried: "Have I heard thee aright? Hath my husband, the king, staked and lost me in his madness? Did he stake and loose aught beside?"

Said the man: "Yudhishthira hath lost all his riches and his kingdom; he staked his brethren and lost them one by one; he staked himself and lost; and then he staked thee, O queen, and lost also. Therefore, come thou with me."

Draupadi rose in her pride and spoke angrily, saying: "If my lord did stake himself and become a slave, he could not wager me, for a slave owns neither his own life nor the life of another. Speak, therefore, unto my husband these words, and unto Duryodhana say: 'Draupadi hath not been won'."

The man returned to the assembly and spake unto Yudhishthira the words which Draupadi had said, but he bowed his head and was silent.

Duryodhana was made angry by the defiant answer of the proud queen, and he said unto his brother Duhsasana: "The sons of Pandu are our slaves, and thy heart is without fear for them. Go thou to the palace and bid the princess, my humble menial, to come hither quickly."

Red-eyed and proud Duhsasana hastened to the palace. He entered the inner chambers and stood before Draupadi, who was clad in but a single robe, while her hair hung loosely.

Said the evil-hearted Kaurava: "O princess of Panchala with fair lotus eyes, thou hast been staked and lost fairly at the game of hazard. Hasten, therefore, and stand before thy lord Duryodhana, for thou art now his bright-eyed slave."

Draupadi heard and trembled. She covered her eyes with her hands before the hated Duhsasana; her cheeks turned pale and her heart sickened. Then suddenly she leapt up and sought to escape to an inner room. But the evil-hearted prince seized her by the hair, for he no longer feared the sons of Pandu, and the beautiful princess quivered and shook in her loose attire like to a sapling which is shaken by the storm wind. Crouching on her knees, she cried angrily, while tears streamed from her lotus eyes: "Begone! O shameless prince. Can a modest woman appear before strangers in loose attire?"

Said stern and cruel Duhsasana: "Even if thou wert

4

THE ORDEAL OF QUEEN DRAUPADI

From the painting by Warwick Goble

naked now, thou must follow me. Hast thou not become a slave, fairly staked and fairly won? Henceforth thou wilt serve among the other menials."

Trembling and faint, Draupadi was dragged through the streets by Duhsasana. When she stood before the elders and the chieftains in the pavilion she cried: "Forgive me because that I have come hither in this unseemly plight. . . ."

Bhishma and Drona and the other elders who were there hung their heads in shame.

Unto Duhsasana Draupadi said angrily: "Cease thy wickedness! Defile me no longer with unclean hands. A woman's hair is sacred."

Sacred indeed were the locks of the Pandava queen, for they had been sprinkled with water sanctified by mantras at the imperial sacrifice.

Weeping, she cried: "Hear and help me, O ye elders. You have wives and children of your own. Will you permit this wrong to be continued. Answer me now."

But no man spake a word.

Draupadi wept and said: "Why this silence? . . . Will no man among ye protect a sinless woman? . . . Lost is the fame of the Kauravas, the ancient glory of Bharata, and the prowess of the Kshatriyas! . . . Why will not the sons of Pandu protect their outraged queen? . . . And hath Bhishma lost his virtue and Drona his power? . . . Will Yudhishthira no longer defend one who is wronged? . . . Why are ye all silent while this deed of shame is done before you?"

As she spake thus, Draupadi glanced round the sons of Pandu one by one, and their hearts thirsted for vengeance. Bhishma's face was dark, Drona clenched his teeth, and Vidura, white and angry, gazed upon Duhsasana with amaze while he tore off Draupadi's veil and addressed her with foul words. When she looked towards the Kaurava brethren, Duhsasana said: "Ha! on whom darest thou to look now, O slave?"

Shakuni and Karna laughed to hear Draupadi called a slave, and they cried out: "Well spoken, well spoken!"

Duhsasana endeavoured to strip the princess naked before the assembly; but Draupadi, in her distress, prayed aloud to Krishna, invoking him as the creator of all and the soul of the universe, and entreated him to help her. Krishna heard her, and multiplied her garments so that Duhsasana was unable to accomplish his wicked purpose.

Karna spake to Draupadi and said: "'Tis not thy blame, O princess, that thou hast fallen so low. A woman's fate is controlled by her husband; Yudhishthira hath gambled thee away. Thou wert his, and must accept thy fate. Henceforward thou wilt be the slave of the Kaurava princes. Thou must obey them and please them with thy beauty. . . . 'Tis meet that thou shouldst now seek for thyself a husband who will love thee too well to stake thee at dice and suffer thee to be put to shame. . . . Be assured that no one will blame a humble menial, as thou now art, who looks with eyes of love upon great and noble warriors. Remember that Yudhishthira is no longer thy husband; he hath become a slave, and a slave can have no wife. . . . Ah! sweet Princess of Panchala, those whom thou didst choose at thy swayamvara have gambled and lost thee; their kingdom they have lost, and their power also."

At these words Bhima's bosom heaved with anger and with shame. Red-eyed he scowled upon Karna; he seemed to be the image of flaming Wrath. Unto Yudhishthira he spake grimly, saying: "If you hadst not staked our freedom and our queen, O king and elder brother, this son of a charioteer would not have taunted us in this manner."

Yudhishthira bowed his head in shame, nor answered a word.

Arjuna reproved Bhima for his bitter words; but Pritha's mighty son, the slayer of Asuras, said: "If I am not permitted to punish the tormentor of Draupadi, bring me a fire that I may thrust my hands into it."

A deep uproar rose from the assembly, and the elders applauded the wronged lady and censured Duhsasana. Bhima clenched his hands and, with quivering lips, cried out:

"Hear my terrible words, O ye Kshatriyas. . . . May I never reach Heaven if I do not yet seize Duhsasana in battle and, tearing open his breast, drink his very life blood! . . ."

Again he spoke and said: "If Yudhishthira will permit me, I will slay the wretched sons of Dhritarashtra without weapons, even as a lion slays small animals."

Then Bhishma and Vidura and Drona cried out: "Forbear, O Bhima! Everything is possible in thee."

Duryodhana gloried in his hour of triumph, and unto the elder of the Pandava brethren spake tauntingly and said: "Yudhishthira, thou art spokesman for thy brethren, and they owe thee obedience. Speak and say, thou who dost ever speak truly, hast thou lost thy kingdom and thy brethren and thine own self? O Yudhishthira, hast thou lost even the beauteous Draupadi? And hath she, thy wedded wife, become our humble menial?"

Yudhishthira heard him with downcast eyes, but his lips moved not. . . . Then Karna laughed; but Bhishma, pious and old, wept in silence.

Then Duryodhana cast burning eyes upon Draupadi, and, baring his knee, invited her, as a slave, to sit upon it.

Bhima gnashed his teeth, for he was unable to restrain his pent-up anger. With eyes flashing like lightning, and in a voice like to thunder he cried out: "Hear my vow! May I never reach Heaven or meet my ancestors hereafter if, for these deeds of sin, I do not break the knee of Duryodhana in battle, and drink the blood of Duhsasana!"

The flames of wrath which leapt on the forehead of Bhima were like red sparks flying from tough branches on a crackling fire.

Dhritarashtra was sitting in his palace, nor knew aught of what was passing. The Brahmans, robed in white, were chanting peacefully their evening mantras, when a jackal howled in the sacrificial chamber. Asses brayed in response, and ravens answered their cries from all sides. Those who heard these dread omens exclaimed: "*Swashti! Swashti!*"[1]

Dhritarashtra shook with terror, and when Vidura had told him all that had taken place, he said: "The luckless and sinful Duryodhana hath brought shame upon the head of Rajah Drupada's sweet daughter, and thus courted death and destruction. May the prayers of a sorrowful old man remove the wrath of Heaven which these dark omens have revealed."

Then the blind maharajah was led to Draupadi, and before all the elders and the princes he spoke to her, kindly and gently, and said: "Noble queen and virtuous daughter, wife of pious Yudhishthira, and purest of all women, thou art very dear unto my heart. Alas! my sons have wronged thee in foul manner this day. O forgive them now, and let the wrath of Heaven be averted. Whatsoever thou wilt ask of me will be thine."

Said Draupadi: "O mighty maharajah, thou art merciful; may happiness be thy dower. I ask of thee to set at

[1] Similar to "Amen".

liberty now my lord and husband Yudhishthira. Having been a prince, it is not seemly that he should be called a slave."

Dhritarashtra said: "Thy wish is granted. Ask a second boon and blessing, O fair one. Thou dost deserve more than a single boon."

Said Draupadi: "Let Arjuna and Bhima and their younger brethren be set free also and allowed to depart now with their horses and their chariots and their weapons."

Dhritarashtra said: "So be it, O high-born princess. Ask yet another boon and blessing and it will be granted thee."

Said Draupadi: "I seek no other boon, thou generous monarch: I am a Kshatriya by birth, and not like to a Brahman, who craveth for gifts without end. Thou hast freed my husbands from slavery: they will regain their fortunes by their own mighty deeds."

Then the Pandava brethren departed from Hastinapur with Pritha and Draupadi, and returned unto the city of Indra-prastha.

The Kauravas were made angry, and Duryodhana remonstrated with his royal sire and said: "Thou hast permitted the Pandava princes to depart in their anger; now they will make ready to wage war against us to regain their kingdom and their wealth; when they return they will slay us all. Permit us, therefore, to throw dice with them once again. We will stake our liberty, and be it laid down that the side which loseth shall go into exile for twelve full years, and into concealment for a year thereafter. By this arrangement a bloody war may be averted."

Dhritarashtra granted his son's wish and recalled the Pandavas. So it came to pass that Yudhishthira sat down once again to play with Shakuni, and once again Shakuni brought forth the loaded dice. Ere long the game ended, and Yudhishthira had lost.

Duhsasana danced with joy and cried aloud: "Now is established the empire of Duryodhana."

Said Bhima: "Be not too gladsome, O Duhsasana. Hear and remember my words: May I never reach Heaven or meet my sires until I shall drink thy blood!"

Then the Pandava princes cast off their royal garments and clad themselves in deerskins like humble mendicants. Yudhishthira bade farewell to Dhritarashtra and Bhishma and Kripa and Vidura, one by one, and he even said farewell to the Kaurava brethren.

Said Vidura: "Thy mother, the royal Pritha, is too old to wander with thee through forest and jungle. Let her dwell here until the years of your exile have passed away."

Yudhishthira spoke for his brethren and said: "Be it so, O saintly Vidura. Now bless us ere we depart, for thou hast been unto us like to a father."

Then Vidura blessed each one of the Pandava princes, saying: "Be saintly in exile, subdue your passions, learn truth in your sorrow, and return in happiness. May these eyes be blessed by beholding thee in Hastinapur once again."

Pritha wept over Draupadi and blessed her. Then the Princess of Panchala went forth with loose tresses; but ere she departed from the city she vowed a vow, saying: "From this day my hair will fall over my forehead until Bhima shall have slain Duhsasana and drunk his blood; then shall Bhima tie up my tresses while his hands are yet wet with the blood of Duhsasana."

The Pandava princes wandered towards the deep forest, and Draupadi followed them.

CHAPTER XVI

Second Exile of the Pandavas

The Gift of the Sun God—Life in the Jungle—Bhima and the Ape God—Flowers of Paradise—Draupadi's Complaint to Krishna—Reproved by Yudhishthira—Arjuna wrestles with the God Shiva—His Celestial Weapon—Visit to Indra's Heaven—Battle with Sea Giants—Sages in the Forest—Duryodhana captured by Gandharvas—Pandavas rescue him—His Desire to perish—The Rival Sacrifice—Karna's Vow—Adventure at Sacred Pond—Pandavas in Virata—Adventures of Brethren—The Cattle Raid—Kauravas defeated—Marriage of Arjuna's Son—End of Exile.

YUDHISHTHIRA lamented his fate to the Brahmans as he wandered towards the forest. "Our kingdom is lost to us," he said, "and our fortune; everything is lost; we depart in sorrow, and must live on fruits and roots and the produce of the chase. In the woods are many perils—many reptiles and hungry wild animals seeking their prey."

A Brahman advised the deposed rajah to call upon the sun god, and Yudhishthira prayed: "O sun, thou art the eye of the universe, the soul of all things that are; thou art the creator; thou art Indra, thou art Vishnu, thou art Brahma, thou art Prajapati, lord of creatures, father of gods and man; thou art fire, thou art Mind; thou art lord of all, the eternal Brahma."

Then Surya[1] appeared before Yudhishthira and gave unto him a copper pot, which was ever filled with food for the brethren.[2]

[1] The sun god.

[2] Like the "Pot of Worth" possessed by the Celtic Finn-mac-Coul.

For twelve long years the Pandavas lived in the woods with their wife Draupadi, and Dhaumya, the Brahman. Whatever food they obtained, they set apart a portion for the holy men and ate the rest. They visited holy shrines; they bathed in sacred waters; they performed their devotions. Ofttimes they held converse with Brahmans and sages, who instructed them in pious works and blessed them, and also promised them that their lost kingdom would be restored in the fullness of time.

They wandered in sunshine and in shade; they dwelt in pleasant places, amidst abundant fruits and surrounded by flowers. They suffered also from tempests and heavy rains, when their path would be torn by streams, and Draupadi would swoon, and all the brethren would be faint and weary and in despair. Then Bhima would carry them all on his back and under his arms.

The gods appeared unto the brethren during their exile. Dharma, god of wisdom and holiness, addressed Yudhishthira his son many questions, which he answered piously and well. Hanuman, son of Vayu, the wind god, was made manifest before Bhima. It chanced that the strong Pandava, who was also Vayu's son, was hastening on his way and went swift as the wind; the earth shook under him and trees fell down, and he killed at one touch of his foot tigers and lions and even great elephants that sought to obstruct his path.[1] Hanuman shrank to the size of an ape, but his tail spread out in such great proportions across Bhima's path, that he was compelled to stay his course and stand still. He spake to Bhima then and told the tale of Rama and Sita. Then he grew suddenly as lofty as Vindhya mountain and transported his brother, the

[1] Like the Celtic giant Caoilte, who went swifter than the March wind, and the Teutonic storm-giant Ecke, who gave chase to Dietrich in his character as Thunor (Thor).—See *Teutonic Myth and Legend*, Chapter xxxviii.

Pandava, to the garden of Kuvera,[1] King of Yakshas, lord of treasure, who dwells in Mount Kailasa in the Himalayas; then Bhima procured sweet-scented flowers, which gave youth to those who had grown aged and turned grief into joy, and these he gave unto Draupadi.

Krishna came to visit the Pandavas in the forest, and Draupadi lamented before him, saying: "The evil-hearted Duryodhana dared to claim me for his slave. Fie! fie! upon the Pandavas because that they looked on in silence when I was put to shame. Is it not the duty of a husband to protect his wife? . . . These husbands of mine, who have the prowess of lions, saw me afflicted, nor lifted a hand to save."

Draupadi wept bitter tears from her exquisite coppery eyes, but Krishna at length comforted her, saying: "Thou wilt yet live to see the wives of those men who persecuted thee lamenting over their fallen husbands as they welter in their life blood. . . . I will help the Pandavas, and thou wilt be once again a queen over kings."

Krishna said to Yudhishthira: "Had I been at Dwaraka when thou wert called upon to visit Hastinapur, this unfair match would not have taken place, for I would have warned Dhritarashtra. But I was waging a war against demons. . . . What can I do, now that this disaster is accomplished? . . . It is not easy to confine the waters after the dam hath burst."

After Krishna returned to his kingdom, Draupadi continued to lament her fate. She said to Yudhishthira: "The sinful, evil-hearted Duryodhana hath a heart of steel. . . . O king, I lie on the ground, remembering my soft luxurious bed. I, who sit on a grass mat, cannot forget my chairs of ivory. I have seen thee in the court of

[1] Like the Teutonic elf-king Laurin, whose wonderful rose garden is among the Tyrolese mountains.—*Teutonic Myth and Legend.*

monarchs; now thou art a beggar. I have gazed upon thee in thy silken robes, who art now clad in rags. . . . What peace can my heart know now, O king, remembering the things that have been? My heart is full of grief. . . . Doth not thy wrath blaze up, seeing thy brothers in distress and me in sorrow? How canst thou forgive thy cruel enemy? Art thou devoid of anger, Yudhishthira? . . . Alas! a Kshatriya who doth not act at the right moment—who forgiveth the foeman he should strike down, is the most despised of all men. The hour hath now come for thee to seek vengeance; the present is not a time for forgiveness."

Said the wise Yudhishthira: "Anger is sinful; it is the cause of destruction. He that is angry cannot distinguish between right and wrong. Anger slayeth one who should be reverenced; it doth reverence to one who should be slain. An angry man may commit his own soul to hell. Know thou that wise men control their wrath so as to achieve prosperity both in this world and in the next. A weak man cannot control his wrath; but men of wisdom and insight seek to subdue their passions, knowing that he who is angry cannot perceive things in their true perspective. None but ignorant people regard anger as equivalent to energy. . . . Because fools commit folly, should I who seek wisdom do likewise? . . . If wrongs were not righted except by chastisement, the whole world would speedily be destroyed, for anger is destruction; it maketh men to slay one another. O fair Draupadi! it is meet to be forgiving; one should forgive every wrong. He who is forgiving shall attain to eternal bliss; he who is foolish and cannot forgive is destroyed both in this world and in the next. Forgiveness is the greatest virtue; it is sacrifice; it is tradition; it is inspiration. Forgiveness, O beautiful one! is holiness; it is Truth; it is Brahma. By forgiveness the universe is made steadfast. . . . The wise man who learns how to forgive attaineth to Brahma (the highest god). O Draupadi, remember thou the verses of the sage—

> 'Let not thy wrath possess thee,
> But worship peace with joy;
> Who yieldeth to temptation
> That great god will destroy'.

He who is self-controlled will attain to sovereignty, and the qualities of self-control are forgiveness and gentleness. O let me attain with self-control to everlasting goodness!"

Said Draupadi: "I bow down before the Creator and Ordainer of life and the three worlds, for my mind, it seems, hath been dimmed. By deeds men are influenced, for deeds produce consequences; by works are they set free. . . . Man can never gain prosperity by forgiveness and gentleness; thy virtue hath not shielded thee, O king; thou art following a shadow. . . . Men should not obey their own wills, but the will of the god who hath ordained all things. . . . Yet O, methinks, as a doll is moved by strings, so are living creatures moved by the lord of all; he doth play with them as a child with a toy. . . . Those who have done wrong are now happy, and I am full of grief and in sore distress. Can I praise thy god who permits of such inequality? What reward doth thy god receive when he alloweth Duryodhana to prosper —he who is full of evil; he who doth destroy virtue and religion? If a sin doth not rebound on the sinner, then a man's might is the greatest force and not thy god, and I sorrow for those who are devoid of might."

Yudhishthira made answer: "Alas! thy words are the words of an unbeliever. I do not act merely for the sake of reward. I give because it is right to give, and

I sacrifice because it is my duty so to do. I follow in the paths of those who have lived wise and holy lives, because that my heart turneth toward goodness. I am no trader in goodness, ever looking for the fruits thereof. The man who doubteth virtue will be born among the brutes;[1] he will never attain to everlasting bliss. O do not, thou fair one, doubt the ancient religion of thy people! God will reward; he is the giver of fruits for deeds; virtue and vice bear fruits. . . . The wise are content with little in this world; the fools are not content although they receive much, because they will have no joy hereafter. . . . The gods are shrouded in mystery; who can pierce the cloud which covers the doings of the gods? Although thou canst not perceive the fruits of goodness, do not doubt thy religion or the gods. Let thy scepticism give room to faith. O do not slander the great god, but endeavour to learn how to know him. Turn not away from the Supreme One who giveth eternal life, O Draupadi."

Said Draupadi: "I do not slander my god, the lord of all, for in my sorrow I but rave. . . . But yet I hold that a man should act, lest by inaction he is censured. Without acts no one can live. He who believeth in chance and destiny and is inactive, liveth a life of weakness and helplessness which cannot last long. Success comes to him who acts, and success depends on time and circumstance. So hath a wise Brahman taught me."

Bhima then spoke, charging Yudhishthira with weakness, and pleading with him to wrest the sovereignty from Duryodhana: "O thou art like froth," he cried; "thou art unripe fruit! O king, strike down thine enemies! Battle is the highest virtue for a Kshatriya."

[1] In the next life in this world, according to the belief in transmigration of souls.

Said Yudhishthira: "Verily, my heart burneth because of our sufferings. But I have given my pledge to remain in exile, and it cannot be violated, O Bhima. Virtue is greater than life and prosperity in this world; it is the way to celestial bliss."

Then they were all silent, and they pondered over these things.

Now the Pandavas had need of celestial weapons, for these were possessed by Drona and Bhishma and Karna. In time, therefore, the holy sage Vyasa appeared before Arjuna and bade him to visit Mount Kailasa, the high seat of the gracious and propitious god Shiva, the three-eyed, the blue-throated, and to perform penances there with deep devotion, so as to obtain gifts of arms. So Arjuna went his way, and when he reached the mountain of Shiva he went through great austerities: he raised his arms aloft and, leaning on naught, stood on his tiptoes; for food he ate at first withered leaves, then he fed upon air alone. Great was the fervour of his austerities, and from the ground smoke issued forth. The Rishis pleaded with Shiva, fearing disaster from the penances of Arjuna. Then the god assumed the form of a hunter and went towards Indra's warrior son, whom he challenged to single combat. First they fought with weapons; then they wrestled one with another fiercely and long, and in the end Arjuna was cast upon the ground and he swooned. When that brave Pandava regained consciousness he made a clay image of Shiva, prostrated himself and worshipped the gracious one, and made an offering of flowers. Soon afterwards he beheld his opponent wearing the garland he had given, and he knew that he had wrestled with Shiva himself. Arjuna fell down before him, and received from the god a celestial weapon named Pasupata. Then a great storm broke forth, and the earth shook, and the spirit of the weapon stood beside Arjuna, ready to obey his will.

Next appeared Indra, king of gods, Varuna, god of waters, Yama, king of the dead, and Kuvera, lord of treasures, and they stood upon the mountain summit in all their glory; unto Arjuna they gave gifts of other celestial weapons.

Thereafter Indra transported his son to his own bright city, the celestial Swarga, where the flowers always bloom and sweet music is ever wafted on fragrant winds. There he beheld sea-born Apsaras, the heavenly brides of gods and heroes, and music-loving Gandharvas, who sang songs and danced merrily in their joy. And Urvasi, a fair Apsara of faultless form, with bright eyes and silken hair, looked with love upon Arjuna; but she sought in vain to subdue him, whereat she spoke scornfully, saying: "Kama, god of love, hath wounded me with his arrows, yet thou dost scorn me. For this, O Arjuna, thou wilt for a season live unregarded among women as a dancer and musician."

Arjuna was troubled, but Indra said: "This curse will work out for thy good."

Arjuna abode in Indra's fair city for the space of five years. He achieved great skill in music and in dance and song. And he was trained also to wield the celestial weapons which the gods had given unto him.

Now the demons and giants who are named the Daityas and Danavas were the ancient enemies of Indra. Certain of them there were who had their dwellings in the lowest division of the underworld beneath the floor of ocean, which is called Patala. And a day came when Arjuna waged war with them. He rode forth in Indra's great car, which went through the air like to a bird, and Matali was the driver. When he reached the shore of the sounding sea, the billows rose against him like great mountains, and the waters were divided; he saw demon fish and giant tortoises, and vessels laden with rubies. But he paused not, for he was without fear. The mighty Arjuna was eager for battle, and he blew a mighty blast upon his war shell: the Daityas and Danavas heard him and quaked with terror.[1] Then the demons smote their drums and sounded their trumpets, and amidst the dread clamour the wallowing sea monsters arose and leapt over the waves against Indra's great son. But Arjuna chanted mantras; he shot clouds of bright arrows; he fought with his bright celestial weapons, and the furies were thwarted and beaten back. Then they sent fire against him and water, and they flung rocks like to great peaks; but he fought on until in the end he triumphed, and slew all that stood against him nor could escape.

Thereafter the valiant hero rode speedily towards the city of demons and giants which is named Hiranyapura. The women came out to lure him, calling aloud, and their voices were like the voices of cranes. He heard but paused not. All these evil giant women were driven before him; in confusion they fled, terrified by the clamour of Indra's celestial car and the driving of Matali, and their ear-rings and their necklaces fell from their bodies like to boulders tumbling and thundering adown mountain steeps.

Arjuna reached the city of Hiranyapura and entered it; and he gazed with wonder on mighty chariots with ten thousand horses, which were many-coloured like to gaily-plumaged peacocks, beautiful and stately and proud. And he wrecked the dwellings of the Daityas and Danavas.

[1] Like Dietrich von Bern, he assumes the character of the thunder god, and reminds us of Thor going eastward to battle against the Jotuns.

Indra praised his warrior son for his valour in overcoming the demons and giants of ocean, and he gave unto him a chain of gold, a bright diadem, and the war shell which gave forth a mighty blast like to thunder.[1]

During the years that Arjuna had his dwelling in Indra's celestial city, Yudhishthira and his three younger brethren, with Draupadi and the priest Dhaumya, abode a time in the forest of Kamyaka. Great sages visited them there, and from one Yudhishthira obtained skill in dice. Others led the wanderers to sacred waters, in which they were cleansed of their sins, and they achieved great virtues. And the sages related unto them many tales of men and women who suffered and made self-sacrifices, undergoing long exiles and performing penances so as to attain to great wisdom and win favour from the gods.

Thereafter the exiles went northward towards the Himalayas, and at length they beheld afar off the dwelling of Kuvera, lord of treasure and King of Yakshas. They gazed upon palaces of crystal and gold; the high walls were studded with jewels, and the gleaming ramparts and turrets were adorned by dazzling streamers. They saw beauteous gardens of bright flowers, and soft winds came towards them laden with perfume; wonderful and fair were the trees, and they were vocal with the songs of birds.

Kuvera walked forth and spake words of wisdom unto Yudhishthira, counselling him to be patient and long-suffering, and to wait for the time and the place for displaying Kshatriya prowess.

The exiles wandered on, and one day, when they sighed for Arjuna, they beheld the bright car of Indra,

[1] For slaying a sea giant, the Celtic Finn-mac-Coul was awarded by the king of Erin the "Horn of Worth", which could be heard "over seven hills". Like Arjuna's war shell, it was evidently the "thunder horn".

and they worshipped Matali, the charioteer. Then Indra came with his hosts of Apsaras and Gandharvas, and when they had adored him, the god promised Yudhishthira that he would yet reign in splendour over all men.

Arjuna appeared, and he was received with rejoicing, and all the Pandavas returned together to Kamyaka. There they were visited by Markandeya, the mighty sage, whose life endures through all the world's ages, and he spake of the mysteries and all that had taken place from the beginning, and revealed unto them full knowledge of the Deluge.

Now while the Pandavas were enduring great suffering in the forest, Karna spake to Duryodhana and prevailed upon him to spy upon their misery. So Dhritarashtra's son went forth, as was the custom every three years, to inspect the cattle and brand the calves. And with him went Karna and many princes and courtiers, and also a thousand ladies of the royal household. When, however, they all drew nigh to the forest, they found that the Gandharvas and Apsaras, who, as it chanced, had descended to make merry there, would not permit the royal train to advance. Duryodhana sent messages to the Gandharva king, commanding him to depart with all his hosts; but the celestial spirits feared him not, and issued forth to battle. A great conflict was waged, and the Kauravas were defeated. Karna fled, and Duryodhana and many of his courtiers and all the royal ladies were taken prisoners.

It happened that some of Duryodhana's followers who took flight reached the place where the Pandavas were, and told them how their kinsmen had been overcome. Then Arjuna and Bhima and the two younger brethren went forth against the Gandharvas and fought with them until they were compelled to release the royal prisoners. In this manner was the proud Duryodhana humbled by those against whom he had cherished enmity.

Yudhishthira gave a feast to the Kauravas, and he called Duryodhana his "brother", whereat Duryodhana made pretence to be well pleased, although his heart was stung with deep mortification.

After this the sullen and angry Duryodhana resolved to end his life. His friends remonstrated with him, but he said: "I have naught to live for now, nor do I desire friendship, or wealth, or power, or enjoyment. Do not delay my purpose, but leave me each one, for I will eat no more food, and I will wait here until I die. Return, therefore, unto Hastinapur and reverence and obey those who are greater than me."

Then Duryodhana made a mat of grass, and, having purified himself with water, sat down to wait for the end, clad in rags and absorbed in silent meditation.

But the Daityas and Danavas[1] desired not that their favourite rajah should thus end his life lest their power should be weakened, and they sent to the forest a strange goddess, who carried him away in the night. Then the demons, before whom Duryodhana was brought, promised to aid him in the coming struggle against the Pandavas, and he was comforted thereat, and abandoned his vow to die in solitude. So he returned speedily unto Hastinapur and resumed his high position there.

Soon afterwards, when the princes and the elders sat in council with the maharajah, wise old Bhishma praised the Pandava princes for their valour and generosity, and advised Duryodhana to offer them his friendship, so that the kinsmen might ever afterwards live together in peace. Duryodhana made no answer, and, smiling bitterly, rose up and walked out of the council chamber. Bhishma

[1] Demons and giants.

was made angry thereat, and departed also and went unto his own house.

Then Duryodhana sought to rival the glory of Yudhishthira by holding an Imperial sacrifice. Duhsasana, with evil heart, sent messengers unto Yudhishthira, inviting him to attend with his brethren; but Yudhishthira said: "Although this great sacrifice will reflect honour on all the descendants of King Bharata, and therefore upon me and my brethren, I cannot be present because our years of exile have not yet come to an end."

He spoke calmly and with dignity, but Bhima was made angry, and exclaimed: "Messengers of Duryodhana, tell thy master that when the years of exile are over, Yudhishthira will offer up a mighty sacrifice with weapons and burn in consuming flames the whole family of Dhritarashtra."

Duryodhana received these messages in silence. And when the sacrifice, which was called Vaishnava, was held, Karna said unto Duryodhana: "When thou has slain the Pandavas and canst hold thy Rajasuya[1], I will be present also to do homage unto thee."

Then Karna took a vow and said: "I will neither eat venison nor wash my feet[2] until I have slain Arjuna."

Spies hastened unto the Pandavas and related all that had taken place at the sacrifice, and also the words which Karna had spoken. When Yudhishthira heard of the terrible vow which Karna had vowed, he sorrowed greatly, for he knew that a day must come when Arjuna and Karna would meet in deadly conflict.

One day thereafter Surya, god of the sun, warned

[1] Dhritarashtra being still alive and the Pandavas having refused to attend, Duryodhana was unable, as he desired, to perform the greater sacrifice.

[2] A necessary religious act of purification before prayer. Karna thus imperilled his soul's welfare to be avenged upon his rival.

Karna that Indra had resolved to divest him of his celestial armour and ear-rings. "But," said Surya, "thou canst demand in exchange a heavenly weapon which hath power to slay gods and demons and mortal men."

So it came that Indra stood before Karna, disguised as a Brahman, and asked for his armour and ear-rings. Having vowed to give unto the Brahmans whatsoever they might ask of him, Karna took off his armour and ear-rings and gave them unto the king of the gods, from whom he demanded in exchange an infallible weapon. Indra granted his request, but smiled[1] and went upon his way, knowing well that the triumph of the Pandavas was now assured.

It chanced that one day after this that Jayadratha[2], Rajah of Sindhu, passed through the wood when the Pandavas had gone a-hunting. He beheld Draupadi with eyes of love, and, despite her warnings, carried her away in his chariot.

When the Pandavas returned and were told by a bondmaiden what had taken place, they set out in pursuit of the Rajah of Sindhu, who left his chariot when they drew nigh, and concealed himself in a thicket.

Bhima then said unto Yudhishthira: "Return now with Draupadi and our brethren. Although the rajah should seek refuge in the underworld, he will not escape my vengeance."

Said Yudhishthira: "Remember, O Bhima, that although Jayadratha hath committed a grievous sin, he is our kinsman, for he hath married the sister of Duryodhana."

Draupadi said: "He is worthy of death, for he is the

[1] A supernatural gift in such circumstances carried with it fatal consequences.

[2] *Pron.* jay-a-drat'ha.

worst of kings and the vilest of men. Have not the sages said that he who carries off the wife of another in times of peace must certainly be put to death."

When Bhima found Jayadratha, he cast him down and cut off his hair except five locks; then the strong warrior promised to spare the rajah's life if he would do homage to Yudhishthira and declare himself his slave.

So the Rajah of Sindhu had to prostrate himself before Yudhishthira as a humble menial. Thereafter he departed in his shame and went unto his own country.

When the twelfth year of exile was nigh to an end, the Pandava brethren bethought them to leave the forest. But ere they went a strange and dread adventure threatened them with dire disaster. It chanced that a stag carried away upon its antlers the twigs with which a Brahman was wont to kindle his holy fire. The Brahman appealed to Yudhishthira to pursue the animal, and the Pandavas endeavoured in vain to kill it or recover the sacred twigs. Weary with the chase, they at length sat down to rest. They were all athirst, and one of them climbed a banyan tree to look for signs of water, for birds ever flutter over pools. When it was discovered that a pond was nigh, Yudhishthira sent Nakula towards it. The young man approached the water, and ere he stooped he heard a Voice which said: "Answer thou what I shall ask of thee ere thou dost drink or draw water."

But Nakula's thirst was greater than his fear, and he drank of the waters; then he fell dead.

Sahadeva followed him, wondering why his brother tarried. He too gazed greedily upon the pool, and he too heard the Voice, but heeded not and drank; and he fell dead also.

Arjuna next went towards the water. The Voice spake to him, and he answered with anger: "Who art thou that wouldst hinder me thus? Reveal thyself, and mine arrows will speak to thee."

Then he drew his bow, and his shafts flew thick and fast as raindrops. But his valour was as naught, for when he drank he also fell dead like the others. Bhima followed him, and stooped and drank, unheeding the Voice, and he was stricken down like to Arjuna and Nakula and Sahadeva.

At length wise Yudhishthira approached the pond. He beheld his brethren lying dead, and sorrowed over them. Then, as he drew nigh to the water, the Voice spake once again, and he answered it, saying: "Who art thou?"

The Voice said: "I am a Yaksha. I warned thy brethren not to drink of this water until they had answered what I should ask of them, but they disregarded my warning and I laid them in death. If thou wilt answer my questions thou canst, however, drink here nor be afraid."

Said Yudhishthira: "Speak and I will answer thee."

The Voice said: "Who maketh the sun to rise? Who keepeth him company? Who maketh the sun to go down? In whom is the sun established?"

Said Yudhishthira: "Brahma maketh the sun to rise; the gods accompany him; Dharma maketh the sun to set; in truth is the sun established."

The Voice said: "What sleepeth with open eyes? What moveth not after birth? What is that which hath no heart? What is that which swelleth of itself?"

Said Yudhishthira: "A fish doth sleep with open eyes; an egg moveth not after birth; a stone hath no heart; a river swelleth of itself."

The Voice said: "What maketh The Way? What

is called Water? What is called Food? What is called Poison?"

Said Yudhishthira: "They that are pious make The Way; space is called water; the cow is food[1]; a request is poison."

The Voice said: "Who is spoken of as the unconquered enemy of man? What is spoken of as the enemy's disease? Who is regarded as holy? Who is regarded as unholy?"

Said Yudhishthira: "Man's unconquered enemy is anger, and his disease is covetousness; he who seeketh after the good of all is holy; he who is selfishly cold is unholy."

The Voice said: "Who are worthy of eternal torment?"

Said Yudhishthira: "He who sayeth unto the Brahman whom he hath asked to his house, I have naught to give; he who declareth the Vedas to be false; he who is rich and yet giveth naught to the poor."

Many such questions did the Voice address to wise Yudhishthira, and he answered each one patiently and with knowledge. Then the Yaksha revealed himself in the form of Dharma, god of wisdom and justice, for behold! he was the celestial sire of Yudhishthira. Unto his son he granted two boons; and Yudhishthira desired that his brethren should be restored to life, and that they should all have power to remain unrecognized by anyone in the three worlds for the space of a year.

Ere the Pandavas left the forest, Yudhishthira invoked the goddess Durga[2], giver of boons, saying: "O slayer of

[1] Babu P. C. Roy comments on this head: "The cow is the only food in this sense. The cow gives milk. The milk gives butter. The butter is used in *Homa* (the offering). The Homa is the cause of the clouds. The clouds give rain. The rain makes the seeds to sprout forth and produce food."

[2] A form of the goddess Kali, wife of Shiva.

the Buffalo Asura, thou art worshipped by the gods, for thou art the protector of the three worlds. Chief of all deities, protect thou and bless thou us. Confer victory upon us, and help us in our distress."

The goddess heard Yudhishthira, and confirmed the promise of Dharma that the Pandava brethren and Draupadi would remain unrecognized during the thirteenth and last year of their exile.

Then the wanderers concealed their weapons in a tree, and went together towards the city of Virata[1] so that they might conceal themselves. According to the terms of banishment, they would have to spend a further twelve years in the jungle if the Kauravas discovered their whereabouts.

The Pandavas found favour in the eyes of the rajah. Yudhishthira became his instructor in the art of playing with dice, because he was wont to lose heavily. Bhima was made chief cook. Arjuna, attired as a eunuch, undertook to teach dancing and music to the ladies of the harem. Nakula was given care of horses, and Sahadeva of kine. The queen was drawn towards Draupadi, who offered to become a bondwoman on condition that she should not have to wash the feet of anyone, or eat food left over after meals; and on these terms she was engaged. The queen feared that Draupadi's great beauty would attract lovers and cause dispeace; but the forlorn woman said that she was protected by five Gandharvas, and was without fear.

Bhima soon won much renown by reason of his matchless strength. At a great festival he overcame and slew a wrestler from a far country who was named Jimúta, and he received many gifts. The rajah took great pride in him, and was wont to take him to the

[1] *Pron.* vir-at'a.

apartments of the women, where he wrestled with caged tigers and lions and bears, slaying each one at desire with a single blow. Indeed, all the brothers were well loved by the monarch because of their loyal services.

It chanced that the queen's brother, Kichaka[1], a mighty warrior and commander of the royal army, was smitten with love for beautiful Draupadi, and at length he sought to carry her away. But one night Bhima waited for him when he came stealthily towards Draupadi, and after a long struggle the strong Pandava slew him. Then Bhima broke all this prince's bones and rolled up his body into a ball of flesh.

Great was the horror of Kichaka's kinsmen when they discovered what had happened, and they said: "No man hath done this awful deed; the Gandharvas have taken vengeance."

In their wrath they seized Draupadi, to burn her on the pyre with the body of Kichaka; but Bhima disguised himself and went to her rescue, and he scattered her tormentors in flight, killing many with a great tree which he had uprooted.

The rajah was terror-stricken, and spake unto the queen, and the queen thereafterwards asked Draupadi to depart from Virata. But the wife of the Pandavas begged to remain in the royal service yet a time; and she said that her Gandharva protectors would serve the rajah in his greatest hour of peril, which, she foretold, was already nigh to him. So the queen bore with her, and Draupadi tarried there.

Soon afterwards the Rajah of Trigartis, hearing that mighty Kichaka was dead, plotted with the Kauravas at Indra-prastha to attack the city of Virata with purpose to capture the raj. Duryodhana agreed to aid him, so the

[1] *Pron.* kee-chak'a ("ch" as in "change").

Rajah of Trigartis invaded the kingdom from the north, while the Kauravas marched against Virata from the south.

It came to pass that on the last day of the thirteenth year of the Pandavas' exile the first raid took place from the north, and many cattle were carried off. Yudhishthira and Bhima, with Nakula and Sahadeva, offered to give their help when it became known that the Rajah of Virata had been captured by his enemies. The Pandavas went forth to rescue the monarch, and they routed the raiders and rescued their prisoner; they also seized upon the Rajah of Trigartis, and forced him to submit with humility to his rival ere he was allowed to return to his own city.

Meanwhile the Kauravas had advanced from the south. Uttar[1], son of the Rajah of Virata, went against them, and Arjuna was his charioteer. When the young man, however, beheld his enemies, he desired to flee, but his driver compelled him by force to remain in the chariot.

Then Arjuna procured his own weapons from the tree in which they were concealed. Thus, fully armed, he rode against the Kauravas, who said: "If this be Arjuna, he and his brethren must go into exile for another twelve years."

Bhishma said: "The thirteenth year of concealment is now ended."

The Kauravas, however, persisted that Arjuna had appeared ere the full time was spent.

Indra's great son advanced boldly. Suddenly he blew his celestial war shell, and all the Kauravas were stricken with fear, and they swooned and lay on the field like men who slept. Arjuna forbore to slay them, and he commanded Uttar to take possession of their royal attire.

[1] *Pron.* oot'ar.

Then the great archer of the Pandavas returned to the city with the rajah's son.

Now when the monarch discovered how Arjuna had served him by warding off the attack of the Kauravas, he offered the brave Pandava his daughter, Uttara, for a bride; but Arjuna said: "Let her be given unto my son."

It was then that the Pandava brethren revealed unto the Rajah of Virata who they were. All those who had assembled in the palace rejoiced greatly and honoured them.

To the marriage of Abhimamju, son of Arjuna and Subhadra, came many great rajahs. Krishna came with his brother Balarama, and the Rajah Drupada came with his son Dhrishta-dyumna.

Now the Rajah of Virata resolved to aid Yudhishthira in obtaining back his kingdom from the Kauravas, who protested that their kinsmen had been discovered ere yet the complete term of exile was ended.

Shakuni, the cunning gambler, and the vengeful Karna supported the proud and evil-hearted Duryodhana in refusing to make peace with the Pandava brethren, despite the warnings of the sages who sat around the Maharajah Dhritarashtra.

CHAPTER XVII

Defiance of Duryodhana

The Council at Virata—Speeches of Kings and Princes—Army to be raised for the Pandavas—Krishna's Attitude—His Army on one side and Himself on the other—Ambassador visits Kauravas—Pandavas invited to Hastinapur—A Deadlock—Krishna visits Hastinapur—Elders counsel Peace—Duryodhana refuses to Yield—Plot to seize Krishna—A Revelation of Divine Power—Krishna's Interview with Karna—Pritha informs Karna of his Birth—Karna refuses to desert Duryodhana—His Resolution and Promise.

Ere the wedding guests departed from Virata, after merrymaking and song and dance, the elders and princes and chieftains assembled in the council chamber. Drupada was there with his son, and Krishna with his brother Balarama and Satyaki his kinsman, and all the Pandava brethren were there also, and many others both valiant and powerful. Bright and numerous as the stars were the gems that glittered on the robes of the mighty warriors. For a time they spake kindly greetings one to another, and jested and made merry. Krishna sat pondering in silence, and at length he arose and spake, saying:

"O rajahs and princes, may your fame endure for ever! Thou knowest well that Yudhishthira was deprived of his kingdom by the evil trickster Shakuni. He hath endured twelve years of exile, and hath served, like his brethren, as a humble menial for a further year in the palace of the Rajah of Virata. After long suffering Yudhishthira desires peace; his heart is without anger, although he hath endured great shame. The heart of Duryodhana, however, still burns with hate and jealous wrath; still, as in his youth, he desires to work evil by deceit against the Pandava brethren. Now, consider well, O ye monarchs, what Yudhishthira should do. Should he call many chieftains to his aid and wage war to punish his ancient foes? Or should he send friendly messengers to Duryodhana, asking him to restore the kingdom which he still continues to possess?"

Balarama then spoke and said: "Ye pious rajahs! ye have heard the words of my brother, who loveth Yudhishthira. It is true, indeed, that the Kauravas have wronged the Pandavas. Yet I would counsel peace, so that this matter may be arranged between kinsmen. Yudhishthira hath brought his sufferings upon his own head. He was unwise to play with cunning Shakuni, and also to continue playing, despite the warnings of the elders and his friends. He hath suffered for his folly. Now let a messenger be sent to Duryodhana, entreating him to restore the throne unto Yudhishthira. I do not advise war. What hath been gambled away cannot be restored in battle."

Next arose Satyaki, the kinsman of Krishna. He said: "O Balarama, thou hast spoken like to a woman. Thou remindest me that weaklings are sometimes born to warriors, like to barren saplings sprung from sturdy trees. Timid words come from timid hearts. Proud monarchs heed not counsel so weakly as thine. O Balarama! canst thou justify Duryodhana and blame the pious-hearted and gracious Yudhishthira? If it had chanced that Yudhishthira while playing with his brethren had been visited by Duryodhana, who, having thrown the dice, achieved success, then the contest would have been fair in the eyes of all men. But Duryodhana plotted to ruin his kinsman, and invited him to Hastinapur to play with the evil-hearted Shakuni, who threw loaded dice. But that is ended. Yudhishthira hath fulfilled his obligation; his exile is past, and he is entitled to his kingdom. Why, therefore, should he beg for that which is his own? A Kshatriya begs of no man; what is refused him he seizeth in battle at all times. . . . Duryodhana still clings to Yudhishthira's kingdom, despite the wise counsel of Bhishma and Drona. Remember, O Balarama, it is not sinful to slay one's enemies, but it is shameful to beg from them. I now declare my advice to be that we should give the Kauravas an opportunity to restore the throne of Yudhishthira; if they hesitate to do so, then let the Pandavas secure justice on the battle-field."

Drupada, Rajah of Panchala, then arose and said: "Ye monarchs, I fear that Satyaki hath spoken truly. The Kauravas are a stubborn people. Methinks it is useless to entreat Duryodhana, whose heart is consumed with greed. It is vain to plead with Dhritarashtra, who is but as clay in the hands of his proud son. Bhishma and Drona have already counselled in vain. Karna thirsts for war, and Duryodhana intrigues with him and also with false and cunning Shakuni. Methinks it were idle to follow the advice of Balarama. Duryodhana will never yield up what he now possesseth, nor doth he desire peace. If we should send to him an ambassador who will speak mild words, he will think that we are weak, and become more boastful and arrogant than heretofore. My advice is that we should gather together a great army without delay: the rajahs will side with him who asketh first. Meanwhile let us offer peace and friendship unto Duryodhana: my family priest will carry our message. If Duryodhana is willing to give up the kingdom of

Yudhishthira, there will be peace; if he scorns our friendship, he will find us ready for war."

Krishna again addressed the assembly and said: "Drupada hath spoken wisely. The Pandavas would do well to accept his counsel. If Duryodhana will agree to restore the raj unto Yudhishthira, there will be no strife or bloodshed. . . . You all know that the Pandavas and Kauravas are my kinsmen; know also that they are equally dear unto me. . . . I will now go hence. When ye send out messengers of war, let them enter my kingdom last of all."

After Krishna had returned home, he was visited by Duryodhana and Arjuna, for both parties desired greatly his help in the war. He spake to the rival kinsmen and said: "Behold, I stand before you as in the balance; I have put myself on one side, and all my army is on the other. Choose now between you whether you desire me or my forces. I shall not fight, but will give advice in battle."

Then Duryodhana asked for the army, but Arjuna preferred to have Krishna alone. And Krishna promised to be Arjuna's charioteer.

Duryodhana sought to prevail upon Balarama to aid him, but Krishna's brother said: "I have no heart for this war. I spake to Krishna in thy favour, but he answered me not. Well, thou knowest that thou hast wronged Yudhishthira, and that it would well become thee to act justly in this matter. Do thy duty, and thy renown will be great."

Duryodhana departed in sullen anger from Balarama.

In time Drupada's priest appeared in the city of Hastinapur, and the elders and princes sat with Dhritarashtra to hear his message. Said the Brahman: "Thus speaketh the Pandavas—'Pandu and Dhritarashtra were brothers: why, therefore, should Dhritarashtra's sons possess the whole kingdom, while the sons of Pandu are denied inheritance? Duryodhana hath ever worked evil against his kinsman. He invited them to a gambling match to play with loaded dice, and they lost their possessions and had to go into exile like beggars. Now they have fulfilled the conditions, and are prepared to forget the past if their raj is restored to them. If their rightful claim is rejected, then Arjuna will scatter the Kauravas in battle.'"

Bhishma said: "What thou hast said is well justified, but it is wrong to boast regarding Arjuna. It would be wise of thee not to speak of him in such manner again."

Angrily rose Karna and said: "If the Pandavas have suffered, they are themselves to blame. It is but fitting that they should plead for peace, for they are without followers. If they can prove their right to possessions, Duryodhana will yield; but he will not be forced by vain threatenings, or because the Rajahs of Panchala and Virata support them. O Brahman! tell thou the Pandavas that they have failed to fulfil their obligations, for Arjuna was beheld by us before the thirteenth year of banishment was completed. Let them return to a jungle for another term, and then come hither and submit to Duryodhana and beg for his favours."

Said Bhishma: "Thou didst not boast in this manner, O Karna, when Arjuna opposed thee at the Virata cattle raid. Remember that Arjuna is still powerful. If war comes, he will trample thee in the dust."

Dhritarashtra reproved Karna for his hasty speech, and said unto Bhishma: "He is young and unaccustomed to debate; be not angry with him."

Then the blind old monarch sent his minister and charioteer, Sanjaya, to the Pandavas to speak thus: "If you desire to have peace, come before me and I will do justice. Except wicked Duryodhana and hasty Karna all who are here are well disposed to you."

When Sanjaya reached the Pandavas, he was astonished to behold that they had assembled together a mighty army. He greeted the brethren and delivered his message.

Said Yudhishthira: "We honour Dhritarashtra, but fear that he has listened to the counsel of his son Duryodhana, who desires to have us in his power. The maharajah offers us protection, but not the fulfilment of our claims."

Krishna then spake, saying: "The Pandavas have assembled a mighty army, and cannot reward these soldiers unless they receive their raj. It is not yet too late to make peace. Deliver unto the Kauravas, O Sanjaya, this message: 'If you seek peace, you will have peace; if you desire war, then let there be war.'"

Ere Sanjaya left, Yudhishthira spoke to him and said: "Tell thou Duryodhana that we will accept that portion of the raj which we ourselves have conquered and settled: he can retain the rest. My desire is for peace."

Many days went past, and the Pandavas waited in vain for an answer to their message. Then Yudhishthira spake to Krishna, saying: "We have offered to make peace by accepting but a portion of our kingdom, yet the Kauravas remain silent."

Said Krishna: "I will now journey unto Hastinapur and address the maharajah and his counsellors on thy behalf."

Yudhishthira said: "Mayst thou secure peace between kinsmen."

Then Draupadi entered and, addressing Krishna, said:

"Yudhishthira is too generous towards the Kauravas in offering to give up part of his kingdom unto them. He entreateth them overmuch, as well, to grant him that which belongs not unto them. If the Kauravas wage war, my sire and many other rajahs will assist the Pandavas. . . . Oh! can it be forgotten how Duhsasana dragged me by the hair to the Gambling Pavilion, and how I was put to shame before the elders and the princes?" . . .

She wept bitterly, and Krishna pitied her. "Why do you sorrow thus?" he asked with gentle voice. "The time is drawing nigh when all the Kauravas will be laid low, and their wives will shed tears more bitter than thine that fall now, O fair one."

Messengers who arrived at Hastinapur announced the coming of Krishna. Wise Vidura counselled that he should be welcomed in state, whereupon Duryodhana proclaimed a public holiday, and all the people rejoiced, and decorated the streets with streamers and flowers.

Vidura was well pleased, and he said to Duryodhana: "Thou hast done well. But these preparations are in vain if thou art unwilling to do justice unto the Pandavas."

Duryodhana was wroth, and said: "I will give naught except what they can win in battle. If the success of the Pandavas depends upon Krishna, then let us seize Krishna and put him in prison."

Dhritarashtra was horror-stricken, and cried out: "Thou canst not thus treat an ambassador, and especially an ambassador like unto Krishna."

Bhishma rose up and said: "O maharajah, thy son desireth to work evil and bring ruin and shame upon us all. Methinks disaster is not now afar off."

So saying, he departed unto his own house, and Vidura did likewise.

All the Kauravas went forth to meet the royal ambassador save Duryodhana, who scarcely looked upon Krishna when he arrived at the palace.

Krishna went to the house of Vidura, and there he saw Pritha, who wept and said: "How fares it with my sons, whom I have not beheld for fourteen years? How fares it with Draupadi? In sorrow have I heard of their sufferings in desolate places. Ah! who can understand mine own misery, for every day is full of weariness and grief unto me?"

Said Krishna: "Be comforted, O widow of Pandu! Thy sons have many allies, and ere long they will return in triumph to their own land."

Thereafter Krishna went to the house of Duryodhana, who sat haughtily in the feasting chamber. At length Dhritarashtra's son spake unto his kinsman, who ate naught. He said: "Why art thou unfriendly towards me?"

Said Krishna: "I cannot be thy friend until thou dost act justly towards thy kinsmen, the Pandavas."

When Krishna went again to the house of Vidura, the aged counsellor said to him: "'Twere better if thou hadst not come hither. Duryodhana will take no man's advice. When he speaketh he doth expect all men to agree with him."

Said Krishna: "It is my desire to prevent bloodshed. I came to Hastinapur to save the Kauravas from destruction, and I will warn them in the council chamber on the morrow. If they will heed me, all will be well; if they scorn my advice, then let their blood be upon their own heads."

When the princes and the elders sat with Dhritarashtra in the council chamber, Narada and other great Rishis appeared in the heavens and were invited to come down and share in the deliberations, and they came down.

Krishna arose, and in a voice like thunder spake forth, saying: "I have come hither not to seek war, but to utter words of peace and love. O maharajah, let not your heart be stained with sin. Thy sons have wronged their kinsmen, and a danger threatens all: it approacheth now like an angry comet, and I can behold kinsmen slaying kinsmen, and many noble lords laid in the dust. All of you here gathered together are already in the clutch of death. O Dhritarashtra, man of peace, stretch forth thine hand and avert the dread calamity which is about to fall upon thy house. Grant unto the Pandavas their rightful claim, and thy reign will close in glory unsurpassed and in blessed peace. . . . What if all the Pandavas were slain in battle! Would their fall bring thee joy? Are they not thine own brother's children? . . . But, know thou, the Pandavas are as ready for war as they are eager for peace; and if war comes, it will be polluted with the blood of these thy sons. O gracious maharajah, let the last years of thy life be peaceful and pleasant, so that thou mayst be blessed indeed."

Dhritarashtra wept and said: "Fain would I do as thou hast counselled so wisely, O Krishna, but Duryodhana, my vicious son, will not listen to me or obey, nor will he give heed unto his mother, nor to Vidura, nor unto Bhishma."

Next Bhishma spoke, and he addressed Duryodhana, saying: "'Twould be well with thee if thou wouldst follow the advice of Krishna. Thou art evil-hearted and a wrongdoer; thou art the curse of our family; thou takest pleasure in disobeying thy royal sire and in scorning to be guided by Krishna and Vidura. Soon thy sire will be bereft of his kingdom because of thy deeds; thy pride will bring death to thy kinsmen. Hear and follow my advice; do not bring eternal sorrow to thine aged parents."

Duryodhana heard these words in anger, but was silent.

Then Drona spake to him and said: "I join with Bhishma and Krishna in making appeal unto thee. Those who advise thee to make peace are thy friends; those who counsel war are thine enemies. Be not too certain of victory; tempt not the hand of vengeance; leave the night-black road of evil and seek out the road of light and welldoing, O Duryodhana."

Next Vidura rose up. He spoke with slow, gentle voice, and said: "Thou hast heard words of wisdom, O Duryodhana. . . . I sorrow deeply in this hour. My grief is not for thee, but for thine aged sire and thine aged mother, who will fall into the hands of thine enemies; my grief is for kinsmen and friends who must die in battle, and for those who will thereafter be driven forth as beggars, friendless and without a home. The few survivors of war will curse the day of thy birth, O Duryodhana."

Again Bhishma spoke. He praised the valour of the Pandavas, and said: "It is not yet too late to avoid calamity. The field of battle is still unstained by the blood of thousands; thine army hath not yet met the arrows of death, O Duryodhana. Ere it is too late, make thy peace with thy kinsmen, the Pandavas, so that all men may rejoice. Banish evil from thine heart for ever; rule the whole world with the heirs of Pandu."

Dhritarashtra still wept. . . . The Rishis counselled peace like the elders.

Then angry Duryodhana spoke, while his eyes burned bright and his brows hung darkly, and said: "Krishna counsels me to be just, yet he hateth me and loveth the Pandavas. Bishma scowls upon me, and Vidura and Drona look coldly on; my sire weeps for my sins. Yet what have I done that ye, O elders, should turn my sire's affection from me? If Yudhishthira loved gambling and staked and lost his throne and freedom, am I to blame? If he played a second time after being set at liberty, and became an exile, why should he now call me a robber? Pallid and inconstant is the star of the Pandavas' destiny: their friends are few, and feeble is their army. Shall we, who fear not Indra even, be threatened and browbeaten by the weak sons of Pandu? No warrior lives who can overcome us. A Kshatriya fears no foeman; he may fall in battle, but he will never yield. So have the sages spoken. . . . Hear me, my kinsmen all! My sire gifted Indra-prastha to the Pandavas in a moment of weakness. Never, so long as I and my brother live, will they possess it again. Never again will the kingdom of Maharajah Dhritarashtra be severed in twain. It has been united, and so will remain for ever. My words are firm and plain. So tell thou the Pandavas, O Krishna, that they ask in vain for territory. Nor town nor village will they again possess with my consent. I swear by the gods that I will never humble myself before the Pandavas."

Said Krishna: "How canst thou speak in such a manner, O Duryodhana? How canst thou pretend that thou didst never wrong thy kinsmen? Be mindful of thine evil thoughts and deeds."

Duhsasana whispered to his elder brother: "I fear, if thou dost not make peace with the Pandavas, the elders will seize thee and send thee as a prisoner to

Yudhishthira. They desire to make thee and me and Karna to kneel before the Pandavas."

Angry was Duryodhana, and he rose and left the council chamber. Duhsasana and Karna and Shakuni followed him.

Krishna then turned to Dhritarashtra and said: "Thou shouldst arrest these four rebellious princes and act freely and justly towards the Pandavas."

The weak old maharajah was stricken with grief, and he sent Vidura for his elder son. Then came Queen Gándhári and remonstrated with Duryodhana; but when she had spoken he answered not, and went away again.

Shakuni and Karna and Duhsasana waited outside for Duryodhana, and they plotted to lay hands on Krishna so that the power of the Pandavas might be weakened. But to Krishna came knowledge of their thoughts, and he informed the elders who were there.

Once again the maharajah summoned Duryodhana before him, and Krishna said: "Ah! thou of little understanding, is it thy desire to take me captive? Know now that I am not alone here, for all the gods and holy beings are with me."

Having spoken thus, Krishna suddenly revealed himself in divine splendour. His body was transformed into a tongue of flame; gods and divine beings appeared about him; fire issued from his mouth and eyes and ears; sparks broke from his skin, which became as radiant as the sun. . . .

All the rajahs closed their eyes; they trembled when an earthquake shook the palace. But Duryodhana remained defiant.

Krishna, having resumed his human form, then bade farewell to the maharajah, who lamented the doings of Duryodhana. The divine one spake and said: "O

Dhritarashtra, thee I forgive freely; but alas! a father is often cursed by the people because of the wicked doings of his own son."

Ere Krishna left the city he met Karna and spake to him, saying: "Come with me, and the Pandavas will regard thee as their elder brother, and thou wilt become the king."

Said Karna: "Although Duryodhana is a rajah, he rules according to my counsel. . . . I know, without doubt, that a great battle is pending which will cover the earth with blood. Terrible are the omens. Calamity awaits the Kauravas. . . . Yet I cannot desert those who have given me their friendship. Besides, if I went with thee now, men would regard me as Arjuna's inferior. Arjuna and I must meet in battle, and fate will decide who is the greater. I know I shall fall in this war, but I must fight for my friends. . . . O mighty one, may we meet on earth again. If not, may we meet in heaven."

Then Krishna and Karna embraced one another, and each went his own way.

Vidura spake to Pritha, mother of the Pandavas, and said: "O mother of living sons, my desire is ever for peace, but although I cry myself hoarse, Duryodhana will not listen to my words. Dhritarashtra is old, yet he doth not work for peace; he is intoxicated with pride for his sons. When Krishna returneth to the Pandavas, war will certainly break out; the sin of the Kauravas will cause much bloodshed. I cannot sleep, thinking of approaching disaster."

Pritha sighed and wept. "Fie to wealth!" she said, "that it should cause kinsmen to slaughter one another. War should be waged between foemen, not friends. If the Pandavas do not fight, they will suffer poverty; if they go to war and win, the destruction of kinsmen will not bring triumph. My heart is full of sorrow. And alas! it is Karna who supports Duryodhana in his folly; he hath again become powerful."

Pritha lamented the folly of her girlhood which caused Karna to be, and she went forth to look for him. She found her son bathing in sacred waters, and she spoke, saying: "Thou art mine own son, and thy sire is Surya. I hid thee at birth, and Radha, who found thee, is not thy mother. It is not seemly that thou shouldst in ignorance plot with Duryodhana against thine own brethren. Let the Kauravas this day behold the friendship of thee and Arjuna. If you two were side by side you would conquer the world. My eldest son, it is meet that thou shouldst be with thy brethren now. Be no longer known as one of lowly birth."

A voice spoke from the sun, saying: "*What Pritha hath said is truth. O tiger among men, great good will be accomplished if thou wilt obey her command.*"

Karna remained steadfast, for his heart was full of honour. He said unto Pritha, his mother: "O lady, it is now too late to command my obedience. Why didst thou abandon me at birth? If I am a Kshatriya, I have been deprived of my rank. No foeman could have done me a greater injury than thou hast done. Thou hast never been a mother to me, nor do thy sons know I am their brother. How can I now desert the Kauravas, who trust in me in waging this war. I am their boat on which to cross a stormy sea. . . . I will speak without deceit unto thee. For the sake of Duryodhana I will combat against thy sons. I cannot forget his kindness; I cannot forget mine own honour. Thy command cannot now be obeyed by me. Yet thy solicitation to me will not be fruitless. I have power to slay Yudhishthira, and Bhima, and Nakula, and Sahadeva, but I promise they shall not fall by my hand. I will fight with Arjuna alone. If I slay Arjuna, I will achieve great fame; if I am slain by him, I will be covered with glory."

Said Pritha: "Thou hast pledged the lives of four of thy brethren. Be that remembered to thee in the perils of battle. Blessed be thou, and let health be given thee."

Karna said: "So be it," and then they parted, the mother going one way and the son another.

After this the Pandavas and Kauravas gathered together their mighty armies and marched to the field of battle.

CHAPTER XVIII

The Battle of Eighteen Days

Armies on the Battlefield—Bhishma leads the Kauravas—Karna refrains from fighting—Bhishma's Triumphant Charge—Arjuna's Success—Slaughter of Princes—Bhima in Peril—Iravat is slain—The Rakshasa Warrior—Duryodhana desires Karna as Leader—The Fall of Bhishma—Drona as Leader—How Abhimanyu perished—Arjuna's Revenge—The Night Battle—Drupada and Drona are slain—Karna's Vow—Bhima drinks Duhsasana's Blood—Karna's Combat with Arjuna—The Fall of Karna—The Last Day of Battle—Duryodhana in Hiding—Discovered by Pandavas—Bhima overcomes Duryodhana—Wrath of Balarama—Krishna intervenes—Drona's Son in Pandava Camp—A Night of Slaughter.

Soon after Krishna had returned from Hastinapur, Duryodhana sent a challenge to the Pandavas. His messenger spake, saying: "You have vowed to wage war against us. The time has come for you to fulfil your vow. Your kingdom was seized by me, your wife Draupadi was put to shame, and you were all made exiles. Why do you not now seek to be avenged in battle? Where is drowsy Bhima, who boasted that he would drink the blood of Duhsasana? Duhsasana is weary with waiting for him. Where is arrogant Arjuna, who hath Drona to meet? When mountains are blown about like dust, and men hold back the wind with their hands, Arjuna will take captive the mighty Drona. . . . Of what account was the mace of Bhima and the bow of Arjuna on the day when your kingdom was taken from you, and you were banished like vagabonds? . . .

Vain will be the help of Krishna when you meet us in battle."

Krishna answered the messenger, saying: "Vainly dost thou boast of prowess, but ere long thy fate will be made known unto thee. I will consume thine army like to fire which consumeth withered grass. Thou wilt not escape me, for I will drive the chariot of Arjuna. And let Duhsasana know that the vow of Bhima will ere long be fulfilled."

Said Arjuna: "Tell thou Duryodhana, 'It is unseemly for warriors to boast like women. . . . It is well that Duhsasana cometh to battle.'"

When the messenger spake these words to Duryodhana, Karna said: "Cease this chatter! Let the drums of war be sounded."

So on the morrow at red dawn the armies of the Kauravas and the Pandavas were assembled for battle on the wide plain of Kuru-Kshetra. Bhishma, with his large palmyra standard decked with five stars, had been chosen to lead Duryodhana's army, and Karna, who had quarrelled with him, vowed not to fight so long as the older warrior remained alive. "Should he fall, however," Karna said, "I will go forth against Arjuna."

The army of the Pandavas was commanded by Dhrishta-dyumna, son of Drupada, and brother of Draupadi. Among the young heroes were Arjuna's two sons, the noble and peerless Abhimanyu, whose mother was Krishna's fair sister Subhadra, and brave Iravat, whose mother was Ulupi, the serpent nymph, daughter of the king of the Nagas. Bhima's Rakshasa son, the terrible Ghatotkacha, who had power to change his shape and create illusions, had also hastened to assist his kinsmen. Krishna drove the chariot of Arjuna, who carried his celestial bow, named Gandiva, the gift of the god Agni;

and his standard was the image of Hanuman, the chief ape god, who was the son of Vayu, the wind god. Now the army of Duryodhana was more numerous than the army of Yudhishthira.

Drona led the right wing of the Kaurava forces, which was strengthened by Shakuni, the gambler, and his Gandhari lancers. The left wing was led by Duhsasana, who was followed by Kamboja cavalry and fierce Sakas and Yavanas mounted on rapid steeds. The peoples of the north were there and the peoples of the south, and of the east also.[1] Blind old Dhritarashtra was in the rear, and with him was Sanjaya, his charioteer, who related all that took place, having been gifted with divine vision by Vyasa.

Ere yet the conflict began, Yudhishthira walked unarmed towards the Kauravas, whereat his kinsmen made merry, thinking he was terror-stricken. But Pandu's noble son first spake to Bhishma and asked permission to fight against him. Bhishma gave consent. Then he addressed Drona in like terms, and Drona gave consent also. And ere he returned to his place, Yudhishthira called out before the Kaurava army: "Whoso desireth to help our cause, let him follow me." When he had spoken thus, Yuyutsu, the half-brother of Duryodhana, made answer: "If thou wilt elevate me, I will serve thee well." Said Yudhishthira: "Be my brother." Then Yuyutsu followed Yudhishthira with all his men, and no man endeavoured to hold him back.

When the armies were being set in order for battle, Arjuna bade Krishna to drive his chariot to the open space on which the struggle would take place. Indra's

[1] The late Professor H. H. Wilson considered that the Kamboja were troops of Khorasan, Balkh, and Bokhara, that the Sakas, the Sacæ of the ancients, were some of the Scythians from Turkestan and Tartary, and that the Yavanas, "Ionians", were the Greeks of Bactria. The peoples of south and east included half-breeds and aborigines.

mighty son surveyed the hosts, and when he saw his kinsmen, young and old, and his friends and all the elders and princes on either side ready to fall upon one another, his heart was touched, and he trembled with pity and sorrow. He spake to Krishna, saying: "I seek nor victory, nor kingdom, nor any joy upon earth. Those for whose sake we might wish for power are gathered against us in battle. What joy can come to us if we commit the crime of slaying our own kinsmen?"

So saying, Arjuna let fall his celestial bow and sat down on the bench of his chariot with a heart full of grief.

Krishna admonished Arjuna, saying: "Thou art a Kshatriya, and it is thy duty to fight, no matter what may befall thee or befall others. So I command thee who am responsible for thy doings. He who hath wisdom sorroweth not for the living or for the dead. As one casteth off old raiment and putteth on new, so the soul casteth off this body and entereth the new body. Naught existeth that is not of the soul."

After long instruction, Krishna revealed himself to Arjuna in his celestial splendour and power and said: "Let thy heart and thine understanding be fixed in me, and thou shalt dwell in me hereafter. I will deliver thee from all thy sins. . . . I am the same unto all creatures; there is none hateful to me—none dear. Those who worship me are in me and I am in them. Those who hate me are consigned to evil births: they are deluded birth after birth, nor ever reach unto me."[1]

Arjuna gave ear unto the counsel of Krishna, and prepared for the fray.

[1] A long section of the *Mahábhárata* occurring here, and forming a sort of episode or discussion by itself, is called "Bhagavadgita", and is dealt with more fully in Chapters VI, VII.

Loudly bellowed the war shells, and the drums of battle were sounded. The Kauravas made ready to attack with horsemen, footmen, and charioteers, and elephants of war. The Pandavas were marshalled to meet them. And the air was filled with the shouting of men, the roaring of elephants, the blasts of trumpets, and the beating of drums: the rattling of chariots was like to thunder rolling in heaven. The gods and Gandharvas assembled in the clouds and saw the hosts which had gathered for mutual slaughter.

As both armies waited for sunrise, a tempest arose and the dawn was darkened by dust clouds, so that men could scarce behold one another. Evil were the omens. Blood dropped like rain out of heaven, while jackals howled impatiently, and kites and vultures screamed hungrily for human flesh. The earth shook, peals of thunder were heard, although there were no clouds, and angry lightning rent the horrid gloom; flaming thunderbolts struck the rising sun and broke in fragments with loud noise. . . .

The undaunted warriors never faltered, despite these signs and warnings. Shouting defiance, they mingled in conflict, eager for victory, and strongly armed. Swords were wielded and ponderous maces, javelins were hurled, and numerous darts also; countless arrows whistled in speedy flight.

When the wind fell and the air cleared, the battle waxed in fury. Bhishma achieved mighty deeds. Duryodhana led his men against Bhima's, and they fought with valour. Yudhishthira fought with Salya, Rajah of Madra[1]; Dhrishta-dyumna, son of Drupada, went against Drona, who had captured aforetime half of the Panchala king-

[1] Although the brother of Madri, mother of the two younger Pandava princes, he was an ally of the Kauravas.

dom with the aid of the Pandavas. Drupada was opposed to Jayadratha, the Rajah of Sindhu, who had endeavoured to carry off Draupadi, and was compelled to acknowledge himself the slave of Yudhishthira. Many single combats were fought with uncertain result.

All day the armies battled with growing ardour. When evening was coming on, Abhimanyu, son of Arjuna, perceived that the advantage lay with the Kauravas, chiefly because of Bhishma's prowess. So he went speedily against that mighty warrior, and cut down the ensign of his chariot. Bhishma said that never before had he beheld a youthful hero who could perform greater deeds. Then he advanced to make fierce attack upon the Pandava army. Victoriously he went, cutting a blood-red path through the stricken legions; none could resist him for a time. The heart of Arjuna was filled with shame, and he rode against Bhishma, whose advance was stayed. The two heroes fought desperately until dusk. Then Bhishma retired; but Arjuna followed him, and pressed into the heart of the Kaurava host, achieving great slaughter. The truce was sounded, and the first day's battle came to an end.

Yudhishthira was despondent because that the fortunes of war seemed to be against him; in the darkness he went unto Krishna, who bade him to be of good cheer, and Yudhishthira was comforted.

On the morning of the second day Bhishma again attacked the Pandava forces, shattering their ranks; but Arjuna drove him back. Perceiving this, Duryodhana lamented to Bhishma that he had quarrelled with Karna. The old warrior made answer: "Alas! I am a Kshatriya, and must fight even against my beloved kinsman." Then he rode against Arjuna once more, and the two warriors contended fiercely and wounded one another.

Drupada's son waged a long combat with Drona, and Bhima performed mighty deeds. He leapt on the back of an elephant and slew the son of the Rajah of Maghadha[1]; and he slew the rajah and his elephant also with a single blow of his mace.

Towards evening a furious combat was waged by Abhimanyu, son of Arjuna, and Lakshmana, son of Duryodhana. The young Pandava was about to achieve the victory, when Duryodhana came to his son's aid with many rajahs. Shouts were raised: "Abhimanyu is in peril; he will be overcome by force of numbers!" Arjuna heard these words, and rode to the rescue. Thereupon the Kauravas cried out in terror: "Arjuna! Arjuna!" and scattered in flight. That evening Bhishma spake unto Drona and said: "Methinks the gods are against us."

On the third day the army of the Pandavas advanced in crescent formation and drove back the Kaurava army. Many were slain, and rivers of blood laid down the dust; horses writhed in agony, and the air was filled with the shrieking and moaning of wounded men. Terrible were the omens, for headless men rose up and fought against one another; then the people feared that all who contended in that dread battle would be slain.

When he beheld the broken cars, the fallen standards, and the heaps of slain elephants and horses and men, Duryodhana said to Bhishma: "Thou shouldst yield thy place to Karna. Methinks thou art partial to Arjuna and the Pandavas."

Said Bhishma: "Thy struggle is in vain, foolish Duryodhana. None can wipe out the stain of thy sins; of no avail is cunning against a righteous cause. Verily, thou shalt perish because of thy folly. . . . I have no

[1] Behar.

fear of battle, and I will lead the Kauravas until I triumph or fall."

Then angry Bhishma urged his charioteer to attack the enemy; and he drove back all who opposed him, even Arjuna. The fighting became general, nor did it end until night obscured the plain.

Bhima was the hero of the fourth day of battle. He swept against the Kauravas like a whirlwind; in vain were darts thrown and arrows shot at the strong Pandava. He wounded both Duryodhana and Salya, Rajah of Sindhu. Then fourteen of Duryodhana's brethren rushed to combat with him. Like the lion who licks his lips when he beholds his prey drawing nigh, Bhima awaited them. Brief and terrible was the conflict, and ere six princes fled in terror, eight were slaughtered by the mighty Pandava.

Another day dawned, and Arjuna and Bhima advanced in triumph until they were met and held back by Drona. Once again the sons of Duryodhana and Arjuna sought out one another. Mighty were their blows and swift, and for a time all men watched them, wondering greatly. At length Lakshmana was grievously wounded, and was carried from the field by his kinsmen. Abhimanyu returned in triumph to Yudhishthira. On that same day were slain by Bhuri-sravas the ten great sons of Satyaki, Krishna's kinsman.

Another day dawned, and it was a day of peril for Bhima. Confident of victory, he pressed too far into the midst of the Kaurava host, and was surrounded by overwhelming numbers. Drupada perceived his peril and hastened to help him, but neither could retreat. Then Arjuna's fearless son, the slayer of Lakshmana, with twelve brave chieftains shattered the Kaurava hosts and rescued Bhima and Drupada from the surging warriors who thirsted for their blood.

The seventh day was the day of Bhishma. None could withstand him in his battle fury. The Pandavas quailed before him, nor could Bhima or Arjuna drive him back. Ere night fell, the standard of Yudhishthira was cut down, and the Kauravas rejoiced greatly, believing that they would achieve a great victory.

On the day that followed, however, the tide of battle turned. As Bhishma advanced, his charioteer was slain, and the steeds took flight in terror. Then confusion fell on the Kaurava army. For a time the Pandavas made resistless advance amidst mighty slaughter. Then the six Gandhari princes advanced to beat back the forces of Yudhishthira. On milk-white steeds they rode, and they swept like to sea birds across the ocean billows. They had vowed to slay Iravat, son of Arjuna and the Naga princess. The gallant youth feared them not and fought triumphantly, stirred with the joy of battle; he slew five of the princes, but the sixth, the eldest prince, struck down Arjuna's son, who was plucked thus rudely from life like to a fair and tender lotus. Terrible was the grief of Arjuna when he was told that his son had fallen. Then with tear-dimmed eyes he dashed upon the foe, thirsting for vengeance; he broke through the Kaurava ranks, and Bhima, who followed him, slew more of Duryodhana's brethren.

Bhima's terrible son, the Rakshasa Ghatotkacha, also sought to be avenged when Iravat fell. Roaring like the sea, he assumed an awesome shape, and advanced with flaming spears like the Destroyer at the end of Time, followed by other Rakshasas. Warriors fled from his path, until Duryodhana went against him with many elephants; but Ghatotkacha scattered the elephant host. Duryodhana fought like a lion and slew four Rakshasas, whereupon Bhima's son, raging furiously, his eyes red as fire, dashed against Duryodhana; but that mighty Kaurava shot arrows like angry snakes, and he wounded his enemy. Then a rajah urged his elephant in front of Duryodhana's chariot for protection. Ghatotkacha slew the great animal with a flaming dart. Next Bhishma pressed forward with a division to shield Dhritarashtra's son, and the Rakshasa fought fiercely; he wounded Kripa, and with an arrow severed the string of Bhishma's bow. Then the Panchalas hastened to aid Bhima's son, and the Kauravas were scattered in flight.

Duryodhana was stricken with sorrow, and went to the snow-white tent of Bhishma that night and spoke, saying: "Forgive my harsh words, O mighty chieftain. The Pandavas are brave in battle, but they are unable to resist thee. If, however, thou dost love them too well to overcome them utterly, let Karna take thy place, so that he may lead the hosts against our enemies."

Said Bhishma: "Alas! Duryodhana, thy struggle is of no avail. The just cause must win; they who fight for the right are doubly armed. Besides, Krishna is with the Pandavas: he drives Arjuna's car, and not even the gods could strike them down. Thou art confronted by utter ruin, O proud and foolish prince. I will fight as I have fought until the end, which is not now far off."

On the next day Bhishma was like a lordly elephant which treads down the marsh reeds; he was like a fire which burns up a dry and withering forest. In his chariot he advanced triumphantly, and great was the carnage which he wrought.

Yudhishthira was in despair, and spake to Krishna when night fell. Krishna said: "Bhishma has vowed that he will not slay one who had been born a woman, knowing that the righteous would defame him if he slew a female. Let Sikhandin[1] be therefore sent against him with Arjuna."

Arjuna said: "Alas! I cannot fight behind another, or achieve the fall of Bhishma by foul means. I loved him as a child; I sat upon his knee and called him 'Father'. Rather would I perish than slay the saintly hero."

Said Krishna: "It is fated that Bhishma will fall on the morrow, a victim of wrong. As he hath fought against those whom he loveth, so must thou, Arjuna, fight against him. He hath shown thee how Kshatriyas must ever wage war, although their foemen be hated or well beloved."

Arjuna, being thus admonished, went forth on the tenth day with Sikhandin, born a woman and made a male by a Yaksha.

Once again Duryodhana sought to prevail upon Bhishma to give place to Karna, and Bhishma answered him in anger: "This day will I overcome the Pandavas or perish on the field of battle."

Then the ancient hero advanced and challenged Arjuna. A terrible conflict ensued, and it lasted for many hours; all the warriors on either side stopped fighting and looked on. At length Sikhandin rushed forward like a foaming billow, and when Bhishma saw him his arms fell, for he could not contend against one who had been born a woman. Then the arrows of Arjuna pierced Bhishma's body, and the peerless old hero fell from his chariot wounded unto death. . . . The sun went down, and darkness swept over the plain.

There was great sorrow on the blood-drenched plain

[1] A daughter of Drupada who exchanged her sex with a Yaksha. She was a re-incarnation of the Princess Amba of Kasi, who, with her two sisters, was captured by Bhishma at the swayamvara. Her sisters were the mothers of Pandu and Dhritarashtra.

that night. Arjuna wept as a son weeps for a father, and he carried water to Bhishma. Yudhishthira cursed the day on which the war began. To the dying chieftain came Duryodhana and his brethren also. Friends and enemies lamented together over the fallen hero.

Bhishma spake to Duryodhana, saying: "Hear the counsel of thy dying kinsman; his voice speaketh as from the dead. If thy heart of stone can be moved, thou wilt bring this slaughter of kinsmen by kinsmen to an end now. Restore unto Yudhishthira his kingdom and make thy peace with him, and let Pandavas and Kauravas be friends and comrades together."

He spoke in vain, for his words stirred the heart of Duryodhana to hate his kinsmen the Pandavas with a deeper hatred than before.

Karna came to the battlefield, and Bhishma said unto him: "Proud rivals have we two been, jealous one of the other, and ever at strife. My voice faileth, yet must I tell thee that Arjuna is not greater than thou art on the battlefield. Nor is he of higher birth, for thou art the son of Pritha and the sun god Surya. As Arjuna is thine own brother, 'twould be well for thee to bring this strife to an end."

But Bhishma spoke in vain. Karna hated his brother, and thirsted for his life.

A guard was set round Bhishma, who lay supported by a pillow of arrows, waiting the hour of his doom. Nor did he die until after the great conflict was ended.

The Kauravas held a council of war, and they chose Drona to be their leader. The battle standard of the Brahman was a water jar and a golden altar upon a deer-skin. He vowed before Duryodhana that he would take Yudhishthira prisoner.

On the first day of Drona's command, and the eleventh

day of the great war, Abhimanyu was foremost in the fight. He dragged a chieftain by the hair out of his chariot, and would have taken him prisoner, but Jayadratha, the rajah who had endeavoured to abduct Draupadi, intervened, and broke his sword upon the young man's buckler. Jayadratha fled, and Salya, Rajah of Madra, attacked Arjuna's noble son. But Bhima dashed forward and engaged him in fierce combat. Both were mighty wielders of the mace; they were like two tigers, like two great elephants; they were like eagles rending one another with blood-red claws. The sound of their blows was like the echoing thunder, and each stood as steadfast as a cliff which is struck in vain by fiery lightning. . . . At length both staggered and fell, but Bhima at once sprang up to strike the final blow. Ere he could accomplish his fierce desire, however, Salya was rescued by his followers and carried to a place of safety. . . . Thereafter the battle raged with more fury than ever, until night fell and hid from sight all the dead and the living.

Drona sought to fulfil his vow on the second day of his command, and he prompted Susarman, the rajah who had invaded Virata when the Pandavas were servants there, to send a challenge for single combat to Arjuna. Susarman selected a place apart. Arjuna fought many hours, until he put the boastful rajah and his followers to flight; then he taunted them for their cowardice. Meanwhile Drona had dashed upon Yudhishthira, who, when confronted by certain downfall, leapt on the back of a swift steed and escaped from the battlefield. But it was no shame for a Kshatriya to flee before a Brahman.

Duryodhana went against Bhima: he was wounded after a brief combat, and retreated from the field. Many warriors then pressed against Bhima, but Arjuna had returned after fighting Susarman, and drove furiously against the Kauravas; in triumph he swept over the blood-red plain. Karna watched his rival with jealous wrath and entered the fray. The fire burned redly in his eyes, and he attacked Arjuna, resolved to conquer or to die. Uncertain and long was the conflict, and when night fell the two great warriors withdrew relunctantly from the field.

Drona on the morrow arranged his army like to a spider's web, and once again Susarman challenged Arjuna, so as to draw him from the battle-front. It was the day of Abhimanyu's triumph and the day of his death. Yudhishthira sent Arjuna's son to break the web of foemen, and he rode his chariot against elephants and steeds with conquering fury. Duryodhana attacked the youthful hero with a band of warriors, but fell wounded by Abhimanyu, who also slew the warriors. Salya next dashed against Arjuna's son, but ere long he was carried from the field grievously wounded. Then Duhsasana came forward, frowning and fierce.

Abhimanyu cried out: "Base prince, who plotted with Shakuni to win the kingdom of Yudhishthira and put Draupadi to shame, I welcome thee, for I have waited long for thee. Now thou wilt receive meet punishment for thy sins."

As he spake, the fearless youth flung a dart, and Duhsasana fell stunned and bleeding, but was rescued from death by his followers.

Proudly rode Lakshmana, son of Duryodhana, against Arjuna's son, and fought bravely and well; but he was cut down, and died upon the battlefield.

Then it was that the evil Jayadratha, who had vowed to be the slave of Yudhishthira in the forest, advanced stealthily with six warriors to fight with the lordly youth. Round him they surged like howling billows; alone stood

Abhimanyu, and seven were against him. His charioteer was slain and his chariot was shattered; he leapt to the ground and fought on, slaying one by one. . . . Perceiving his peril, the Pandavas endeavoured to rescue Arjuna's son; but Jayadratha held them back, and Karna aided him. At length Abhimanyu was wounded on the forehead, blood streamed into his eyes and blinded him, and he stumbled. Ere he could recover, the son of Duhsasana leapt forward and dashed out his brains with a mace. So died the gallant youth, pure as he was at birth. He died like to a forest lion surrounded by hunters; he sank like to the red sun at evening; he perished like to a tempest whose strength is spent; he was spent out even like a fire which has consumed a forest and is extinguished on the plain; Abhimanyu was lost as is the serene white moon when shrouded in black eclipse.

So that day's battle ended, and Abhimanyu slumbered in the soft starlight, lifeless and cold.

When it was told to Arjuna that his son was slain, the mighty warrior wept silently and lay upon the ground. At length he leapt up and cried: "May the curse of a father and the vengeance of a warrior smite the murderers of my boy! . . . May I never reach heaven if I do not slay Jayadratha on the morrow. . . ." A spy hastened to the camp of the Kauravas and told of the vow which Arjuna had taken. Jayadratha trembled with fear.

Early next morning Arjuna spake to Krishna, saying: "Drive swiftly, for this will be a day of great slaughter." He desired to find Jayadratha; with him went Bhima and Satyaki. Many warriors engaged them in battle, for the Kauravas hoped to contrive that the sun should go down ere Arjuna could fulfil his terrible vow.

Mounted on an elephant, Duhsasana opposed Arjuna; but the lordly tusker took flight when the rattling chariot drew nigh. Drona blocked the way; but Arjuna refused combat, saying: "Thou art as a father unto me. . . . Let me find the slayer of my son. . . ." He passed on. Then Duryodhana came up and engaged him. Karna fought with Bhima, and Bhurisrava attacked Satyaki. Long waged the bitter conflicts, and at length Krishna perceived that his kinsman was about to be slain. He called to Arjuna, who cast a celestial weapon at Bhurisrava, which cut off both his arms; then Satyaki slew him. Many warriors confronted Arjuna thereafter, and many fell. But the day wore on and evening drew nigh, and he could not find Jayadratha. At length Arjuna bade Krishna to drive furiously onward, and to pause not until he found the slayer of his son. The chariot sped like to a whirlwind, until at length Arjuna beheld the evil-hearted Jayadratha; he was guarded by Karna and five great warriors, and at that time the sun had begun to set.

Karna leapt forward and engaged Arjuna; but Krishna, by reason of his divine power, caused a dark cloud to obscure the sun, whereupon all men believed that night had fallen. Karna at once withdrew; but Arjuna drove on, and as the sun shot forth its last ray of dazzling light, he dashed upon Jayadratha as a falcon swoops down upon its prey. Brief was the struggle, for ere daylight faded utterly, Arjuna overthrew the slayer of his son and cut off his head. Bhima uttered a roar of triumph when he saw the head of Jayadratha held aloft, and the Kauravas sorrowed greatly because that their wicked design had been thwarted.

Night fell, but the fighting was renewed. In the darkness and confusion men slew their kinsmen, fathers cut down their sons, and brothers fought against brothers. Yudhishthira sent men with torches to light up the blood-red plain, and the battle was waged for many hours. Swords were splintered and spears were lost, and warriors threw great boulders and chariot wheels against one another. All men were maddened with the thirst for blood, and the night was filled with horrors.

At length Arjuna called for a truce, and it was agreed that the warriors should sleep on the battlefield. So all lay down, the charioteer in his chariot, the horseman on his steed, and the driver of the elephant on his elephant's back. . . .

Duryodhana reproached Drona because that he did not slay the Pandavas in their sleep. . . . "Let Karna," he said, "lead the hosts to victory."

Said Drona: "Thou art reaping the red harvest of thy sins. . . . But know now that on the morrow either Arjuna will fall or I will be slain by him."

When the bright moon rose in the heavens the conflict was renewed. Many fell on that awful night. Ghatotkacha, the Rakshasa son of Bhima, was foremost in the fray, and he slaughtered numerous Kaurava warriors. At length Karna went against him, and then the air was filled with blazing arrows. Each smote the other with powerful weapons, and for a time the issue hung in the balance. Ghatotkacha created illusions, but Karna kept his senses in that great fight, even after his steeds had been slain; he leapt to the ground, then flung a celestial dart, the gift of Indra, and Ghatotkacha, uttering terrible cries, fell down and breathed his last breath. The Kauravas shouted with gladness, and the Pandavas shed tears of sorrow.

Ere the night was ended, Drona slew his ancient enemy Drupada, Rajah of Southern Panchala, and he cut down also the Rajah of Virata.

Ere dawn broke, Dhrishta-dyumna, son of Drupada,

went forth to search for Drona, the slayer of his beloved sire.

Said Bhima: "Thou art too young to strike down so great a warrior as Drona. I will fight with him until he is wearied, then thou canst approach and be avenged."

Bhima struggled with the sage, his preceptor, for many hours; then Dhrishta-dyumna engaged him, but neither could prevail over the slayer of Drupada.

At length the Pandava warriors shouted falsely: "Aswatthaman, son of Drona, is slain."

When Drona heard the dread tidings, he fainted in his chariot, and vengeful Dhrishta-dyumna rushed forward and cut off his head. Then the son of Drupada threw the head of Drona towards Duryodhana, saying: "Here is the head of thy mighty warrior; I will cut off the heads of each Kaurava prince in like manner."

The fall of Drona was like the sinking of heaven's sun; it was like the drying up of the ocean; the Kauravas fled away in fear.

Terrible was the grief of Aswatthaman when he approached at eventide and found that his sire had been slain. Night fell while he sorrowed, and he vowed to slay Dhrishta-dyumna and all his kindred.

Karna was then chosen to be the leader of the Kaurava army, and Duryodhana hailed him with joy and said: "Thou alone canst stem the tide of our disasters. Arjuna hath been spared by Bhishma and by Drona because that they loved him. But the arm of Karna is strengthened by hatred of the proud Pandava archer."

When morning broke over the plain of Kuru-kshetra, the first battle of Karna began, and it continued all day long. Countless warriors were slain; blood ran in streams, and the dead and mangled bodies of men and elephants and horses were strewn in confusion. The air was darkened with arrows and darts, and it rang with the shouts of the fighters and the moans of the wounded, the bellowing of trumpets, and the clamour of drums.

At length evening came on and the carnage ended. . . . . Duryodhana summoned a council of war and said: "This is the sixteenth day of the war, and many of our strongest heroes have fallen. Bhishma and Drona have fallen, and many of my brethren are now dead."

Said Karna: "To-morrow will be the great day of the war. I have vowed to slay Arjuna or fall by his hand."

Duryodhana was cheered by Karna's words, and all the Kauravas were once more hopeful of victory.

In the morning Karna went forth in his chariot. He chose for his driver Salya, Rajah of Madra, whose skill was so great that even Krishna was not his superior.

Arjuna was again engaged in combat with Susarman when Karna attacked the Pandava army. So the son of Surya went against Yudhishthira and cast him on the ground, saying: "If thou wert Arjuna I would slay thee."

Bhima then attacked Karna, and they fought fiercely for a time, until Arjuna, having overcome Susarman, returned again to combat with Karna.

Duhsasana, who put Draupadi to shame, came up to help Karna, and Bhima sprang upon him. Now Bhima had long desired to meet this evil-hearted son of the blind maharajah, so that he might fulfil his vow. He swung his mace and struck so mighty a blow that the advancing chariot was shattered. Duhsasana fell heavily upon the ground and broke his back. Then Bhima seized him and, whirling his body aloft, cried out: "O Kauravas, come ye who dare and rescue the helper of Karna."

No one ventured to approach, and Bhima cast down Duhsasana's body, cut off his head, and drank his blood as he had vowed to do. "Ho! ho!" he cried, "never have I tasted a sweeter draught. . . ."

Many Kaurava warriors fled, and they cried out: "This is not a man, for he drinketh human blood."

All men watched the deadly combat which was waged between the mighty heroes Arjuna and Karna. They began by shooting arrows one at another, while Krishna and Salya guided the chariots with prowess and care. The arrows of Arjuna fell upon Karna like to summer rain; Karna's arrows were like stinging snakes, and they drank blood. At length Arjuna's celestial bow Gandiva was struck and the bow-string severed. . . .

Arjuna said: "Pause, O Karna. According to the rules of battle, thou canst not attack a disabled foeman."

But Karna heeded not. He showered countless arrows, until his proud rival was wounded grievously on the breast.

When Arjuna had restrung his bow, he rose up like to a stricken and angry tiger held at bay, and cast a screen of arrows against his foe. But Karna feared him not, nor could Arjuna bear him down. The issue hung in the balance. . . .

Then suddenly a wheel of Karna's chariot sank in the soft ground, nor could Salya urge the horses to advance.

Karna cried out: "Pause now, O Arjuna, nor wage unequal war. It is not manly to attack a helpless enemy."

Arjuna paused; but Krishna spake quickly, saying: "O Karna, thou speakest truly; but was it manly to shoot arrows at Arjuna whilst he engaged himself restringing his bow? Was it manly to scoff at Draupadi when she was put to shame before elders and princes in the gambling hall? Was it manly of thee and six warriors to surround Abhimanyu so as to murder him without compassion?"

When Arjuna heard his son's name, his heart burned with consuming wrath. Snatching from his quiver a crescent-bladed arrow, he drew his bow and shot it at Karna, whose head was immediately struck off.

So fell in that dread combat a brother by a brother's hand.

The Kauravas fled in terror when Karna was slain, and Kripa said unto Duryodhana: "Now that our greatest warriors are dead, it would be well to sue for peace."

Said Duryodhana: "After the wrongs I have done the Pandavas, how can I ask or expect mercy at their hands? Let the war go on till the end comes."

Salya was then chosen as the leader of the Kaurava army, which had greatly shrunken in numbers, and on the morning of the eighteenth day of the war the battle was waged with fury. But the Pandavas were irresistible, and when Duryodhana perceived that they were sweeping all before them, he fled away secretly, carrying his mace. He had power to hide under water as long as he desired, by reason of a mighty charm which had been conferred upon him by the demons; so he plunged into a lake and lay concealed below the waters.

Salya was slain by Yudhishthira, and he fell like to a thunder-splintered rock. Sahadeva overthrew false Shakuni, the gambler, who had played against Yudhishthira with loaded dice, and Bhima cut down all Duryodhana's brethren who had survived until that last fateful day. Of all the Kaurava heroes there then remained alive only Aswa-thaman, son of Drona, Kripa, and Kritavarman, and the hidden Duryodhana.

At length Bhima discovered where Duryodhana was

concealed. Yudhishthira went to the lake side and urged him to come forth and fight.

Said Duryodhana: "Take my kingdom now and have pleasure in it. Depart and leave me, for I must retire to the jungle and engage in meditation."

Yudhishthira said: "I cannot accept aught from thee except what is won in battle."

Said Duryodhana: "If you promise to fight one by one, I will come out of the water and slay you all."

Yudhishthira said: "Come forth, and the battle will be fought as thou dost desire. Now thou hast spoken as becomes a Kshatriya."

Still Duryodhana tarried, and Bhima shouted: "If thou dost not come out of the lake at once, I will plunge in and drag thee to the shore."

Then Duryodhana came forth, and the Pandavas laughed to see him, for he was covered with mire, and water streamed down from his raiment.

Said Duryodhana: "Soon will your merriment be turned to grief."

Now, all during the time of the Pandava exile, Duryodhana had practised with the mace, so that he became the equal of Bhima. But he had no one to support him there. The other survivors remained in hiding. Then Balarama appeared, and he caused the combat to be waged in the middle of the blood-red plain; he was Duryodhana's supporter.

The warriors fought like two fierce bulls, and smote one another heavy blows, until their faces were reddened with blood. Once Duryodhana almost achieved victory, for he struck Bhima on the head so that all present thought that the Pandava hero had received his deathblow. Bhima staggered but recovered himself, and soon afterwards he struck Duryodhana a foul blow upon the knee, which smashed the bone so that he fell prostrate. Thus was the vow of Bhima fulfilled. . . .

He danced round Duryodhana a time, then, kicking his enemy's head, cried out at length: "Draupadi is avenged."

Yudhishthira was wroth; he smote Bhima on the face and said: "O accursed villain, thou wilt cause all men to speak ill of us."

Then Arjuna led Bhima away, and Yudhishthira knelt beside Duryodhana and said: "Thou art still our ruler, and if thou wilt order me to slay Bhima, thy command will be obeyed. Thou art now very nigh unto death, and I sorrow for the Kaurava wives and children, who will curse us because that thou hast been laid low."

Said Balarama: "Bhima hath broken the laws of combat, for he smote Duryodhana below the waist."

Krishna said: "My brother, did not Duryodhana wrong the Pandavas with foul play at dice? And did not Bhima, when he beheld Draupadi put to shame, vow to break the knee of Duryodhana?"

Said Balarama: "So thou dost approve of this? . . . Can I forget that Bhima kicked the head of our wounded kinsman, the rajah?"

Krishna stayed the vengeful hand of Balarama, and prevailed upon him to take vows not to fight against the Pandavas.

When night fell, the dying Duryodhana was visited on the battlefield by Aswatthaman, son of Drona, and Kripa, and Kritavarman. Unto Aswatthaman he gave permission to attack the Pandavas while yet they slumbered. . . . Then Drona's son went forth in the darkness to glut his hunger for vengeance because that his sire had been slain. . . . The pale stars looked down on the dead and the dying as Aswatthaman crossed the battleplain and went stealthily towards the tents of his foemen, with Kripa and Kritavarman.

At the gate of the Pandava camp an awful figure rose up against the conspirators. Aswatthaman was not afraid, and he fought with his adversary until he perceived that he was the god Shiva, the Blue-throated Destroyer. Then Drona's son drew back, and on an altar he kindled a fire to worship the all-powerful deity. Then, having naught else to sacrifice, he cast his own body upon the flames. By this supremely pious act Shiva was propitiated; he accepted Drona's son and entered his body, saying: "Hitherto, for the sake of Krishna, have I protected the sons of Draupadi, but now their hour of doom hath come."

Then Aswatthaman rushed into the camp and slaughtered with the cruel arm of vengeance. Rudely he awakened Dhrihsta-dyumna, who cried out: "Coward! wouldst thou attack a naked man?"

Aswatthaman answered not his father's slayer, but took his life with a single blow. . . . Through the camp he went, striking down each one he met, and shrieks and moans arose on every side.

Draupadi was awakened by the clamour, and her five young sons sprang up to protect her. Aswatthaman slew each one without pity. . . . Then he lit a great fire to discover those who had concealed themselves, and with reeking hands he completed his ghastly work of slaughter. Meanwhile Kripa and Kritavarman, with weapons in their hands, kept watch at the gate, and cut down all who endeavoured to escape.

Now the Pandava princes slept safely on that night of horror in the camp of the Kauravas, so that they escaped the sword of Drona's son.

When his fell work was accomplished, the bloodthirsty Aswatthaman cut off the heads of Draupadi's five sons and carried them to Duryodhana, who rejoiced greatly, believing that they were the heads of Yudhishthira and his brethren. But when he perceived that the avenger of night had slain the children of Draupadi instead, he cried out: "Alas! what horror hast thou committed? Thou hast slain innocent children, who, had they lived, would have perpetuated our name and our fame. My heart burns with anger against the sires and not their harmless sons."

Duryodhana groaned heavily: his heart was oppressed with grief, and, bowing down his head, he died sorrowing.

Then Aswatthaman and Kripa and Kritavarman fled away, fearing the wrath of the Pandavas.

CHAPTER XIX

Atonement and the Ascent to Heaven

Draupadi's Sorrow—The Vengeful Maharajah—Bhima is Forgiven—Dead Burned on Battlefield—Atonement for Sin—The Horse Sacrifice—Arjuna's Wanderings—A Woman turned to Stone—The Amazons—Fathei and Son Conflict—The Wonderful Serpent Jewel—Return of the Horse—The Sacrifice Performed—Maharajah Retires to the Forest—Meeting of Mournful Relatives—The Vision of the Dead—Widows Drown Themselves—A Forest Tragedy—Dwaraka Horrors—End of Krishna and Balarama—City Destroyed by the Sea—Farewell of the Pandavas—The Journey to Heaven—Yudhishthira Tested by Deities—Vision of Hell—The Holy Life.

WHEN it was told to the Pandava brethren that their camp had been raided in darkness by the bloodthirsty Aswatthaman, Yudhishthira exclaimed: "Alas! sorrow upon sorrow crowds upon us, and now the greatest sorrow of all hath fallen. Draupadi mourns the death of her brother and her five sons, and I rear she will perish with grief."

Draupadi came before her husbands and, weeping bitterly, said: "For thirteen cruel years you have endured shame and exile so that your children might prosper. But now that they are all slain, can you desire to have power and kingdom?"

Said Krishna: "O daughter of a rajah, is thy grief so great as is Pritha's and Gandhari's, and as great as those who lament the loss or their husbands on the battlefield? Thou hast less cause than others to wail now."

Draupadi was soothed somewhat, but she turned to

Bhima and said: "If thou wilt not bring to me the head of Aswatthaman, I will never again look upon thy face."

Said Yudhishthira: "Aswatthaman is a Brahman, and Vishnu, the greatest of the gods, will punish him if he hath done wrong. If we should slay him now, O Draupadi, thy sons and thy brother and thy sire would not be restored unto thee."

Draupadi said: "So be it. But Aswatthaman hath a great jewel which gleams in darkness. Let it be taken from him, for it is as dear unto him as his life."

Then Arjuna went in pursuit of Aswatthaman and found him, and returned with the jewel.

To the battlefield came blind old Dhritarashtra, mourning the death of his hundred sons. And with the weeping maharajah were Queen Gandhari and the wives of the Kaurava princes, who sorrowed aloud. Wives wept for their husbands, their children wailed beside them, and mothers moaned for their sons. Bitter was the anguish of tender-hearted women, and the air was filled with wailing on that blood-red plain of Kurukshetra.

When Queen Gandhari beheld the Pandavas she cried out: "The smell of Duryodhana is upon you all."

Now Dhritarashtra plotted in his weak mind to crush the head of Bhima, the slayer of Duryodhana. When he embraced Yudhishthira he said: "Where is Bhima?" and they placed before him an image of the strong Pandava. Dhritarashtra put forth his arms, and he crushed the image in his embrace and fell back fainting. Then he wailed: "Alas! Bhima was as a son unto me. Although I have slain him, the dead cannot return."

Well pleased was the maharajah when it was told to him that Bhima still lived; and he embraced his son's slayer tenderly and with forgiveness, saying: "I have no children now save the sons of Pandu, my brother."

Pritha rejoiced to meet her five sons, and she embraced them one by one. Then she went towards the sorrowing Draupadi, who fainted in her arms. Thereafter they wept together for the dead.

The bodies of the slain rajahs and princes were collected together, and wrapped in perfumed linen and laid each upon a funeral pyre and burned, and the first pyre which was kindled was that of Duryodhana. The Pandavas mourned for their kinsmen. Then they bathed in the holy Ganges, and took up water and sprinkled it in the name of each dead hero. Yudhishthira poured out the oblation for Karna, his brother, and he gave great gifts to his widows and his children. Thereafter all the remaining bodies of the slain were burned on the battlefield.[1]

Yudhishthira was proclaimed rajah in the city of Hastinapur, and he wore the great jewel in his crown. A great sacrifice was offered up, and Dhaumya, the family priest of the Pandavas, poured the Homa offering to the gods on the sacred fire. Yudhishthira and Draupadi were anointed with holy water.

In the days that followed, Yudhishthira lamented over the carnage of the great war, nor could he be comforted. At length Vyasa, the sage, appeared before him and advised that he should perform the horse sacrifice to atone for his sins.

Then search was made for a moon-white horse with yellow tail and one black ear, and when it was found a plate of gold, inscribed with the name of Yudhishthira, was tied upon its forehead. Thereafter the horse was

[1] No widows were burned with their husbands, for the Sati (or Suttee) ceremony had not yet become general in India; nor did the Brahmans officiate at the pyres.

let loose, and was allowed to wander wheresoever it desired. A great army, which was led by Arjuna, followed the horse.

Now it was the custom in those days that when the sacred horse entered a raj[1], that raj was proclaimed to be subject to the king who performed the ceremony. And if any ruler detained the horse, he was compelled to fight with the army which followed the wandering animal. Should he be overcome in battle, the opposing rajah immediately joined forces with those of the conqueror, and followed the horse from kingdom to kingdom. For a whole year the animal was allowed to wander thus.

The horse was let loose on the night of full moon in the month of Choitro.[2]

Arjuna met with many adventures. He fought against a rajah and the son of a rajah, who had a thousand wives in the country of Malwa, and defeated them. But Agni, who had married a daughter of the rajah, came to rescue his kin. He fought against Arjuna with fire, but Arjuna shot celestial arrows which produced water. Then the god made peace, and the rajah who had detained the horse went away with Arjuna. Thereafter the horse came to a rock which was the girl-wife of a Rishi who had been thus transformed because of her wickedness. "So will you remain," her husband had said, "until Yudhishthira performs the Aswa-medha ceremony." The horse was unable to leave the rock. Then Arjuna touched the rock, which immediately became a woman, and the horse was set free.

In time the horse entered the land of Amazons, and the queen detained it, and came forth with her women warriors to fight against Arjuna, who, however, made peace with them and went upon his way. Thereafter

[1] Royal territory. [2] The Easter full moon.

the holy steed reached a strange country where men and women and horses and cows and goats grew upon mighty trees like to fruit, and came to maturity and died each day. The rajah came against Arjuna, but was defeated. Then all the army fled to the islands of the sea, for they were Daityas, and Arjuna plundered their dwellings and obtained much treasure.

Once the horse entered a pond, and was cursed by the goddess Parvati, and it became a mare; it entered another pond and became a lion, owing to a Brahman's spell.

In the kingdom of Manipura the horse was seized, and soldiers armed with fire weapons were ready to fight against the Pandavas and their allies. But when the rajah, whose name was Babhru-váhana, discovered that the horse bore the name of Yudhishthira, he said: "Arjuna is my sire;" and he went forth and made obeisance, and put his head under the foot of the Pandava hero. But Arjuna spurned him, saying: "If I were thy sire, thou wouldst have no fear of me."

Then the rajah challenged Arjuna to battle, and was victorious on that day.[1] He took all the great men prisoners, and he severed Arjuna's head from his body with a crescent-bladed arrow. The rajah's mother, Chitrangada, was stricken with sorrow, as was also Ulupi, the daughter of Vasuka, the king of serpents, who had borne a son to Arjuna. But Ulupi remembered that her sire possessed a magic jewel which had power to restore a dead man to life, and she sent the rajah of Manipura to obtain it from the underworld. But the Nagas refused to give up the jewel, whereupon Arjuna's mighty

[1] Here we meet with the familiar father-and-son-combat theme of which the stories of the Persian Sohrab and Rustem, the Germanic Hildebrand and Hadubrand, and the Celtic Cuchullin and Conlaoch are representative variants. Arjuna had effected a temporary exogamous marriage according to matriarchal customs.

son fought against them with arrows which were transformed into peacocks; and the peacocks devoured the serpents. Then the Naga king delivered up the magic jewel, and the rajah returned with it. He touched the body of Arjuna with the jewel, and the hero came to life again, and all his wounds were healed. When he departed from Manipura city the rajah, his son, accompanied him.

So from kingdom to kingdom the horse wandered while the army followed, until a year had expired. Then it returned to Hastinapur.

Yudhishthira had meantime lived a life of purity and self-restraint. Each night he lay upon the ground, and always slept within the city. Beside him lay Draupadi, and a naked sword was ever betwixt them.

Great were the rejoicings of the people when the horse came back: they made glad holiday, and went forth to welcome the army with gifts of fine raiment and jewels and flowers. Money was scattered in the streets, and the poor were made happy, being thus relieved generously in their need.

Yudhishthira embraced Arjuna and kissed him and wept tears of gladness, and welcomed Arjuna's son, Babhru-váhana, Rajah of Manipura, and also the other rajahs who had followed the sacred horse.

Twelve days after the return of Arjuna, and on the day when Magha's full moon marked the close of the winter season, the people assembled in great multitudes from far and near to share Yudhishthira's generous hospitality and witness the Aswa-medha ceremony, which was held upon a green and level portion of consecrated ground. Stately pavilions, glittering with jewels and gold, had been erected for the royal guests, and there were humbler places for the Brahmans. In thrones of gold sat Maharajah Dhritarashtra and Rajah Yudhishthira, and the other rajahs had thrones of sandalwood and gold. The royal ladies were ranged together in their appointed places. Wise Vyasa was there, and he directed the ceremony. And Krishna, the holy one, was there also.

When all the guests were assembled, Yudhishthira and Draupadi bathed together in the sacred waters of the Ganges. Then a portion of ground was measured out, and Yudhishthira ploughed it with a golden plough. Draupadi followed him, and sowed the seeds of every kind which is sown in the kingdom, while all the women and the Brahmans chanted holy mantras. Then a golden altar was erected with four broad layers of golden bricks, and stakes of sacred wood from the forest and from Himalaya, and it was canopied and winged with gold-brocaded silk.

Then eight pits were dug for Homa[1] of milk and butter to be made ready for the sacrificial fire, and in skins were wrapped up portions of every kind of vegetable and curative herb which grew in the kingdom, and these were placed in the Homa pits.

On the ground there were numerous sacrificial stakes, to which were tied countless animals—bulls and buffaloes and steeds, wild beasts from forest and mountain and cave, birds of every kind, fishes from river and lake, and even insects.

The priests offered up animals in sacrifice to each celestial power, and the feasting was beheld by sacred beings. The Gandharvas sang, and the Apsaras, whom the Gandharvas wooed, danced like sunbeams on the grass. Messengers of the gods were also gathered there, and Vyasa and his disciples chanted mantras to celestial music. The people lifted up their voices at the sound

[1] Offerings.

of rain drum and the blast of the rain trumpet. Then bright was the lustre of Yudhishthira's fame.

When all the kings and royal ladies and sages took their places to be blessed by the horse sacrifice, Yudhishthira sat on his throne, and in his hand he held the horn of a stag.

Vyasa sent four-and-sixty rajahs with their wives to draw water from the holy Ganges. Many musicians went with them beating drums and blowing trumpets and playing sweet instruments, and girls danced in front, going and returning. And all the rajahs and their wives were given splendid raiment by Yudhishthira, and necklaces of jewels also, and he put betelnut in their mouths one by one. To the Brahmans were gifted much gold and many jewels, and elephants, horses, and kine, and they were well pleased.

Yudhishthira then sat naked in his throne, and each one who had drawn holy water poured a quantity over his head; and they poured what remained over the head of the sacred white horse.

Nákula held the horse's head, and said: "The horse speaketh."

Those who were about him asked in loud voices: "What doth the horse reveal?"

Said Nákula: "Thus speaketh the horse—'In other such ceremonies the horse which is sacrificed departs unto Swarga[1], but I shall rise far above Swarga, because that Krishna is here'."

Then Dhaumya, having washed the horse, gave a scimitar to Bhima with which to strike off the head at a single blow. But ere this was done, Dhaumya pressed an ear of the holy animal, and milk flowed forth. Then he said to Bhima: "Pure indeed is the horse; verily the

[1] Indra's heaven.

gods will accept the sacrifice. Strike now, O strong one."

Bhima raised the scimitar and severed the head, which immediately ascended unto heaven and vanished from before the eyes of all. Great was the wonder and the joy of the assembled multitude.

Krishna and other rajahs and sages then cut open the horse's body, from which a bright light issued forth. They found that the animal was pure, and Krishna said unto Yudhishthira: "This, thy sacrifice, is acceptable unto Vishnu."

Draupadi was made Queen of the Sacrifice, and mantras were chanted, and she was adored and given rich offerings, because of her virtue and her wisdom.

The body of the slain steed was divided, and the flesh gave forth the odour of camphor. Priests lifted portions in their ladles and placed these on the sacrificial fire, and they made Soma. And Rajah Yudhishthira and all his brethren stood in the sin-cleansing smoke and breathed its fragrance.

Dhaumya cried out, as he laid a piece of flesh on the altar fire: "O Indra, accept thou this flesh which hath turned to camphor."

When he had uttered these words, Indra, accompanied by many gods, appeared before the people, who made obeisance with fear and secret joy. Indra took from Vyasa portions of the flesh and gave these to each of the gods. Then he vanished from sight with all his companions.

Vyasa blessed Yudhishthira, and Krishna embraced him.

Said Krishna: "Thy fame will endure for ever."

Yudhishthira made answer: "Unto thee do I owe all these blessings."

Thereafter Krishna and the rajahs poured holy water over the heads of Yudhishthira and Draupadi.

All the fragments of the herbs which had been provided for Homa were then ground into powder. And Yudhishthira gave balls of the powder to each one present, so that they might eat of the sacred herbs and share in the blessings of the Aswa-medha. He ate his own portion last of all. The fragments of the offerings which remained were burnt on the altar.

Then Pritha and all the maidens who were with her made merry, while the musicians played gladsome airs.

Yudhishthira distributed more gifts. Unto Vyasa he assigned an estate, and bestowed upon the Brahmans who officiated many animals and pearls and slaves. To the rajahs he gave war elephants and steeds and money, and to the rajahs' wives bridal-night gifts of raiment and jewels and gold.

Bhima feasted all the Brahmans, and Yudhishthira wept as he bade farewell to Krishna, his friend in peace and in war, who departed in his chariot unto sea-washed Dwaraka.

There was prosperity in the kingdom under Yudhishthira's wise and just government; but blind old Dhritarashtra never ceased to mourn the death of Duryodhana, his first-born, and at length he retired to live in a humble dwelling in the jungle. With him went Queen Gandhari, and Pritha, the mother of the Pandavas, and Vidura, and others who were of great age.

Years went past, and a day came when Yudhishthira and his brethren and their wife Draupadi journeyed to the dwelling-place of their elders. They found them all there save Vidura, who had departed to a sacred place on the banks of the Ganges to undergo penance and wait for the coming of Yama, god of the dead. Then all the kinsfolk, young and old, went forth to find Vidura; but when they came to him he was wasted with hunger and great age, nor could he speak unto them. They waited beside him until he died, and then they mourned together. This new sorrow awakened old-time grief, and they spoke of all those who had fallen in the great war. Fathers and mothers lamented for their sons, and wives for their husbands. . . .

While they wept and moaned together, the great sage Vyasa came nigh and spoke, saying: "Verily, I will soothe all your sorrows. . . . Let each one bathe at sunset in the holy waters of the Ganges, and when night falls your lost ones will return to you once again."

Then they all sat waiting on the river bank until evening came on. Slowly passed the day; it seemed to be as long as a year.

At length the sun went down, and they chanted mantras and went into the Ganges. Vyasa bathed beside the old Maharajah Dhritarashtra and Yudhishthira. . . . Then all came out and stood on the bank.

Suddenly the waters began to heave and foam, and Vyasa muttered holy words and called out the names of the dead one by one. . . . Soon all the heroes who had been slain arose one by one. In chariots they came, and on horseback and riding upon lordly elephants. They all uttered triumphant cries; drums were sounded and trumpets were blown; and it seemed as if the armies of the Pandavas and Kauravas were once again assembled for battle, for they swept over the river like a mighty tempest.

Many of the onlookers trembled with fear, until they beheld Bhishma and Drona, clad in armour, standing aloft in their chariots in splendour and in pride; then came Arjuna's son, the noble Abhimanyu, and Bhima's Asura

5

THE RETURN OF THE HEROES SLAIN IN BATTLE

From the painting by Warwick Goble

son. Soon Gandhari beheld Duryodhana and all his brethren, while Pritha looked with glad eyes upon Karna, and Draupadi welcomed her brother Dhrishta-dyumna and her five children who had all been slain by vengeful Aswatthaman. All the warriors who had fallen in battle returned again on that night of wonder.

With the host came minstrels who sang of the deeds of the heroes, and beautiful girls who danced before them. All strife had ended between kinsmen and old-time rivals; in death there was peace and sweet companionship.

The ghostly warriors crossed the Ganges and were welcomed by those who waited on the bank around Vyasa. It was a night of supreme and heart-stirring gladness. Fathers and mothers found their sons, widows clung to their husbands, sisters embraced their brothers, and all wept tears of joy. The elders who were living conversed with those who were dead; the burdens of grief and despair fell from all hearts after lone years of mourning; the past was suddenly forgotten in the rapture of beholding those who had died.

Swiftly passed the night as if it had endured but for an hour. Then when dawn began to break, the dead men returned to their chariots and their horses and their elephants and bade farewells. . . .

Vyasa spoke to the widows and said that those of them who desired to be with their husbands could depart with them. Then the Kaurava princesses and other high-born ladies, who never ceased to mourn for their own, kissed the feet of the Maharajah Dhritarashtra and Queen Gandhari and plunged into the Ganges with the departing hosts. . . . Vyasa chanted mantras, and all the drowned widows were transported to heaven with their husbands. . . .

The Pandavas returned to Hastinapur, and when two years had gone past a new sorrow fell upon them. One day Narada, the sage, stood before Yudhishthira and told that a great fire had swept through the jungle, and that Dhritarashtra, and Gandhari, and Pritha, and all who were with them, had perished.

Soon afterwards the Pandavas came to know, by reason of dread omens which appeared, that a great calamity was drawing nigh, but no man could tell what it was or when it would take place.

Ere long it became known that the city of Dwaraka was doomed to be destroyed. A horror in human shape was beheld in the night; it was coloured yellow and black, its head was bald and its limbs misshapen, and men said it was Yama, god of the dead. . . . Visions of headless men contending in battle were beheld at sunset. . . . The moon was eclipsed, a dread tempest ravaged the land, and a plague of rats afflicted the city.

Krishna forbade all the people, on pain of death, to drink wine, and commanded them to perform devotions on the seashore. . . .

Then the night was haunted by a black woman with yellow teeth who grinned horribly at house doors. All the inhabitants of the city were stricken with terror. . . . Evil spirits came also and robbed the jewels of the women and the weapons of the men. . . . At length the chakra[1] of Krishna went up to heaven, and his chariot and horses followed it. . . . The end of the Yádavas was not afar off, and the day came when Apsaras called out of heaven: "Depart from hence," and all the people heard them.

When the people gathered on the seashore they held a feast, and being allowed to drink wine for one day, they drank heavily and began to quarrel. At length Satyaki slew Kritavarman, who had gone to the Pandava camp with Drona's son on the night of slaughter. Then

[1] Celestial weapon.

Kritavarman's friends killed Satyaki and one of Krishna's sons. Krishna slew the rebels, but he could not quell the tumult and the fighting which ensued; fathers slew their sons, and sons their fathers, and kinsmen contended fiercely against kinsmen.

Then Krishna and Balarama left the city, and both died in the jungle. From Balarama's mouth issued a mighty snake, for he was the incarnation of the world serpent. . . . Krishna was mistaken for a gazelle by a hunter, who shot an arrow which pierced his foot at the only spot where he could be mortally wounded. He then departed to his heaven, which is called Goloka.

Ere Krishna had left Dwaraka he caused messengers to hasten for Arjuna, who came speedily, to find the women wailing for the dead. Then Vasudeva, father of Krishna, died, and Arjuna laid the body of the old man upon the pyre, and he was burned with four of his widows, who no longer desired to live. The bodies of Krishna and Balarama were cremated also.

Arjuna then set forth towards Indra-prastha with a remnant of the people; and when they had left Dwaraka, the sea rose up and swallowed the whole city, with those who had refused to depart from it. . . . Such was the end of the power of the Yadavas.

Deep gloom fell upon the Pandavas after this, and Vyasa, the sage, appeared before them, and revealed that their time had come to depart from the world.

Then Yudhishthira divided the kingdom. He made Parikshit, son of Abhimanyu, Rajah of Hastinapur; and Yuyutsu, the half-brother of Duryodhana, who had joined the Pandava army on the first day of the great war, was made Rajah of Hastinapur. He counselled them to live at peace one with another.

The Pandavas afterwards cast off their royal garments

and their jewels and put on the garb of hermits, and the bright-eyed and faithful Draupadi did likewise. Yudhishthira departed first of all, and his brethren walked behind him one by one, and Draupadi went last of all, followed by a hound. They all walked towards the rising sun, and by the long circuitous path which leads to Mount Meru, through forests and over streams and across the burning plains, never again to return.

One by one they fell by the way, all save Yudhishthira. Draupadi was the first to sink down, and Bhima cried: "Why hath she fallen who hath never done wrong?"

Said Yudhishthira: "Her heart was bound up in Arjuna, and she hath her reward."

Sahadeva was next to fall, and then Nakula. At length Yudhishthira heard the voice of Bhima crying in distress: "Lo! now the noble Arjuna hath fallen. What sin hath he committed?"

Said Yudhishthira: "He boasted confidently that he could destroy all his enemies in one day, and because he failed in his vow he hath fallen by the way."

The two surviving brothers walked on in silence; but the time came when mighty Bhima sank down. He cried: "O Yudhishthira say, if thou canst tell, why I have fallen now."

Said Yudhishthira: "O wolf-bellied one, because of thy cursing and gluttony and thy pride thou hast fallen by the way."

Yudhishthira walked on, calm and unmoved, followed by his faithful hound. When he drew nigh to sacred Mount Meru, the world-spine, Indra, king of the gods, came forth to welcome him, saying: "Ascend, O resolute prince."

Said Yudhishthira: "Let my brethren who have fallen

by the way come with me also. I cannot enter heaven without them, O king of the gods. Let the fair and gentle princess come too; Draupadi hath been a faithful wife, and is worthy of bliss. Hear my prayer, O Indra, and have mercy."

Said Indra: "Thy brethren and Draupadi have gone before thee."

Then Yudhishthira pleaded that his faithful hound should enter heaven also; but Indra said: "Heaven is no place for those who are followed by hounds. Knowest thou not that demons rob religious ordinances of their virtues when dogs are nigh?"

Said Yudhishthira: "No evil can come from the noble. I cannot have joy if I desert this faithful friend."

Indra said: "Thou didst leave behind thy brethren and Draupadi. Why, therefore, canst thou not abandon thine hound?"

Said Yudhishthira: "I have no power to bring back to life those who have fallen by the way: there can be no abandonment of the dead."

As he spake, the hound was transformed, and behold Dharma, god of justice, stood by the rajah's side.

Dharma said: "O Yudhishthira, thou art indeed mine own son. Thou wouldst not abandon me, thy hound, because that I was faithful unto thee. Thine equal cannot be found in heaven."

Then Yudhishthira was transported to the city of eternal bliss, and there he beheld Duryodhana seated upon a throne. All the Kauravas were in heaven also, but the rajah could not find his brethren or fair Draupadi.

Said Indra: "Here thou shalt dwell, O Yudhishthira, in eternal bliss. Forget all earthly ties and attain to perfection; thy brethren have fallen short, therefore they sank by the way."

Yudhishthira said: "I cannot remain here with the Kauravas who have done me great wrong. Where my brethren are, there would I be also with our wife Draupadi."

Then a celestial being conducted Yudhishthira to the abode of his brethren and the Princess of Panchala. He entered the forest of the nether regions, where the leaves were like to sharp weapons and the path was covered with knives. Darkness hung heavily, and the way was miry with blood and strewn with foul and mutilated corpses. Shapes of horror flitted round about like to shadows; fierce birds of prey feasted upon human flesh. The damned were burning in everlasting fires, and the air reeked with foul odours. A boiling river went past, and Yudhishthira saw the place of torture with thorns, and the desert of fiery sand: he gazed mutely upon each horror that was unfolded before his eyes.

Fain would Yudhishthira have turned back, but he heard in the darkness the voices of his brethren and Draupadi bidding him to stay a little while to comfort them while they suffered torment.

Then Yudhishthira said to the celestial being: "Depart now from me, for I must remain here to assuage the sufferings of my brethren and Draupadi."

As he spake the gods appeared, and the scene of horror vanished from before the eyes of Yudhishthira, for it was an illusion conjured up to test his constancy.

Then Yudhishthira was led to the heavenly Ganges, and having bathed in its sacred waters, he cast off his mortal body and became a celestial. Then, rejoicing, he entered Swarga, the celestial city of Indra, and was welcomed by Krishna in all his divine glory, and by his brethren and by Draupadi, and all whom he had loved upon earth.

Indra spoke and said: "This is the beautiful and immortal one, who sprang from the altar to be thy wife, and these bright beings are her five children. Here is Dhritarashtra, who is now the king of the Gandharvas; there is Karna, son of Surya, the peerless archer who was slain by Arjuna. Here cometh towards thee Abhimanyu, son of Arjuna; he is now the star-bright companion of the lord of night. . . . Here are Pandu, thy sire, and Pritha, thy mother, now united in heaven. Behold! also, Yudhishthira, the wise Bhishma, whose place is with the Vasus round my throne: Drona sits with Dharma, god of wisdom. Here are all the peerless warriors who fell in battle and have won heaven by their valour and their constancy. So may all mortals rise to eternal bliss, casting off their mortal bodies and entering by the shining door of the celestial city, by doing kindly deeds, by uttering gentle words, and by enduring all suffering with patience. The holy life is prepared for all the sons of men."

Thus ends sublimely the story of the Great War of the Bharatas.

CHAPTER XX

Nala and Damayanti

A Noble Prince and Fair Princess—Swan Messengers of Love—A Royal Romance—The Love-sick Maiden—Indra and the Rishis—The Swayamvara —Gods Descend from Heaven—Nala's Mission—Interview with Damayantí— A Faithful Lover—Gathering of Rajahs—Gods Rejected by Damayantí—The Choice of Nala—Wedding Gifts of the Gods—The Royal Marriage—Kali the Demon—Plot to Ruin Nala.

ONCE upon a time there reigned in Nishadha[1] a great rajah of choicest virtues whose name was Nala. He had great skill in taming steeds; he was a peerless archer, and was devoted to truth. Nala commanded a mighty army: like to the sun was his splendour, and he was exalted over all other kings as is the monarch of the gods. He had withal great piety, and he was deeply read in the Vedas, but he was ever a passionate lover of dice. Many a high-born lady spoke his praises, for he was generous of heart, and self-controlled, and the guardian of law. Indeed, Nala was a very present Manu.[2]

Now there ruled over the neighbouring state of Vidarbha the mighty rajah Bhíma, the terrible in strength, who was likewise of choicest virtues. He was childless, and he yearned for children. For long he had been wont to perform many holy deeds intent upon offspring, but

[1] The south-eastern division of Central India.

[2] An incarnation of Manu, the first lawgiver.

without avail.[1] It chanced, however, that one day there came to his court a Bráhman named Damana, and hospitable welcome was accorded him by the child-desiring Bhíma, for the seer was feasted in the hall with the rajah and his royal consort. Thereafter a boon was conferred upon the queen: she became the mother of one sweet girl, the pearl of maidens, who was named Damayantí, and of three noble sons, Dama, Danta, and the renowned Dam'ana, who all grew great and powerful.

When fair Damayantí had attained the full bloom of her beauty, she was unequalled throughout the world for her brilliance and for her grace. Upon the faultless and slender-waisted maiden there waited, as about Indra's queen, a hundred female slaves and a hundred virgin handmaids, and she shone among them, decked with jewels and rich ornaments, like to the goddess of beauty, unrivalled and without a peer. Never among the gods, or the Yakshas, or among mortal men was a maiden more fair ever heard of or ever beheld than soul-disturbing Damayantí, who disturbed the souls of the gods.

In presence of Bhima's sweet daughter the high-born ladies of Vidarbha took joy in constantly praising Nala, that tiger among rajahs. Likewise before Nishadha's king was Damayantí ever extolled because of her beauty. So it fell that, hearing much of each other's virtues, the silent passion of love was nurtured in both their hearts.

Impatient grew Nala as his love increased, and he was wont to wander in a grove within his palace garden musing secretly upon the maiden of faultless form. One day he saw disporting in the grounds a flock of beautiful swans with wings all flecked with gold. The rajah crept

[1] It was a religious necessity to have offspring. A son performed the funeral rites which rescued his father's soul from hell.

forward softly and seized one, and much he marvelled to hear it cry out in human language.

"Slay me not, O gentle king, and to thee I will render a service, for I will praise thee in the presence of Damayantî so that ever after she shall think of no other mortal man but thee."

Immediately Nala set the bird at liberty, and it flew away rejoicing with its bright companions towards Vidarbha. When they reached the ladies' garden of Bhima's palace they settled down at the feet of Damayantî, who was reposing in the shade with her virgin handmaids. All the fair young women gazed in wonder on the swans, admiring their graceful forms and their plumage gleaming with gold, and ere long they began to pursue them among the trees. Then of a sudden the bird which Damayantî followed spoke to her in human language and said:

"Damayantî, hear! The noble king Nala dwells in Nishadha. Comely is he as a god, nor can his equal be found in the world. Thou art the pearl of women, and he is the pride of men. If thou wert wed to him, then would perfect beauty and noble birth be united. Blessed indeed would be the union of the peerless with the peerless."

Wondering, the maiden listened while the bird conversed thus strangely, and then she said: "Speak also unto Nala in this manner."

The swan made answer: "So be it," and thereupon took flight with the others to Nishadha, where it related unto Nala all that had taken place.

Ever after that day Damayantî ceased to live for herself alone; all her thoughts were given up to Nala. She desired most to sit apart in silent reverie; the bloom faded from her cheeks, and she grew dejected and melancholy. Indeed, the maiden yielded up her soul to sorrow,

6

DAMAYANTI AND THE SWAN

From the painting by Warwick Goble

and much she sighed in secret, gazing upward and meditating, for love had taken possession of her heart; nor did she find pleasure in sleep, or in gentle converse, or in merry banquets. In the midst of her broken slumbers she was wont to weep and cry out: "Oh, woe is me!"

The virgin handmaidens read her heart, and they went before her sire and told that his gentle daughter was pining for the monarch among men. When Bhima heard this, he pondered deeply what should be done for Damayantí, and he perceived that her time for the swayamvara[1] had come. So he summoned all the high-born rajahs upon earth, saying: "O heroes of the world, come ye to the swayamvara."

Then did the whole land resound with the trampling of elephants and horses and the rumbling of chariots, for the stately princes, fōllowed by their armies, swarmed towards the court of Bhima. By the strong lord of Vidarbha were they welcomed with honour, and they sat upon their thrones.

Now it happened that at this time these two wise sages, Nárada and Párvata,[2] ascended Mount Meru to Swarga, the heaven of Indra, and they saluted the Cloud-compeller within his palace. The immortal lord bade them welcome, and asked how it fared with the world. Narada said it fared well with the world and with all the mighty kings. Then Indra spake, saying: "Where are all the royal heroes? Why do they not come hither as my honoured guests?"[3]

The wise sage made answer and said: "O Cloud-compeller, the great rajahs cannot appear before thee

[1] The ceremony at which a princess made public choice of a husband from among a number of suitors gathered together.

[2] Two of the ten Rishis (saints) who were sons of Bráhma. Narada was a messenger of the gods. Parvata was his great rival.

[3] Indra wonders that no battle-slain heroes are arriving at the Indian Valhal.

because even now they are hastening one and all to the swayamvara of Damayantí, the renowned daughter of Bhima, the fairest woman upon earth. O slayer of drought demons, every king seeks to woo this maid of transcending beauty, for she is the pearl of all the world."

As Narada spake, the other gods drew nigh and listened to his stately utterance. Then together they exclaimed with rapture: "We also will go thither. . . ." In an instant they were hastening through the air in their chariots towards the city of Vidarbha to mingle with the wooers of Bhima's fair daughter.

Meanwhile Nala had set forth with joy, his heart full of love for Damayantí. The gods beheld him standing upon the surface of the earth with radiance like to the sun, and they arrested their course, gazing in mute wonder, for he was as comely as the god of love. Then, dropping down through the blue air, they hailed the stately hero, saying: "Do as we now beseech thee, O most excellent of princes; be thou the bearer of our message."

Nala adored the gods with folded hands and promised to obey their will, saying humbly: "Who are ye that now command my service?"

Indra spoke and said: "Lo! we are the dread guardians of the world. I am Indra, lord of heaven; yon is Agni, god of fire; here is Varuna, king of the waters; and there is Yama, lord of the dead.[1] Thou must inform Damayantí that we have come to woo her and say to her: '*Choose for thine husband one of the celestial beings*'."

Nala made answer with folded hands, saying: "Send me not, I entreat thee, upon this mission. How can I who am enamoured with the maiden, plead aright the cause

[1] At the period the poem was composed there were only four "guardians"; later there were eight.

of another. In mercy spare me, ye gods—spare me this unwelcome service."

But the gods would not be moved from their purpose. They reminded Nala he had already promised to do their will, and they therefore urged him to set forth without delay lest he should belie his words.

Then the lord of Nishadha pleaded: "The palace of Bhima is strongly guarded, and I cannot enter there."

Indra said: "Thou wilt indeed enter."

And lo! even as the god spake, Nala found himself standing before Damayantī in her secret bower.

The beauteous maiden was surrounded by her virgin band, and he gazed upon her faultless limbs and slender waist and into her entrancing eyes. Her shining beauty excelled even the tender rays of the moon. The love of Nala grew deeper and stronger as he looked upon the smiling princess; but he curbed his passion, remembering his mission.

All the maidens gazed with wonder and joy at the noble form, and in their hearts they exclaimed: "Oh! the splendid one; oh! the strong and mighty hero—who is he? . . . Is he god, or Yaksha, or Gandharva?" But they spoke not a word, for they were made bashfully silent by reason of his beauty.

Nala smiled upon Damayantī, and first she smiled softly in return; then she exclaimed in her wonder: "Who art thou that hast come hither like a celestial being to awaken all my love. Speak and tell, O sinless lord. How didst thou contrive to enter the palace unseen, for surely all the chambers are strongly guarded by stern orders of the king?"[1]

The rajah made answer, saying: "O thou fairest one, know now that I am even Nala, and that I come hither as

[1] Evidently the zenana system was in vogue prior to the Mohammedan conquest.

the messenger of the gods Indra and Agni, Varuna and Yama, and through their power have I entered here, unseen nor stayed, for it is their desire that I should say unto thee: '*Choose, O princess, for thine husband one of the celestial beings*'. Such is the purpose of my mission from the great world guardians. Having heard me, thou mayst decide as thou wilt."

Damayantí at once did homage to the gods. Then she smiled upon Nala and spoke, saying: "Lo! I am thine already, and whatsoever I possess is thine also. O give me thy love in return, Nala. For know that my heart's love was increased by the endearing words of the swan, and it is because of thee that the rajahs are all gathered here now. If thou wilt despise me, I will suffer death for thy sake by fire, or by water, or even by the noose[1]."

The rajah made answer and said: "Wilt thou despise these, the gods, and choose for thine husband a mortal who is more lowly than the dust they walk upon? Let thy heart aspire to them. Remember, too, that the man who incurs the anger of the world's dread guardians will meet with certain death. From such a fate oh shield me, thou fairest one! . . . So choose one of the perfect gods, and thou shalt have robes unsullied by dust, garlands that never fade, and celestial joy without end."

Trembling, and with tear-dimmed eyes, Damayantí said: "I do homage with due humility to all the gods, but oh! I desire thee for my husband, thee and thee only."

But Nala spake, saying: "I am charged with the mission of the celestial beings, and cannot plead for myself now. But afterwards I will come to claim thee,

[1] Death by hanging was not regarded as a special disgrace.

and will speak boldly, O bright one, so remember me in thine heart."

The maiden smiled through her tears. "Ah!" she said, "I see now a way of escape. . . . When thou comest to the swayamvara, enter thou together with the gods, and I will name thee as mine own, so that no sin may be charged against thee."

Then Nala returned to the gods, who waited him eagerly, and he told them all that the maiden had said, word for word. "In thy wisdom," he added, "thou wilt judge of what remains, O ye excelling gods."

When at length the day of happy omen, the day of the swayamvara, arrived, Bhima summoned at noontide all the love-sick rajahs, and they passed through the court of golden columns and under the bright portal arch, and entered the Hall of State like to lions on the mountains. The rajahs were then seated on their thrones, adorned with garlands and with dangling ear gems. The arms of some were robust and powerful like the battle mace; those of others were delicate and smooth as a serpent. With profuse and flowing hair, shapely noses, and arching eyebrows, the faces of these great lords were radiant as the stars in heaven. As a mountain cave is full of tigers, so was Bhima's great Hall full of rajah tigers on that day.

When Damayantí entered in state, every eye and every soul was entranced by her dazzling beauty; all these lords of earth gazed upon her with unmoving eyes. . . . The name of each rajah was proclaimed in turn, and Nala, looking about her, was suddenly stricken with dismay, for she perceived that there were present five Nalas who were undistinguishable in form and attire one from another. The four gods who desired to win her had each assumed the likeness of her beloved one.

Whichsoever of these she gazed upon, he seemed to be her rajah, and in her secret heart she wailed: "How can I discern Nala among the celestial beings?"

In her sore distress the trembling maiden folded her hands and did homage before the gods, to whom she prayed, saying:

> "When I heard the sweet words of the swans, I pledged my heart to Nala. I adjure thee by this truth, O ye gods. Oh! reveal my lord.
>
> "From my faith I have never swerved either by word or by deed. I adjure thee by this truth, O ye all-knowing Powers. Oh! reveal my lord.
>
> "The gods have destined that Nala should be mine husband. I adjure thee by this truth. Oh! reveal my lord.
>
> "The vow which I so pledged to Nala is holy, and I must ever keep it. I adjure thee by this truth. Oh! reveal my lord.
>
> "O ye mighty ones, ye guardians of the world, assume now your forms divine, so that I may know Nala, the monarch of men."

The gods heard the sad maiden's piteous prayer and marvelled greatly. They perceived that her resolve was firm, that she was constant in truth and in love, and was holy and wise, and that she remained faithful to her lord. So they revealed the tokens of their greatness.[1] . . . Then Damayantí was able to discern the four celestial beings because their skins were without moisture and their eyes never winked, there was no dust on their garlands and their feet did not touch the earth.

[1] Deities cast no shadows, they never perspired, nor did their feet touch the ground when walking. Their eyes never winked.

7

DAMAYANTI CHOOSING A HUSBAND

From the painting by Warwick Goble

She also knew Nala because he cast a shadow; there was dust on his raiment, and his garland was beginning to fade; drops of moisture stood on his skin, and his eyelids moved.

Gazing first upon the celestial beings and then upon him who was her heart's desire, Damayantí named Nala as her lord. She modestly touched the hem of his garment and threw round his neck a wreath of bright flowers, and thus chose him for her husband.

All the rivals of Nala uttered cries of sorrow, but the gods and the sages exclaimed aloud: "Well done! Well done!" and honoured the lord of Nishadha.

Nala spake in his joy to fair Damayantí, saying: "Since thou, O maiden with serene smile, hast chosen me for thine husband in the presence of the gods, know that I will be a faithful consort who will ever take delight in thy words. I am thine, and so long as my life endures I will be thine only."

So did the lord of Nishadha pledge his faith, and the heart of the maiden was made glad. The happy pair then did homage before the gods, and these resplendent guardians of the earth bestowed, in their joy, eight surpassing gifts upon Nala. Indra gave him power to behold the godhead in the sacrifice, and power to walk unhindered by any obstacle wheresoever he desired; Agni gave him power over fire, and power over the three worlds;[1] Varuna gave him power over water, and power to obtain fresh garlands at will; and Yama gave him subtle skill in preparing food, and eminence in every virtue. Each of the gods also conferred his double blessing upon Nala, and thereafter they departed.

All the rajahs wondered greatly when they beheld the maiden's choice confirmed in this manner, and they

[1] Heaven, earth, and the underworld.

went away as they came, with joy, and returned unto their own domains.

Bhima rejoiced greatly when the happy bridal was celebrated in pomp and with state, and he bade Nala adieu with great courtesy when that great lord of Nishadha, after fitting sojourn at Vidarbha, set out to return to his native city with the pearl of women whom he had won.

Now it chanced that when the gods had left the swayamvara they met in the midst of the blue air Kali[1], the demon of evil, who was accompanied by the wicked spirit Dwápara. Indra, the slayer of giants, spoke and said: "Whither art thou going with Dwápara, O Kali?"

Kali made answer: "We are hastening to the swayamvara, for it is my desire to obtain Damayantí as my bride."

Smiling, the king of gods spake, saying: "The bridal is now arranged and ended, for lo! the fair Damayantí has chosen Nala for her husband in our presence."

When he heard these words, the heart of Kali was made angry, and he exclaimed: "Since she has preferred a mortal in presence of the celestial beings, let her choice be her own doom."

But the gods said: "Know thou that our consent was freely given, because Damayantí has chosen for herself a husband endowed with all the virtues, and equal even to the guardians of the world. If anyone should chance to curse Nala, the curse will recoil fatally, and the curser will be cast into the torments of the dark lake of hell." Having spoken thus, the bright deities ascended the heavens.

Then said Kali to Dwapara: "I cannot now control my fierce wrath. Lo! I will be avenged upon Nala, for

[1] Dowson regards the demon Kali as the personification of the Kali Yuga.

I will enter his body, and he will be bereft of his kingdom and of his bride. Thou, Dwapara, wilt enter the dice and give me thine aid."

So was a malignant compact arranged between the demon of evil and his darksome ally, and together they went towards Nishadha to haunt the stately palace of Nala, waiting for the fatal moment.

CHAPTER XXI

Wanderings in the Forest

Nala Possessed by a Demon—A Brother's Challenge—The Game of Dice—The Rajah's Stakes—Alarm of Citizens—Damayantí's Grief—Flight of Children—A Kingdom Gambled away—The Exiled King—His Faithful Wife—Departure to the Forest—Damayantí Deserted—Seized by a Serpent—Rescued by a Huntsman—A Terrible Curse—Forest Perils—Appeal to a Tiger—The Holy Mountain—Prophecy of Hermits—Address to the Asoka Tree—The Caravan—Disasters of a Night—Damayantí's Flight to Chedi.

For twelve bright years Nala and Damayantí lived happily together. The great rajah ruled his people justly; he offered up every sacrifice to the gods, and he gave sumptuous gifts to holy men. Fair Damayantí became the mother of a beauteous daughter, who was named Indrasena, and of a comely son, who was named Indrasen. So were the blessings of life showered upon the blissful pair.

But at length there came a day when, after performing an unclean act, Nala sipped holy water and went to prayer with unwashed feet.[1] The watchful Kali seized this fatal opportunity, and straightway entered the rajah and possessed his inmost soul. Then that evil demon summoned Push'kara, the brother of Nala, saying: "Come now and throw dice with the king. I will give thee mine aid, so that thou wilt be enabled to win the whole realm for thyself."

[1] The ceremony of purification included the sipping of water and the washing of feet.

Pushkara at once challenged his brother, whereupon the wicked spirit Dwapara entered the dice.

Nala gave ready consent to take part in the game of hazard, for he was swayed by evil Kali. Then the two rivals began to play together in the presence of Damayantí.

The great rajah staked his wealth, and he was worsted; he staked his golden treasures and he staked his chariots, and still he was worsted; he staked his rich attire, and he continued to lose. The passion for dice had possessed Nala like to sudden madness, and it was in vain that his friends endeavoured to restrain him.

In time rumours of dire happenings went abroad through the city, whereupon the rajah's faithful subjects, accompanied by high counsellors of state, assembled at the palace gate with desire to prevail upon him to cease playing. They urged upon Damayantí to intervene, and the spirit-broken daughter of Bhima approached Nala in anguish and in dismay, and with tear-choking voice she spoke to him, saying: "All thy subjects are gathered without, for they cannot endure the thought that misfortune should fall upon thee."

Nala heard her, but answered not a word, because his soul was clouded by evil Kali. Then the wise men said: "It is not he;" and they departed to their homes in sorrow and in shame. . . .

So the play went on; daily it went on through many weary months, and Nala was always worsted.

When, in the end, Damayantí perceived that all the treasures were lost, she sent for the faithful charioteer, Várshneya, and spoke to him, saying: "Hasten now and yoke Nala's speedy and much-loved steeds, and place my children in the chariot. Then drive quickly to the city of my kindred and leave them in care of my father, the

Rajah Bhima. When thou hast done me that service, O Varshneya, thou mayst go wheresoever thou wilt."

So the charioteer conveyed the beauteous girl Indrasena and the comely boy Indrasen to the city of Vidarbha, and he delivered them safely unto Bhima, whom he informed fully regarding the fall of Nala. Thereafter he departed, sorrowing greatly, and went to the city of Ayodhyá,[1] where he took service with the renowned Rajah Rituparna.

Nala played on; he continued to throw the dice, until at length he had lost all his possessions. Then Pushkara smiled and spoke to his stricken brother, saying: "Now, throw but one more hazard. Where is your stake? Ah! you have naught left now save Damayantí. Let us throw the dice for her."

At these words Nala's heart was rent in twain. Mute with sorrow, he gazed upon his brother. . . . He arose and stripped off his rich vestments one by one in the presence of his lamenting friends. Then slowly and in silence he went forth, naked and alone. Damayantí, wearing but a single garment, followed him behind. Together they stood at the city gates.

Then Pushkara, who had become rajah, caused to be proclaimed throughout the city the dread decree: "*Whosoever giveth food or drink unto Nala shall be immediately put to death*".

In their terror the people could not give further help to the fallen king, and for three days and three nights he drank water only. Then he plucked wild fruit and roots from the earth, and these he ate. Nala thereafter wandered away from Nishadha, an outcast among men, and Damayantí followed him behind.

[1] Ayodhyá signifies "invincible" city. It is identified with the modern Oude.

Tortured by hunger, the fallen king at length beheld on the ground a flock of birds with gold-flecked wings, and he said in his heart: "Now I will make me a welcome feast."

So he crept forward and flung over them his single garment; but they rose in the air, carrying it away with them. As they went they cried out mockingly in human language and said: "Know now, O foolish king, that we are the dice. We came hither on purpose to despoil thee utterly, for so long as thou hadst left a single garment our joy was incomplete."

Thereupon Nala spoke to Damayantí in his anguish, saying: "O blameless one, by whose anger have I been driven from my kingdom and rendered thus unable to procure any food? Listen now to my counsel. The roads diverge here before us, and one leads southward past the caves of holy hermits, which are stored with food, towards the kingdom of thy royal sire."

Anxiously did Nala point out the way and urge upon Bhima's fair daughter to take refuge in Vidarbha ere he would enter the great forest.

Weighed down by her heavy sorrow, Damayantí made answer with tear-choking voice: "Alas! thy words of counsel cause my heart to break and my limbs to fail me. How can I leave thee all alone in trackless forest when thou hast lost thy kingdom and thy riches, and whilst thou art athirst and tortured by hunger? Rather let me comfort thee, O my husband, when in thy grief, and, famine-stricken as thou now art, thou dost ponder wearily over thy lost happiness, for in truth have wise physicians said that a wife is the only balsam and the only healing herb for her husband's sorrow."

Said Nala: "Thou hast spoken truly. There is indeed no medicine for a stricken man like to his wife's love. Think not that I desire to part from thee. . . . Would that I could abandon myself!"

Damayantí wept and said: "If thou wouldst not leave me, why, O king, dost thou make heavier my sorrow by pointing out the way to Vidarbha? Thou art too noble to abandon me, yet thou dost show me the road southward. If it is meet that I should return unto my father, come thou with me and he will bid thee welcome, and we could dwell together happily in his palace."

Nala made answer sadly: "Ah! never can I return in my shame to that city where I have appeared aforetime in pride and in splendour."

Then, comforting Damayantí, Nala wandered on with her through the deep forest, and they made one garment serve them both. Greatly they suffered from hunger and from thirst, and when at length they came to a lonely hut, they sat down on the hard ground, nor had they even a mat to rest upon. Damayantí was overcome with weariness, and soon she sank asleep; she lay all naked on that bare floor. But there was no rest for Nala; he thought with pain of his lost kingdom and the friends who had deserted him, and of the weary journey he must make in the midst of the great forest. "Ah! were it better to die now and end all," he mused, "or to desert her whom I love? She is devoted unto me more deeply than I deserve. Perchance if she were abandoned she would return to Vidarbha. She is unable to endure my sufferings and the constant sorrow which must be mine."

Long he pondered thus, until Kali swayed him to desert his faithful wife. So he severed her garment and used half of it. He turned away from the fair princess as she lay fast asleep.

Repenting in his heart, Nala returned speedily and gazed upon fair Damayantí with pity and with love. He wept bitterly, saying: "Ah! thou dost sleep on the bare hard ground whom neither sun nor storm hath ever used roughly. O my loved one, thou hast ever awakened to smile. How wilt thou fare when thou dost discover that thy lord hath abandoned thee in the midst of the perilous forest? . . . May sun and wind and the spirits of the wood protect thee, and may thou be shielded ever by thine own great virtue!"

Then the distracted rajah, prompted by Kali again, hastened away; but his heart was torn by his love, which drew him back. . . . So time and again he came and went, like to a swing, backward and forward, until in the end the evil spirit conquered him, and he departed from Damayantí, who moaned fitfully in her sleep; and he plunged into the depths of the forest.

Ere long the fair princess awoke, and when she perceived that she was all alone she uttered a piteous scream and cried out: "Oh! where art thou, my king, my lord, my sole protector? . . . I am lost; oh! I am undone. I am helpless and alone in the perilous wood. . . . Ah! now thou art but deceiving me. Do not mock me, my lord. Art thou hidden there among the bushes? Oh, speak! . . . Why dost thou not make answer? . . . I do not sorrow for myself only. I cannot well endure that thou shouldst be alone, that thou shouldst thirst and be an hungered and very weary, and without me to give thee comfort. . . ."

So she wailed as she searched through the forest for Nala, now casting herself upon the ground, now sitting to pine in silence, and anon crying out in her grief. At length she said: "Oh, may he who causeth Nala to suffer endure even greater agony than he endureth, and may he live for ever in darkness and in misery!"

Hither and thither she wandered, seeking her lord,

and ever was she heard crying: "Alas! O alas! my husband."

Suddenly a great serpent rose up in its wrath and coiled itself round her fair body. . . .

"Oh! my guardian," she cried, "I am now undone. The serpent hath seized me. Why art thou not near? . . . Ah! who will comfort thee now in thy sorrow, O blameless Nala?"

As she lamented thus, a passing huntsman heard her cries; he broke through the jungle and beheld Damayantí in the coils of the serpent. . . . Nimbly he darted forward and with a single blow smote off the monster's head, and thus rescued the beauteous lady from her awesome peril. Then he washed her body and gave her food, and she was refreshed.

"Who art thou, O fair-eyed one?" he asked. "Why dost thou wander thus alone in the perilous wood?"

Damayantí of faultless form thereupon related to the huntsman the story of her sorrow. As she spoke, his frail heart was moved by her great beauty, and he uttered amorous words with whining voice. . . . Perceiving his evil intent, she was roused to fierce anger. Her chastity was her sole defence, and she cursed him so that he immediately fell down dead like to a tree that has been smitten by lightning and is suddenly blasted.[1]

Freed thus from the savage huntsman of wild beasts, the lotus-eyed Damayantí wandered on through the deep forest, which resounded everywhere with the song of the cricket. All around her were trees of every form and name, and she beheld shady arbours, deep valleys, and wooded hill summits, and lakes and pools, loud resounding waterfalls, and great flowing rivers. The forest was drear and appalling: it was full of lions and tigers, of

[1] The power of a curse is illustrated in Southey's *Curse of Kehama.*

countless birds and fierce robbers. She saw buffaloes and wild boars feeding, and the fierce and awesome forms that were there also—serpents and giants and terrible demons. . . . But, protected by her virtue, she wandered on all alone without fear. Her sole anxiety was for Nala, and she wept for him, crying: "Ah! where art thou? O blameless one, remember now thy vows and thy plighted faith. Remember the words which the gold-winged swan addressed unto thee. . . . Am I not thy loved one? . . . Oh! why dost thou not make answer in this dark and perilous forest? The savage beasts are gaping to devour me. Why art thou not near to save? . . . I am weak and pallid and dust-stained, and have need of thee, my protector. . . . Whom can I ask for Nala? The tiger is before me, the king of the forest, and I am not afraid. I address him, saying: 'Oh! I am lonely, and wretched, and sorrowful, seeking for my exiled husband. If thou hast seen him, console me; if thou hast not seen him, devour me, and set me free from this misery.' . . . But the tiger turns down to the river bank, and I wander onward towards the holy mountain, the monarch of hills.

"'Hear me!' I cry. I salute thee, O Mountain. . . . I am a king's daughter and the consort of a king, the illustrious lord of Nishadha, the pious, the faultless one, who is courageous as the elephant. . . . Hast thou seen my Nala, O mighty Mountain? . . . Ah! why dost thou not answer me? . . . Comfort thou me now as if I were thine own child. . . . Oh! shall I ever behold him again, and ever hear again his honey-sweet voice, like music, saying: 'Daughter of Vidarbha,' while it doth soothe all my pain with its blessed sound? . . ."

Having thus addressed the mountain, Damayanti turned northward and wandered on for three days and three nights. Then she reached a holy grove, and entered it humbly and without fear. She beheld there the cells of hermits and their bright sacred fires. The holy men were struck with wonder by reason of her beauty, and they bade her welcome, saying: "Art thou a goddess of the wood, or of the mountain, or of the river? O speak and tell."

Damayantí made answer: "I am not a goddess of the wood, or a mountain spirit, or yet a river nymph, but a mortal woman."

Then she related to the holy men the story of her sorrow and her wandering, and these seers spoke to her and said: "A time cometh soon, a time of beauty, when thou wilt again behold Nala in splendour and sin-released ruling over his people."

When they had spoken thus, all the holy men vanished, and their sacred fires vanished also. Damayantí stood a while in silent wonder, and in her heart she said: "Have I seen a vision? . . ." Then she went towards another region.

Lamenting for Nala, the fair one came to a beauteous asoka tree[1]: its green branches were gemmed with gleaming fruit, and were melodious with the songs of birds. "O happy tree," she cried, "take away all my grief. . . . Say, hast thou beheld my Nala, the slayer of his enemies, my beloved lord? Oh! hast thou seen my one love, with smooth, bright skin, wandering alone in the forest? Answer me, O blessed Asoka, so that I may depart from thee in joy. Ah! hear and speak thou happy tree. . . ."

So, wailing in her deep anguish, Damayantí moved round the asoka. Then she went towards a lonelier and more fearsome region. . . . She passed many a river and

[1] A (not) soka (sorrow). This beautiful tree has exquisitely coloured and abundant blossom, varying from rich orange red to primrose yellow. It is sacred to Siva.

many mountains, and she saw numerous birds and deer as she wandered on and on, searching for her lost lord.

At length she beheld a great caravan of merchants. Ponderous elephants and eager camels, prancing horses and rumbling cars came through a river. The river banks were fringed by cane and tangled undergrowth; the curlew called aloud there, and the osprey; red geese were clamouring; turtles were numerous, as were the fish and the serpents likewise. All the noble animals of the caravan came splashing noisily across the ford.

The great concourse of travellers stared with wonder on the slender-waisted, maniac-like woman, clad in but half a garment, smeared with dust and pale and sorrowful, her long hair all matted and miry. Some there were who fled from her in fear. But others took pity and said: "Who art thou, O lady, and what seekest thou in the lonely forest? Art thou a goddess of the mountain, or of the forest, or of the plain? . . . We pray for thy protection; be mindful of our welfare so that we may prosper upon our journey."

Then Damayantí told the story of her misfortune and sorrow, and all the travellers gathered round about to hear—boys and young men and grey-haired sages. "Oh! have you beheld my lord, my Nala?" she cried unto them.

The captain of the band answered her "Nay"; and she asked him whither the caravan was bound, whereat he said: "We are going towards the realm of Chedi, over which Subáhu is king." When the merchants resumed their journey, Damayantí went with them.

Through the forest they travelled a long distance, and at eventide they reached the green shore of a beautiful wide lake which sparkled with bright lotus blooms.[1] The camp was pitched in the middle of a deep grove. Gladly did the men bathe with their wearied animals in the delicious, ice-cool waters.

At midnight all slept. . . . In the deep silence a herd of wild forest elephants, with moisture oozing from their temples,[2] came down to drink from the gurgling stream which flowed nigh to the camp. When they scented the tame elephants lying crouched in slumber, they trumpeted aloud, and of a sudden charged ponderously and fell upon them like to mountain peaks tumbling into the valleys beneath. . . . Trees and tents were thrown down as they trampled through the camping ground, and the travellers awoke panic-stricken, crying: "Oh! Alas! Ah! Oh!" Some fled through the forest; others, blind with sleep, stood gasping with wonder, and the elephants slew them. The camp was scattered in the dire confusion; many animals were gored; men overthrew one another, endeavouring to escape; many shrieked in terror, and a few climbed trees. Voices were heard calling: "It is a fire!" and merchants screamed, "Why fly away so speedily? Save the precious jewels, O ye cowards."

Amidst the tumult and the slaughter Damayantí awoke, trembling with fear, and she made swift escape, nor suffered a wound. In the deep forest she came nigh to the few men who had found refuge, and she heard them say one to another:

"What deed have we done to bring this misfortune upon us? Have we forgotten to adore Manibhadra[3], the high king of the Yakshas? Worshipped we not, ere we set forth, the dread spirits which bring disasters? Was

[1] They are coloured red, white, and blue.

[2] Rutting elephants. The seasonal juice is odorous, and issues from minute holes on each side of the elephant's temples.

[3] Manibhadra, the demi-god, was worshipped by travellers, and resembles Kuvera, god of wealth.

it doomed that all omens should be belied? How hath it come that such a disaster hath befallen us?"

Others who had been bereft of their kindred and their wealth, and were in misery, said: "Who was she—that ill-omened, maniac-eyed woman who came amongst us? In truth she seemed scarcely human. Surely it is by reason of her evil power that disaster hath befallen us. Ah! she is a witch, or she is a sorceress, or mayhap a demon. . . . Without doubt she is the cause of all our woes. . . . Would that we could find her—oh the evil destroyer! Oh the curse of our host! . . . Let us slay the murderess with clods and with stones, with canes and with staves, or else with our fists. . . ."[1]

When the terrified and innocent Damayantí heard these fearsome threats, she fled away through the trees, lamenting her fate, and wailing: "Alas! alas! my terrible doom doth haunt me still. Misfortune dogs my footsteps. . . . I have no memory of any sin of thought or deed—of any wrong done by me to living beings. Perchance, oh, alas! I did sin in my former life, and am now suffering due punishment. . . . For I suffer, indeed. I have lost my husband; my kingdom is lost; I have lost my kindred; my noble Nala has been taken from me, and I am far removed from my children, and I wander alone in the wood of serpents."

When morning broke, the sorrowful queen met with some holy Brahmans who had escaped the night's disaster, and she went with them towards the city of Chedi.

The people gazed with wonder on Damayantí when she walked though the streets with her dust-smeared body and matted hair. The children danced about her as she wandered about like to a maniac, so miserable and weary and emaciated.

[1] A curious glimpse of Hindu ideas regarding demi-gods or demons.

It chanced that the sorrowing woman came nigh to the royal palace. The mother of the king looked forth from a window, and beheld her and said: "Hasten, and bid this poor wanderer to enter. Although stricken and half-clothed she hath, methinks, the beauty of Indra's long-eyed queen. Let her have refuge from those staring men."

Damayantí was then led before the queen mother, who spoke gently, saying: "Although bowed down with grief, thou art beautiful of form. Thou fearest not anyone. Who art thou so well protected by thine own chastity?"

Bhima's daughter wept, lamenting her fate, and related all that had befallen her, but did not reveal who she was. Then the queen mother said: "Dwell thou here with me, and our servants shall go in quest of thy husband."

Damayantí said: "O mother of heroes, if I abide here with thee I must eat not of food remnants, nor do menial service, nor can I hold converse with any man save the holy Brahmans who promise to search for my husband."

The royal lady made answer: "As thou desireth, so let it be." Then she spake to Sunanda, her daughter, saying: "This lady will be to thee a handmaiden and a friend. She is of thine own age and thy worthy peer. Be happy together."

At these words the Princess Sunanda was made glad, and she led the strange woman unto her own abode, where sat all her virgin handmaidens.

There Damayantí dwelt for a time, waiting for her lost husband.

CHAPTER XXII

Nala in Exile

Nala's Wanderings—The Magic Fire—King of Serpents Rescued—Nala Transformed—His Service as a Charioteer—Life in Ayodhya—The Evening Song of Sorrow—Search for Damayantí—How she was Discovered—Her Departure from Chedi—Search for Nala—A Woman's Faith—Journey to the Swayamvara—The Tree Wonder—Demon Leaves Nala's Body—The Coming of the Chariot—Damayanti's Vow.

Soon after Nala had fled into the forest depths, deserting the faithful Damayantí, he beheld a great fire which blazed furiously. As he drew nigh he heard a voice crying over and over again from the midst of the sacred flames: "Hasten, Nala! Oh, hasten, Nala, and come hither!"

Now, Agni had given Nala power over fire, so crying: "Have no fear," he leapt through the flames. . . . In the space within that blazing circle be beheld the king of serpents lying coiled up in a ring with folded hands and unable to move.[1] "Lo! I am Karkotaka," the serpent said, "and am suffering this punishment because that I deceived the holy sage Nárada, who thereupon cursed me, saying: 'Thou wilt remain here in the midst of the flames until Nala cometh nigh to free thee from my curse'. . . . So do I lie without power to move. O mighty rajah, if thou wilt rescue me even now, I will reward thee abundantly with my noble friendship, and help thee to attain great

[1] This serpent was a demi-god with human face and hands. It ruled its kind in the underworld, and recalls the Egyptian king serpent in the story of the shipwrecked sailor. —See *Egyptian Myth and Legend.* It is also called Vasuka and Shesha.

happiness. Oh lift me all speedily from out of this fiery place, thou noble rajah!"

When he had spoken thus, Karkotaka, king of the serpents, shrank to the size of a man's finger, whereupon Nala uplifted and carried him safely through the flames to a cool and refreshing space without.

The serpent then said: "Now walk on and count thy steps, so that good fortune may be assured to thee."

Nala walked nine steps, but ere he could take the tenth the serpent bit him, whereat the rajah was suddenly transformed into a misshapen dwarf with short arms.

Then Karkotaka said: "Know now that I have thus changed thy form so that no man may know thee. My poison, too, will cause unceasing anguish to the evil one who possesseth thy soul; he will suffer greatly until he shall set thee free from thy sorrow. So wilt thou be delivered from thine enemy, O blameless one. . . . My poison will harm thee not, and henceforth, by reason of my power, thou wilt have no need to fear the wild boar, or any foeman, or a Brahman, or the sages. Ever in battle thou wilt be victorious. . . . Now, go thy way, and be called 'Váhuka, the charioteer'. Hasten thou unto the city of Ayodhya[1] and enter the service of the royal Rajah Rituparna, the skilful in dice. Thou wilt teach him how to subdue horses, and he will impart to thee the secret of dice. Then wilt thou again have joy. Sorrow not, therefore, for thy wife and thy children will be restored unto thee, and thou wilt regain thy kingdom."

Then the serpent gave unto Nala a magic robe, saying: "When it is thy desire to be as thou wert, O king, think of me and put on this garment, and thou wilt immediately resume thy wonted form."

[1] Oudh.

Having spoken thus, the king of serpents vanished from sight. Thereupon Nala went towards the city of Ayodhyá, and he stood in the presence of the royal Rajah Rituparna, unto whom he spoke thus: "My name is Váhuká. I am a tamer of steeds, nor is my equal to be found in the world; and I have surpassing skill in cooking viands."

The rajah welcomed him and took him into his service, saying: "Thou shalt cause my horses to be fleet of foot. Be thou master of mine own steed, and thy reward will be great."

He was well pleased and gave unto Váhuka for comrades Várshneya, who had been in Nala's service, and Jívala also. So the transformed rajah abode a long time at Ayodhya, and every evening, sitting alone, he sang a single verse:

Where is she all worn but faithful, weary, thirsty, hung'ring too?
Thinks she of her foolish husband? . . . Doth another man her woo?

Ever thus he sang, and his comrades heard him and wondered greatly. So it came that one evening Jívala spoke to Nala and said: "For whom do you sorrow thus, O Váhuka? I pray you to tell me. Who is the husband of this lady?"

Nala answered him with sad voice and said: "Once there was a peerless lady, and she had a husband of weakly will. And lo! as they wandered in a forest together, he fled from her without cause, and yet he sorrowed greatly. Ever by day and by night is he consumed by his overwhelming grief, and brooding ever, he sings this melancholy song. He is a weary wanderer in the wide world, and his sorrow is without end; it is never still. . . . His wife wanders all forlorn in the forest. Ah! she deserved not such a fate. Thirsting and anhungered she wanders alone because her lord forsook her and fled; wild beasts are about her, seeking to devour; the wood is full of perils. . . . It may be that she is not now alive. . . ."

Thus did Nala sorrow in his secret heart over Damayantī during his long sojourn at Ayodhya, while he served the renowned Rajah Rituparna.

Meanwhile King Bhima was causing search to be made for his lost daughter and her royal husband. Abundant rewards were offered to Bráhmans, who went through every kingdom and every city in quest of the missing pair. It chanced that a Brahman, named Sudeva, entered Chedi when a royal holiday was being celebrated, and he beheld Damayantī standing beside the Princess Sunanda and the queen mother at the royal palace.

Sudeva perceived that her loveliness had been dimmed by sorrow, and to himself he said as he gazed upon her: "Ah! the lady with lotus eyes is like to the moon, darkly beautiful; her splendour hath shrunken like the crescent moon veiled in cloud—she who aforetime was beheld in the full moonlight of her glory. Pining for her lost husband, she is like to a darksome night when the moon is swallowed; her sorrow hath stricken her like to a river which has become dry, like to a shrunken pool in which lotus blooms shrivel and fade; she is, indeed, like to withered lotus. . . . Doth Nala live now without the bride who thus mourns for him? . . . When, oh when shall Damayantī be restored once again unto her lord as the moon bride is restored unto the peerless moon?[1] . . . Methinks I will speak. . . ."

[1] The moon is masculine, and the marriage occurs at a certain phase. In Egypt the moon is male, but was identified with imported female deities. In Norse mythology Mani is moon god; there was, however, an earlier moon goddess, Nana. In Ireland and Scotland the moon was not individualized—that is, not in the Gaelic language.

The Brahman then approached Damayantí and said: "I am Sudeva. Thy royal sire and thy mother and thy children are well. . . . A hundred Brahmans have been sent forth throughout the world to search for thee, O noble lady."

Damayantí heard him and wept.

The Princess Sunanda spoke to her queen mother, saying: "Lo! our handmaid weeps because that the Brahman hath spoken unto her. . . . Who she is we shall speedily know now."

Then the queen mother conducted the holy man to her chambers and spoke to him, saying: "Who is she—this mysterious and noble stranger, O holy man?"

Sudeva spoke in answer: "Her name is Damayantí, and her sire is King Bhima, lord of Vidarbha. Her husband is Nala. . . . From birth she has had a dark beauty spot like to a lotus between her fair eyebrows. Although it is covered with dust, I perceived it, and so I knew her. By Brahma was this spot made as the sign of his beauty-creating power."

The queen mother bade Sudeva to remove the dust from the beauty spot of Bhima's daughter. When this was done, it came forth like to the unclouded moon in heaven, and the royal lady and her daughter wept together and embraced the fair Damayantí[1].

Then the queen mother said: "Lo! thou art mine own sister's daughter, O beauteous one. Our sire is the Rajah Sudáman who reigns at Dasárna[2]. . . . Once I beheld thee as a child. . . . Ah! ask of me whatsoever thou desirest and it shall be thine."

The words for moon in A. Saxon and German are masculine; in Gaelic they are feminine.

[1] The Gaelic Diarmid had similarly a beauty spot on his forehead. Women who saw it immediately fell in love with him.

[2] Dasarna, "Ten Forts", in the south-eastern part of Central Hindustan.

"Alas! I am a banished mother," Damayantí said with fast-flowing tears. "Permit me, therefore, to return unto my children who have been orphaned of mother and sire."

The queen mother said: "Be it so."

Then Damayantí was given an army to guard her on her journey towards her native city, and she was welcomed there by all her kindred and friends with great rejoicing. King Bhima rewarded Sudeva with a thousand kine, and a town's revenue for a village.[1]

When Damayantí was embraced by her mother she said: "Now our chief duty is to bring home Nala."

The queen wept, and spoke to her husband, the royal Bhima, saying: "Our daughter still mourns heavily for lost lord and cannot be comforted."

Then Bhima urged the Brahmans to search for Nala, offering munificent reward when that he should be found. Damayantí addressed these holy men ere they departed and said unto them: "Wheresoever thou goest, speak this my message over and over again:

"*Whither art thou gone, O gambler, who didst sever my garment in twain? Thou didst leave thy loved one as she lay slumbering in the savage wood. Lo! she is awaiting thy return: by day and by night she sitteth alone, consumed by her grief. Oh hear her prayer and have compassion, thou noble hero, because that she ever weepeth for thee in the depths of her despair!*"

So the holy men went through every kingdom and every city repeating the message of Damayantí over and over again; but when they began to return one by one, each told with sadness that his quest had been in vain.

[1] A Bráhman village settlement.

Then came unto Vidarbha that Brahman, the wise Parnada, who had sojourned a time in the city of Ayodhya. He addressed the daughter of Bhima, saying: "Unto Rituparna I spake regarding thy husband, repeating thy message, but he answered not a word. So I went out from before him. Thereafter there came to me his charioteer, a man with short arms and misshapen body. His name is Váhuka, and he is skilled in driving the swift chariot and in preparing viands. He sorrowed greatly, and with melancholy voice spoke unto me these words:

'*In the excess of her sorrow a noble woman will compose herself and remain constant, and so win heaven by her virtues. She is protected by the breastplate of her chastity, and will suffer no harm. Nor will she yield to anger although she be deserted by her lord, whose robe the birds have taken away, leaving him in sore distress. She will not be moved to wrath against her husband, the sorrow-stricken and famine-wasted, who hath been bereft of his kingdom and despoiled of happiness.*'

When I heard the stranger's speech I came speedily hither to repeat it unto thee."

Damayantí at once went and spoke to her mother privately, for she was assured that Vahuka, the charioteer, was her royal lord. Then she gave of her wealth to the Brahman, saying: "Thou wilt get more if Nala returns home." The wise Parnada was weary with travel, and he departed to his own village.

Neither Damayantí nor her mother made known unto King Bhima their discovery nor yet their immediate purpose. Secretly the wife of Nala spake to Sudeva and said: "Hasten thou unto the city of Ayodhya, and appear before the Rajah Rituparna as if thou hadst come by chance, and say unto him: '*Once again is the daughter of Bhima to hold her swayamvara. All the kings and all the sons of kings are hastening as aforetime to Vidarbha. To-morrow at dawn she will choose for herself a new lord, for no one knoweth whether Nala liveth or not.*'"

So Sudeva went unto Ayodhya and spake as Damayantí desired of him, and then said: "If thou wouldst win the princess, O Rituparna, thou must go swiftly, for when the sun rises she will choose her a second husband."

Rituparna at once sent for Vahuka, and said: "O skilled charioteer, I must needs hasten to Vidarbha in a single day, because that the fair Damayantí holdeth her swayamvara at dawn to-morrow."

At these words the heart of Nala was torn with grief, and he said unto himself: "Is this but a stratagem to deceive me? Or is she whom I wronged estranged in mind? Hath she grown fickle of heart, she who hath been soul-stricken by grief in the depths of despair?"

Then he spake unto Rituparna and said: "As thou desirest so will I do, O Rituparna. I will drive thee in a single day to Vidarbha."

Having promised thus, he went forth and selected four steeds of high courage with the ten good marks,[1] which were as swift as the wind. He yoked them in haste, spake to them soothingly, and then set forth with Rituparna and Varshneya also at full speed. The rajah sat in silent wonder as the chariot went swiftly, and to himself he said: "Vahuka hath the god-like skill of the charioteer of heaven. . . . Can he be Nala, who hath taken himself another body? If he is not Nala, he is one who hath equal skill. Great men are wandering at times to and fro in disguise—gods who are hidden in human form."

[1] Ten twists or "eddies" of hair called A-vartas—one on forehead, two on breast, one on each flank hollow, &c.

So the rajah marvelled and thought, while he rejoiced in the matchless skill of the misshapen charioteer.

Swiftly they went. Over hills and rivers and over forests and lakes the chariot glided like to a bird through the air. . . . Of a sudden the rajah's robe was swept away, and he cried to the charioteer, saying: "Stop at instant, so that Varshneya may hasten back and recover my garment."

Nala paused not, and said: "Thy robe is now five miles behind us, and we cannot wait to recover it."

So they went on with all speed. Ere long Rituparna beheld a lofty fruit tree, named Vibhítak, and he said to Vahuka: "Now, skilful charioteer, thou shalt perceive my ability in numbers. No single mind is accomplished in every kind of knowledge. On two branches of yonder fruit tree are fifty million leaves and two thousand and ninety-five berries."

Vahuka said: "The leaves and the fruit are invisible to me. But I will tear off a branch and count the berries while Varshneya doth hold the bridle."

"But," urged the rajah, "we cannot pause on our journey."

Vahuka said: "Thou mayst stay with me, or thou canst let Varshneya drive thee at full speed."

Then the rajah spoke soothingly, saying: "O matchless charioteer! I cannot go on without thee to Vidarbha. I trust in thee. If thou wilt promise that we will reach the city ere night falls, I will do even as you desire."

The transformed Nala made answer: "I will indeed make haste when I have counted the berries."

So the horses were drawn up, and Nala tore a branch from the tree. Having counted the berries, he found they were in number even as the rajah had said, and he exclaimed: "Wonderful, indeed, is thy power, O Rituparna! Fain would I know thy secret."

Now the rajah was eager to proceed on his way, and he said: "I know the secret of the dice, and am therefore skilled in numbers."

"Then," said Nala, "if thou wilt impart to me thy secret, I will give thee knowledge in steeds."

Rituparna made answer thereat: "So be it;" and he forthwith informed the charioteer in the science of dice.

Now when Nala grew skilful in dice, Kali immediately passed out of his body, and Nishadha's fallen king vomited forth the serpent poison and was made weak with the struggle. Released from the venom, Kali resumed his wonted form, but he was beheld by Nala alone, who sought to curse him.

In his terror, the evil demon folded his hands and said: "Do not injure me, O king, and I will give thee matchless fame. . . . Know thou that Damayantí cursed me heavily in her wrath when thou didst desert her in the forest, and I have ever since endured great agony. Night and day, too, have I been scorched by the poison of the king of serpents. . . . Now I seek thy pity. I come to thee that thou mayst be my refuge. Lo! I promise, if thou wilt not curse me, that he who henceforth faileth not to praise thee, will have no dread of me in his heart."

Nala's wrath subsided, and he permitted Kali to enter the cloven fruit tree. Then he leapt into the chariot and drove on, and Kali returned unto his own place.

The chariot flew on like a bird, and the soul of Nala was elated with gladness. But he still retained the form of Vahuka.

At eventide the watchmen on the walls of Vidarbha

proclaimed the coming of Rituparna, and King Bhima gave permission that he should enter by the city gate.

All that region echoed the thunder of the rumbling chariot. Nala's horses, which Várshneya had driven from Nishadha, and were within the city, careered and neighed aloud as if Nala were beside them once again.

Damayantí also heard the approaching chariot, and her beating heart was like a cloud which thunders as the rain cometh on. Her soul was thrilled by the familiar sound, and it seemed to her that Nala was drawing nigh.[1] . . . On the palace roofs peacocks craned their necks and danced,[2] and elephants in their stalls, with uplifted trunks, trumpeted aloud as if rain were about to fall.

Damayantí said: "The sound of the chariot fills my soul with ecstasy. Surely my lord cometh. Oh, if I see not soon the moon-fair face of Nala I will surely die, for, thinking of his virtues, my heart is rent with sorrow. Unless he cometh now I will no longer live, but will perish by fire."

[1] This recalls: "He came even unto them. . . . The driving is like the driving of Jehu the son of Nimshi; for he driveth furiously."—2 *Kings*, ix, 20.

[2] The Indian peacock is sensitive to rain, and goes round "dancing" when it is coming on.

CHAPTER XXIII

The Homecoming of the King

Damayanti's Suspicions—Maid Interviews the Charioteer—The Message Repeated—A Husband's Emotion—Wonders Performed by Nala—Wife's Final Test—Children Visit their Father—Interview in the Palace—Nala Reproaches Damayanti—Her Confession and Vindication—Message from the Gods—Husband and Wife Reunited—Nala Returns to Nishadha—The Second Gambling Match—Nala Wins back his Kingdom—Erring Brother Forgiven—King and Queen Once More.

WITH sorrowful anxiety Damayantí ascended to the roof terrace of the lofty palace to gaze upon the chariot as it entered the middle court. She saw Rituparna stepping down, and Varshneya, who followed him, while Váhuka began to unyoke the foaming steeds.

King Bhima, who knew naught of his daughter's stratagem, received the royal Rajah of Ayodhya with much courtesy, and said: "I bid thee welcome, O king. . . . Why hast thou come hither?"

Now Rituparna wondered greatly that he beheld no kings or kings' sons, or even signs that a swayamvara was about to be held, but he kept his counsel and said: "I have come to salute thee, O Bhima."

The royal sire of Damayantí smiled thereat and said unto himself: "He hath not come so speedily through many cities for such a purpose. But we shall know betimes why he hath made this journey."

Rituparna was conducted to his chamber for rest and

refreshment by a company of royal servants, and Várshneya went with them.

Meanwhile Vahuka led his horses to the stables, and Damayantí descended to her chamber, thinking again and again that the sound of the coming chariot was like to the sound of Nala drawing nigh. So she called her fair handmaid, who was named Keśiní, and said unto her: "Go forth and speak to the misshapen charioteer with short arms, for methinks he is Nala. . . . Ask thou him who he is, and be mindful of his answer."

The handmaiden went forth and spoke unto Váhuka, saying: "Lo! the Princess Damayantí would fain know whence ye come and for what purpose."

Said Vahuka: "King Rituparna hath heard that the swayamvara is to be held at dawn to-morrow, so he set forth from Ayodhya and came hither swifter than the wind. I am his charioteer."

Keśiní asked him: "Who is the third man who hath come?"

Said Váhuka: "Várshneya is his name. He departed unto Ayodhya when Nala fled away. . . . I am skilled in taming steeds and in preparing viands."

The handmaiden then asked: "And doth this Varshneya know whither Nala hath fled and how he fares. Hath he told thee aught regarding him?"

Said Vahuka: "Várshneya carried away the children of Nala from Nishadha, but he knows not aught of the rajah, O fair one. Indeed, no man knoweth. He hath assumed a strange form, and wanders disguised about the world. . . . Nala alone knoweth, nor will he reveal himself."

Keśiní then spake, saying: "When the holy Brahman went unto the city of Ayodhya he uttered those words of Damayantí once and once again:

'*Whither art thou gone, O gambler, who didst sever my garment in twain? Thou didst leave thy loved one as she lay slumbering in the savage wood. Lo! she is awaiting thy return. By day and by night she sitteth alone, consumed by her grief. Oh! hear her prayer and have compassion, thou noble hero, because that she ever weepeth for thee in the depths of her despair.*'

Now speak again, I pray thee, the words which thou didst utter to the Brahman, for they gave healing to the stricken heart of Damayantí. Fain would the princess hear that speech once more."

Then was the soul of Nala rent with grief, hearing the message of Damayantí, and with tearful voice he said, repeating his former utterance:

"*In the excess of her sorrow a noble woman will compose herself and remain constant, and so win heaven by her virtues. She is protected by the breastplate of her chastity, and will suffer no harm. Nor will she yield to anger, although she be deserted by her lord, whose robe the birds have taken away, leaving him in sore distress. She will not be moved to wrath against her husband, the sorrow-stricken and famine-wasted, who hath been bereft of his kingdom and despoiled of happiness.*"

Nala could scarce restrain his emotion as he spoke these words. Then the fair Keśiní hastened unto Damayantí and told all.

In her distress the princess said unto her handmaiden: "Go thou and observe this man closely, and return betimes to inform me of all he doeth. When he doth prepare viands for his royal master let no fire be given unto him nor any water."

Keśiní hastened forth to watch the charioteer, and

when she returned she said: "O princess, this man is like unto a god. When he approacheth a low-built entrance he doth not stoop; the portal rises before him. Much flesh was given unto him to prepare viands for Rituparna. He but gazed on the empty vessels and they were filled with water. No fire was lit, and he took a handful of withered grass and held it up to the sun, whereupon it blazed instantly, and oh! the marvel, his fingers were unscorched by the flames. Water flows at his will, and as quickly it vanisheth. And lo! I beheld another marvel. When he lifted up flowers that had faded they were immediately refreshed, so that they had greater beauty and richer fragrance than before."[1]

Damayantí was fully assured that Váhuka was no other than her husband in altered form, and, weeping, she said softly: "Ah! go once again to the kitchen, fair Keśiní, and obtain without his knowledge a small portion of the food which he hath prepared."

Ere long the handmaiden returned with a morsel of well-cooked meat, and when Damayantí, who had ofttimes tried the food which had been cooked by her husband, tasted thereof, she uttered a loud cry in her anguish, and said: "Yon charioteer is Nala!"

Then she sipped water of ablution,[2] and sent her two children with Keśiní to the kitchen. Immediately that the charioteer beheld Indrasena and her brother he embraced them tenderly: he gazed lovingly upon the children, who were as beautiful as the children of the gods, and his soul was deeply moved, while tears ran down his cheeks. Seeing that the handmaiden observed him closely, he said: "Ah! the little ones are so like unto

[1] The powers given Nala by the gods as marriage gifts are here illustrated.

[2] A part of the ceremony of purification. The mouth was washed after eating, drinking, expectorating, slumbering, &c.

mine own children that I could not restrain my tears. . . . Let us part now, O innocent maiden; we are in a land of strangers, and if thou comest so often men will speak ill of thee."

When Damayantí was told how the charioteer had been so profoundly moved when he saw the royal children, she sent Keśiní unto her mother, the queen, for she was impatient to behold her husband once again. The handmaiden spake to the queen, saying: "Lo! we have observed the charioteer closely, and believe that he is Nala, although misshapen of form. Damayantí is fain he would come before her, with or without the knowledge of her sire, and that quickly."

The queen at once went unto Bhima and told him all, and the rajah gave permission that the charioteer should be summoned. In an instant word was sent unto Nala, and soon he stood before Damayantí and gazed upon her, and was moved to anguish. The princess was clad in a robe of scarlet, and her hair was thrown into disarray and defiled with dust: she wept and trembled with emotion.

At length Damayantí spoke, saying: "O Váhuka, hast thou ever heard of a noble and upright man who fled away, abandoning his sleeping wife in a forest? Innocent was she, and worn out with grief. Who was he who thus forsook his wife but the lordly Nala? . . . What offence did I give unto him that he should have deserted me while I slept? Was he not chosen by me as mine husband even before the gods? . . . How could he abandon her who loved him—the mother of his children? . . . Before the celestial beings he pledged his faith. How hath he kept his vow?"

She spoke with broken voice, and her dark eyes were dewed by sorrow.

Nala made answer, gazing upon his beloved wife, and said: "My kingdom I lost by the dice, but I was innocent of evil, because Kali possessed my soul, and by that demon was I also swayed to desert thee, O timid one! But thou didst smite him with thy curse when thou wert in the forest mourning for me, yet he remained in my body until, in the end, he was conquered by my long-suffering and devotion. Lo! now, O beauteous one, our grief is nigh to its end. The evil one hath departed, and through love of thee I come hither right speedily. . . . But how," he asked sternly, "may a high-born lady choose her another husband, as thou wouldst fain do, even now, O faint heart? The heralds have gone up and down the land saying: '*The daughter of Bhima will hold her second swayamvara because such is her fancy.*' And for this reason Rituparna made haste to come hither."[1]

Damayantí shook with emotion when these hard words were spoken, and she addressed Nala, saying: "Do not suspect me, O noble one, of such shameful guilt. It was for thee and thee alone that the Bráhmans went forth repeating the message which I addressed unto them. Lo! when I learned of the words thou didst speak unto the wise Parnada, I conceived this stratagem with purpose to bring thee hither. Faithful of heart have I remained, nor ever have I thought evil of thee. I call upon the wind to slay me now if I have sinned: on the sun I call also and on the moon, which enters into every thought of living beings. Let these three gods who govern the three worlds[2] speak now to prove my words, or else turn against me."

[1] According to the laws of Manu, second marriages were unlawful. Apparently, however, they were permissible at the early period of the poem, at least in some districts.

[2] Heaven, the earth, and the underworld.

Then the wind which the princess had adjured spake from without and said: "O Nala, Damayantí hath done no evil, nor hath she thought on evil. For three long years she hath treasured up her virtue in its fullness. She speaketh what is true even now. Thou hast found the daughter of Bhima: the daughter of Bhima hath found thee. Take now thine own wife to thy bosom."

Even as the wind was speaking, flowers fell out of heaven all around them,[1] and the soft music of the gods floated down the wind. Nala marvelled greatly, and gazed with love upon the innocent Damayantí. Then he put on the holy garment and thought upon the king of serpents. Immediately he resumed his own form, and the daughter of Bhima beheld her lost husband once again.

Damayantí shrieked and embraced Nala, and she hid her face in his bosom. He was again travel-worn and dust-stained as he clasped her to his heart, and she sighed softly. Long they stood there, speaking no words, in silent ecstasy. . . . The children were brought in and Nala embraced them once more.

Then did the queen, who rejoiced greatly, inform Bhima of Nala's return, and he said: "When he has performed his ablutions he will be re-united to Damayantí on the morrow."

The whole night long the happy pair sat together in the palace relating all that had befallen them during the years that they were parted one from another.

On the morn that followed Nala was again wedded to Damayantí, and thereafter he paid homage to Bhima. The glad tidings of his return spread swiftly through the city, and there was great rejoicing. Soon all the houses were decorated with banners and garlands; the streets

[1] A sign of divine approval and favour.

were watered and strewn with flowers. The altars of the gods were also adorned.

When Rituparna came to know that his charioteer, Váhuka, was the Rajah of Nishadha, he was well pleased, and he went into Nala's presence and said: "May thou have joy with thy queen to whom thou art re-united. Have I ever done aught unjustly unto thee whilst thou wert in my palace? If so, I now seek thy forgiveness."

Said Nala, "No injustice have I ever suffered from thee, mine old friend and kinsman. . . . I give thee fully all I have—my skill in steeds."

Rituparna was grateful unto Nala for his gift. He gave in return fuller instruction in the science of dice, and thereafter departed to his own city.

When a month had gone past Nala took leave of King Bhima and went towards Nishadha with one great chariot, sixteen elephants, fifty armed horsemen, and six hundred foot soldiers. The whole force entered the city boldly and made the earth to shake. Nala at once went before Pushkara and said: "I would fain throw dice with thee once again. I have much wealth and will stake all my treasure and even Damayantí upon the hazard. Thou, Pushkara, must stake thy kingdom. Let us stake everything; let us play for our lives. And know, too, that, according to ancient law, he who wins a kingdom by gambling must accept the challenge to play the counter game. . . . If thou wilt not play, then let us settle our difference in single combat."

Pushkara restrained from smiling, for he was confident of success, so with haughty contempt he made answer:

"It is joy to me that thou dost again possess great treasure to enable thee to play. It is joy also to me that I can win Damayantí with faultless limbs. Soon, indeed, will Bhima's daughter be decorated with the treasure which I shall win; she shall stand by my side as Apsarás, queen of heaven, stands beside Indra. Long have I waited for thee so that I might win Damayantí and be fully satisfied."

Nala would fain have drawn his sword, but composed himself, and, with angry eyes and scornful smile, he said: "Cease this idle chatter and let us play. Thereafter thou wilt have no desire to speak."

Immediately the two brothers set to the game, and Nala won at a single hazard all that he had lost. Then he smiled and said: "Now the whole kingdom is mine once again. Fallen monarch! never wilt thou behold the fair Damayantí because thou art become her slave. . . . Know now, that thou didst not triumph heretofore by reason of thine own skill, but because Kali aided thee, nor didst thou perceive this, O fool! . . . But fear not that I will take vengeance. . . . I give thee back thy life. Thou wilt have an estate and revenues and my friendship, because I remember, O Pushkara, that thou art my brother. . . . Mayst thou live for a hundred years!"

Then Nala embraced his brother, who did homage with hands folded, saying: "May thy splendour endure for ever! May thou live for ten thousand years! Thou hast given me my life and a city in which to live."

Pushkara remained with Nala for a month, and then went his way to his own domain.

All Nishadha rejoiced because that their rightful king had returned. The counsellors of state did homage before Nala, and said: "There is great joy now in city and country, and the people come to honour thee even as Indra is honoured by all the gods."

When the rejoicings were over, and the city of Nishadha was again tranquil, Damayantī returned home escorted by a great army, and she brought great treasures which her royal sire Bhima, the terrible in strength, had conferred upon her. With the long-eyed queen came her children also.

Thereafter Nala lived in happiness like unto the mighty Indra, being happily restored to his kingdom, and once again the monarch among men. He achieved great renown as a ruler, and he performed every holy rite with munificence and devotion.

Kusa grass, sipped holy water, and became absorbed in thought, until visions of the story were revealed before his eyes. Sloka by sloka and book by book, he composed the *Ramayana*; and as long as mountains endure and rivers run towards the sea, so long will it be repeated by the lips of mankind.

Valmiki sang that in days of yore there were two mighty kingdoms in sun-bright Hindustan, and these were Ko'sala, whose King was Dasarat'ha, father of Rama, and Mit'hila,[1] which was ruled over by Jan'aka, the father of beauteous Sita.

Now the capital of Kosala was Ayodhya[2], which shone in splendour like to Indra's celestial city; it had wide streets with large dwellings, richly decorated temples, towering like mountains, and grand and noble palaces. In the palace gardens there were numerous birds and flowers, shady groves of fruit trees, and lakes gemmed with bee-loved lotuses; the soft winds were wont to beat back the white water-blooms from the honey bees as coy maidens are withheld by the impulses of modesty from their eager lovers. Birds disported on the gleaming lakes, kingfishers were angered to behold themselves mirrored in the depths, thinking they gazed upon rivals, and ruffled the waters with their flapping wings. . . . The city of Ayodhya was full of prosperous and happy people.

Maharajah Dasaratha, who was of the Solar Race, dwelt in a stately palace; it was surrounded by strong walls, and guarded by a thousand warriors fierce as flames of consuming fire, and ever watchful like to mountain lions which protect their dens. Eight sage counsellors served the monarch with devotion, and he had two family priests, Vasishtha and Vamadeva.

[1] The kingdoms of Oudh and North Behar.

[2] *Pron.* a-yōd'hya.

But although Dasaratha was mighty and powerful, and prospered greatly, his heart was full of sorrow because that no son had been born to him by either of his three queens, Kausalya, Kaikeyi, and Sumitra. . . . At length he resolved to perform the Aswamedha (horse sacrifice) so that the gods might be prevailed upon to grant him an heir who would perpetuate his race. When his will was made known to the queens, their faces brightened as the lotus brightens at the promise of spring.

So it came to pass that a black horse was let loose on the night of the full moon of the month of Choitro[1]. A Brahman accompanied it, and after wandering for a full year, the animal returned again to the kingdom.[2]

Many rajahs attended the ceremony which took place on the north bank of the Sarayu river. Twenty-one sacrificial posts were set up for the birds, and beasts, and reptiles, which were to be offered up besides the horse, and there were eighteen Homa pits. When the fire was kindled upon the altar, Kausalya, the chief queen, slew the horse with the sacred scimitar, while the Brahmans chanted mantras. . . . All night long Kausalya and Kaikeyi, wives of the Maharajah, sat beside the horse's body, as was needful in performance of the rite. . . . Portions of the flesh were duly given to the fire, and when the ceremony was completed, Dasaratha awarded great gifts of kine and treasure to the Brahmans.

An oblation was afterwards offered to the gods, who came to the place of sacrifice with the music-loving Gandharvas, the Celestial saints, the Siddhas[3], and seven Deva-rishis. Brahma came with Vishnu and Shiva, and

[1] Easter full moon.

[2] As we have seen, Arjuna and an army accompanied the white horse which was sacrificed in the *Mahábhárata.*

[3] The spirits of ancestors.

Indra came also with the hastening Maruts. Ere they departed, the gods promised that four sons would be born to Dasaratha.

After this, Indra and the other gods[1] journeyed to the heaven of Brahma, and spake regarding Ravana[2], the monarch of demons, who had his dwelling in Lanká.[3]

Now Ravana had performed such great penances that Brahma rendered him invulnerable to gods and demons, with the result that the demon made Yama, god of death, his slave, and put Agni and Vayu, and the sun and moon, under subjection; indeed, he oppressed all the gods and obstructed sacrifices and despoiled the Brahmans. So Indra and other minor deities entreated Brahma to deliver them from the sway of Ravana.

Brahma heard the gods, and then conducted them to Vishnu's dwelling in the Ocean of Milk. Indra and the others honoured the Preserver, and cried: "O Lord of the Universe, remove the afflictions which press heavily upon us. Brahma hath blessed Ravana, nor can recall his gift. Save us, therefore, from the oppression of the demon king."

Vishnu spake and said: "Be not afraid, for I shall deliver you all. Ravana entreated Brahma for protection against all beings save the apes and men. Go therefore towards the earth, ye gods, and assume the guise of apes, and lo! I will divide myself into four parts and be born as the four sons of Maharajah Dasaratha. When I shall battle against Ravana, you will hasten to mine aid."

It came to pass that the wives of Dasaratha, who had eaten of sacrificial food, became the mothers of sons—

[1] The Vedic deities. [2] *Pron.* rah'va-na.

[3] He is called a Rakshasa king in the *Ramayana*. Ravana appears to be the Brahmanical conception of Vritra, the ruler of the Danavas or Asuras. Lanká is Ceylon.

Kausalya of Rama, Kaikeyi of Bharata, and Sumitra of Laksh'mana, and Satrughna. The people of the kingdom rejoiced greatly; they danced and sang and decked Ayodhya with streamers and flower garlands.

Of the four children Rama was the most beautiful: lying in his white cradle he was like to a blue lotus bloom amidst the gleaming waves of the Ganges. Vasishtha, the wise Brahman, perceived that he had all the marks of Vishnu, and revealed his knowledge to the Maharajah, by whom the child was well beloved. One evening the full moon rose in all its splendour, and Rama stretched out his hands because he desired to have it for a toy. His mother bought him jewels, but he threw them from him and wailed and wept until his eyes were red and swollen. Many of the women assembled round the cradle in deep concern. One said that the child was hungry, but he refused to drink; another that the Sasti was unpropitious, and offerings were at once made to that goddess; still Rama wept. A third woman declared that a ghost haunted and terrified the child, and mantras were chanted.

When the women found that they were unable to soothe Kausalya's son, the Maharajah was called, but Rama heeded him not. In his despair Dasaratha sent for his chief counsellor, who placed in Rama's hands a mirror which reflected the moon. Then the little prince was comforted, believing that he had obtained the moon; he ceased to weep, and everyone was put at ease once again.

When the children grew older they began to lisp words, and as they were unable to pronounce "peeta" and "mata"[1] they said "pa" and "ma". If Rama were asked his name, he answered "Ama". Sometimes

[1] Father and mother.

the Maharajah sat among his sage counsellors with the little boy upon his knee.

In their third year the princes had their ears pierced, and after that they played with other children. They made clay images of gods and put clay offerings in their mouths, and they broke the images because they would not eat.

Their education began when they were five years old. Vasishtha was the preceptor, and first he worshipped Saraswati, goddess of learning, and instructed his pupils to make offerings of flowers and fruit. They received instruction daily, beginning with the alphabet; then they studied grammar, and at length they mastered eighteen languages; they were also instructed in music and dancing and painting, and in all the sciences. From time to time the princes were examined by their royal sire in the presence of his counsellors. Afterwards they were trained to exercise in arms and take part in military sports, and they became skilled archers, and elephant riders, and horsemen and charioteers. Of all the princes Rama was the most accomplished; he rose above the others like to a flag which flutters proudly above a high dome.

Now when the princes were sixteen years old, their royal sire began to consider what brides should be selected for them. It chanced that while he was discussing this matter one day with his counsellors, Vishwamitra paid a visit to the palace. Dasaratha welcomed him with due honours, and spake saying: "Speak and tell what is thy request so that I may grant it speedily."

That mighty sage, who had been a Kshatriya in former times, but became a Brahman after practising rigid and long austerities, made answer and said: "O Maharajah, the Rakshasas are destroying our sacrificial offerings, and I pray you to permit Rama to return with me to my hermitage, for he is mighty and brave and young and is able to overpower the demons."

Reluctantly did Dasaratha consent, but not until Vasishtha had reassured him, and he commanded that Lakshmana should accompany Rama to the hermitage. Then the princes took leave of their parents and went away with Vishwamitra.

On the first night they abode in a hermitage situated where the river Sarayu pours into the Ganges, and the sage informed the princes that on that very spot Shiva had been wounded by the arrows of Kamadeva, god of love, whom he angrily consumed with the fire that issued from his third eye.

Next day the sage led the two princes towards a dark and fearsome jungle haunted by numerous beasts of prey, in which dwelt the terrible Rakshasa woman named Taraka, mother of Maricha;[1] she was misshapen and horrible, and continually ravaged all that country. Rama twanged his bow to challenge her, and she came towards the princes roaring angrily and throwing boulders. Because she was a female, the sons of Dasaratha were reluctant to cause her death. Rama shot arrows and cut off both her arms, and Lakshmana deprived her of nose and ears. She immediately changed her shape and became invisible, but by the power of sorcery continued to cause many stones to fall in showers about the young heroes. Vishwamitra urged Rama to slay her, and, guided by sound alone, he shot a great arrow which caused her death. Then the sage rejoiced greatly, and embracing Rama kissed his head.

In the morning Vishwamitra chanted powerful man-

[1] The fighting Rakshasas of the *Mahábhárata* are all males. Here the female—the mother of demons—is prominent, as in *Beowulf* and typical Scottish stories.

tras, which caused Celestial weapons to appear for Rama, and the spirits of the weapons stood before the prince with clasped hands and said: "*We are thy servants, O nobly generous one. Good betide thee! Whatever thou dost desire, lo! we shall accomplish for thee.*"[1]

Said Rama: "When I have need of you, I will think of you, and then you will wait upon me."

Thereafter Vishwamitra led the princes to his hermitage, which was situated in a pleasant grove where deer disported and birds sang sweetly. All the sages welcomed them. It chanced that when six days had gone past, the Brahmans prepared to offer up a sacrifice. Suddenly a band of Rakshasas, led by Maricha, son of the hag Taraka and Savahu, rushed towards the altar to defile the offering with bones and blood. Rama thought of his Celestial weapons, and they immediately appeared beside him. He cast one at Maricha which drove him hundreds of miles out to sea, and he threw a fire weapon at Savahu which consumed him; then he attacked and slew all the other demons. . . . The sages rejoiced greatly, and honoured the prince.

Next morning Vishwamitra informed Rama and Lakshmana that he and the other sages purposed to attend a great sacrifice which was to be offered up by Janaka, Rajah of Mithila. "You will accompany us," he said, "and the rajah will show you Shiva's great bow, which neither god nor man can break."

Now, both while they abode at the hermitage and as they journeyed towards Mithila, the princes heard the sacred legends of Vishnu in his dwarf incarnation, of the Churning of the Ocean, of the descent of Ganga through Shiva's hair, and of the cursing of Indra by a sage.

[1] A Gaelic axiom says, "Every weapon has its demon".

At length they reached the capital of Janaka,[1] King of Mithila, who welcomed Vishwamitra, and said: "Who are these courageous young men with the majesty of elephants and the fearlessness of tigers? Comely are they as the twin Aswins."

Said the sage: "These are sons of Dasaratha; they are slayers of Rakshasas, and desire greatly to behold Shiva's mighty bow."

Then the monarch spake to the nobles and warriors, and said: "Bring forth the bow."

His command was immediately obeyed. From an inner hall many stalwart men hauled the stupendous bow on an eight-wheeled iron chariot into the presence of the monarch of Mithila.

"Behold the bow of Shiva!" cried the warriors.

Said Janaka: "Behold the mighty bow which has been treasured by generations of kings. Many rajahs and warriors have endeavoured in vain to bend it; even Rakshasas and Asuras have failed; the gods themselves quail before it. . . . To the rajah who can bend this mighty weapon I will give in marriage my daughter, the beauteous Sita."

Rama gazed with wonder, and then said: "Permit me to lift and bend thy bow."

Wondering greatly at these words, the monarch and many high nobles and strong warriors gathered round about. . . . With smiling face, Rama lifted the bow; then proudly he strung it, whereat those who looked on were all amazed. . . . The prince put forth his strength and bent the bow with resistless force until it snapped in the middle with a terrible noise like to thunder; the earth

[1] "The remains of the capital founded by Janaka, and thence termed Janakpur, are still to be seen, according to Buchanan, on the northern frontier at the Janeckpoor of the maps."—Note to Professor H. H. Wilson's translation of the *Uttara Rama Charita.*

shook and the mountains echoed aloud. . . . At the loud crash, which resembled the roar of Indra's thunderbolt, all who were present fell down stunned and terrified save Janaka and Vishwamitra and the two sons of Dasaratha.

Said the monarch: "Now have mine eyes beheld a great wonder. Peerless is Rama, the noble one, and he shall be given for wife my daughter Sita, who is dearer to me than life. . . . Let speedy messengers hasten unto Dasaratha and bid him to come hither."

When Dasaratha reached Janaka's capital, Rama and Sita were wedded amidst great rejoicings.

Happy were the lovers together. When they arrived at Ayodhya the people welcomed them, and Dasaratha's queens embraced and kissed the soft-eyed bride of peerless fame.

It is told that on their honeymoon they loved to wander in the moonlight. On a night of warmth and beauty they went to the banks of a pond which sparkled with lotus blooms.

Said Rama: "My loved one, graceful art thou as the lotus, thy hair is like silken moss, thine eyes like beautiful bees; fair is thy face as the moon's soft image amidst the waters, thine arms are shapely lotus stalks, and thy bosom is like to buds of sweet lotus, O my peerless bride."

They plunged together into the cool, moon-swept waters, and Rama cast at his bride many fair water blooms. Sita retreated before him until she went beyond her depth; then she clung lovingly to Rama, twining her arms about his neck, nor did he hasten to draw her back, so dearly he loved to be embraced by her.

Hide-and-seek they then played amidst the floating flowers. Rama sank down until his face only was seen, and Sita, who searched for him, knew not whether she saw the face of Rama or a blue lotus bloom on the surface of the pond. Bending down to smell what seemed to be a flower, she touched her lover's lips, and he kissed her sweetly. Then Sita hid herself, and her face was like to a lotus bloom among lotus blooms. Rama kissed her many times ere she moved or smiled. . . . At length they darted merrily from the pond in bright moonlight, their garments dripping sparkling water drops, and then they drank cups of honey; the heart of Sita was intoxicated, and she babbled words of love and sweetness. . . .

Rama and Sita spent happy hours together, sharing supreme joy like to Vishnu and peerless Lakshmi in the bright Celestial regions.

The Maharajah Dasaratha was growing old, and his counsellors and the people began to consider who should be appointed Yuvarajah (Young Rajah), to take over the duties of sovereignty and allow the monarch to spend his closing years in preparation for death, so that he might secure heaven in the next life.

All the sages and chieftains favoured the choice of Rama, and the heart of Dasaratha was filled with joy. The people rejoiced also when it was told to them that Rama was to become their ruler, and they raised shouts of triumph and gladness. Then Rama was sent for, and the Maharajah blessed him and bade him to spend the night in Vishnu's temple with his wife Sita, to prepare for the ceremony of installation on the morrow. That night the city of Ayodhya was illuminated, and the people prepared to decorate the streets with garlands and streamers when the dawn came.

Now there was one who did not rejoice, because that she hated Rama, son of the queen Kausalya. This was the old nurse of Prince Bharata, son of the queen Kaikeyi[1]. Her name was Manthara; she had been the slave of Kaikeyi while that queen yet abode in the palace of her sire, the rajah Aswapati. Ugly and misshapen was Manthara; she was short-necked, flat-breasted, and had legs like a crane; she was big-bellied and humpbacked. When Rama was a child she had offended him and he smote her, and ever afterwards she regarded him with fierce enmity.

It chanced that Kaikeyi was gazing idly from the palace roof on the illuminated and bustling streets, when the hunchbacked slave approached her, and said: "Canst thou be merry, O foolish one, on this night? Thou art threatened by dire misfortune. Dasaratha hath deceived thee. Thy son Bharata hath been sent to thy father's city, so that the son of Kausalya may be installed as Yuvarajah on the morrow. Henceforth thou wilt be the bondswoman of Kausalya, Rama's mother, and thou wilt have to wait obediently on the commands of proud Sita. Hasten now and prevent this dread happening."

Said Kaikeyi: "Why do you hate Rama? He is the eldest son of the chief queen, and Bharata could not become Yuvarajah without the consent of Kausalya's son, who honours me as he honours his own mother."

Manthara fumed with wonder and indignation at these words; then she said: "What madness hath blinded thee? What folly maketh thee heedless of the gulf of sorrow which awaiteth thee and thy son? I am older than thou art, and have seen dark deeds committed in royal houses. Can Bharata become the slave of Rama? Well I know that jealous Rama will drive thy lordly son into exile and mayhap slay him. . . . Arise, thou heedless queen, and save Bharata, lest he be sent to wander alone in the fearsome jungle. Speak thy mandate to the

[1] *Pron.* ky-kay-yee'.

Maharajah, whose heart hath been captivated by thy beauty. . . . Any other woman but thee would rather die than suffer a rival wife to triumph over her."

Said Kaikeyi, whose heart began to burn with jealous anger: "How can I prevail upon Dasaratha to exalt my son and send Rama into exile?"

Then the hunchback reminded Bharata's mother that she had been promised two boons by her husband. In time past Dasaratha had gone to help Indra to wage war against the demons. He was grievously wounded and would have died, but Kaikeyi cured him. So he vowed to grant her two boons, and she said: "When I have need of two favours, I will remind thee of thy promise."

Manthara spake to the queen mother of Bharata, saying: "Now go to the mourning chamber and feign sorrow and anger. The Maharajah will seek thee out, and when he findeth thee demand of him the two boons which he promised aforetime."

So it came to pass that in the mourning chamber Kaikeyi spake to Dasaratha, and said: "Now grant me the two boons as thou didst vow to do, or I shall die this night."

Said the Maharajah: "Speak thy wishes, and they will be granted. May I never achieve bliss if thy desires are not fulfilled."

Kaikeyi said: "Let royal deeds redeem royal words. The first boon I ask is that my son Bharata be installed as Yuvarajah; the second is that Rama be banished for fourteen years to live in the jungle as a devotee clad in a robe of bark."

When Dasaratha heard these awful words he swooned and fell prone like to a tempest-smitten tree. . . . At length he recovered his senses, and opening his eyes, said: "Have I dreamed a fearsome dream? Do demons torture me? Is my mind clouded with madness?" . . .

Hushed and trembling, he gazed upon Kaikeyi as a startled deer gazes at a tigress. . . . He was as helpless as a serpent which hath been mantra-charmed, and for a time he sobbed aloud. . . . At length wrath possessed him, and, red-eyed and loud-voiced, he reproached her, saying: "Traitress, wouldst thou bring ruin to my family? . . . Rama hath never wronged thee; why dost thou seek to injure him? O Kaikeyi, whom I have loved and taken to my bosom, thou hast crept into my house like a poisonous snake to accomplish my ruin. It is death to me to part with my brave and noble Rama, now that I am old and feeble. . . . Have pity on me and ask for other boons."

Said Kaikeyi, coldly and bitterly: "If thou wilt break thy vow now to one who saved thy life, all men will despise thee, and I will drink poison this very night."

Dasaratha was made silent a time. Then he spoke with tears, and said: "Beautiful art thou, O Kaikeyi. Thou hast taken captive my heart. How can this evil desire dwell in thy bosom and darken it with guile? Thou hast entrapped me with the bait of thy beauty. . . . Can a father dishonour his well-loved son? Rather would I enter hell than send Rama into exile. How can I look upon his face again? How can I suffer to behold him parting with gentle Sita? . . . Oh! I have drunk of sweet wine mingled with poison. . . . Have pity on me, O Kaikeyi! I fall at thy feet. . . . I would that Yama would snatch me off in this hour."

Said Kaikeyi: "If thou dost honour truth thou wilt grant the boons I crave, but if thou wouldst rather break thine oath, let me drink poison now."

Dasaratha cried in his grief: "O shadow - robed

Night, decked with stars! arrest the hours that pass by, or else give my heart release. Cover with thy darksome mantle my sorrow and my shame, and hide this deed of crime from the knowledge of mankind. Let me perish ere the dawn; may the sun never rise to shine upon my sin-smeared life."

So he lamented through the night, and unto Kaikeyi he said: "I grant the boons, but I reject thee for ever and thy son Bharata also."

Morning dawned. . . . The city was decorated with streamers and flowers. A golden throne was set up for Rama; the tiger's skin was spread for his feet; the white umbrella waited for him. Elephants and chariot horses were harnessed. . . . The preparations for the sacrifice were completed. . . . The crowds began to gather in the streets waiting for the Maharajah and noble Rama, whom all the people loved.

Towards the palace went Sumantra, the chief counsellor. He entered the chamber in which Dasaratha had spent the night to awaken him and conduct him to the ceremony.

Kaikeyi met the counsellor and said: "Summon Rama hither, for the Maharajah must speak with him."

Wondering greatly, Sumantra hastened to the prince's dwelling and spake the royal command. Said Rama: "I will go quickly. Tarry here, O Sita, and await my return."

Sita followed Rama to the doorway and invoked the gods so that they might bless and protect him.

The multitudes of people hailed the prince as he was driven in his chariot towards the palace, and women threw flowers upon him from the housetops. . . . He entered the gate, driving through the first three courts; he dismounted and walked across the two inner courts; he then bade his followers to remain without, and soon he stood before the Maharajah and made humble obeisance.

Rama beheld his father sitting beside Kaikeyi; his body was bent, his face was worn with grief. Tears fell from Dasaratha's eyes as his son kissed his feet and the feet of Kaikeyi also; he strove to speak while tears streamed from his eyes, but all he could utter was, "Oh! Rama." . . . The sorrow of Dasaratha rose and fell in his heart like to the waves of a stormy sea.

Said Rama: "Oh! have I offended my sire? Speak, mother, and tell. Wherefore do tears fall from his eyes? Why is his face clouded with grief? . . . I would rather die than wound his heart by word or deed."

Kaikeyi said: "The Maharajah is not angered, nor is he grief-stricken, but he fears to speak his purpose until thou dost promise to serve his will."

Said Rama: "O speak and I will obey even if I am asked to quaff poison and die ere my time. My promise is given and my lips have never lied."

Kaikeyi said coldly: "The Maharajah vowed to grant two boons when I cured his wounds and saved his life, although he repents his promise now like to a man of low caste. I have asked him to fulfil his vow, and the boons I crave are that Bharata, whose star is bright, be installed as Yuvarajah, and thou shouldst be banished for twice seven years. . . . If thou art ready to obey thy father's will and preserve his honour, thou wilt depart this day from the city and permit Bharata to govern the kingdom."

Dasaratha's heart was pierced with agony at these words, but Rama heard them unmoved; they fell upon his ears like to sparks falling into the sea. Calmly he spake and said: "I will depart this day in fulfilment of my father's vow. Cheerfully will I obey his command. Let Bharata be summoned quickly from Girivrajah, and I will hasten to the jungle of Dandaka."

Said Kaikeyi: "So be it. . . . But tarry not, for thy sire will neither wash nor eat until thou hast departed hence."

Rama bowed before his sire who was prostrated with sorrow; he bowed before Kaikeyi also. . . . All the royal attendants wept, but Rama was unmoved as is the ocean when a pot of water is drawn from it or poured in.

He went towards Kausalya, his mother, who was engaged making offerings to Vishnu on his behalf, and informed her what had taken place.

Kausalya wept and cried: "O dearly beloved, if thou hadst never been born I would not have to suffer this calamity. . . . My son, I am the chief queen, but Kaikeyi hath supplanted me, and I am disliked and neglected by my husband. . . . I am old and unable to endure the loss of thee, my son. . . . Hath my heart grown hard as rock that it will not break now? Is Yama's mansions so full that I am not called away? I have no desire to live any longer. . . . Can a son obey a sire in his dotage? . . . Rama, Rama, the people will rise in revolt; seize thou the throne, and if thy father remaineth hostile slay him, because he hath become contemptible before all men, being but a woman's slave."

Lakshmana said: "Mother, thy words are just. Who will dare oppose Rama so long as I serve him?"

Said Kausalya: "Hear the words of thy brother, Rama. If thy sire's command must be obeyed so must mine, and I command thee now not to depart to the jungle. If thou wilt not obey me, I will eat no more food and thou wilt be guilty of my death."

Rama said: "I must obey my sire's command. Permit me, therefore, O mother, to depart now. . . . O Lakshmana, I have promised my sire to obey. Do not ask me to break my plighted word."

Still Kausalya pleaded with Rama to remain, and he sought to comfort her, but her grief was too heavy to be removed, for she loved her son dearly and hated her rival Kaikeyi.

With darkened brow and saddened eyes, Rama then went unto Sita and told her all, and said: "My mother is heartbroken, O Sita; she hath need of thee to soothe her grief. O dearly beloved, I must now depart and leave thee. Be ever obedient unto Bharata, nor laud me ever, for a rajah cares not to hear another praised in his presence."

Said Sita: "A wife must ever accompany her husband and share his sufferings. If thou must depart to the forest, it is my duty to go before thee and smooth the thorns in thy path. So long as I am with thee I will be happy even in the jungle. Dearer to me than the palace is the place where I can hold sweet converse with my husband. I will lighten thy burden of sorrow, O Rama, but if thou wilt leave me here alone I will surely die."

Rama spoke of the perils of the jungle, which was full of wild beasts and venomous reptiles, where food was scarce, and, when found, bitter to taste, where they would find no home and would have to lie on the bare ground, and where they would suffer greatly from heat and cold, from tempest and rains. "O Sita," he cried, "thou art dearer to me than life itself. How can I permit thee to suffer for me? My love will grow greater when I know what it is to be separated from thee. . . . Wait here, O loved one, until I return again."

Said Sita: "I know nor fear the perils and sorrows of the jungle. Rather would I sleep with thee on the bare ground than lie here alone on a bed of down. Without thee I have no desire to live. . . . Take me with thee, O Rama, and let me share thy sorrow and thy joys. Sweeter will be the jungle with thee beside me than the palace when thou hast departed."

In vain Rama remonstrated with her, but she refused to be separated from him. She fell at his feet, weeping bitterly, and at length he consented that she should share his sufferings in the jungle.

Then Lakshmana pleaded to accompany Rama also, nor could he be persuaded to remain behind.

Thereafter Rama and Sita and Lakshmana went together, walking barefooted, towards the palace to bid farewell to the Maharajah and his queens.

Rumours of what had happened were passing through the city, and the people gazed with sorrow on Rama, his bride and his brother, and some said: "The Maharajah is possessed by demons." Others said: "Let us desert the city and follow Rama. Then Bharata will have none left to rule over."

Rama entered the palace with his wife and brother, and stood before the Maharajah with folded hands.

Dasaratha lamented and said: "A woman hath deceived me. She concealed her wicked designs in her heart as a fire is concealed by ashes. . . . The evening is late; tarry therefore with thy mother and me until day breaks."

Said Rama: "Kaikeyi commanded me to depart this day to the jungle, and I promised to obey. . . . When fourteen years have gone past we shall return again and honour thee."

The Maharajah and his counsellors desired to send the royal army and the huntsmen and much grain and treasure to the jungle with Rama, although Kaikeyi protested loudly, but Rama refused to have soldiers and followers, and asked for the raiment of bark which he must wear, and for the spade with which to dig roots and the basket to carry them.

The shameless Kaikeyi then went away and returned with three dresses of bark. Rama and Lakshmana immediately cast off their royal garments and all their ornaments, and assumed the rough attire of devotees. But Sita, who from childhood had been clad in silk, wept and said: "How can I wear raiment of bark? I cannot use such attire."

All the women shed tears at these words, and Dasaratha said: "Kaikeyi's command is binding on Rama only, and his wife and brother may assume any garments they desire."

So the robe of bark was taken away from Sita; it was not permitted that she should be put to shame.

Then Rama and Sita and Lakshmana took leave of all those who were in the palace, and, amidst lamentation and wailing, took their departure from the palace. They were conveyed to the frontier of the kingdom in a chariot, and many people followed them from the city, resolved to share exile with Rama. The night was spent on the banks of the Tamasa, and all slept save Rama alone. As soon as dawn came, he awakened Sita and Lakshmana and the charioteer, and together they departed ere the slumbering multitude were aware. The exiles thereafter parted with the charioteer, and crossing the river Tamasa, journeyed on till they saw the sacred Ganges, in which the gods are wont to bathe, and on whose banks many sages had chosen hermitages.

When the people awoke and found that those whom they loved and honoured had hastened away, they returned with hearts full of sorrow to the mourning city of Ayodhya.

CHAPTER XXV

The Rape of Sita

The Maharajah's Doom—Tale of the Hermit's Son—A Curse Fulfilled—Death of Dasaratha—Bharata Refuses the Throne—Visit to Rama in Exile—Loyalty to a Dead Sire—Javala the Sceptic—Bharata Honours Rama's Sandals—Wanderings of the Exiles—A Love-stricken Rakshasa—Jesting ends in Bloodshed—A War of Vengeance—Rama's Great Victory—Ravana's Cunning Plot—The Magic Deer—Rama and Lakshmana Lured from Hermitage—Sita Taken Captive.

Now the Maharajah Dasaratha was doomed to die a sorrowful death. Be it known that in his youth, when he loved to go a-hunting, he heard in the jungle depths one evening a gurgling of water, and thought an elephant or a deer had come to drink from a hidden stream. He drew his bow; he aimed at the sound and discharged an arrow. . . . A human voice uttered a cry of agony. . . . Breaking through the tangled jungle growth, Dasaratha discovered that he had mortally wounded a young hermit who had come to draw water for his aged parents. The poor victim forgave the king and counselled him, saying: "Hasten to my sire and inform him of my fate, lest his curse should consume thee as a fire consumes a withered tree." Then he expired.

Dismayed and sorrowing deeply, Dasaratha went towards the dwelling of the boy's parents, who were blind and old. He heard the father cry: "Ah! why hast thou lingered, my son? I am athirst, and thy mother longs for thee."

In broken accents the king informed the lonesome

parents of their son's death. The sire lamented aloud, and said: "Oh! lead me to my son. Let me embrace him for the last time."

Dasaratha conducted the weeping parents to the spot where the lad lay lifeless and stained with blood. The sire clasped the body, and cried: "Oh! wilt thou not speak and greet me, my son? Thou liest on the ground; thou dost not answer me when I call. Alas! thou canst not love me any longer. . . . Thy mother is here. Oh! thou who wert dutiful and kind, speak but one tender word to her and to me. . . . Who will now read to us each morning the holy books? Who will now find roots and fruits to feed us? . . . Oh! tarry with us yet a little longer, my son. Wait for us ere thou dost depart to the Kingdom of Death—stay but one day longer, and on the morrow thy father and mother will go with thee on the weary and darksome path of no returning. . . . How can we live now that our child and protector is taken from us?"

So the blind old hermit lamented. Then he spake to the king, and said: "I had but this one child and thou hast made me childless. Now slay me also, because Death is blunted and unable to hurt me any more. . . . A father cannot feel greater agony than when he sorrows for a beloved son. This peculiar sharp sorrow thou wilt yet know, O king. As I weep now, and as I am hastened to death, mourning for my son, so wilt thou suffer in like manner, sorrowing for a dearly-beloved and righteous son. Thy death, O Dasaratha, will cleanse thee of this crime."

Having spoken thus, the hermit built the funeral pyre for the dead boy, and when it was lit he and his wife leapt amidst the flames and entered the Kingdom of Death.

After Rama had departed from Ayodhya, his mother, Kausalya, reproached Dasaratha, saying: "Thou wouldst not break thy promise to Kaikeyi, but thou didst break thy promise made to thy counsellors that Rama should be thy successor."

The Maharajah was bowed down with grief, and cried: "Oh! forgive me, Kausalya, because my heart is breaking while I mourn for my beloved son. Oh! do not wound me again, I pray thee."

Kausalya wept and said: "Alas! my grief hath made me speak cruelly to thee."

In the middle of the second night after Rama had departed, Dasaratha awoke and cried: "O Kausalya, I am dying with grief. Mine eyes have grown blind with weeping. Take my hand in thine and speak unto me. Oh! bitterly I grieve now that I cannot look upon Rama ere I die. Happy are they whose eyes behold him . . . My heart beats feebly." . . .

When he had spoken thus, Dasaratha fell back and was silent. Kausalya, mother of Rama, and Sumitra, mother of Lakshmana, knelt beside him, and they swooned when his spirit fled.

In the morning messengers were sent speedily to Bharata, who sojourned in the kingdom of the Kaikeyas with his mother's sire, the rajah Aswapati, bidding him to return without delay. Seven nights passed while the prince journeyed towards Ayodhya. He knew not that Dasaratha had died until he reached the palace. Then Kaikeyi, his mother, informed him without tears. Bharata wept, and flung himself down upon the floor and cried aloud.

Kaikeyi said: "Thou shouldst not thus give way to grief, my son."

Said Bharata: "If the Maharajah were alive, he would

have embraced and kissed me on my return. But where is Rama, who is now as a sire unto me?"

Then Kaikeyi told him all that had taken place, and said: "For thy sake, my son, I have accomplished this. Sorrow not, because thou wilt be installed as ruler here."

Said Bharata: "I have lost my father and my elder brother. Of what good is a kingdom unto me now? O evil-hearted woman, thou hast bereft this house of all joy; thou hast slain my sire and banished Rama. . . . But I will bring my brother back from the jungle; he shall be seated on the throne."

Satrughna sorrowed like Bharata, and when he beheld the wicked hunchback Manthara he threw her down and dragged her across the floor, saying: "This hateful creature is the cause of our calamities. I will slay her."

Kaikeyi flew away in terror, and Bharata said: "Slay her not, because she is a woman. I would have killed my wicked mother, but, had I done so, Rama would ne'er have forgiven me nor have spoken to me again. Spare this wretch, O Satrughna, lest Rama should be angry with thee."

Kausalya, mother of Rama, then approached Bharata and said: "The raj is now thine, O ambitious one. Thy mother hath secured it for thee."

Bharata fell at her feet and vowed that he would never sit on the throne, but would hasten after Rama to entreat him to return.

Then Kausalya wept and embraced him because that he was loyal to his elder brother.

When Bharata had performed the funeral rites for the Maharajah, he left Ayodhya with a strong army to search for Rama.

The two brothers met in the jungle of Chitra-kuta,

and they embraced one another and wept for their dead sire.

In the morning Bharata spake to Rama in the presence of the army, saying: "This raj, which was given unto me against my will, I now gift unto thee, mine elder brother. Accept it and remove the stain of my mother's sin."

Said Rama: "O Bharata, my royal sire, fulfilling his vow, banished me to the jungle and appointed thee to the raj. A faithful son cannot recall the mandate of his sire."

Then Java'li, the Brahmanic counsellor of Dasaratha, spake and said: "O Rama, why dim thine understanding with empty maxims? Thou hast already obeyed thy sire. It is foolish to think that thou shouldst continue this allegiance to one who is dead. A man enters the world alone and departs alone; he owns not friendship to kindred. His parents are to him like a wayside inn which he leaves in the morning; his allegiance to them is temporary. He meets them like a traveller who tarries on his journey and then goes on his way as before. In this world we have only one life to live. If thou wilt refuse this raj thou wilt destroy thy one life. I am sorry for those who scorn the blessings of this world so long as they are alive in the hope that they will reach a Paradise which does not exist. When this life is spent we are extinguished for ever. Alas! that men should make to their ancestors useless offerings. Can a dead man eat thereof? These offerings are a waste of food. If the soul endures and passes into a new body how can it benefit from food eaten by another? These practices were invented by cunning priests with selfish motives. . . . There is no Hereafter. Therefore snatch the joys of life while thou canst, O Rama, take the raj which is offered to thee and return to Ayodhya."

Said Rama, whose heart was filled with anger: "O Javali, thy motive is excellent but thy doctrines are false. A good man is distinguished from an evil man by his deeds. How can I, who have embraced a virtuous life, turn now into the path of evildoing? The gods who read a man's heart would curse me for my sins. Vain are thine idle words; thy reasoning is cunning but false. Truth is our ancient path. Truth endures when all else passes away. The venom of falsehood is more deadly than the venom of a serpent's sting. Thou hast said that there is no Hereafter, and that we should snatch pleasures while life endures. If that is so, why do wise men condemn what is evil if the vicious are simply pursuing the quest of happiness? Why do sages live austere lives, eating fruits and roots, instead of feasting on flesh and drinking wine? There would be no sciences if we believed only those things we behold. Inferential proof must be permitted. Is a woman to consider herself a widow when her husband is out of sight? . . . Know, all of ye, that I will be faithful to the mandate of my sire. I will keep my promise which I cannot recall. Let Bharata reign, for I will dwell in the jungle."

Bharata said: "If my sire's wish must be fulfilled, let me remain in the jungle for fourteen years so that Rama may return to Ayodhya."

Said Rama: "Neither Bharata nor I can recall or change the commands of Dasaratha."

Thereafter Bharata gave to Rama a pair of new sandals decked with gold, saying: "Put these upon thy feet and they shall accomplish the good of all."

Rama put on the sandals and then returned them to his brother, who said: "I will live as a devotee for fourteen years with matted hair and in a robe of bark.

These sandals, O Rama, will be placed upon the throne which I will guard for thee. If thou dost not return when the time of thy penance is ended, I will perish upon the pyre."

The brethren then took leave of one another. Bharata returned to Ayodhya, and to his counsellors spake, saying: "I will dwell outside the city in Nandigrama until Rama returns again."

Then he clad himself in bark and went to the jungle. There he conducted the affairs of government, holding the royal umbrella over Rama's sandals. All presents which were given were first presented to the sandals, because Bharata ruled the kingdom for his elder brother. The sandals of Rama were the symbol of royal authority.

Meanwhile Rama with Sita and Lakshmana went southward towards deeper jungles, visiting various holy sages, and having crossed the Vindhya mountains, they wandered together in the Deccan and Southern India. At Panchavati[1], nigh to the sources of the river Godavari, the royal exiles built a hut with four rooms, and lived peaceful and pious lives. Thirteen years and a half went over their heads.

It came to pass that one day there came to the quiet hermitage a Rakshasa woman, named Surpa-nakha, the sister of Ravana, the demon King of Lanka, Ceylon. She was misshapen and ugly and her voice was harsh and unpleasant. When she beheld Rama, who was comely as a lotus, and of lofty and loyal bearing, her heart was filled with love for him. Made bold with this love, she resolved to assume another form so as to induce him to leave the faithful Sita. . . . In time she stood before the prince in the guise of a young and beautiful woman, and said: "Who art thou who hast

[1] Nasik. About 100 miles from Bombay.

8

RAMA SPURNS THE DEMON LOVER

From the painting by Warwick Goble

come hither with thy bride to dwell in this lone jungle which is haunted by Rakshasas?"

Said Rama: "I am Rama, the elder son of a Maharajah named Dasaratha. I dwell here in exile in fulfilment of my sire's vow, with Sita, my spouse, and Lakshmana, my brother. Why dost thou, O fair one, who art as beautiful as the bride of Vishnu, wander about here all alone?"

Surpa-nakha said: "I am a Rakshasa woman, the sister of Ravana, and have come hither because I love thee. I have chosen thee for my husband, and thou shalt rule over my great empire. Thy Sita is pale and deformed and unworthy of thee, but I am of surpassing beauty and have power to assume any form at will. I must devour Sita and thy brother, so that we may range the jungle together and visit the lofty hills."

Said Rama: "Sita is my beloved bride, nor would I leave her. But Lakshmana hath no consort and is a fit husband for thee."

Surpa-nakha at once departed from Rama, and went and found Lakshmana, who jested with her.

Then the enraged Rakshasa woman sprang towards Sita in jealous anger, but Rama thrust her back. Like to lightning Lakshmana leapt forward with his sword and cut off the ears and nose of the evil-hearted Surpa-nakha, whereat she shrieked and fled away, wailing like to the storm wind. The rocks answered back her awesome cries.

Surpa-nakha hastened to one of her brothers who was named Khara, and when he saw her disfigured and bleeding, he cried: "None but a Celestial could have done this deed. This day will I drink the blood of Indra as a crane drinks milk and water."

Then Surpa-nakha related what had taken place, and

said: "Rama and Lakshmana attacked me to protect the woman Sita, whose life-blood I desired to drink. I entreat thee to bring her to me now."

Khara called upon fourteen Rakshasas and commanded them to capture the three royal hermits who dwelt in Dandaka jungle. They hastened away and Surpa-nakha went with them, but soon she returned wailing, because Rama had slain the Rakshasas with Celestial arrows.

Khara immediately called upon his brother Dush'ana, saying: "Assemble an army of fourteen thousand Rakshasas, and bring my weapons and my chariot with white horses, for, verily, this day I must kill the hateful Rama."

Evil were the omens as the army marched to battle. Jackals howled and birds screamed at dawn; the sky was blood-red, and Rahu endeavoured to swallow the sun and caused an awesome eclipse; a headless horror appeared in mid air. The arrows of Rama emitted smoke, and he said to Lakshmana: "Hasten with Sita to a secret cave in the mountains and protect her there. I will battle with the demons alone."

Lakshmana did as his brother commanded. Then Rama girt on his glowing armour, and, armed with a Celestial bow and many arrows, he awaited the coming of his enemies. When the Rakshasas appeared they quailed before him, because he appeared like to Yama at a Yuga end, but Khara drove on in his chariot, urging his followers to attack; they followed him roaring like a tempest, and they appeared like to black tremendous clouds rushing towards the rising sun.

Thousands of weapons were showered against Rama, who began to discharge flaming arrows, which swept among the Rakshasas like fire in a sun-dried forest, so that many were mangled and slain. Still Khara and his brother continued to attack; but Rama seized a great Celestial weapon and slew Dushana and scattered the demon army in flight. Khara sought to avenge his brother's death, but Rama drew his bow and shot a blazing arrow which consumed him instantly. So was the battle won, and Sita came forth from the cave and embraced her heroic husband and kissed him.

Of all the Rakshasa host only Surpa-nakha escaped alive. She hastened to Lanka and informed the ten-headed King Ravana of the death of his brothers, and said: "Thou canst not defeat Rama in battle. But he may be overcome by guile. He hath a beautiful spouse, whose name is Sita, and she is dearer to him than life. If thou wilt take her captive, Rama can be slain, because he is unable to exist without her."

Said Ravana: "I will bring Sita hither in my chariot."

On the morrow Ravana and his brother Maricha, whom Rama had aforetime driven far across the ocean with a Celestial weapon, went towards the hermitage of the royal exiles in a resplendent chariot which went through the air like a great bird; it was drawn by asses which had the heads of Rakshasas.

Maricha assumed the shape of a golden deer with silvern spots; its horns were tipped with sapphire and its eyes were like to blue lotus blooms. This beautiful animal of gentle seeming grazed below the trees until Sita beheld it with wondering eyes as she came forth to pluck wild flowers. She called to Rama, saying: "A deer of wondrous beauty is wandering through the grove. I long to rest at ease on its golden skin."

Said Rama: "O Lakshmana, I must fulfil the desire of Sita. Tarry with her until I obtain this animal for her."

So speaking, he lifted his bow and hastened away through the trees.

Lakshmana spoke to Sita and said: "My heart is full of misgiving. Sages have told that Rakshasas are wont to assume the forms of deer. Ofttimes have monarchs been waylaid in the forest by artful demons who came to lure them away."

Rama chased the deer a long time hither and thither through the forest, and at length he shot an arrow which pierced its heart. In his agony Maricha sprang out of the deer's body, and cried out in imitation of Rama's voice: "*Sita, Sita, save me! O save me, Lakshmana!*" Then he died, and Rama perceived that he had slain the Rakshasa Maricha, brother of Ravana.

Sita's heart was filled with alarm when she heard the voice of the Rakshasa calling in imitation of her husband. She spake to Lakshmana, saying: "Hasten and help my Rama; he calls for help."

Said Lakshmana: "Do not fear for Rama, O fair one. No Rakshasa can injure him. I must obey his command and remain beside thee. The cry thou hast heard is an illusion wrought by demons."

Sita was wroth; her eyes sparkled and her voice shook as she spake, saying: "Hath thine heart grown callous? Art thou thy brother's enemy? Rama is in peril, and yet thou dost not hasten to succour him. Hast thou followed him to the forest desiring that he should die, so as to obtain his widow by force? If so, thy hope is a delusion, because I will not live one moment after he dies. It is useless, therefore, for thee to tarry here."

Said Lakshmana, whose eyes were filled with tears: "I do not fear for Rama. . . . O Sita! thy words scald me, for thou art as a mother unto me. I cannot answer thee. My heart is free from sin. . . . Alas! that fickle women with poisonous tongues should endeavour to set brother against brother."

Sita wept, and Lakshmana, repenting that he had spoken harshly, said: "I will obey thee and hasten unto Rama. May the spirits of the forest protect thee against hidden enemies. I am troubled because I behold evil omens. When I return, may I behold Rama by thy side."

Said Sita: "If Rama is slain I will die by drowning, or by poison, or else by the noose. I cannot live without Rama."

Ravana kept watch the while, and when he saw Lakshmana leaving the hermitage, he assumed the guise of a forest sage and went towards the lonely and sad-hearted Sita. The jungle had grown silent. Ravana saw that Sita was beautiful as the solitary moon at midnight when it illumines the gloomy forest. He spake, saying: "O woman of golden beauty, O shy one in full bloom, robed in silk and adorned with flowers, art thou Sri, or Gauri,[1] or the goddess of love, or a nymph of the forest? Red as coral are thy lips; thy teeth shine like to jasmine; love dwelleth in thine eyes so soft and lustrous. Slender art thou and tall, with shapely limbs, and a bosom like to ripe fruit. . . . Wherefore, O fair one, with long shining tresses, dost thou linger here in the lonesome jungle? More seemly it were if thou didst adorn a stately palace. Choose thee a royal suitor; be the bride of a king. What god is thy sire, O beautiful one?"

Sita honoured Ravana, believing that he was a Brahman. She told him the story of Rama's exile, and said: "Rest thyself here until the jungle-ranging brethren return to greet thee."

Then Ravana said: "No Brahman am I, but the ruler of the vengeful Rakshasas. I am Ravana, King of Lanka, dreaded by even the gods. Thy beauty, O fair one, clad

[1] Names of the wives of Vishnu and Shiva.

in yellow silk, has taken captive my heart. Be my chief queen, O Sita, and five thousand handmaidens will wait upon thee. Share mine empire and my fame."

Said Sita, whose eyes flashed fiery anger: "Knowest thou Rama, the god-like hero who is ever victorious in strife? I am his wedded wife. Knowest thou Rama, the sinless and saintly one, who is strongly armed and full of valour and virtue? I am his wedded wife. What madness hath prompted thee to woo the wife of so mighty a warrior? I follow Rama as a lioness follows a lion. Canst thou, a prowling jackal, hope to obtain a lioness? Snatch from the jaws of a lion the calf which it is devouring, touch the fang of a cobra when it seizeth a fallen victim, or tear up a mountain by the roots, or seize the sun in heaven before thou dost seek to win or capture the wife of Rama, the avenger."

Ravana boasted his prowess, saying: "I have power to slay even Yama. I can torture the sun and shoot arrows through the earth. Little dost thou know of my glory and my heroism."

Then he changed his shape and stood up in gigantic demon form with vast body and ten heads and twenty arms. . . . Seizing Sita, he soared through the air with her as Garuda carries off the queen of serpents; he placed her in his chariot and went away swifter than the wind.

The unseen spirits of the jungle looked on, and they heard the cries of Sita as she called in vain for Rama and Lakshmana. Jatayus[1], Monarch of Vultures, who lay asleep on a mountain top, heard her and awoke; he darted upon Ravana like to the thunderbolt of Indra. A fierce battle was fought in mid air. Jatayus destroyed the chariot and killed the Rakshasa asses, but Ravana

[1] *Pron.* Jata'yus.

took Sita in his arms, and, soaring higher than the Vulture king, disabled him with his sword.

Then Ravana continued his journey towards Lanka, floating in the air. As he passed over the Mountain of Apes, Sita contrived to cast off her ornaments, and they dropped through the air like falling stars. . . . The five apes found them and said: "Ravana is carrying away some beautiful woman who calls upon Rama and Lakshmana."

When Ravana reached his palace he delivered Sita to a band of Rakshasa women, commanding them to guard her by day and by night.

Long and loudly did Rama lament when he returned to the forest hut and found that it was empty. He knew that Sita had been carried away, but whither he knew not.

CHAPTER XXVI

Rama's Mission Fulfilled

Rama Laments for Sita—The King of Vultures—Story of the Demon—Revelation after Death—Rama forms an Alliance with the Apes—Slaying of Bali—The Rainy Season—Sita's Life in Lanka—Hanuman the Spy—Discovery of Sita—Battle with Giants—Building of Rama's Bridge—The Worship of Shiva—Invasion of Lanka—The War with Demons—A Serpent Noose—How the Sleeping Giant was Slain—Rama and Lakshmana Wounded—Hanuman carries a Mountain to Lanka—Lakshmana Slain and Restored to Life—Ravana seeks to kill Sita—The Fall of Ravana—Sita's Ordeal of Fire—Rama's Return to Ayodhya—Second Exile of Sita—The Horse Sacrifice—Rama's Warlike Sons—Sita Returns to the Earth Mother—Ascent of Rama.

RAMA wept for Sita. He searched hither and thither through the forest, and called on every mountain and tree and on every bird and every beast, asking whither she had gone. When he found a tattered garland which his loved one had worn, he swooned with overpowering grief.

Then Lakshmana sprinkled water drops on his face until he revived. "Alas! my brother," he cried, "do not sorrow thus lest death should snatch thee away."

Said Rama: "Sita is my heart's love. I cannot live without her. For my sake she deserted the royal palace to wander in this fearsome jungle. Now that she is gone, the moments seem longer than years. . . . How can I live on when she is lost to me?"

Lakshmana comforted his brother: then they arose together and continued their vain search. . . . Rama beheld a beauteous lotus in a clear stream, and, blinded with tears, he deemed it was the face of Sita. "O hard-hearted one," he exclaimed, "art thou hiding there among the water blooms? Seekest thou to test my love in this manner? Arise and come to me, my sweet love, nor doubt me any longer."

But the bloom moved not, and Lakshmana led away his grief-distracted brother.

"Mayhap she hath returned to the hut now," Rama cried. Then the brethren hastened to the hermitage, but found it empty as before. . . . Rama wailed in the moonlight and cried to the orb of night: "O moon! mankind welcome thy coolness, but thou dost bring to me naught but sorrow and tears. . . . Thou lookest over the whole world, beholding all living beings. Where, O tell me, where is my beloved one, my lost Sita?"

Rama wandered fitfully through the jungle: the moonbeams and the shadows fluttered around, and it seemed as if the face of Sita were peering from everywhere. So passed a sleepless night, full of mourning and illusions.

On the morrow the brethren went forth again in quest of the lost one. They came to the place where Jatayus lay dying, and that lordly bird spake to Rama and related all that had befallen Sita and himself.

Rama sat on the ground: he embraced the dying Vulture King, and said unto Lakshmana: "Alas! my brother, the noble Jatayus hath given up his life to serve me. I have lost my kingdom and my sire; I have lost Sita, and now our ally, the Rajah of Vultures, is dying. . . . All my friends are passing away. If I were to sit in the shade of a tree, the tree would fall; if I stooped to drink water from a river, verily the river would dry up." . . .

Then he spake to Jatayus, saying: "Whither hath Ravana gone with my well-beloved?"

Said the Vulture: "He went southward towards an unknown forest fastness. . . . Alas! my strength fails, mine eyes grow blind, my life is ebbing from my body."

When he had spoken thus, Jatayus died in Rama's arms, and his soul ascended to the heaven of Vishnu in a chariot of fire.

Thereafter the brethren went towards the south. On their way they met a black demon of monstrous size; his head was in the middle of his body; he had but one eye, and his teeth were numerous and long. Suddenly the misshapen demon stretched out his two great arms, and the brethren fought against the arms.

The demon cried: "Who are ye that dare to combat with me? I welcome ye because I am an hungered this day, and long to feast on human flesh."

Rama and Lakshmana fought on until they cleft both the great arms that were coiled around them, whereat the monster fell upon the ground. Said Rama: "We are Dasaratha's sons, who are exiles in the jungle."

Then the demon revealed that he was Kabandha, and bade them burn his body, so that he might be bereft of his Rakshasa form and nature; thereafter, he promised, he would inform them regarding Sita. The brethren dug a pit and cremated the monster, and from the fire arose Kabandha, the Gandharva, who had been placed under spells. He spake and said: "Ravana dwells in the island of Lanka; he is the King of Rakshasas. If thou wouldst fain overcome him, thou must seek the aid of the ape chief, Sugriva, King of the Vanars, who dwells on Rishyamukha mountain."[1]

When the brethren went towards this mountain,

[1] Among the Nilgiri mountains.

Hanuman, son of Vayu, the wind god, a counsellor of the Ape King, came forth to meet them. He conducted Rama and Lakshmana before Sugriva, to whom they related the story of Sita's abduction.

Said Sugriva: "Some days past I beheld a woman who was borne aloft in the arms of a flying Rakshasa; she threw down her ornaments, which we have preserved with care."

Then the ornaments were brought forth, and they were recognized by Lakshmana, but Rama wept so profusely that he knew not whether he gazed upon the jewels of Sita or not.

Sugriva, who was the son of Surya, the sun god, desired to aid Rama, but he told that his bride and his kingdom had been taken from him by his half-brother Bali, son of Indra, whom he feared.[1] Then Rama promised to slay Bali and restore the kingdom to Sugriva. And as he promised so did he do. Sugriva challenged his brother to single combat, and Rama discharged an arrow which pierced the heart of the usurper. All the apes rejoiced greatly when the rightful King of the Vanars was restored to his throne.

The rainy season came on soon afterwards, and Rama and Lakshmana went to dwell upon the mountain Malyavana, where they found a cave.

Slowly passed the days of waiting. Ofttimes did Rama grieve for Sita. He was wont to speak to Lakshmana, saying: "Delightful is the season of rain and tempest unto those who dwell in happy homes in the midst of their families; it is a time of sorrow to those who suffer separation. . . . Behold the great black clouds like to battling elephants leaping and rolling in heaven. Thunder

[1] These apes are the incarnations of the Vedic deities who sojourned on earth according to Vishnu's command.

roars amidst the mountains. The lightnings flash and sparkle; alas! their golden lustre in the darkness of night reminds me of my lost Sita. . . . Now the wind falls and the earth is bright with rain tears, and I hear the sighing of Sita as she weeps in pain and sorrow. . . . The rainbow comes forth in beauty like to Sita arrayed with jewels and ornaments. . . . Now the earth is refreshed: trees are budding and flowers bloom again in beauty, but I cannot be consoled. Lost is Sita, my dearly beloved; she writhes in the palace of the Rakshasa king as the lightning writhes amidst the black clouds. . . . Ah! I abandoned my throne and kingdom with joy because Sita was with me; now my heart is breaking because she hath been snatched away. . . . See how the shadows gather again; winds roar and rains pour down; as dubious is my future, and dark as is this gloomy day of sorrow. Jatayus hath told that Sita is concealed in a distant fastness. . . . How can I be consoled? I mourn not for myself alone, but chiefly because she whom I love sorrows and suffers in a strange land."

Now, when Sita was dwelling in the palace of the demon king, guarded by Rakshasa women, Ravana approached her again and again, and addressed to her sweet speeches, praising her beauty and endeavouring to win her love. But Sita rejected him with scorn. Although she was his prisoner, he could not win her by force. She was strengthened by her own virtue; she was protected by Brahma's dread decree. Be it known that once upon a time the lustful Ravana had seized by force a nymph of Indra's heaven, whose name was Punjikashthala. When he committed that evil offence, Brahma spake angrily and said that Ravana's head would be rent asunder if ever again he attempted to act in like manner towards another female in heaven or upon earth.

Sita said unto the demon king: "Thou shalt never have me for wife either in this world or in the next. Rather would I die than gratify thy desire."

Angry was Ravana, and he commanded the female Rakshasas to convey Sita to the Asoka grove, believing that her heart would be melted by the beauties of that fair retreat. "Thou wilt provide her with fine raiment," he said, "and with rich ornaments and delicious food, thou wilt praise me before her, and anon threaten her with dire calamity if she refuseth to become my bride."

Sita remembered Rama in her heart by day and by night, and wept and moaned for him, refusing to be comforted.

When the rainy season was drawing to a close, Rama fretted because Sugriva, King of the Vanars, was making no effort to collect his forces and prepare for the recovery of Sita. Instead, he drank wine and spent the days in merriment among his wives. At length Lakshmana visited the palace and threatened Sugriva with death, because he had broken his promise, whereat the monarch summoned speedily his great armies of apes and bears in countless numbers. Four divisions were then sent out to the north and the south, and eastward and westward, to search for Sita.

Success attended the efforts of the army commanded by Hanuman. It chanced that his officers discovered on a mountain summit Sampati, the brother of Jatayus, King of the Vultures. He was wounded and helpless, because his wings had been scorched by endeavouring to soar to the sun so that he might fulfil a vain boast. Although stricken thus, Sampati could still see clearly over vast distances. He had beheld Ravana carrying away Sita across the ocean towards Lanka. This knowledge he communicated through his son to Hanuman. When he rendered such great service to Rama his wings began to grow, and he was enabled once again to take flight athwart the blue heaven.

Hanuman then resclved to visit the distant island with purpose to discover where Sita had been hidden. Assuming gigantic form, he stood upon a mountain top and leapt seaward. The mountain shook when he sprang from it. Over the sea went the wind god's son and that swiftly. But demons endeavoured to arrest his progress through the air. Surasa, mother of the Nagas, rose up with gaping jaws, and cried: "Thou must needs pass through my mouth ere thou wilt go farther, O Hanuman."

The heroic Ape extended his bulk, but the Naga hag opened wider and wider her jaws to prevent him passing Then Hanuman shrank to the size of a man's thumb, and leapt into her mouth and out of it again and again so as to fulfil her conditions, whereat the hag owned that she was defeated and allowed him to pass.

Next arose the she dragon, Sinhika, who clutched the shadow of Hanuman and held him back. Wrathfully she sprang forward to devour him, but again the cunning Ape contracted himself, and entering her mouth, attacked her and wounded her so that she was slain.

Leaping from her body, Hanuman resumed his journey until he arrived at Lanka. Night had fallen but the moon shone brightly. He assumed the form of a cat and crept stealthily through the capital, gazing on the wonders about him. He reached the great palace of Ravana and entered therein. It had shining crystal floors and jewelled stairways of gold and silver. The mansion of Indra was not more beautiful than that resplendent palace of the demon king. Hanuman crept on through the women's chamber, and beheld fair forms "subdued in all the shapes of sleep"; beautiful were they as lotus blooms that await the sun's first kiss ere they open their soft eyelids, or as the lustrous stars on an autumn night gleaming and moving in heaven; it seemed as if a wreath of sweet human blossoms had been thrown carelessly into that perfumed chamber of sleep.

Hanuman wandered on until he reached the Asoka grove. There he beheld the long-lost Sita, the queen of stars. Fierce she demons surrounded her, and some were of fearsome shape; they had dogs' heads and pigs' heads and the faces of horses and buffaloes; some were of great bulk and others were dwarfish; some had but one eye and others had three eyes; the ears of some hung touching the ground; others that were hairy were the most horrible to behold.

When morning came Ravana drew nigh to plead his love, praising the beauty of Sita, but she rejected him, as she had ofttimes done before, whereat the demon grew angry and threatened her with dire tortures and even death. . . . Sita was like to a gentle fawn surrounded by wolves. Yet she was without fear. Rather would she perish than be unfaithful to Rama.

Hanuman kept watch, crouching in the branches of a tree, and at length he found it possible to approach her in secret. At first she feared that Ravana had assumed the form of Hanuman to deceive her, but she was reassured when the Vanar spy showed her the ring of Rama, and related how greatly he sorrowed because she had been taken from him. Then was her heart touched with sorrow mingled with joy. Hanuman offered to carry her away, but in her modesty she refused to touch the body of any male being save Rama. She took from her hair a bright jewel which she gave to Hanuman as a token; and she said that Ravana had allowed her but two months to live if she refused to yield to him.

Hanuman desired, ere he left the city of Ravana, to show his enmity against the demons. Assuming his gigantic form, he uprooted trees and destroyed fair mansions. The guards came out against him and he slew many of them. But, at length, the mighty Indrajit, son of Ravana, hastened forth and shot a magic serpent-shaft which enwrapped Hanuman like a noose, and rendered him helpless. Thus was he taken prisoner, and he was dragged before Ravana, who commanded that the Ape be put to death. But a counsellor intervened and advised that Hanuman should be regarded as an envoy, and treated with dishonour ere he was sent back, so that their enemies might be terrified. Ravana consented to this course, and an oil-soaked cloth was tied round the Ape's great tail and set on fire. But Sita prayed that the fire should not injure Hanuman, and her prayer was heard. The son of Vayu suddenly contracted his body so that his bonds fell from him, and he leapt over the city, setting fire with his flaming tail to many mansions, and so accomplishing great destruction. Then he obtained another brief interview with Sita, and once again leapt over the ocean; he hastened with the good tidings of his journey to Rama, who rejoiced greatly that his loved one had been found.

Preparations were at once begun to rescue Sita. The Vanar armies were marched southward, and they camped on the shore over against Lanka, which lies sixty miles from the mainland. Here they were joined by a new and powerful ally.

Be it known that the mighty deeds of Hanuman had stricken terror to the heart of Ravana. The demon king summoned a council of war to consider what should be done. All his warriors advised him to wage war, except Bibhishana, his younger brother, who censured the monarch for the offence which he had committed against blameless Rama. "Hear my words," he said, "and restore Sita to her rightful lord, or else Rama will swoop down upon thy kingdom, O Ravana, as a falcon who seizeth his prey. Make peace with him now, lest many perish in battle."

Ravana was made angry, and cried: "Alas! for the love of my near relatives, who sorrow at my fame and smile at my peril; they are ever jealous and full of guile, because they hate me in their secret hearts. . . . Evil is thy speech, O Bibishana. Depart from me, false prince, and carry thy treason to our enemies. . . . If thou wert not my brother I would slay thee even now."

Bibhishana was thus banished from the Rakshasa kingdom, and he immediately crossed the sea and joined the forces of Rama.

Rama performed sacrifices to propitiate the God of Ocean, so that the Vanar forces might be enabled to pass over to Lanka, but these proved to be unavailing. Then angrily he seized his bow and shot Celestial weapons into the bosom of the deep. The earth and the sea were immediately convulsed, and darkness covered the heavens; lightning flashed and thunder bellowed aloud; the mountains began to break in pieces. Rama next seized a fiery dart and threatened to dry up the waters of the sea.

At that moment the King of Ocean rose serenely above the weltering billows in all his splendour, attended by shining water snakes. He addressed Rama with great reverence, reminding him that according to ancient laws he must remain unfordable, but counselling him the while to seek the aid of the Vanar chief Nala, son of Vishwakarma, the divine artisan, so that a bridge might be constructed to enable the armies to cross the deep. Then the King of Ocean vanished amidst the waves and the heavens brightened again.

Nala was immediately called upon to give his aid. Assisted by his workmen, this wonderful Vanar, whose body was green, constructed a causeway of rocky islands between the mainland and Lanka (Ceylon), and to this day it is called "Rama's Bridge".[1]

Rama meanwhile set up the Linga symbol of the god Shiva, and worshipped it on that holy island which hath since been called Ramisseram.

In five days the strait was spanned. Then Rama mounted on the back of Hanuman, son of the wind god Vayu, and Lakshmana mounted the back of Angada, son of Bali and grandson of Indra, and led the Vanar hosts across the sea. The apes and bears which composed the great attacking army leapt from island to island, shouting: "Victory to Rama!" "Victory to Lakshmana!" "Victory to Sugriva!" Now the apes were of many colours; they were white and black, green and blue, yellow and red and brown. Sugriva shone like silver, Angada resembled a white lotus; Nila, son of Agni, was red, and Hanuman was yellow as pure gold; Sarambha had also a yellow body, and Nala was green, while Darvindha had a black body, a red face, and a yellow tail. These were all leaders and great warriors of the Vanar host.

The army landed in Lanka unopposed, and encamped on a plain fronting the capital of the Rakshasa king.

The Rakshasas issued forth speedily to attack the apes, and the blowing of horns and beating of drums sounded like to the mighty thunder peals at a Yuga end. Indrajit was the Rakshasa leader. His followers rode on

[1] Also "Adam's Bridge". The green Celtic fairies are similarly credited with making island chains and long jutting promontories which stretch out from opposite shores of arms of the sea.

elephants and lions, on camels and asses, on hogs and hyenas, and on wolves; they were armed with bows and arrows, maces, spears, tridents, swords, and beams, but some had also magic weapons. Roaring and swaying, they drove forward like to long sea-rollers assaulting the shore.

The gigantic apes wielded trees for clubs and threw great boulders, but some depended on their sword-like nails and their long arrowy teeth. They rushed against the demons, shouting "Rama, Rama!" and soon the plain was covered by heaps of writhing bodies and severed limbs, while rivers of blood streamed across it from between the battling hosts. Rama looked on without fear. He reposed his faith on the apes, for he knew that they were incarnations of the gods.

The apes were driven back until Sugriva flung a great tree, which shattered the chariot of Indrajit. Then the Rakshasa leader and his army took flight.

Indrajit obtained a new chariot by offering up in sacrifice a black goat, and returning to the battlefield with his forces he shot arrows at Rama and Lakshmana. Then he threw a serpent noose, which bound the two brothers so that they were unable to move. Great was their peril, but Vayu, god of wind, sent to their aid the great Celestial bird Garuda, the serpent killer, and the snakes which formed the noose fled from before it, whereat the brethren, who had meantime fallen in a swoon, rose up again. Ravana then came forth, but Rama shot arrows which swept the ten crowns from his ten heads, and he retired in his shame and skulked in the city.

The Rakshasas were in desperate straits and bethought them to awaken Kumbha-karna, the mightiest of all the demons. In former days he had terrorized the Universe; he continually devoured human beings, and had defeated

Indra even, but Brahma intervened and decreed that he would sleep for six months and then awaken for one day only. Each time he awoke he devoured a great meal, after which he was again overpowered by slumber.

Thousands of men danced and shouted and blew trumpets beside the great sleeper, but he could not be wakened; elephants were driven over his body, yet he never moved; then beautiful women came and caressed him, and he suddenly opened his eyes and roared like to the sea. His eyes were red with anger, and he cried: "Why have I been awakened before my time?"

The Rakshasas informed Kumbha-karna of the army which surrounded the city, and they brought him much food; greedily he swallowed swine and deer and many human beings and drank rivers of wine. Refreshed, but not yet satisfied, he arose and said: "Where are the apes so that I may devour them?"

He mounted his chariot and went forth to battle. The apes trembled to behold him and fled panic-stricken. . . . Sugriva rallied them quickly, and then they began to fling trees and boulders, but these were all splintered to pieces on the limbs of the giant. He defeated Hanuman, and seized Sugriva and carried him off in his chariot. Thousands of apes were devoured by the mighty Rakshasa.

At length Kumbha-karna went against Rama and a fierce conflict ensued, but in the end Rama discharged flaming arrows and severed his head from his body. The monster staggered backward and fell into the ocean, and great billows arose and tossed angrily in the midst of the swollen deep.

Indrajit thereafter offered up another sacrifice and secured fresh weapons. Rendering himself invisible, he rose high in the air and showered arrows like rain until

Rama and Lakshmana, who were grievously wounded, fell down and pretended to be dead.

When darkness came on, Hanuman and Bibhishana surveyed the battlefield with torches and found that many apes had been wounded and slain. Great was their sorrow, but Sushena, the ape physician, bade Hanuman to hasten to a certain Himalayan mountain to obtain healing herbs. The wind god's son assumed tremendous bulk, and, leaping aloft, went speedily through the air until he reached the place where the herbs grew. He searched for them in vain; then he tore up the mountain, and carrying it in his hand returned again to the battlefield. The physician soon discovered the herbs; then he gave healing to Rama and Lakshmana and the wounded apes, who rose up at once ready and eager to fight as before. Hanuman returned with the mountain and restored it to its place.

When the sun rose, Ravana sent forth young heroes to battle against the apes and bears, but they were all slain. Then Indrajit came to avenge the fallen, but Lakshmana drew his bow and shot an arrow which Indra had given to him. Unerring was his aim, and Indrajit was struck down; his body rolled headless upon the plain.

Ravana lamented for the death of his son, crying: "He was the mightiest of my heroes and the dearest to my heart. All the gods feared him, yet by a mortal was he laid low. . . . O my son, thy widow wails for thee and thy mother weeps in sore distress. Fondly I deemed that when the frailties of old age afflicted me thou wouldst close mine eyelids in death, but youth is taken first and I am left alone to battle against mine enemies."

For a time the mighty demon wept; then he arose in wrath to wreak vengeance. First of all he hastened towards the Asoka grove to slay Sita. But the Rakshasa dames concealed the wife of Rama, and prevailed upon Ravana not to pollute his fame by slaying a woman. One cried to him: "Auspicious is the last day of the waning moon. The hour of thy vengeance is nigh. Turn thee towards the battlefield and great glory will be thine."

Ravana went gloomily away; he mounted his chariot to battle against his enemies, remembering those who had already fallen. Followed by a great army, he swept from the city like to a tempest cloud which darkens the summer heaven. He beheld his brother Bibhishana fighting for Rama, and angrily cast at him a great weapon, but Lakshmana flung a javelin which shattered it in flight. Ravana smiled grimly and shouted to Lakshmana: "Slayer of my son, I welcome thee! Thou hast protected Bibhishana; now protect, if thou canst, thine own self."

Having spoken thus he flung a great dart, which pierced the heart of Lakshmana and pinned him to the earth.

Rama stooped over the fallen hero and cried: "Alas! art thou fallen, my gallant brother? Thy weapons have dropped from thy hands; death claims thee, but, O Lakshmana, thou wilt not die alone. I am weary of battle and of glory, and when my task is ended, I will follow in thy footsteps. . . . The love of wife or friend is easily won, but the love of a faithful brother, equal to thine, is rarely found in this world of illusions. . . . Dearest of brothers, greatest of heroes, wilt thou never awaken from thy deathly swoon or open again thine eyes to behold me? . . . Alas! the lips of Lakshmana are silent and his ears are stopped."

In the darkness of night Hanuman again hastened northward in speedy flight to obtain the mountain which he had aforetime carried to Lanka. The physician found upon it the healing herbs; he pounded them and made a paste which he placed under the nostrils of the unconscious warrior. Then Lakshmana rose up again healed and hale and powerful. Rama rejoiced greatly, and turned against his foes. . . . A night attack was made upon the Rakshasa capital, and the Apes intercepted a sacrifice which Ravana sought to offer up to the gods so as to compel their aid; many fair mansions were given to the flames.

When day came Ravana went forth to battle. Surpanakha, his sister who had caused the war, stood in his way, and he thrust her aside impatiently, whereat she cursed him, saying: "For this thou wilt never again return to the city."

Ravana drove on in battle fury, his heart filled with hatred for his foes and with sorrow for the fallen. Rama went against him in the chariot of Indra, and for a time a dubious conflict was waged. The earth trembled and the ocean shook with fear.

Suddenly Rama darted forward. He drew his bow and shot a swift arrow, which smote off one of Ravana's ten heads, but immediately another appeared in its place.[1] Then the hero seized the flaming weapon which Brahma had created for the protection of the gods; with unerring aim he discharged it in flaming splendour; it struck the demon; it cleft in twain his heart of iron. Roaring in his fierce agony Ravana fell ponderously upon the plain and immediately expired. So was the enemy of gods and men put to death by peerless Rama.

Celestial music was heard in heaven and flowers fell upon the plain of victory: a voice came down the wind, saying: "*O victor of truth and righteousness, thy task is now ended.*"

[1] Like Hydra against which Hercules fought.

The Rakshasa hosts broke in flight when Ravana fell, and Rama entered the city in triumph. Bibhishana burned the body of his fallen brother, and performed the funeral rites. Thereafter he was proclaimed King of Lanka.

When peace was restored, Rama commanded that Sita should be brought forth. She was carried towards the plain concealed in a litter, and all the Apes gathered round to behold her, whereat Rama requested her to alight and walk towards him, and she did so. With folded hands she approached her husband and knelt at his feet, weeping tears of joy.

Clouded was the brow of Rama; he spoke sternly, and said: "Mine enemies are slain, and thou art delivered from captivity, O Sita; but now that my shame is removed I have no desire to behold thee. I cannot receive thee as my wife, because that thou hast dwelt in the house of Ravana."

Said Sita: "Chaste and innocent have I remained. . . . O Rama, if thou hadst informed me of thy doubt, I would have died ere now. Better is death than thy dark suspicion."

Addressing Lakshmana, she then said: "Build for me a funeral pyre so that I may end my grief amidst the flames."

As she desired so did the brother of Rama do. He built the pyre and set it alight. Then Sita invoked Agni:

> If in act and thought, she uttered, I am true unto my name,
> Witness of our sins and virtues, may this fire protect my fame!
>
> If a false and lying scandal brings a faithful woman shame,
> Witness of our sins and virtues, may this fire protect my fame!

32

THE CORONATION OF RAMA AND SITA

If in lifelong loving duty I am free from sin and blame,
Witness of our sins and virtues, may this fire protect my fame!

R. C. Dutt's trans.

Fearlessly she then leapt amidst the flames and vanished, while all lamented around her. Rama cried: "This day have I sinned, because she is innocent."

In that hour a great wonder was wrought. Suddenly the Deva-rishis and Gandharvas and the gods appeared in the air. At the same time the red flames of the mighty pyre were divided, and the god Agni came forth with Sita, whom he delivered to Rama, saying: "*Receive thy wife who is without sin or shame.*"

Rama embraced Sita, and said: "I have never doubted her virtue; she is without sin, and now her purity has been proved before all men."

He wept, and Sita hid her face in his bosom and soft embrace.

The exile of Rama was now ended, and he returned speedily in the car of Indra to Ayodhya, with Sita and Lakshmana and Hanuman.

Bharata welcomed his elder brother, and laid the sandals at his feet, saying: "These are the symbols of thy rule, O Rama; I have guarded the throne for thee. Now take thy crown and govern thy kingdom. I give thee back thine own."

Rama was crowned on the morrow amidst the rejoicings of the people, and prosperity returned once again to the kingdom.

Time went past, but the sorrows of Sita were not ended. The people whispered against the fair queen, doubting her virtue, because that she had been taken away by Ravana, and they wondered Rama had received her back. At length her husband, yielding to the wishes of his subjects, banished the innocent queen from the kingdom. The faithful Lakshmana conducted her towards the southern jungles, and abandoned her nigh to the hermitage of Valmiki, counselling her with tears to take refuge with the saintly poet.

Valmiki received her with pity, and soon afterwards she gave birth to two sons, who were named Lava and Kusa.

Sixteen years went past, and Rama's mind was troubled because that he had slain Ravana, who was the son of Pulastya, the Rishi. So he resolved to perform the Aswamedha (horse sacrifice) to cleanse his soul of sin.

The horse was sent forth to wander through the land, and when it approached the hermitage of Valmiki, Lava and Kusa, the sons of Rama and Sita, took possession of it. They defeated the royal army and wounded Satrughna. Lakshmana hastened forth with another army, but he was also grievously wounded and defeated by the young heroes. Then Rama himself went southward to wage war and recapture the horse. When his sons came forth against him, Rama wondered to find that they were so like to himself in countenance and bearing; his heart was filled with tenderness, and he asked them: "Whose children are you?"

Lava and Kusa greeted him with reverence, and said: "Sita is our mother, but we know not the name of our sire."

Then Rama perceived that the lads were his own sons. . . . Valmiki, the sage, came towards him, and Rama said: "The people spoke evil things against Sita, and it was necessary to prove her innocence. Now let her be taken into my presence, for I know that these noble children are mine."

Valmiki returned to Sita and asked her to go with

him before Rama, but for a time she refused to do so. The sage pleaded with her, and at length she walked forth from the hermitage with downcast eyes and hands uplifted. In the presence of Rama and the people she then invoked the Earth, and cried:

> If unstained in thought and action I have lived from day of birth,
> Spare a daughter's shame and anguish and receive her, Mother Earth!
>
> If in duty and devotion I have laboured undefiled,
> Mother Earth! who bore this woman, once again receive thy child!
>
> If in truth unto my husband I have proved a faithful wife,
> Mother Earth! relieve thy Sita from the burden of this life!
>
> *R. C. Dutt's trans.*

When she had spoken thus, all who heard her wept and sorrowed. And while they gazed upon her with pity and tenderness, the earth suddenly yawned, and from its depths arose a golden throne sparkling with gems and supported by four great serpents, as a rose is supported by green leaves. Then the Earth Mother appeared and hailed Sita with loving words, and led her to the throne, on which she seated herself beside her sinless daughter, the faithful and undefiled wife of Rama. . . . The throne thereafter vanished and the earth closed over it.

So passed Sita from before the eyes of all mankind. Rama flung himself upon the ground in an agony of sorrow. But Brahma appeared and spake to him, saying: "Why dost thou despair, O Lord of all? Well thou knowest that life is but a dream, a bubble of water. . . ."

Rama, however, even after the Aswamedha had been performed, continued to mourn until the Celestial bird

Garuda came for him: then he ascended to heaven, as Vishnu, and found Sita, who was the goddess Lakshmi, the incomparable Sri.

So endeth the story of Rama, whose fame can never die.

INDEX

Vowel Sounds.—*ă*, almost like *u* in *fur*; *ai*, like *i* in *high*; *ä*, as in *palm*; *e*, like *a* in *late*; *ī*, as *e* in *he*; *ō*, as in *shore*; *ū*, as in *pull*; *u*, as in *sun*.